C000134465

CREATING COMMERCIAL WEB $ITES

Kim and Brad Hampton

201 West 103rd Street
Indianapolis, Indiana 46290

PRESIDENT, SAMS PUBLISHING   Richard K. Swadley

PUBLISHING MANAGER   Dean Miller

MANAGING EDITOR   Cindy Morrow

MARKETING MANAGER   John Pierce

ACQUISITIONS EDITOR
Cari Skaggs

DEVELOPMENT EDITOR
Brian-Kent Proffitt

SOFTWARE DEVELOPMENT SPECIALIST
Cari Skaggs

PRODUCTION EDITOR
Carolyn Linn

TECHNICAL REVIEWER
Ian Anderson

EDITORIAL COORDINATOR
Bill Whitmer

RESOURCE COORDINATOR
Deborah Frisby

TECHNICAL EDIT COORDINATOR
Lynette Quinn

FORMATTER
Frank Sinclair

EDITORIAL ASSISTANT
Carol Ackerman

COVER DESIGNER
Tim Amrhein

BOOK DESIGNER
Alyssa Yesh

PRODUCTION TEAM SUPERVISOR
Brad Chinn

PRODUCTION
Stephen Adams, Debra Bolhuis, Kevin Cliburn, Elizabeth Deeter, Jason Hand, Daniel Harris, Louisa Klucznik, Paula Lowell, Casey Price, Dana Rhodes, Laura Robbins, Bobbi Satterfield, Anne Sipahimalani, Ian Smith, Marvin Van Tiem

OVERVIEW

CONTENTS

ACKNOWLEDGMENTS

First and foremost, we each thank the other, for being the best partner possible—in business, writing, and marriage. To our family, friends, and colleagues—who may have thought we were crazy over the years, but still gave us encouragement and support—we thank you. To the folks at Sams.net and Macmillan Publishing, perhaps the most professional and considerate group of people we have ever had the pleasure to work with—thanks for not taking 'no' as an answer. To our clients, who were not only understanding when we told them we were taking time to write a book, but continued to call offering help and support—thank you. We have always tried to treat our clients as friends, and after putting so much of ourselves into our work, it's touching to know how much it has been appreciated. A special thank you to the one member of our team who is always cool and collected, who kept us sane and grounded during the writing of this book and never once complained when he couldn't leave the house for days on end: our dog, Bacchus. Finally, a word to all those who choose to stray from the beaten path: Believe in yourself, and never let the bastards get you down.

ABOUT THE AUTHORS

As members of the so-called Generation X, a young copywriter and aspiring graphic artist faced a job market filled with the unfortunate victims of the downsizing of the late eighties. Rather than just give up, they decided to go it alone, and opened Hampton and Associates in 1991 with a lot of ideas and very little capital. Almost everyone thought they were crazy—that they had a pipe dream that would never pan out—but their communications skills, gut instincts, and aggressive techniques began impressing clients. Before long, they were getting noticed and gaining a reputation for themselves as "down and dirty" marketers. Always searching for alternative ways to market, Kim and Brad began looking at and testing the marcom (marketing communications) potential of some of the online services, as well as Fidonet. At that time, the Internet was the bastion of students and scientists who would "never" allow its commercialization. Things change. By late 1994, H&A began offering marketing design on something called the World Wide Web. Few people had heard of this, and fewer still were willing to invest, but the couple employed the same tenacity that had driven their business from the start and touted the capabilities of this new and powerful medium to anyone within earshot. The news media soon picked up the story of the two "pioneers," and in the first part of 1995, H&A began turning down print design jobs in order to specialize in Internet presence development. Since then, they have applied their no-nonsense marketing skills to develop hundreds of WWW systems and pages for companies ranging from Mom 'n' Pop retail, to manufacturing, to the hi-tech giant Intel. In five years, by straying off the beaten path, Brad and Kim have turned their dreams into a reality. They are now two of the most respected and sought-after designers in the industry. This is the book they wish they'd had when they started out, and they hope it will encourage others to follow their own dreams.

INTRODUCTION

WHY YOU NEED THIS BOOK

There has certainly been enough hype about the so-called Information Superhighway to cause tens of millions of people to scramble for Internet access. There is still quite a bit of controversy as to whether or not the World Wide Web (WWW) and Internet truly are the medium of choice for this superhighway—and there is, of course, a fringe element that believes that we should have no superhighway at all. The fact is, however, a significant number of businesses and individuals, as well as a vast majority of universities and government resources, have already adopted the Internet and WWW as *the* new communications medium. In short, the Internet and WWW are the closest thing we've got to the Information Superhighway, and those who wait to see what may evolve from this risk being left behind.

The WWW makes possible nearly instant, interactive, multimedia communications on a global level. There has never been a communications tool this powerful, and unlike many emerging technologies, the WWW is relatively inexpensive. There are many very good reasons for a company to create a presence on the Internet, and very few reasons not to.

This book is designed to be many things. We have attempted to provide a big enough picture so that decision makers and students, entrepreneurs and employees, writers, doctors, entertainers, and scientists will be able to understand how to make use of the WWW. At the same time, this book is detailed enough so that even seasoned HTML publishers will find design principles, tips, and tools that will improve both the content and success of their work.

WHO SHOULD READ THIS BOOK?

This book can help meet a variety of needs:

◆ If you are an HTML programmer hoping to meet the communications needs of businesses, this book will show you how to develop and publish pages and systems for the retail, business-to-business, and corporate environments.

◆ If you are a writer, graphic artist, or marketing professional who wishes to break into the HTML design market, this book is for you.

◆ If you are a businessperson seeking an understanding of WWW marketing and how it may relate to your business, you will find this book an excellent overview of the medium.

◆ Most importantly, if you have been assigned the task of developing Internet communications for your company, regardless of your background, you will find this book to be a step-by-step manual for successfully designing and implementing an Internet marketing system.

HOW TO USE THIS BOOK

Each chapter of this book details a different facet of Internet marketing. We have designed the book to be useful in many ways:

- ◆ The book can be read from beginning to end as an instructional manual.
- ◆ Each chapter of the book can be read as needed, and the book can serve as a reference.
- ◆ Someone needing to develop an Internet presence in a hurry (as in, "I want to have a Web site up before next week's trade show") can skim through the book, follow the Quick & Dirty Guides, and be online with an acceptable system in a matter of days.
- ◆ Someone wanting an overview of WWW marketing can browse through the chapters in any order and get a solid understanding of how the Internet has affected business communications, and learn how to use this tool for their own ventures.

Every chapter contains information and guidelines, as well as tips, tricks, diagrams, and examples. At the end of the chapter is a summary of the points addressed and, where applicable, a Quick & Dirty Guide for cutting corners and getting things up and going ASAP.

WHAT THIS BOOK IS NOT

This book is not "How to Get Rich on the Internet." There are an ever-increasing number of books that propose that simply being on the WWW will enable someone to make millions of dollars overnight. We'll go out on a limb here and say that that's not very likely to happen.

Neither is this book a primer on writing HTML code. While the entire library of HTML tags are included throughout the book, it is assumed that you either know basic HTML or that you are leaving the HTML coding to someone else. While it is certainly possible to learn HTML by reading this book, it's best that you have some practice before launching a commercial communications system.

Finally, this book is not designed to provide a complete understanding of marketing communications. It's preferable that you either have some background in business communications, or that you have resources that can help you in this regard. It's impossible to provide a complete graphic art and copywriting education within one book.

To put it simply, don't expect that if you have absolutely no background in business or computers, you can read this book and suddenly become a commercial Web designer. Although we have made every effort to present the information in a way that is accessible and understandable for everybody, you must learn to walk before you can run.

CONVENTIONS IN THIS BOOK

All listings and lines of code appear in a `monospace` font for ease of reading. All filenames, directory names, Internet addresses, commands, and other words and symbols that appear in programs are set in the same monospace font. A `monospace italic` font is used for placeholders, indicating that the user must substitute something in their place. A **`monospace bold`** font is used to emphasize sections of code that illustrate the use of certain attributes and tags in Appendix H, "Comparative HTML Reference Guide."

The first occurrence of new terms is highlighted by the use of an *italic* font.

WHAT YOU NEED TO CREATE COMMERCIAL WEB PAGES

In the list of things you need, you will see that an Internet access account ranks right up there with a computer and a modem. We are referring to a SLIP (Serial Line Internet Protocol) or PPP (Point-to-Point Protocol) connection at least, and not a text-only (Shell) account. If you haven't done so already, find an ISP (Internet Service Provider) in your area and get online. We assume that if you are reading this book, you are already connected to the Internet, you have been on the Web, and are familiar with how to navigate cyberspace. Furthermore, we expect that you have used e-mail, Usenet, and other Internet services.

Of course, a book about developing Web sites should have its own, and this one does. It contains updated information, resources, and links that will be of interest to our readers. The site is also the place to contact the authors with questions and comments. Turn your browsers to `http://www.hampton.org`. See you there!

The CD-ROM accompanying this book also has resources for you to use, including shareware software and HTML templates. This will be incredibly valuable to people who are looking for ways to get a system up and running as quickly as possible, but it is not everything you need to develop extensive, high-caliber commercial Web systems—it's simply a starting point.

To develop HTML, convert and create graphics, pre-test pages, upload pages to a server, and test them again, you will need the following:

◆ A computer workstation (IBM, MAC, or UNIX)

◆ A modem that transmits and receives at a minimum speed of 14.4Kbps

◆ An Internet access account

◆ An ASCII text editor

◆ A bitmap graphics manipulation program

◆ A WWW server (your own, or space on another) with a constant IP address

◆ A collection of WWW browsers (including Netscape and Microsoft)

◆ An FTP (File Transfer Protocol) application

Now that you know what this book is and is not, how it is arranged, and what you will need, let's get going.

TELL US WHAT YOU THINK!

As a reader, you are the most important critic of our books. We value your opinion and want to know what we're doing right, what we could do better, what areas you'd like to see us publish in, and any other words of wisdom you're willing to pass our way. You can help us make strong books that meet your needs and give you the computer guidance you require.

Do you have access to CompuServe or the World Wide Web? If so, check out our CompuServe forum by typing GO SAMS at any prompt. If you prefer the World Wide Web, check out our site at http://www.mcp.com.

Note:

If you have a technical question about this book, call the technical support line at (800) 571-5840, ext. 3668.

As the team leader of the group that created this book, I welcome your comments. You can fax, e-mail, or write me directly to let me know what you did or didn't like about this book, as well as what we can do to make our books stronger. Here's the information:

Fax: 317/581-4669

E-mail: opsys_mgr@sams.mcp.com

Mail: Dean Miller
            Sams Publishing
            201 W. 103rd Street
            Indianapolis, IN 46290

Developing a Commercial Web Site

PART I

Marketing on the WWW: A Little Background

Before we leap into developing a Web site, it's important that we look into the different issues that have created the current marketing situation on the Internet. As with many things, in order to look forward, we must first look back.

## CHAPTER one

A Prehistoric History of Marketing

Marketing goes back a very long way—in fact, it probably goes back to the days of the caveman. Here's a little story to illustrate how it might have worked back then.

Zog, a cavewoman, lived in a cave on a particularly bumpy section of a particularly bad pass through some particularly difficult terrain.

As it happens, this pass was a trade route between two budding civilizations. Because this section of the pass was so bumpy, the carts the traders used to carry their wares and produce often lost wheels and broke down right in front of Zog's cave. Zog would watch as the traders made new wheels of stone or wood, but she didn't think much of it.

One day, a cart came by and one of its stone wheels crumbled into dust just in front of Zog's cave. This time, though, the cart's owners obviously had no idea what they were doing. Zog applied the skills she'd learned from watching others, and before long, had made a serviceable wheel, which she traded with the cart's owners for some food.

Zog got an idea. Making wheels was much easier than digging up roots and grubs, and it paid better. Zog began making wheels and storing them in her cave. She knew there was a market for wheels, and every time someone broke down in front of her cave, she'd roll out another wheel and arrange a trade. Zog was in business.

Zog grew wealthy, but she found that running out to tell people she could help them got tiring, so she decided to advertise. Zog carved an enormous stone wheel and placed it in front of her cave so that everyone coming through the pass could see it. It worked, and Zog profited.

Zog identified a market (she saw the need for wheels), developed a plan for meeting the needs of that market (she made the wheels), set up a pricing structure (she traded wheels), and developed a method for communicating to that market through availability advertising (the giant wheel). Our friend Zog has addressed the four Ps of marketing—Place, Product, Price, and Promotion—and has established an effective basic marketing structure.

Of course, nothing is that simple. It wasn't long before another caveman set up shop just across the path from Zog. In Zog's case, she probably would have simply beaten her competition to death (as most business people would like to do when confronted by competition), but to make a point, let's say she had to use other means. Zog's competitor also built a giant wheel, and Zog had to paint her wheel red so that it would stand out. Zog began marking her wheels with an X, made little toy wheels with little Xs on them, and did everything she could to make people know "Zog wheel best wheel." She offered guarantees and coupons, set up distributorships, hired salespeople, and on and on.

The point of all this is that, while the tools have evolved and the markets and lines of communication have become more complex, the basics of marketing haven't changed much since Zog. Whether it's via print, radio, direct mail, television, multimedia

CD-ROM, or the World Wide Web, "Zog Make Wheel" and "Zog Wheel Best Wheel" are the basic messages of most promotional marketing campaigns.

WHAT IS THE INTERNET?

The Internet (or Net) is a network of computers that share a common communications protocol (TCP/IP), which enables computers of different types to exchange information. It is this cross-platform compatibility that makes the Net so powerful and has caused it to grow at such an exponential rate.

So, what is a network? It's more than just linking things together; it's the *way* they're linked together. In the case of the Internet, it's the way thousands of computers are linked together. This seems very basic, and people use the term "network" every day, but few people understand the concept.

Imagine you had four computers and that each computer had a line running to each other computer, as in Figure 1.1. Each computer could transfer information to any other computer, but the cables get messy and expensive. It's similar to having a separate telephone for each person you call, rather than having one telephone by which you could call anyone.

In Figure 1.2, each computer connects to only one line. This is a network (were there more computers, the "net" aspect would become more apparent). In a network, each computer has access to the information on the line. In order to keep things straight, each computer must be given a name or *address*.

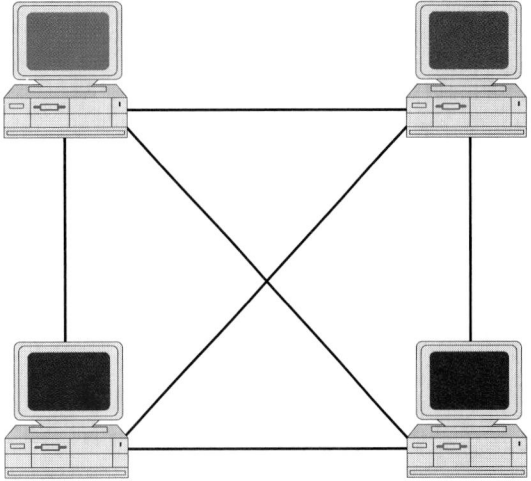

Figure 1.1.
An inefficient computer network.

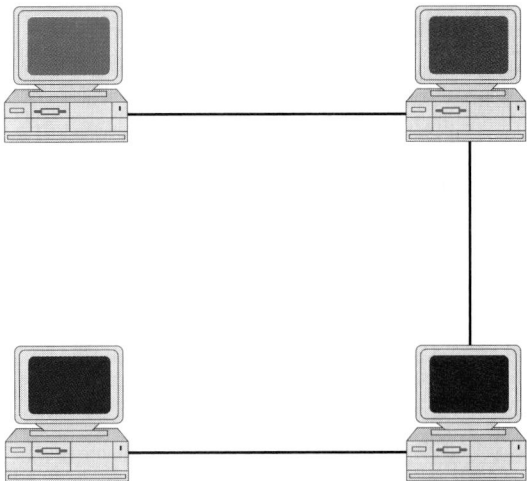

Figure 1.2.
A simplified computer network.

Imagine that Computer C wants some information from Computer A. Computer C sends a message like "Computer A, send me file xxx12." Although the other computers have access to the request, they ignore it because it's addressed to A. This addressing scheme is called a protocol. The Internet Protocol (the IP in TCP/IP) uses a series of numbers to designate an address. This is called the IP address, and each computer connected to the Net has an IP address.

WHO MADE THE INTERNET?

Many believe the Internet is a new concept, but it actually originated in the 1960s as the Advanced Research Projects Agency Network (ARPANET), funded by the Department of Defense. ARPANET enabled a global network of government personnel, scientists, and researchers to collaborate and exchange critical information with each other.

The idea was that, by sharing research, scientists from different disciplines could avoid reinventing the wheel (no offense to Zog). This is to say that a group working on a new type of rocket engine could—rather than requesting literature via mail or conducting research themselves—simply connect to a different computer and download the information they wanted on, say, ignition switches.

In the 1980s, the National Science Foundation (NSF) gave the ARPANET a complete upgrade by implementing a more modern, higher-speed network. This upgraded architecture was given the name Internet, which linked government supercomputers, educational institutions, and research facilities. As a whole, the Internet functioned as a broad-based educational and research network.

There were originally four basic functions on the Internet: e-mail, Usenet, Telnet, and file transfer. E-mail is, obviously, electronic mail—direct communication. Usenet is an electronic bulletin board, a public forum where people can post and view messages. Telnet enables a person to actually use another computer (the TCP part of TCP/IP stands for *Transfer Command Protocol*) for such things as accessing databases. File transfer enables people to send computer files from one system to another.

As it stands now, the Internet is an international network connecting tens of millions of people around the world. Governments, universities, private citizens and, of course, businesses use the Net every day for communication, education, entertainment, and commerce. You'd think that the people originally involved with the Net would have been happy to see it grow so quickly; many weren't.

Note:
Loosely defined, a geek is someone who knows about computers—especially if he or she knows more about computers than you do.

You see, up until a few years ago, the environment on the Internet was very elitist. Even after universities began providing students with access, there was an air of separatism amongst the Netters. Of course, nearly everyone involved in the community was a hard-core UNIX geek, and user-friendly was a laughable term, so the Net community remained rather private. However, the Internet was set up as an open, public network. The plan was that by creating an open-ended network, the resources could continue to grow exponentially. This caused some big problems.

You see, the geeks who made use of the Net felt they owned it. They not only used it for professional and educational purposes, but as a social forum. The best example of this is on the Usenet, where thousands of bulletin boards (newsgroups) existed that not only discussed scientific matters, but things like *Star Trek* and dirty jokes. For many people, the Net was their main form of social interaction, and they were very threatened by the idea that more and more people were joining their private club without any invitation.

Note:
Just a historical note: While the Internet was being built, another global network, known as Fidonet, had also been developed to allow amateurs to network. The framework of this relied on BBSs (Bulletin Board Systems) and private, long distance phone calls to keep information current and available. Everyone involved pretty much saw Fidonet as the bastard child of the Internet, and as the Internet became available to the masses, Fidonet faded.

MARKETING ON THE INTERNET

There is not a long history of using the Internet for marketing purposes—about two years. There were a few enterprising minds who began posting the equivalent of chain letters and "make money fast" pyramid schemes on the Usenet, but it wasn't until 1994 that many people tried to exploit the power of the Net for financial gain.

In April 1994, a husband and wife legal team posted an advertisement on nearly every one of the 8,000+ Usenet groups that were active at that time. As mentioned earlier, the Net was very much an elitist community at that time, and the action of these two lawyers shook that community to the core.

Again, the Net was seen by many users as a "private club." They didn't want to see cyberspace soiled by the filth of commercialism. In reaction to the posting, the lawyers received death threats, their server was repeatedly sabotaged by hackers, and they were portrayed online and in computer magazines as greedy, slimy parasites (even more so than other lawyers). They also brought in more than $100,000 in business within a few weeks—and suddenly, the business world was looking at the Internet with great interest.

One of the funniest things about the whole question of commercialism on the Internet is that the main argument against what the lawyers did was that they were "wasting bandwidth." Bandwidth is the term used to signify the amount of computer and telecommunications resources available on the Internet. While the lawyers' little advertisement was a rather long sales pitch, it certainly took fewer resources than an ongoing discussion on whether Captain Kirk is cooler than Captain Picard.

By the way, what the lawyers did—posting the same message to many newsgroups—is now called *spamming* (as in *to spam, he spams, she spammed*), and it is not something to practice. It's somewhat like putting flyers on every car windshield in a giant parking lot—it's a nuisance. While spamming will certainly get you a lot of attention, it is likely to make you more infamous than famous, and will put you in the crosshairs of some very angry electronic terrorists. Luckily, April 1994 was also about the time that the World Wide Web became a viable commercial reality.

WHAT IS THE WWW?

The core of the World Wide Web (WWW or Web) is a special language and set of protocols for receiving, sending, and displaying information via the Internet. This is called HTTP (Hypertext Transfer Protocol). Contrary to what many people imagine, the Web is not a physical entity. A good analogy might be to think of the Internet as the telephone system, and the WWW as the way in which you use the telephone (dial seven digits, wait for the person to answer, speak, and so on). The Internet is the physical network, and the WWW is one of the ways it is used.

The term *Web* stems from the way in which HTML (Hypertext Markup Language, the language of the WWW) works. Hypertext is a system that enables a programmer to make simple text interactive by allowing it to directly refer to something else. For instance, a line of text in an encyclopedia might define the Chesapeake Bay Retriever as "a breed of dog originally from the Chesapeake Bay region of the Eastern United States." The same definition in hypertext might look this way: "*a breed of dog originally from the Chesapeake Bay region of the Eastern United States.*" (See Figure 1.3.)

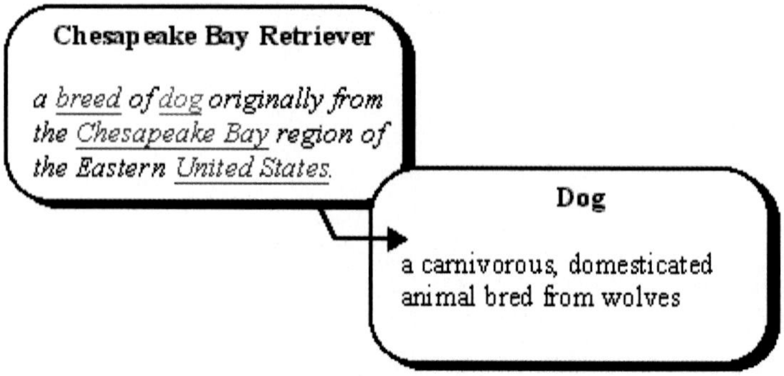

Figure 1.3.
A hypertext link.

By selecting one of the underlined words, the reader is requesting more information on that subject. Exactly what additional information is given depends on how the hypertext document was designed. A CD-ROM encyclopedia might simply link the underlined text to the definition of the word (Dog: a carnivorous, domesticated animal bred from wolves), or it may link to the complete history of dogs.

Basically, hypertext is a way of presenting information in a simple, interactive, and intuitive manner. It enables people to get the information in their own way, and at the level of detail they require. In doing this, hypertext provides a way to organize large amounts of information and to communicate this information effectively.

The original idea behind the WWW was to take the huge resources of the Internet and provide ways to access as little or as much of it as someone might want. It required the people designing the hypertext "pages" (the files that contain the information) to seek out and provide links to other "pages" for cross-reference. Because of the vastness of the Internet, this is no small task.

To use the same example, the dog part of the previous definition might link out to a computer system at the American Kennel Club, or to a page on the same system as the original page that contains a poem about dogs. Where the link takes the user is up to the author—which is you, dear reader—and this is an issue we address throughout the book. The fact that it *can* link elsewhere, that you or I or anyone with a computer and a phone line can be reading about a type of dog on a page stored at one computer, click on a word, and suddenly be reading a completely different file from a completely different machine thousands of miles away— *that* is little short of a miracle.

Now, imagine that you had a page with several links to pages on several different computer systems. If you tried to draw a diagram of the page links on a map, you might draw lines from the computer with the first page, to the computers holding the other pages it is linked to, to the computers holding the other pages they each link to, and so on. Pretty soon your map would begin to look like a tangled mess of lines coming from one central point (the original page). It looks a little like a spider's web, thus the name World Wide Web.

At first, the Web simply connected text. Although this is itself an incredible feat, it wasn't really enough to make Mr. and Ms. Average American run out and buy a computer, and only the high-tech firms made much use of it for communications. What made the World Wide Web feasible for business communications, and what made it the incredible communications tool that everyone is talking about, is what cave dwellers learned thousands of years before the written word. The giant leap that brought the Internet out of the computer room and into the offices and boardrooms and kitchens of the world was the development of the technology to a point that it could also show graphics (as in Figure 1.4). As any good caveman (or cavewoman) could tell you, a picture is worth a thousand words.

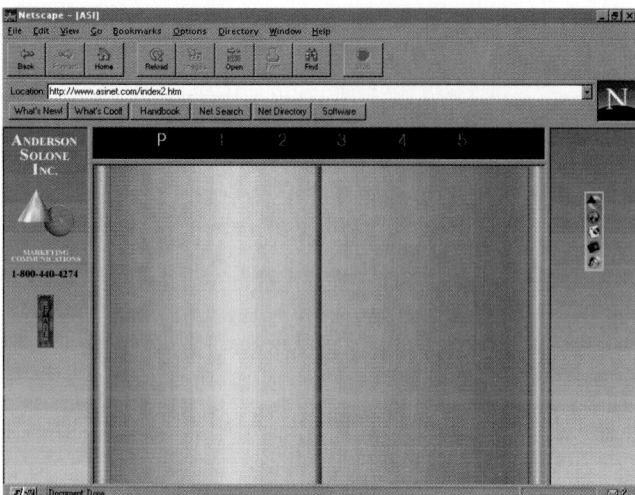

Figure 1.4.
A graphical Web site.

Unlike spamming the Usenet, where your message is copied over and over again and sent to every system on the Net, the WWW works by request. People only receive the information they ask for. While there are still some hard core fanatics who hate the fact that the Internet is now commercialized, there is little they can say when the commercial applications of the Internet take place on a by-request-only basis.

WHAT IS EFFECTIVE MARKETING COMMUNICATION?

Again, the basic components of marketing are the four Ps: Place (selection and design of distribution channels to reach a market), Product (design and development of the product), Price (determining the price), and Promotion (all aspects of generating or enhancing demand for the product, including, but not limited to, advertising). For the most part, the marketing communications we are discussing in relation to the WWW focuses on the fourth P, promotion. However, by use of the WWW, design, development, pricing, and distribution all can be addressed.

Many people think of marketing as simply advertising, and although advertising is a crucial part of marketing, it is only one aspect. We prefer an overall approach. When we speak of *marcom*, short for marketing communications, we are addressing advertising, publicity, customer service, interoffice communications, and a whole variety of other ways in which information is transferred.

For the purpose of this book, *marcom* can be defined as "any and all communications that lead to the presentation of goods or services for commercial sale." Putting an ad in the paper is advertising; writing a press release is publicity; visibly contributing to the local zoo is public relations; and keeping in touch with clients is customer relations. All of these things fall under the umbrella of marketing.

CURRENT INTERNET STATISTICS— WHO'S OUT THERE?

Any good marketing campaign needs to address the issue of demographics. Demographics uses statistical information to help define a market. These statistics are generally collected via surveys, which are then extrapolated to paint a picture of the entire audience. Before we look into the Internet itself, let's discuss how statistics work in general.

A NOTE ON STATISTICS

"There are three kinds of lies: lies, damned lies, and statistics."—Benjamin Disraeli

We begin this section with our favorite quote on statistics. Our point is not that all statistics are useless; on the contrary, they can contain data that can lead to valuable insights. However, they can be (and have been) skewed in order to promote a certain ideal. Organizations can "put a spin" on statistics in order to paint a picture that is beneficial to them while seemingly keeping the factual integrity of the statistics intact.

"Four out of five dentists use Brand X!" Wow, Brand X must be really good, right? Or maybe Brand X is sent free to dentists, and when asked if they had used the sample, 80 percent of the dentists said yes, they had tried it. The statistic is still "true," but it just doesn't have the same impact if you say "Four out of five dentists used our free sample!" Or how about, "Studies show, no aspirin is stronger than Bitter Aspirin"? Well, the studies show that no aspirin is weaker, either; aspirin is aspirin.

In surveys and tests, the actual data and the way in which that data is presented (the extrapolation) can vary wildly. There is a science to statistics that is based on the idea that by collecting enough data, you can apply that data to the entire population. However, the science and protocols used in statistical studies are open enough to allow for erroneous information.

Imagine you performed a telephone survey in which you asked people whether they put their toilet paper on the roller overhand or underhand. When you were finished, say you had 10,000 responses from across the United States (which is a statistically significant number). Of the 10,000, say 75 percent of the respondents hung their toilet paper overhand. Does this mean that 75 percent of the people in the United States hang their toilet paper that way? No, it doesn't.

What this survey would show is that 75 percent of the type of people *who would have taken the time to answer the survey* hang their toilet paper that way. See the difference? So there is a big issue concerning the way in which data is collected, as CommerceNet/Nielsen found out.

RESULTS OF THE COMMERCENET/ NIELSEN SURVEY

Know your audience—this is the first step in any successful marketing campaign. The results of the CommerceNet/Nielsen Internet Demographics Survey provide the most definitive answers to date about the Internet; it is arguably the most widely used and accepted company for Internet statistics. But before we delve into those figures, here are a few words of caution.

CONSIDER THE SOURCE

One goal of the CommerceNet/Nielsen Internet Demographics Study was to test the validity of results collected via Internet-based questionnaires. CommerceNet and Nielsen hypothesized that there would be fundamental differences in the results of a survey conducted online versus results collected via telephoning a nationally representative sample. The company also speculated that the results from the Internet-based questionnaire would be skewed by heavy users. The graphs in Figures 1.5–1.7 illustrate a few key comparisons of the results from the two surveys that support these hypotheses.

Figure 1.5.
Comparing the
frequency of Internet
usage.

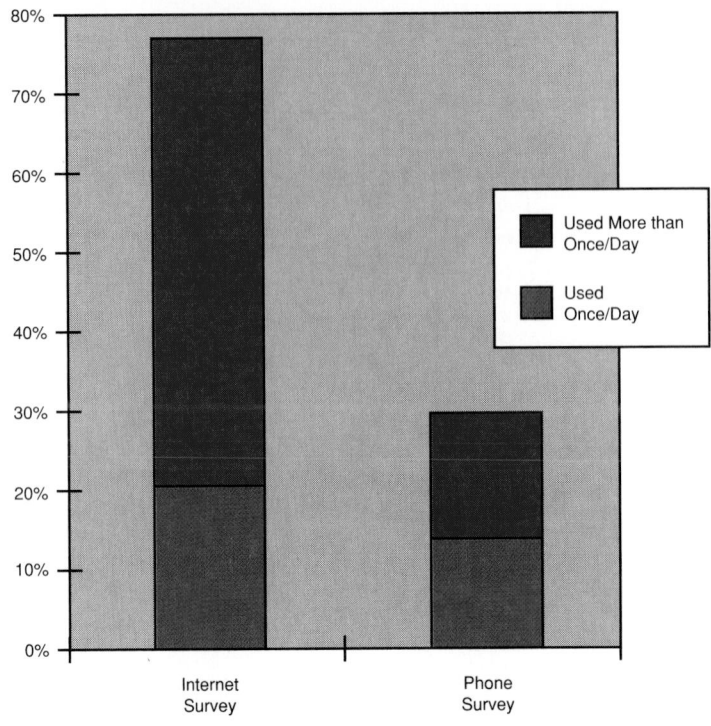

Figure 1.6.
Comparing the skills
of Internet users.

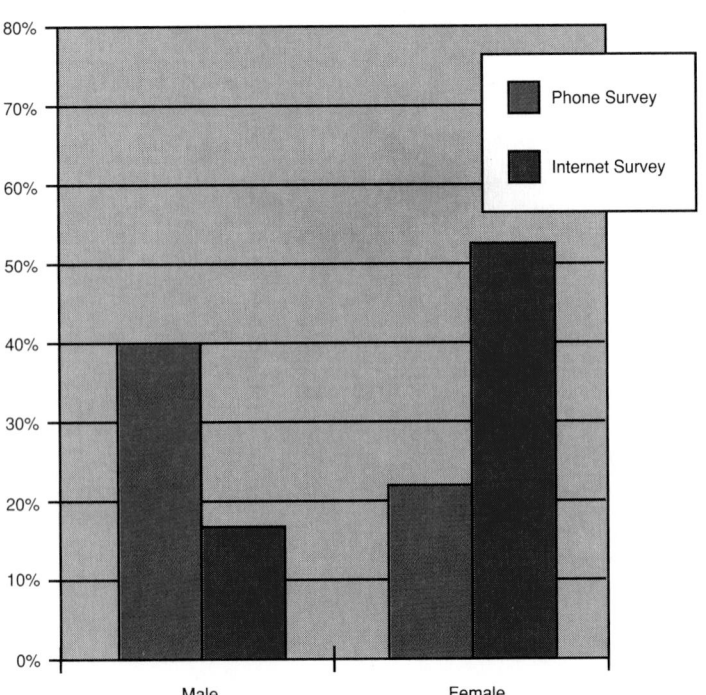

Figure 1.7.
Comparing the gender of Internet users, phone versus online survey.

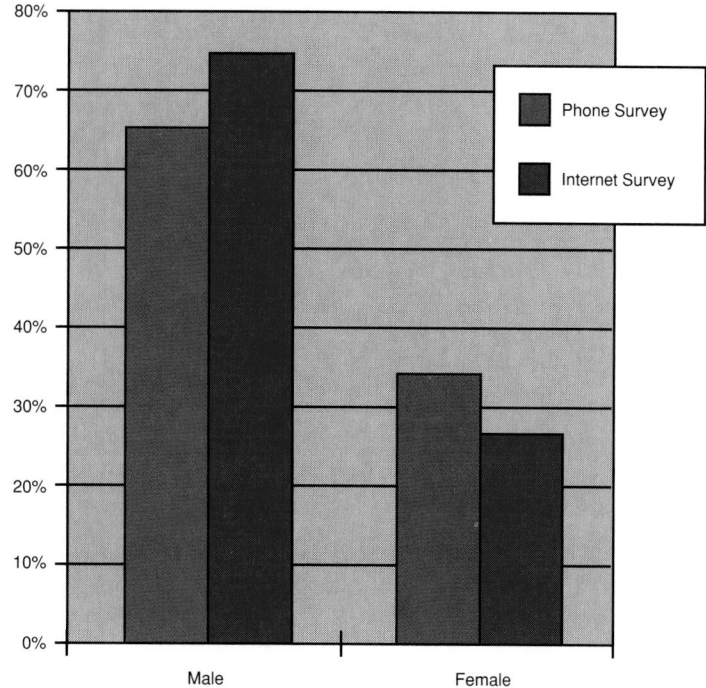

As these results appear to indicate, studies based on data collected from the Internet alone cannot be used to project the population as a whole. These examples show that projections from WWW site surveys differ from the results of surveys of the broader users. The WWW site studies, for instance, overstate Internet usage, overestimate the skill level of the Internet users, and downplay the size of the female market for Internet services. The use of such inaccurate information could result in miscalculations in businesses' current use of the Internet and ongoing Internet plans. This is not to say that these WWW-based surveys have no value. It is, however, extremely important to understand the limitations of information gathered from WWW site questionnaires.

It is important to keep these issues in mind when viewing statistical information in books and magazines, as well as statistics that are available on the Internet itself. We should also note the obvious question of these statistics' timeliness, which is why we list URLs in the back of this book, in addition to posting updated links to statistical information at our Web site .www.hampton.org. Now, the results.

LOCATIONS OF INTERNET AND ONLINE USAGE

Respondents who had used the Internet in the three months prior to the survey were asked when they had last used it. Those who had used the Internet within the previous 24 hours were then asked to identify the access location.

- ◆ Sixty-six percent indicated that they had last used the Internet at work.
- ◆ Forty-four percent had most recently accessed it from home.
- ◆ Eight percent had most recently used the Internet at school.

Persons who used the Internet in the 24-hour period used an average of 1.2 access locations. Even though a higher percentage of people have access in the home, people use the Internet more frequently and for greater durations at work than at home. (Note that the survey period was in August when, presumably, most students would be out of class and therefore not using the Internet in the same manner they would during the normal school year.)

Hours of Usage

Overall usage of both the Internet and online services was significant. On average, all persons 16 and older in the United States and Canada who had used the Internet in the previous three months had used it for 5 hours and 28 minutes per week. The average person with online service access (who had ever used it) used the service for an average of 2 hours and 29 minutes per week. To provide a common base for a more direct comparison, the average minutes per week among all persons (in United States and Canada, 16 and, older) was calculated. The average for the Internet was 35 minutes per week per person in the United States and Canada and for online services, 24 minutes per week per person. In total, the Internet is receiving 46 percent more usage than online services.

To obtain a better understanding of Internet usage, these results were compared to the viewing of rented videotapes. Although on the surface it appears small, the 35 minutes of Internet usage per week per is similar to the total time spent in viewing rented videotapes.

Duration of Usage

Although persons 16 and older with a direct Internet connection made up only 44 percent of those with access, they accounted for 60 percent of persons who had used the Internet in the three-month period and 73 percent of those who had used it in the 24-hour period. The differences in usage between the Internet and online services may be much more a function of having the meter running on online services than it is content or other issues. (Note that, in this survey, direct Internet access is a connection through an Internet service provider, or via an employer's direct access to the Internet; indirect access is an entry to the Internet via commercial online services.)

Gender Differences

Users of both the Internet and online services are primarily male. Males comprise 66 percent of users of the Internet (see Figure 1.8). In addition, males tend to use the Internet with both greater frequency and duration than females, accounting for approximately 77 percent of the total usage. Males comprise 59 percent of the users of online services and are responsible for 63 percent of the total usage. There is less of a gender skew on online services than there currently is with the Internet.

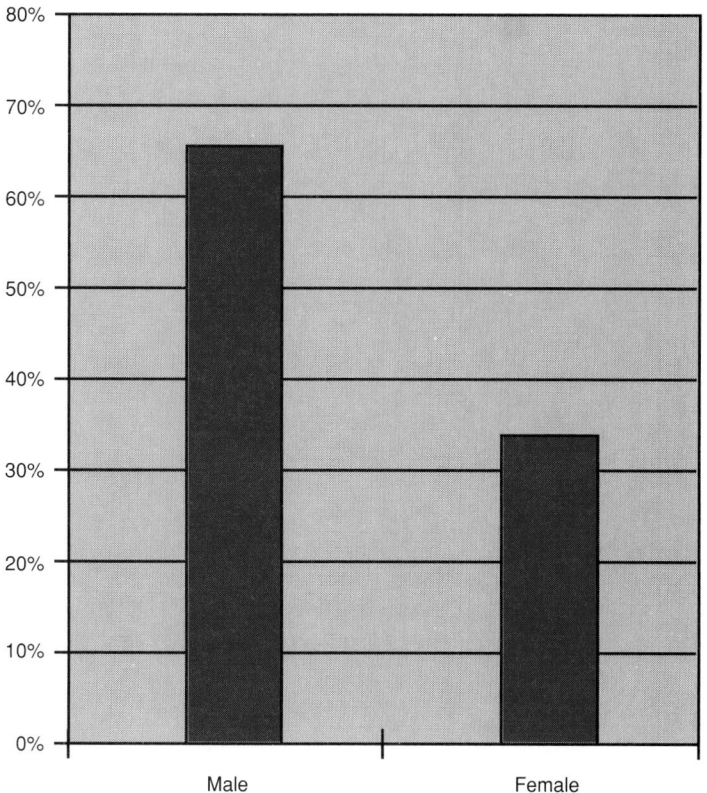

Figure 1.8.
Gender differences
on the Internet.

USES OF THE INTERNET

Those persons who used the Internet in the 24 hours before the survey used it more often to access the WWW than to send e-mail. The percent of Internet users who indicated frequent use of Internet applications other than e-mail during the three-month period studied was also considerable, as shown in Table 1.1.

Table 1.1. Use of Internet applications in a 24-hour period.

Use of Internet	Percentage of Users
To access the WWW	72 percent
To send e-mail	65 percent
To download software	31 percent
To participate in an interactive discussion	21 percent
To partake in a noninteractive discussion	36 percent
To use another computer	31 percent
To utilize real-time audio or video	19 percent

WWW Usage and Demographics

Of those individuals 16 years of age or older in the United States and Canada who had used the Internet during the three months preceding the survey, 76 percent had at some time used the World Wide Web. This is equivalent to more than 8 percent of total 16+ populations in the United States and Canada having used the WWW.

WWW users are clearly upscale, compared with the population as a whole. For example

- Twenty-five percent of WWW users earn household incomes of more than $80,000, whereas only 10 percent of the total U.S. and Canadian population have that level of income.

- Fifty percent of WWW users consider themselves to be in professional or managerial occupations. In contrast, 27 percent of the total U.S. and Canadian population categorize themselves to have such positions.

- Sixty-four percent of WWW users have at least a college degree, while the U.S. and Canadian national level is 29 percent.

Table 1.2 outlines some of these statistics.

Table 1.2. Comparing WWW users to the population of the United States and Canada.

Age	WWW Users	Total Population
16–24	22 percent	18 percent
25–34	30 percent	21 percent
35–44	26 percent	22 percent
45–54	17 percent	16 percent
55 or older	5 percent	21 percent

Education	WWW Users	Total Population
Less than High School	4 percent	11 percent
High School	8 percent	33 percent
Technical School	1 percent	3 percent
Some College	24 percent	24 percent
Completed College	29 percent	17 percent
Some Post Grad	9 percent	3 percent
Post Grad	26 percent	8 percent

Occupation	WWW Users	Total Population
Professional	37 percent	18 percent
Technical	12 percent	6 percent
Admin/Managerial	14 percent	9 percent
Clerical	3 percent	6 percent
Sales	5 percent	5 percent
Service Worker	2 percent	4 percent
Laborer	2 percent	7 percent
Craftsperson	1 percent	3 percent
Homemaker	1 percent	11 percent
Military	2 percent	1 percent
Full-time Student	16 percent	8 percent
Retired/Not Working	2 percent	17 percent

Household Income	WWW Users	Total Population
Under $10K	1 percent	7 percent
$10–19.9K	4 percent	9 percent
$20–29.9K	7 percent	12 percent
$30–39.9K	10 percent	14 percent
$40–49.9K	10 percent	11 percent
$50–59.9K	11 percent	9 percent
$60–69.9K	9 percent	6 percent
$70–79.9K	10 percent	4 percent
$80–89.9K	7 percent	3 percent
$90–99.9K	4 percent	2 percent
$100K or over	14 percent	5 percent
Don't Know/Refuse	14 percent	17 percent

Survey participants were then asked if they had *ever* used the Web to search for various kinds of information, purchase products, or browse, as Table 1.3 illustrates.

Table 1.3. Percentage of Web users who use the Web in various ways.

Use of Web	Percentage
Search for information on products/services	55 percent
Search for information on companies/organizations	60 percent
Search for other information	73 percent
Purchase products or services	14 percent
Browse or explore	90 percent

BUSINESS USES

Approximately half of all persons 16 and older in the United States and Canada who have used the WWW have done so for business purposes. Table 1.4 presents a breakdown of those business functions.

Table 1.4. Percentage of users who have utilized the Internet for various business functions.

Business Function	WWW Users
Collaborating with others	54 percent
Publishing information	33 percent

continues

Table 1.4. continued

Business Function	WWW Users
Gathering information	77 percent
Researching competitors	46 percent
Selling products or services	13 percent
Purchasing products or services	23 percent
Providing customer service and support	38 percent
Communicating internally	44 percent
Providing vendor support and communications	50 percent

KEY CONCLUSIONS OF THE STUDY

- Seventeen percent (37 million) of total persons aged 16 and over in the United States and Canada have access to the Internet.
- There is a sizable base of Internet users in the United States and Canada.

  24 million Internet users (16 years of age or older)

  18 million WWW users (16 years of age or older)
- WWW users are a key target for business applications. They are upscale, professional, and well educated.

  Approximately 2.5 million people have made purchases using the WWW.
- The Internet is skewed male in terms of both usage and users.
- Access through work is an important factor for both the Internet and online services.
- Internet users average 5 hours and 28 minutes per week on the Internet.
- Total Internet usage exceeds usage of online services and is approximately equivalent to the playback time per person of rented videotapes.
- The use of the Internet differs from that of commercial online services.
- Internet-based surveys do not represent the population as a whole.

Now you have the most reliable information available about the Internet. This is enough data to convince most businesses that the WWW and Internet represent a viable, high-quality market. Of course, this is only one of many reasons a company may wish to develop an Internet presence. In the following section, we address a few more.

THIRTEEN REASONS TO PUT A BUSINESS ON THE WORLD WIDE WEB

Having worked on many, many marketing campaigns, we have come to abhor the business evangelists who claim to have narrowed down the entire art and science of conducting business into something like the "Seven Keys to Success." We don't want you to think for a second that this list is anything like that.

What this list represents are some of the very good reasons we've found for doing business on the Internet. However, we loathe the idea that people might try to limit themselves and their campaigns to these few items. Simply think of these as a starting-off point.

1. **To establish a presence.**

   Globally, approximately 50 million people have access to the World Wide Web. Quite simply, there are few businesses that can ignore a market of this size. In the near future, having an e-mail address and Web site will be like having a phone number and business card—crucial to even small companies.

2. **To network.**

   By linking your pages with those of your networked contacts, you are referring clients back and forth. If, for instance, your product complements, is used within, or uses a product from another manufacturer, a potential client can get a complete package of information with just a few clicks of a mouse.

3. **To provide availability advertising.**

   There's little doubt that the most used resource directory is the Yellow Pages. Imagine a book of Yellow Pages that covers the globe—all a client would need to do is tell it what he or she was looking for, and it would automatically open to your listing. That's exactly how the WWW works.

   Not only can you list basic information (your business expertise, location, hours, how to contact you, methods of payment, and so on), but you can update this information instantly (time-sensitive specials, current interest rates, announcements, and press releases). You can even have an entire catalog, including full-color photographs and graphics, available for instant viewing and ordering.

4. **To augment traditional advertising.**

   Imagine including a brochure with every business card, piece of letterhead, print or broadcast ad, and even in your telephone's on-hold messages. By including your WWW address, that's exactly what you can do. A WWW address, such as www.hampton.org, is small enough to fit anywhere, yet it provides instant access to your entire sales argument. Furthermore, an instant e-mail response can be built into Web pages to get and give feedback while the questions are still fresh in your customer's mind, without the cost and lack of response of business reply mail.

   If you read any of the nation's largest magazines and newspapers, you'll notice more and more WWW addresses printed within advertisements. The reason for this is simple: The WWW allows a much higher degree of communication for the advertising investment—"more bang for the buck."

5. **Customer service.**

   People wiser than we have often said that it's easier to keep an old customer than to get a new one. Keeping an open line of communication is one of the most important ways to serve your customers. Via the WWW, you can post information, troubleshooting tips, request forms, and the like that will enable you to "keep your finger on the pulse" of your customers.

6. **Publicity.**

The media is perhaps the most advanced profession today in regard to electronic communication because their main product is information, and they can get it more quickly, cheaply, and easily online. Because of this, online press kits are becoming more and more common. Most pressrooms have gone digital in the past decade, so it is much easier for them to simply take a press release and photos from a Web site than it would be for them to strip-in hardcopy. The easier you make it for the press, the more likely you are to have your press releases turn into articles in a timely fashion.

7. **To open international markets.**

We were recently confronted by an issue where a foreign customs official held a package of print proofs for ransom. If these proofs had been made available on the WWW, this could not have happened. As the United States is discovering, digital information has little respect for international boundary lines. Because of this, markets that may have once been too difficult to approach can now be very profitable.

With a Web site, you can open up a dialogue with international markets as easily as with the company across the street. We'll go so far as to say that you should decide how you want to handle the international business that will come your way before you start a Web site, because it is a good possibility that your online marketing will bring international opportunities—whether it is part of your plan or not. We once posted an ad for an old Jeep on a local Usenet group (not even the Web) and were contacted by people as far away as the Netherlands.

Another added benefit: If your company has offices overseas, it can access (and even add to) the home office's information for the price of a local phone call. So the Internet and Web make possible easier international communications *within* a company as well.

8. **To test market new services and products.**

The advertising costs of rolling out a new service or product can be enormous. Many times, because of the cost of printing and mailing, companies hold off releasing new products until the next generation of their catalog. On the Web, new products and services can be released globally and instantly; updating a Web page to include a new item costs a fraction of what it would to print a new catalog. The Internet's two-way communication also enables you to receive immediate feedback from your markets.

9. **To reach a highly desirable demographic market.**

The demographic of the WWW user is probably the highest mass-market demographic available. College educated, high income, credit card holders (most ISPs require credit card deposits)—it's no wonder that magazines that deal with the Internet and WWW are easily able to get high-revenue ads on a regular basis.

10. **To reach the specialized market.**

Thinking of selling nude photos of George Bush? With millions of Internet users, even the most narrowly defined interest group will be represented. And, because of the search capabilities of the WWW, your potential customers will be able to find you.

11. **To provide 24-hour, 7-day accessibility.**

A fax may come in from Tokyo at 2:00 in the morning. By the time someone comes in to open the office, the sale is lost. By accessing your WWW system, however, the same potential client could have surveyed your brochure and placed an order—for less than it cost to send the fax.

12. **To save money.**

Say your company prints 10,000 copies of a brochure. You send 2,000 out via the mail, give 2,000 to the sales staff, and put 6,000 in a warehouse for later use. Over the next few months, you add new products/services, you move offices, or you add partners. You now have thousands of outdated brochures.

One of the main reasons that so many of the largest corporations in the world have rushed to the WWW is to try to contain print and print-storage costs.

13. **To sell.**

Obviously, sales is the most important part of any business—so why didn't we make this the first item on the list? Because a good businessperson will have seen that all of the other points listed add up to increased sales. The WWW is perhaps the most powerful marketing tool ever devised, but it is only a tool. Even the most perfect promotional system can't make up for a poor product or service, inept staff, or any of the hundreds of intangible stumbling blocks that lie in the way of successful sales. However, with the powerful communication tools and enormous market available in Internet marketing, there's far less of a gamble.

The fact is that clients can find you; review your information in text, pictures, and even sound and video; contact your sales staff; and place an order from their own desks within a matter of minutes, 24 hours a day. No other form of business communication provides this degree of sales support.

SKIPPING AHEAD

OK, Mr. or Ms. Smartypants, so you think you're above all this basic stuff? Well, you may be right. While we have designed this book with the idea that it will be useful to everyone, we understand that you may be at a different stage of the game.

The best advice we can give on this point is to read what you have time for. If you're already staring down the throat of a deadline, for example, you may not have time to read anything but the Quick & Dirty Guides. If, on the other hand, you're trying to get a solid understanding of this medium and you've got the time, you'll want to cover every chapter.

What we're trying to say is that you should feel free to skip ahead, but understand that you'll be missing quite a bit more than just some basic overview if you decide to do so.

QUICK & DIRTY GUIDE
The Quick and Easy Way to Get You Up and Running

First of all, we should admit that the nature of this book suffers a kind of identity crisis. On the one hand, there are no quick and easy ways to set up effective marketing campaigns. On the other hand, we know there are times when the priority is not the best campaign but *any* campaign. So, this book is designed to help overcome the same crisis we often face as marketing professionals—*you want it good, or you want it fast?*

By following the Quick & Dirty Guides in each chapter, you can meet your deadline. You can then come back to read the full chapter, taking the time to ponder every detail when you're not sweating bullets at 3 a.m. Unfortunately, there are not always easy options, and many steps have no quick-fix substitutes; in these cases, we offer guides to efficiency.

SUMMARY

In this chapter, we've scratched the surface of marketing and discussed the evolution of the Internet as a medium for marketing communications. We've also discussed some of the key points that make the World Wide Web such an excellent marketing tool. Now that we have a general idea of how marketing can be applied to the Net, we can begin narrowing things down. In the following chapter, we explore some of the possibilities of WWW communications and begin planning a Web site.

Developing an Effective Web Strategy

Ready, set, go! Now we're going to build a Web site. As with any project, the planning phase is crucial to success. Rushing in blindly, slapping some graphics on a page of text, and posting it are the steps to producing a *bad* Web site. If you've surfed the Web much, you've noticed that that is the way many sites are developed—but not ours, and not yours.

This part of the book is not about developing a marketing strategy; that is covered in Part II, "Designing a Site that Succeeds." This part of the book is about developing a strategy for getting *on* the Web. However, you'll have to have some idea of the scope of the project before you can begin laying down a plan. It's really a catch-22 situation—how can you develop a plan before you have a budget, and how can you set a budget before you have a plan?

To try to overcome this dilemma, we want to briefly address the communications possibilities of the WWW in the broadest scope. We want you to begin thinking of the possibilities right now, so that you can keep your options open while you deal with the costs of development. By doing this, we hope that you'll have a good idea of what you want to do by the time we get to Part II.

Your site will be developed to suit a purpose—as will ours. You are trying to communicate something, and to do that, you'll have to decide what that something is, whom you want to communicate with, and how you'll provide the communication. First things first: What do you want to communicate?

ASSESSING YOUR GOALS

The first step in any marketing project is to assess your goals—you've got to know where you want to end up before you decide on how to get there. As mentioned earlier, there are many ways

of utilizing the WWW, so it is important to decide what you want to do before discussing how you want to do it.

The best thing to do is to begin taking notes. Keep in mind that marketing on the Web isn't just about sales, it's about providing information, public relations, customer service, and more. Set your goals reasonably and in detail. Don't just write down "make lots of money." Instead, you should be addressing how you would intend to make lots of money:

- Do you want to increase awareness about a product or service?
- Do you want to reach new markets?
- Do you want to provide a simple way to order your product/ service?
- Do you want to improve relations with existing customers?

In the case of `hampton.org`, for instance, we wanted to do several things:

- Provide online resources for HTML development.
- Provide hotlist links to other resources.
- Provide a gathering place for our readers.
- Provide for reader feedback.

After you've made a list of things *you'd* like to achieve, you can begin to design a way of achieving them. The next step in this is to figure out who it is you're talking to.

VIEW YOURSELF AS OTHERS WOULD VIEW YOU

When planning your site, try to look at things from the customer/ client point of view, not your own. Ask around, get advice and suggestions from your customers and clients. Ask them what they would like to see.

Don't just get one opinion, get dozens. Ask anyone you can, and take notes. You may get different opinions from each person you ask, but that's OK. One of the most powerful aspects of WWW marketing is that you can address many different types of people within a single Web site. Because the WWW is interactive, people can choose their own path through your Web site, and thus customize their own presentation.

DEVELOPING YOUR STRATEGY

After you've formed an idea of what you want to say, and who you want to have listening, you can begin to decide how you're going to communicate. A big pitfall we've noticed in WWW design is that authors often seem to limit themselves to what is available through traditional media. This is to say that many people see a Web page as a billboard, while others fill page after page with dense text. Divorce yourself from the concept of traditional communication; we've just begun to understand the possibilities of interactive media, and setting your sites too low is easy to do.

Again, the WWW enables you to reach several different types of people, at varying levels of communication. We address this in more detail in Part II of this book, but you should already be thinking of the possibilities. To get you started, here are just a few of the ways the Internet and WWW can be used:

- **Publications:** Newsletters, product information
- **Company profiles:** Who you are, what you do, where you are
- **Staff recruitment:** Simplifying your hiring process
- **Education or Tutorials:** Guides to your product or service, customer support, product training
- **Corporate Information:** Stockholder reports, financial statements, and so on
- **Public Relations:** Community service; for example, sponsoring a page within your site
- **Online Presentations:** Marketing productions with multimedia, sound, video
- **Catalogs/Online Ordering**
- **Networking:** Links to your distributors, suppliers, associations, and so on
- **White Papers:** Technical information on your product
- **Prospect Generation:** Feedback forms, mailing lists
- **Customer Service:** Product support via e-mail, online chat, even video conferencing
- **Internal Communications**: Intranet

You'll notice that many of these things cross over, and many lead to whole new possibilities. The idea is that you should be thinking in terms of a blank canvas—let the gears start turning. You'll run into technological and budget limitations as this book continues, and these will help you narrow things down. For now, your imagination is your best tool.

STARTING SMALL OR HITTING IT BIG

Now we're going to start chipping away at the grand ideas you've begun developing. Were this a perfect world, you'd have all the money, time, and resources necessary to make the perfect Web site. Well, guess what? We don't know how much you have to spend, how long a timeframe you have to work with, or whom you can rely upon for input and assistance. All we can hope for is to give you the tools necessary for making the right decisions.

One of the many great things about WWW design is that your Web site has a chance to evolve. While your grand ideas of an elaborate Web site may not become reality for quite some time, you can lay the foundations early on. While you will probably not be able to do everything you want on your first Web site, you can keep all these things in mind as you continue to develop your site—before and after it is first published. In this way you can think big, but start small.

Starting small is a good idea, especially if you have limited resources. You have a better chance of success if you leave such things as your very own server, bells and whistles, CGI scripts, online transactions, internal search engines, and online databases until after you have established a working site. By keeping it simple and adding on slowly, you can get online more quickly, start with a limited investment, have more time for a hands-on approach to each aspect of the project, and greatly reduce your chance of system bugs. Most importantly, starting small allows you to build your site based on your own online market research.

There are a few situations when releasing a major Web site is advantageous. If you have the resources (budget, talent, and time), you can orchestrate a release that can really wow the masses. You just can't beat a well-timed promotion, and combining your Web release with other media (direct mail, print, and so on) can give you a slam-dunk. So, if you do have the resources, and you are planning on the WWW being part of a major campaign, it might be in your best interest to pull out all the stops.

WHAT'S ALL THIS GOING TO COST?

Here's where we get down to the nitty-gritty. Take out those notes you've made of intended uses for your site, take a look at your marketing budget, and let's see if you can afford it. You don't have a marketing budget? What are you thinking? We cannot overstate the importance of determining costs and setting an online marketing budget before proceeding any further. We are always amazed to find companies who go blindly into the online world with Java this and multimedia that all over the place, only to find they have no budget left to promote the thing. Or worse, we've seen people who put so much time, effort, and expense into the bells and whistles of a site that they don't have the resources to develop content. Thus, their very gee-whiz site doesn't do much good.

Don't forget, there is a huge cost difference between putting up simple product information and conducting business and transactions on the Web. Keep this in mind if you're working on a limited budget. There is good news, however: Internet marketing is relatively cheap (compared to print, radio, television, direct mail), and with the help of this book you can cut costs even further by doing most (and even all) of the work yourself. You can also use the Internet to save money on telephone bills, mail, printing, avoiding customer returns, and so on. In fact, cost avoidance is the reason many companies are drawn to the Web in the first place.

In figuring costs, you have a few options.

OPTION 1: MAKE A BROAD BALLPARK ESTIMATE

With the aid of the following information, guesstimate where your company fits in. This is, of course, the simplest way to do things—though too broad for most uses.

If you do everything yourself, have a small site, and go with a cheap hosting service, you may be able to get online for as little as $125 (we consider domain name registration a necessary expense); then there are your monthly Web site and dial-up fees (which can be as low as $30 a month). This equals a minimum of $485 for the first year. Impossible, you say? Well, here is a breakdown of the way we got our first site up and running cheaply:

Domain registration	$100 (actually, we lucked out on this one—Internic was not yet charging this fee)
Virtual host setup fee	$25
Software	$0

Note:

We used mostly shareware or freeware available on the Net for our first system, much of which is included on the CD-ROM that came with this book. While this was adequate when we were first starting out, we have since invested thousands of dollars in specialized (mainly graphics and 3-D rendering) software. Since we were already an established design firm, we also had the graphics and copywriting skills in-house.

Also, shareware isn't free. If you feel that you will continue to use a shareware product, you are obligated to pay for it.

Time (and a lot of it)	$0
First-year online fees	$360
Total	$485

If you are sure of your do-it-all-yourself plan, you can skip now to the Quick & Dirty Guide at the end of this chapter.

For those of you who will need some help, Web sites vary hugely in price and size. For the year, small companies can expect to pay from $3,500 for a small site on a hosting service, up to $15,000 and beyond. Midsize companies can expect to spend from $4,500 to $75,000 on up, while large companies can expect costs to range anywhere from $75,000 to more than $1 million for a corporate Web site, servers, marketing development, design team, and so forth. For most companies, a good base would be 10 percent of your marketing budget (which should be 10 percent of your sales), so if your company sales are about $1 million a year, your marketing budget should be around $100,000, and you should be thinking of spending around $10,000 on your Web site.

Here's what some of the big guns have paid:

Organization	Cost	Reference	Note
Information Solutions, Inc.	$15,000	*Business Journal of Milwaukee*, 8/12/95, "Communications Medium for the 21st Century"	Development cost
Saturn	$20,000	*ADWEEK*, 1/15/96, "After the Year of the Web"	Initial cost; site then expanded
Hyatt Hotels	$52,000	*Newsday*, 4/10/95, "Doing Business on the Internet"	For initial setup on TravelWeb
COM	$81,000	COM *Talk*, Spring '95 Boston University College of Communications Newsletter	Financed by a research and development grant
Times Mirror Magazine, SKInet	$100,000	*Interactive Marketing News*, 9/29/95, "Don't Surf Net...Ski on It"	Development cost
Scholastic	$130,000	*Interactive Age*, 5/8/95, "Breaking the Silence"	Information from Director of Network Development
Hitachi America	$250,000	*Interactive Marketing News*, 9/29/95, "Hitachi America Launches..."	Expects to spend $45K/mo. site maintenance

Organization	Cost	Reference	Note
Procter and Gamble	$300,000	*ADWEEK*, 1/15/96, "After the Year of the Web"	Estimated for each major brand, average development cost
Annheuser Busch	$600,000	*ADWEEK*, 1/15/96, "After the Year of the Web"	
Virtual Vineyards	$1 million+	*Interactive Week* 1/15/96	One of the most productive sites in online sales
General Motors	$13 million	*ADWEEK*, 1/15/96, "After the Year of the Web"	Estimate $2–3 million per division

OPTION 2: MAKE A NARROW BALLPARK ESTIMATE

You'll have to decide whether to use your own server or a virtual hosting service. (See Chapter 4, "Deciding on a Server: Maintain Your Own or Hire It Out.") We recommend using a hosting service, as it is less expensive (by far, as you'll see) and will free you to spend your budget and time on other issues.

Now take out your list of intended uses for your site, and guess what resources you may need to make it all happen. Use Table 2.1 as a guide; for more precise figures (specific to you), contact a few Internet consultants for ballpark estimates.

The following list is not intended to be a shopping list for developing your site. Obviously, the purpose of this book is to help you avoid many of these costs. The list is simply to let you know how expensive things can get, so that you won't be led into setting too low a budget.

Table 2.1. Web development costs.

Item	Estimated Cost
Web server hardware, software, connection	$29,000–$220,000
Information systems manager (annual salary)	$30,000–$75,000
Virtual hosting service (annual)	$385–$14,000
PC workstation	$1,900–$4,000

continues

Table 2.1. continued

Item	Estimated Cost
Internet access (annual, ranging from telephone dial-up to high-speed, dedicated line)	$180–$7,000
Creative design and development	$20,000–$450,000
Project manager on salary	$55,000–$150,000
HTML programmer on salary	$35,000–$75,000
Graphic designer on salary	$35,000–$65,000
Research	$0–$35,000
Domain name registration	$100
Online marketing director	$55,000—$150,000
Additional software	$0–$15,000

OPTION 3: MAKE A SPECIFIC RANGE ESTIMATE

Take out your notes of intended uses for your site, and make a list of hardware, software, personnel, and services you will need (don't forget maintenance costs). Now (once you have read the remainder of this chapter) begin getting your bids.

Beware: Companies often grossly underestimate their costs. Even if you have taken the time to outline the most detailed of estimates, there are bound to be a few unexpected costs or time delays. Always allow a cushion in your estimate; the less experience you have, the more cushion you should allow.

There are many ways to keep costs down other than doing it all yourself:

Use a hosting service. (We have heard of no company who has set up their own quality, high-speed T1 server for under $50,000.)

Keep it simple; leave the extras for your revisions.

Use few high-end graphics, and use them wisely (also cuts download time).

Forget all the bells and whistles at the beginning (not only saves money and bandwidth, but decreases your chance for "bugs").

Use brand logos and designs that are already used in company marketing and convert them to use on the Web. (This also helps customers and clients recognize and "feel at home" on your site and gives a continuity to your overall marketing collateral.)

Cut print, phone, and mail costs in other areas by using the Internet.

Do It All Yourself or Hire a Consultant/Subcontractor/Employee

While it is very ambitious to do it all yourself, there can be a great advantage in recruiting help. Ultimately, you will want to develop Web expertise in-house, but in the beginning it is often preferable to hire outside help, particularly if you want to get your site up quickly or plan a site that involves complicated scripts and programming. Luckily, there are many resources available to you.

Internet Consultants

Good Internet consultants are worth their weight in gold, which is what you'll often pay for their services. The expertise of an experienced Internet marketing consultant can be invaluable to a company; a consultant can save you time and money, help your organization gain the most from your site, and market your site to bring in new and existing customers.

Even companies with large information systems departments can reap great advantages by using an Internet consultant. We may be biased in this regard, but the simple fact is the WWW is a very new media; computer professionals who graduated as recently as two years ago had little or no education on it. In addition, many computer professionals have been too busy working in information systems to research, learn about, and publish on the Web. The right consultant can bring together the overall picture of a site, from the computer, marketing, creative, *and* business perspectives. A consultant can manage your entire project, organize your staff and/or subcontractors, purchase hardware and software, and design and develop your site from the ground up. He or she can either work closely with you to make step-by-step decisions, or you can opt to take a totally hands-off approach.

You may be reading this book in order to become that Internet consultant yourself, and we have made every effort to enable you to do this. However, if you have the resources, hiring someone to at least assist on your first project isn't a bad idea. Even if you don't need much help, paying someone for a couple of hours of consulting may help you to put things in perspective and save time and money down the road.

Finding a good consultant can be a project itself. Begin by asking your friends and colleagues for referrals; ask them if they were pleased with the work performed. If you have no luck there, your next step should be the Internet itself. There are sites where consultants list their services; a good place to start may be Yahoo!'s listing of Internet consultants at http://www.yahoo.com/Business_and_Economy/Companies/Internet_Services/Internet_Consulting.

When looking for a consultant, make sure the applicants have overall knowledge and experience (not only with the Internet, but marketing, business practices, and design), and that they can demonstrate this knowledge to you at the interview, with references, a portfolio, and a URL list. Call their references before making a final decision, and ask them whether the work was done on time and on budget, if they are happy with their system, and whether they would recommend the consultant. Most importantly, *ask them if the site was effective*.

Do not fall into the trap of getting a computer geek to design your pages unless you have the resources to provide this person with ongoing design consultation. There is a world of difference between knowing HTML and knowing how to design an effective commercial Web system. Also, make sure that you can communicate with the consultant. If your conversations with the consultant end with your feeling as if you don't know anything, you don't have a good consultant. Consultants may know everything you need to know, but if they can't say things in terms you understand, they're not consulting.

You should expect to pay well for an online professional. Fees can range from $65 to $200 an hour, and vary from region to region. Internet professionals are in high demand, particularly in big cities, so rates will generally be higher there. You can't judge by price alone—don't think that the more someone charges, the better he or she is. We've seen and met many high-priced "experts" whose only experience is in developing small, cheap, cookie-cutter sites. This is not the person to deal with.

Note:
Beware of HTML designer/consultants who have huge client lists. It's better to have produced multiple page systems for a few clients than to have produced single-page systems for multiple clients.

Before preparing a contract, sit down with your consultant. Set aside a couple of hours to write out all your ideas and expectations. Your consultant may have ideas on setting up your site differently, which you should discuss prior to preparing a contract. This will allow the consultant to give you an accurate timeline and bid—and will save you *many* wasted hours.

Some things that may be covered in the bid:

- Site content diagram with section titles (Note: Because of the complexity allowed in HTML design, it can be difficult to develop a clear diagram. An experienced consultant will have already addressed this problem in previous projects.)

- Storyboard of site concept graphically detailing each page's look

- Writing of the copy—whether it involves adapting copy from other collateral or starting from scratch

- Graphics production, conversion, and/or adaptation

- HTML programming

- Special scripting or programming

- Server costs (setup costs: hardware, software, connections)

- Marketing costs (online and offline)

- Maintenance costs (server and service)

The contract will generally take one of two forms:

1. **Retainer agreement**, which is based on a minimum of hours worked. Make sure the work that is to be done is clearly spelled out in the contract, not only the hours. You may also want final approval of any subcontractors the consultant wishes to hire.

2. **Contract agreement**, which is preferable. The consultant works as a general contractor, devising a complete Internet strategy. The consultant bids on the project, and once you accept a bid, the

consultant handles it from there. Make certain that not only the work to be done but also the services or products included (hosting service fees, computer hardware, and so on) are clearly noted in the contract.

Generally, consultants and subcontractors are paid a percentage upon signing the contract (20–50 percent), and are then paid percentages (progress payments) along the way. As always in business, it's a good idea to consult your attorney before signing *any* contract.

COMPUTER CONSULTANT/ CONTRACTOR ISSUES

Another option for finishing your Web project is enlisting the aid of a computer consultant—a geek. If you want to do most of the work yourself, but need some help with the heavy programming, a good geek may be just the ticket. This is especially the case if you already have marketing and design resources.

Obviously, you'll be looking for some specialized skills here, so don't think that the office software-loading person will fit the bill. You're looking for someone with skills and training who can either handle your questions and problems, or at least be able to find resources faster than you could yourself.

Here are some tips for finding the right computer consultant for you.

1. **Begin by asking around**. A good place to start is people you know who have a computer consultant already. Ask them what areas of expertise their computer consultant has, the person's strong and weak points, if they have been happy with the results, and if the person meets their deadlines. Again, you're not looking for just anyone; you need someone with a strong (preferably cross-platform) networking background.

2. **Look to the WWW**. If you can't get a good referral, your next step should be the Web itself. Computer consultants are listed all over the place. A good place to start is Yahoo!'s computer consultants list at `http://www.yahoo.com/Business_and_Economy/Companies/Computers/Consulting/`.

3. **Students for hire**. If you have come this far and still have had no luck finding someone within your price range, your next stop could be your local college or university. As we mentioned earlier, the Internet was founded on research, and most institutions of learning offer free access to the students and faculty. Therefore, these people were some of the first to use and master the Internet. If you are fortunate enough to have a college with a good computer department near you, this can be your ticket to the land of plenty. Head straight for the computer department or student employment office.

Keep in mind that these are students; do not expect the same level of professionalism you would from experienced consultants. Be cautious using them for tasks with a large amount of responsibility, or if you have a tight deadline. It is also extremely important in the case of working with a student to set up a timeline and have frequent progress meetings. The greatest flaw we have seen (in our business as well as from personal experience) in new consultants is that they can easily lose sight of the forest for the trees. The same detail-oriented fascination with the work that has allowed them to excel in computer science often leads them away from focusing on the big picture. They may be able to pull things off by working all-nighters (as we all have done from time to time), but you will all be better off sticking to an incremental timeline.

4. **Consider your long-range needs.** Once you have established a relationship with a computer consultant you trust, you'll never want to let him or her go. For this reason, make sure you consider your long-range needs, not just the immediate crisis. Look for a computer consultant who has the ability to service most or all of the needs you predict.

5. **Find the best computer consultant for you.** Every consultant has a specialty; the trick is finding the one with the right specialty for *your* needs. There is a huge difference between a PC repair specialist and, say, a network systems administrator. Ask them their specialty, and allow them to explain their specific strong points and weaknesses. It is important to allow them to state their specialty, rather than telling them what you need. Many computer consultants like to bill themselves as a "Jack of all trades"; be very skeptical of this, it usually means that they are (as the saying goes) "master of none."

6. **Consider their partnerships.** Many good computer consultants, knowing the importance of specializing, develop partnerships with other consultants or organizations. Do not take this as an admission of their weaknesses, but rather as a sign of their forethought. If you cannot find a computer consultant to meet all of your needs (as is often the case), look for one with established partnerships with other qualified professionals who have the necessary expertise to fill in the gaps.

7. **Test them out.** If possible, test your new computer consultant with a small project. Here's where you can see what they are really made of. Many can talk the talk, but… Make sure they can make things happen before committing to a long-term contract or large project. Be very honest about this—tell them what you're doing and establish a strict deadline. If they can't make it happen knowing a contract depends on it, it's never going to happen.

8. **Details, details, details.** It's extremely important to take the time to cover details with your computer consultant, explaining exactly what you want done and any ideas or expectations you have. It's also a great idea to sketch out your ideas on paper. (Yeah, yeah—we know you're busy, but this is important.) Even the best computer consultant is not a mind reader, and if you don't make your expectations clear from the beginning, you have no one to blame for your disappointment but yourself. It is also important to take the time for preparation before meeting with your consultant. If you plan on developing an online purchasing system, for instance, gather all of the necessary information your consultant needs to make it possible, and make sure that all the information is up-to-date. Doing this will not only increase your chances of satisfaction, it will also allow the consultant to establish a more realistic time and budget estimate.

Again: It's incredibly important to get someone you can talk with. If the person you're considering leaves you feeling confused, or if he or she comes across with an attitude of conceit, keep looking. Don't get stuck in a situation where you're paying someone to *know*; you're paying someone to *do*, and part of that *doing* requires working *with* you.

9. **Consider other options.** Don't get too stuck on specific software or hardware. If you've heard you need a UNIX, Visual Basic, or Perl specialist, ask yourself, as well as your consultant, why? Many companies hire UNIX geeks because they were told they needed one, only to find that's not what they really needed at all. Discuss with the computer consultant what software and hardware he or she feels will get the job done in the best possible manner. A good consultant will know the right tools for the right job, and is the best source of information on the subject. Do not assume that the applications you have in mind are the best for the job. (As in: "I spent $5,000 for that software, and that's the software we're going to use!") After all, that's why you wanted the expert in the first place, right?

10. **Write out the specifics.** With the assistance of an attorney, clearly outline which parts of the project the computer consultant will be responsible for, how much is to be paid and how, the all-important deadline (and penalties for missing it), who suffers the cost of unfinished work, who benefits from time or money left over at the end of a proposed project—and don't forget any confidentiality issues you have. Set up milestones, and just as you would an employee, *check up on them*.

SERVER-SIDE ISSUES

If you plan on using a virtual host, there may be services available to you that can save you time and money. For instance, many hosts now include CGI scripts, secure credit card transactions, mailbots, and shopping services in their monthly fees. Even HTML programming can often be had for reduced rates (but beware, these are usually very basic, low-quality, cookie-cutter sites). If you require these services, keep them in mind while shopping for a host. (See Chapter 5, "Virtual Domain Hosts.") In some (rare) cases, your ISP (Internet Service Provider) can also act as your computer consultant—as long as the ISP fits your other criteria.

EMPLOYEE ISSUES

There are advantages to having your staff in-house; just be sure to qualify them as you would anyone else. Some questions to ask yourself if Joe the computer guy (you know, the one who has a "bitchin' system at home" and always knows the answer to computer questions) says he can design your Web site:

- ◆ Has he published commercial sites on the Web before?
- ◆ Does he have enough technical expertise to get the job done?
- ◆ Does he have design experience?
- ◆ Does he have experience in marketing?
- ◆ Does he understand basic business practices?
- ◆ Can he meet a deadline?

If he doesn't meet all these requirements, that's OK—just have him work on the part he has experience or expertise in and have him read this book. Think of the time in training as an investment in your online future. Whatever decision you make, setting clear deadlines from the beginning will be to everyone's advantage. Have we said this enough? Deadline, deadline, deadline!

If you are looking to hire someone for your team, there are some great resources on the Web for just that purpose. One of our favorites is the Online Career Center at www.occ.com. The site's home page is shown in Figure 2.1.

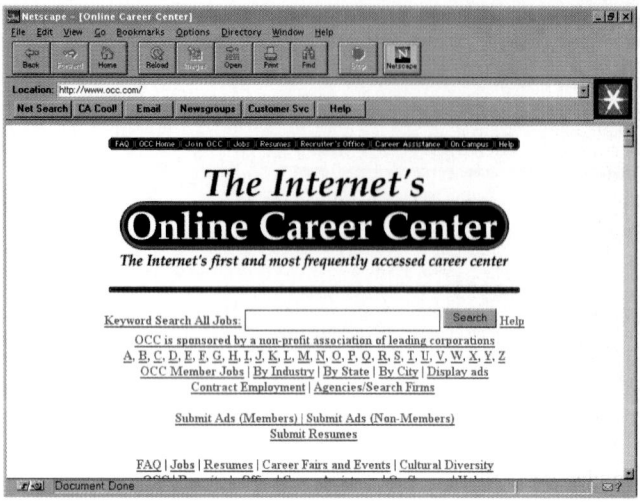

Figure 2.1.
One of the many employee resources on the WWW.

If you address the same issues listed for consultants, you'll have a good start on the selection process for hiring an employee.

GRAPHIC DESIGN SERVICES

Of course, you can design your own graphics. Will they be as good as a professional graphic designer's? Maybe, but probably not. Graphic design is more than making pretty pictures. A good commercial artist will know how human beings perceive color, how people read a page, and so on. Commercial art is about communication, and if you find you just don't have the flair, graphic design services may be just the ticket.

A good place to begin your search for graphic design services is, again, the Web itself; there are listings all over the place. Start at http://www.yahoo.com/Business_and_Economy/Companies/ Graphic_Design/ and work on from there. You can also look in the phonebook for graphic designers and find someone locally. As always, get references from people applicants have worked with and URLs where you can view their work.

There's a catch-22 involved here. Graphic design for the computer screen is different in many ways from graphic design for print, so it is a very good idea to find someone who has experience in creating graphics specifically for computer presentations. On the other hand, the Internet is so hot right now that many people with very little design experience are billing themselves as artists, just because they can make some "cool-looking" graphics. It's been our experience that it's easier to teach a design professional to work within the constraints of computers than it is to get a computer professional to learn commercial art. Either way, Chapter 12, "Working with Graphics," will help both you and your designer (even if you're the same person) develop graphics especially for online marketing.

We recommend you pay graphic designers per graphic and set a clear deadline. It is far simpler for all concerned. The graphic designer should be in direct contact with the HTML programmer, as well as the marketing director. This is vital in saving time, as well as in improving the effectiveness of your site.

You can also choose to purchase stock graphics, but these are not specific to you and generally can also be bought by other companies. They are usually less expensive than a custom design and can be useful for graphics that are not vital to your company image (such as bulleted lists and small icons). Because they are not designed specifically for your system, however, stock graphics can make your site look piecemeal. We make it a policy never to use stock graphics unless they will be used as part of other, more complex custom graphics such as a composite. (See Chapter 12.)

COOPERATIVE EFFORTS

Many smaller companies have found that working in cooperation with friends and colleagues in their Internet venture can be advantageous. For instance, if you're developing a system for a Bed and Breakfast that bills separately owned wineries as a major attraction, and those wineries don't already have pages you can link to, it may be to your advantage to get them involved.

Some potential advantages are

- Sharing a consultant.
- Sharing a common site (which generates additional traffic for each of you).
- Cooperative promotional efforts.
- Developing complementary links to and from each other's sites; more on this in Chapter 22, "International Markets."

There are also drawbacks:

- Only partial control over the site (if shared).
- Sketchy ownership legalities regarding the site.
- Only partial control over who resides on the system. (Your "partner" might want to link to other companies that provide the same service as you, or vice versa.)

Most importantly, if you decide to embark on a cooperative venture:

- Have your own home site (in addition to the shared site).
- Register your own domain name for your site (and own it outright).
- Discuss and write out a clear agreement with all parties involved.
- Give your lawyer a call.

BARTERING

Everyone has strengths and weaknesses. Thanks to the online community, you can meet hundreds and even thousands of people whose strengths are your weaknesses, and vice versa. When you do meet them, keep in touch, as you'll be needing them soon enough. We often use good old-fashioned bartering to get things done in a crunch such as HTML programming for graphic design, animation for a CGI script, football tickets for an icon, and so on.

We've done this quite often, and it has worked well for us in some cases. In other cases, we've found that people seem to move a little more slowly working for barter, and that valuing your services can be a headache. When arranging a barter, make sure you both have a clear understanding of your projects and timelines. And, as with all subcontractors, make sure the people are qualified. You don't want to spend your time doing something for someone else, only to find they're not qualified to complete their part of the bargain.

MAPPING OUT A TIMELINE

Now that you have your team assembled, it's time to map out a timeline to keep you on track.

1. Write down the deadline you set for each member of the team (even if it is just you).

2. Have each team member write out the timelines for their projects and the best days for production meetings. They can either specify dates when individual segments will be done (preferred), or a certain percentage completed. It should look something like Figure 2.2.

Figure 2.2.
A timeline
worksheet.

Timeline for our Web Site

To:	The person in charge
From:	The graphic designer
Project:	Graphics design for our web site: Banners 1-7, Icons 1-7, Large graphics 1-5, Graphic for display ad.
Due:	September 19th

Timeline:

August 1:	Receive sketches from marketing
August 7:	Banner 1 complete
August 8:	Banner 2 complete
August 9:	Banner 3 complete
August 12:	Banner 4 complete
August 13:	Banner 5 complete
August 14:	Banner 6 complete
August 15:	Banner 7 complete
August 19:	Icon 1& 2 complete
August 20:	Icon 3&4 complete
August 21:	Icon 5&6 complete
August 22:	Icon 7 complete
August 26:	Large graphic 1 complete
August 28:	Large graphic 2 complete
August 30:	Large graphic 3 complete
Sept. 3:	Large graphic 4 complete
Sept. 5:	Large graphic 5 complete
Sept. 12:	Graphic for display ad complete

Note: My most convenient days for production meetings are Tuesdays and Thursdays.

3. Take the timelines from your team and compile them into a team timeline.

4. Decide what dates would be best for production meetings and mark those on your timeline. (See Figure 2.3.)

5. Give each member of the team a copy of this master timeline, along with ways to contact all of the other members of the team.

6. Schedule and keep regular production meetings.

7. Keep the individual timelines to use as a progress guide at production meetings.

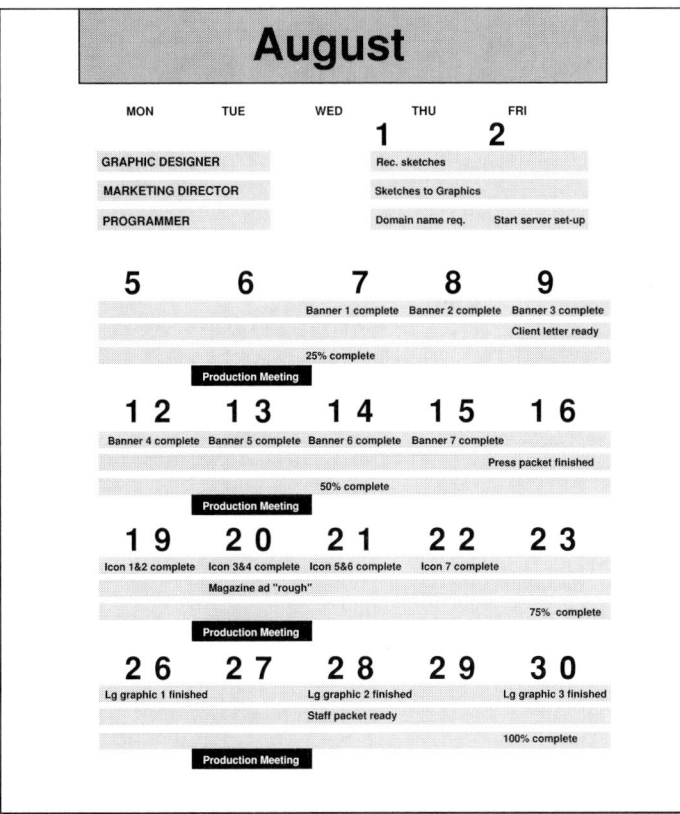

Figure 2.3.
Of course, you needn't get this fancy when developing your timeline. You can simply use any calendar you have on hand, and write the dates on that.

QUICK & DIRTY GUIDE
A Checklist for Getting Started

If at this point your strategy is to get a page up and to consider your real strategy later, here is a checklist to help you get started:

1. Decide who will do what.

2. E-mail potential hosts, outlining the services you need and asking them for specific pricing. (See Chapter 5.)

3. Make a list of possible domain names, and check with InterNIC to see what's available. (See Chapter 3, "Your Domain.")

4. Decide on a virtual host who offers the services you need. (See Chapter 5.) To save time, find one who will register your domain name for you *immediately*.

Q&D A Checklist for Getting Started

5. Sign up for your site. Tell them the domain name you want and what mailbox names you would like to start with. Ask them how long it will take to get you set up. Discuss any special needs you have (CGI, access logs, mail autoresponders). Ask them to set-up FTP access and contact you once they know the location of your directories on the server.

6. Sketch out a simple site diagram and storyboard. (See the Chapter 7 Quick & Dirty Guide, "Real-Life Examples.")

7. Gather all the software you may need (HTML helpers, graphics, FTP, and so on). Much of this is on the CD-ROM included with this book.

8. Write your copy in a text editor.

9. Develop your HTML template (see the Chapter 9 Quick & Dirty Guide, "Developing Your Own Templates") or have this done for you.

10. Cut and paste your copy into your templates.

11. Put everything in one directory to save time.

12. Create or convert your graphics (or hire this out).

13. Create any image maps you need. (See the Chapter 12 Quick & Dirty Guide, "Easy Image Mapping.")

14. Test your site on your own system.

15. Upload your files to your server.

16. Test your site.

17. Market your site off the Internet. (See the Chapter 20 Quick & Dirty Guide, "The Eight Most Important Things You Can Do to Market Your Site Offline.")

18. Market your site online. (See the Chapter 21 Quick & Dirty Guide, "Register with More than 200 Search Engines in Under 30 Minutes.")

19. Now sit down when you have a chance, and read this book thoroughly.

20. Update your system as time permits.

SUMMARY

In this chapter we have begun to address some of the important decisions you need to make before you design your site and some of the issues that will help you make those decisions.

In the next chapter, we discuss what to consider when you set up your domain.

Your Domain

Just like in the real world, your domain is where you exist. It is your street address on the Information Superhighway, and it is a crucial aspect of doing business on the Internet. A domain name is actually an alias; it represents an IP address (which is a series of numbers). The domain name is kept in a database, which lists the server IP address where it resides (as in yourdomain.com = 222.222.44.55). There are servers set up to deal with this translation, called Domain Name Servers (DNSs).

Again, a domain name is much like a street address. Here's an example from the real world for comparison. Suppose you were opening an office, and you had the choice between the following two addresses:

Rocket Science Unlimited
1 Rocket Science Dr.
Anytown USA

or

Rocket Science Unlimited
2100 18th Street
Small Business Building #14
Suite 343
Maildrop #16
Anytown USA

Assuming the office space at these two addresses were identical, which would you prefer? You would probably choose the address that made it look like you owned the entire block, rather than just a cubbyhole in a giant complex. You will want to do the same thing on the Net.

You can place systems on the WWW without your own domain name, but they must be placed under another domain. The following WWW examples are similar to the preceding street addresses in what they communicate: `http://www.rocket_science.com` or `http://www.someone_else.com/pub/users/business/janedoe/rocket_science`.

By using the second address, you're telling the world that you're small. You're also making it very difficult for someone to get to your page because you are making them type in a very long string of text. If your intended customers get just one letter wrong, they'll get an error message. Obviously, we recommend that you register a domain as soon as possible.

DOMAIN NAMES

Again, your domain name is your address, but it is more than that. In your domain name, you have an opportunity to make a statement. What you decide can say something about what you do, who you are, and so on. Think of it as a trademark, service mark, or tagline.

YOUR VIRTUAL TAGLINE

So, what line of business are you in? Architect, restauranteur, T-shirt shop owner? Your address can say at least a little about who you are and what you do. As an example, say your name is Mary Smith and that you own a gourmet coffee house called About a Cup. You know you want to register your own domain name, so you make a list:

```
marysmith.com
snuggles.com (named after your cat)
coffee.com
gourmetcoffee.com
thebestcoffee.com
coffee-online.com
aboutacup.com
```

about_a_cup.com
beverages.com
and so on...

You see that some of these, like `coffee-online.com`, tell people what you do; the `aboutacup.com` domain uses your company name; and `thebestcoffee.com` makes a statement about your product. But `snuggles.com` and `marysmith.com` will have no meaning to anyone who doesn't know you (or your cat). You have an opportunity to send a message with your domain name—to communicate. Take advantage of that opportunity.

WHAT'S IMPORTANT IN CHOOSING A NAME?

There are other considerations in choosing from a list of domain names. One of the biggest problems people run into is when they choose a domain name that they have never tried to say aloud. Again using the fictitious business About a Cup as an example, suppose that you decided to use a domain name that incorporated your business name.

Imagine a customer calls and wants your WWW address. "About a cup, as one word, dot com" (`aboutacup.com`) is a lot easier to say than "about, underscore, a, underscore, cup, dot, com" (`about_a_cup.com`), and much less likely to be screwed up by the person on the other end of the line.

You should also keep your name as short as possible. UNIX allows for very long text strings in a domain name, but you shouldn't go wild with it. While it may be possible to make a domain name like `mary.smith.and.snuggles.the.cat.about.a.cup.com`, it's clearly a stupid thing to do ("our address is mary, dot, smith, dot, and, dot, snuggles, dot, the, dot, cat, dot, about, dot, a, dot, cup...Hello? Are you still there?").

The extensions to the address—the .com, .net, .edu, .gov, .org, and so on—say what kind of enterprise is associated with the domain name. The .com extension means that the domain name is private or a commercial enterprise, and you will probably have to use this extension for your domain name. The other extensions represent network service provider, educational institution, government institution, and nonprofit organization, respectively.

MAKING YOUR LIST, CHECKING IT TWICE (DOMAIN SEARCH)

After you have decided on a list of possible names, you'll need to check them against the list of names currently in use. The way to do this is to access the InterNIC database.

InterNIC is the Internet registration database, the main governing body on the Internet. The reason for having a single database is simple: Somebody has to keep it all straight. As mentioned earlier, a domain name is an alias for a numerical address, and if there were more than one database, things would get pretty confusing.

Originally, InterNIC was governed and paid for by the National Science Foundation. With so many nonscientific individuals and organizations now on the Net, the NSF decided that it would no longer foot the bill for keeping the database up and running. InterNIC is now run by Network Solutions and AT&T (though they still report to the NSF) and is paid for by annual registration fees.

To access InterNIC, either point your browser to `http://www.internic.net`, `http://rs.internic.net`, or `http://ds.internic.net` via the WWW (see Figures 3.1 and 3.2), or use a Telnet client to access `rs.internic.net`. While the InterNIC can be accessed in many ways (including FTP, WAIS, and more), the Web and Telnet are the best ways to go, with Telnet being faster.

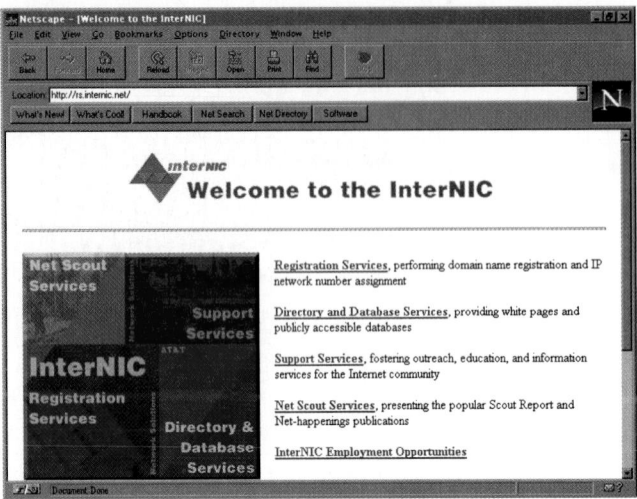

Figure 3.1.
The page at `http://rs.internic.net`.

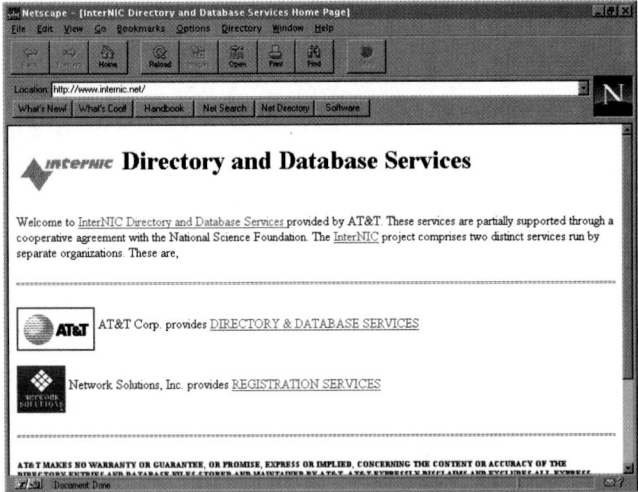

Figure 3.2.
The page at `http://www.internic.net` (and `http://ds.internic.net`).

If you have never used a Telnet client, now is the perfect opportunity to try. Telnet turns your computer into a dumb terminal, which means that all of the processing is done on the server side, and your computer performs only input/output functions (unlike a Web browser that relies on system resources for encoding/decoding, holding a cache of stored information, and so on).

To access the InterNIC database via Telnet, use your Telnet client to connect to `rs.internic.net`. (See Figure 3.3.) After you are connected, you will see an introduction screen that gives some basic information followed by an input prompt.

Since you are only looking to see whether a domain name is taken or not, you will be using the `whois:` command. Type in `whois:` followed by the domain name you want to check. (example: `whois: hampton.org`). If the domain name is already in use, InterNIC will give you information on the company that has registered the domain. If the domain name is not in use, InterNIC will report back `[no match for "yourname.com".]`, and you'll be able to proceed with registration.

If you choose to access the InterNIC database via the WWW, you can either access the pages for InterNIC and follow the links to the `whois:` search, or you can directly access the domain search page at `http://rs.internic.net/cgi-bin/whois`, as shown in Figure 3.4, and follow the instructions.

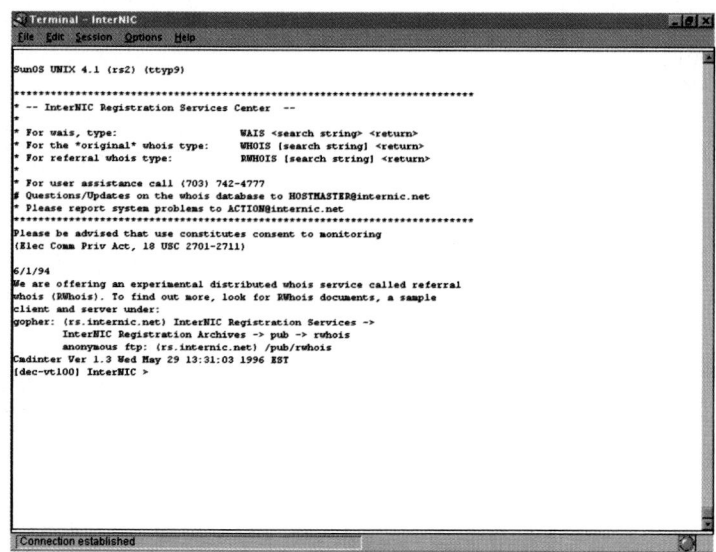

Figure 3.3.
Accessing `rs.internic.net` via Telnet.

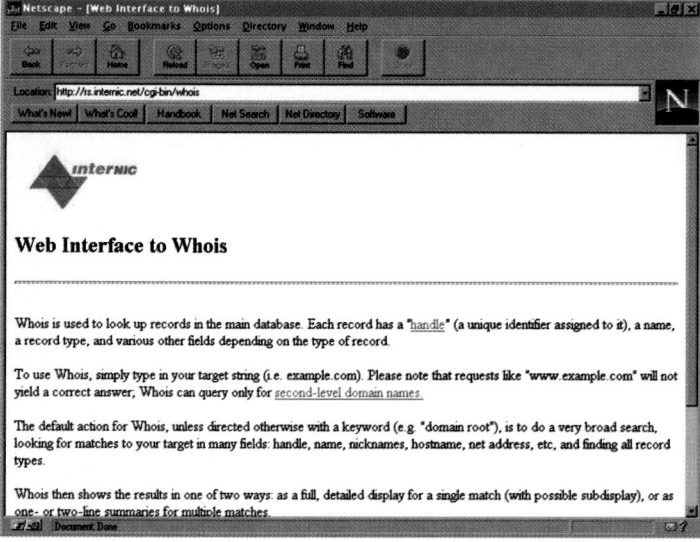

Figure 3.4.
Accessing InterNIC Whois via the WWW.

Note:
Sometimes it takes several weeks to process a domain name registration. Even though the name is not yet on the database, it may already be taken. After you attempt to register the name, InterNIC will inform you if this is the case.

DOMAIN REGISTRATION

The next step is to register your domain name. InterNIC charges a $100 fee for this, which covers your registration for two years (as long as it is in use; a name not in use may be deleted after 90 days). InterNIC didn't begin charging this fee until 1995, and there was quite a bit of hubbub about the fact that people had to pay money for what was once free. The fact of the matter is that $50 a year is very little, and not worth whining about.

WHERE DO I REGISTER?

There are two ways to register:

1. Through your service provider
2. Directly through InterNIC

If you choose to go through a service provider, the provider will generally charge you for the trouble. Filling out the necessary form takes about 10 minutes, and some service providers will charge you an arm and a leg for doing this. It's hard to compare apples to apples in pricing this "service" because providers package the service differently.

Some service providers include the InterNIC fees within the service package, some do not. Some providers include the domain name setup (setting up their server for your domain name), and some add this fee on to your monthly/yearly service costs. The only way to compare prices is to itemize the costs.

We've gone both ways with this, and we have found that going directly through InterNIC is simple, gives us control over the registration process, and enables us to track the costs. While it is still necessary to have chosen a service provider prior to registration (InterNIC must have server IP addresses before it will register the name), InterNIC will deal directly with *you* throughout the registration process. Your service provider is also more likely to believe that you know what you're doing and to charge you less for the setup on their end. This can either be because they are less likely to think that they can pull one over on you, or because they know you're less likely to be calling them every day with stupid questions about the registration process.

There is, unfortunately, another reason for registering your domain yourself. You should be the administrative contact for the domain name; this gives you the power to do what you want with it (such as move the name to another server). There have been cases where unscrupulous service providers

register your domain under their own name. If, after you've spent all the time and money involved in creating your site and promoting the address, you find that the service is lacking, you can't move to another server (at least, not without a lot of hassle). If you register yourself, and make sure you're the administrative contact, you have control.

Finally, you really should know how the whole thing works, and dealing directly with InterNIC will give you some great insight.

HOW DO I REGISTER?

If you are registering through an ISP, the provider will lead you through the process. If you are registering yourself, you'll need to follow these steps:

1. Obtain the domain name registration form. You can get this form via either the WWW or FTP. If you choose to work from the Web, point your browser to http://rs.internic.net/rs-internic.html. (See Figure 3.5.) You can then choose the type of form you need and whether you want to fill out a form online (see Figure 3.6) or download the text version.

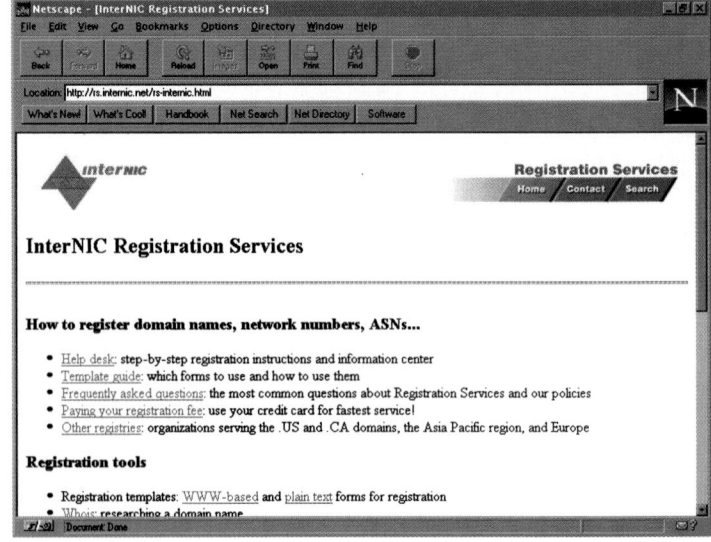

Figure 3.5.
Registration Services main page.

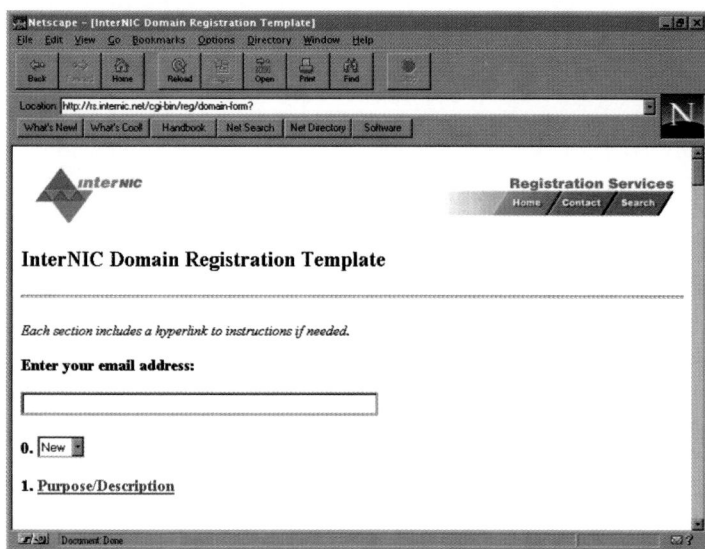

Figure 3.6.
InterNIC domain registration template via the WWW.

If you prefer, you can access the InterNIC FTP server and download the text file template(s) yourself (see Figure 3.7). This is often faster and easier. The templates are available via anonymous FTP (check the anonymous login on your FTP client) at rs.internic.net/templates.

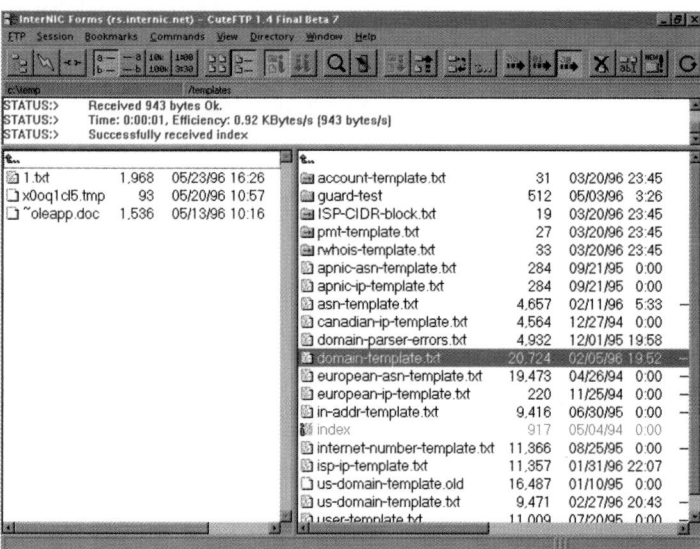

Figure 3.7.
Getting the domain registration template via FTP.

2. Fill out the form *completely*. You will need to get the name of your ISP's technical contact, and the IP addresses of the primary and secondary domain name servers that your ISP will be using. Other than that, most of the information is basic.

3. Submit the form immediately via e-mail, or use the WWW form's SUBMIT function to generate a request form.

Note:
Submitting the InterNIC form does not submit your request. All this does is fill out a template, which will be e-mailed to you. You must then send this completed form to hostmaster@rs.internic.net in order to have your request processed.

4. You will get an instant reply from InterNIC after the request has been submitted. This reply will give you an NIC registration number, which is the only thing you and InterNIC have to go by in referring to your request. DO NOT LOSE THIS NUMBER. If you do, you will have no way to check on the status of your request. The response will also tell you how big the backlog is, and how long you can expect it to take before your domain name is registered.

CHECKING UP

It may become necessary for you to check up on the domain name registration process. You will receive an e-mail message after your name is registered. If you don't get this within a reasonable amount of time (based on the approximate turn-around time given on the instant reply), follow up.

You can either e-mail InterNIC at hostmaster@rs.internic.net, or call them at (703) 742-4777. If you e-mail them, make sure that the NIC registration number is in both the subject line and the body of the e-mail message. If you choose to call, have this number in front of you.

We've gone through this registration process many times and have had to follow up on a few occasions. Even though ours was one of thousands of requests being processed at any given time, we have only experienced the very best service from the representatives at InterNIC. They have always been friendly, courteous, and ultimately professional. There are more than a few companies who could learn quite a bit about customer service from these folks.

Again, we've addressed the domain name registration early in the book, because it's best to get started on the process ASAP. You'll have plenty to do while you wait for the registration to go through.

QUICK & DIRTY GUIDE
Temporary Solutions

If you need to have a page up before your domain name registration is complete, your ISP should be able to do at least one of two things:

1. Place your pages in a directory where they can be accessed by the public (like www.ISP.com/~yourname), or

2. Set up a temporary domain name (also called vanity domain name—as in vanity license plates), which need not go through InterNIC (such as www.yourname.com/home.html).

Either way, you will have to decide on a way to move your pages after your own domain name is set up. To do this, you can either alias the original address (so that people looking up your old name will be automatically sent to your new domain), or you can put a We've Moved page up in your old location, with a link to the new site (this is often better, in that you can tell people to note the new address for future access).

SUMMARY

In this chapter, we have covered these key points:

- You will probably want to register a domain name.

- A domain name is like your address, and it can say something about your company.

- Make sure that your domain name is simple to say aloud, and make it as short as possible.

◆ Once you've decided on a list of
  potential names, check them against
  the InterNIC database, to see if
  they're available.

◆ You will have to register your
  domain name after you've decided
  on a server.

Now that we have this out of the way, we can
return to the server issues.

Deciding on a Server: Maintain Your Own or Hire It Out

Now that we have determined what you can afford (see Chapter 2, "Developing an Effective Web Strategy"), let's determine what you need and where to go from here.

## CHAPTER four

AN OVERVIEW OF SERVER ISSUES

A Web server is a program that resides on a computer on the Internet. When a Web browser (client) connects to a server and requests a file, the server processes that request and sends the file back to the browser, along with information telling the browser how to view the file (file type). Servers use HTTP (HyperText Transfer Protocol) to communicate; that's why people often refer to them as HTTPD servers.

Note:
The D in HTTPD server stands for Daemon. DAEMON is an acronym for Disk And Execution MONitor, and it's a program that sits in the background, waiting for specific input before responding. For example, sending an e-mail message to a nonexistent user invokes the target computer's mailer daemon, which would then reply to the sender with an error message saying that no user by that name exists.

Web servers not only store information, they also can be used to run scripts and programs based on information provided by the reader via the Web browser. For example, say you want to offer free issues of your company newsletter. You set up a Web form called Request free issue, which requires that mailing and company information be entered by your readers. The reader fills out this form and clicks the Submit button. This form information is then sent to a program on the server computer, which processes the request and e-mails the reader a free issue. You

can also set the program up to send you an e-mail with the information the customer provided, for use in a database. The programs or scripts used to perform these functions are called gateway scripts/programs or CGI (Common Gateway Interface) scripts, and are used for most of the forms and search engines you see on the Web. (Chapter 11, "Integrating HTML with CGI," covers this in more detail.)

Web servers reside on all types of computers, from old beat up PCs, to mega-UNIX networks, and all points in between. They are usually directly connected to the Internet via a high-speed (T1 or better) line, but can use slower speed connections (even modems) when performance is not an issue. For our purposes, performance is definitely an issue.

Many specialized companies and ISPs (Internet Service Providers) have space on their servers that they make available to the public (for a fee, of course). These are called WWW service providers, or virtual hosts. We highly recommend using a virtual host if possible.

WHAT IS A VIRTUAL HOST?

Throughout this book we refer to companies who host commercial Web sites on their server as *virtual hosts*. We should perhaps define this term.

There are a growing number of Internet Service Providers (ISPs) and specialized companies hosting Web sites, their services being as varied as their prices. Many companies offer bare-bones services, which are geared toward personal sites and are usually too limited for commercial purposes. Virtual hosts are those hosts that rent space on their server and alias to your domain name (see Chapter 3, "Your Domain"). Most virtual hosts also offer FTP access (to post and update your site), CGI bins, access logs, multiple POP accounts (mailboxes), and so on. We consider these other functions necessary for a successful commercial Web site, so we speak of and recommend only these types of services.

> **Note:**
> Unless you own a huge telecommunications company, you will be using an ISP to some degree. Your local dial-up provider is an ISP, and it uses a larger ISP, who may be using yet another ISP. Suffice it to say that whether or not you are using a virtual host, you will require an ISP.

ASSESSING YOUR SERVER NEEDS

Should you pay a service to host your site, or buy your very own server? That all depends on your special needs, time constraints, equipment resources, and budget. There is a huge difference between setting up your own server and renting space on somebody else's.

While it is relatively simple to pay a fee and post your pages on a virtual server, building your own server requires installing powerful computers, setup and customization of specialized software, and setting up a direct Internet connection. This all takes time and money, and lots of it! Maintaining a server is another important consideration. 24-hour Internet access also means 24-hour maintenance. Will it be the end of the world if your server goes down for a few hours? How about 12 hours? Often businesses selling server systems will bill them as "maintenance free," but don't believe it! You have to be prepared for system failures and have someone around to do cleanup.

Of course, there are many advantages to having your own server. First of all, it's yours! You can put any dandy new software you want on it, run hundreds of custom CGI scripts, lock out anyone you wish, post hundreds of documents, build specialized database front ends, have thousands of site hits per day, rent Web space for extra income, or run your own company intranet (more on this in Chapter 25, "Maintaining Your System").

Whether you need all these things is questionable. Large corporations, those interested in making the Internet a main focus of their marketing plan, gearheads wanting a new toy, and those wanting to make WWW hosting a secondary business will benefit the most from their own server. Also, if you're lucky enough to work for a company that already has the resources for a WWW server, you'll definitely want to take advantage of this. For the most part, however, we advise against having your own server (you don't need to own a telephone company to use a telephone).

THE NEED FOR GROWTH POTENTIAL

Whether you decide to use a service or maintain your own server, it is important to keep the future in mind. If you decide to use a service, you can always build your own server later on, after your site is established, as long as you register your own domain name.

Keeping an eye to the future is even more important when planning your own server (as you'll see in Chapter 6, "Your Very Own Server"). If you invest in the cheapest server you can find, you may find it no investment at all. If you buy something that you believe will work for years to come, you may find that the path of technology will make your system obsolete in a few months (Murphy's law of computer purchasing).

QUICK & DIRTY GUIDE
Choosing a Server

Virtual Hosting Service

PROS	CONS
Inexpensive	Someone else has control over security
No server maintenance	Must deal with sometimes inhospitable hosts
Easy to switch	May have to pay for hidden extras
Can get online more quickly	Dependent on service for upkeep
Extra services (CGI, access logs, and so on)	Little software program adaptability
No systems administrator needed	More difficult to gain direct access to logs

Your Very Own Server

PROS	CONS
Often easier to implement new technologies	Full-time systems administrator needed
More control over site security	Can be expensive (setup and monthly cost)
Can rent Web space	Responsible for managing server
Have systems administrator in house	More time needed to set up
Complete control over content	Difficult to change your mind
Provide direct database connection to your mainframe (possible security issue)	Security challenges (especially if you want to connect your server to the company mainframe)
Complete control over content	No easy CGI setup
Can be used as intranet	More staff required

SUMMARY

The decision whether to use a virtual hosting service or to buy your own server depends on your special needs, time constraints, and most importantly, your budget. If you're part of a large company that plans on a massive Web site with tons of traffic, or if you intend to rent out Web space, or to host a company intranet, investing in a server might be a good idea. However, if you plan a typical Web site with average traffic, or if your budget is limited, a hosting service is your best bet—at least for the time being.

In the next chapter, we address the issues you need to consider when you choose a virtual host. Chapter 6 deals with setting up your own server.

Virtual Domain Hosts

We hope you've taken our advice and chosen to place your system on a third-party server. There are so many ISPs and specialized companies that offer Web hosting services, it would seem a very simple task to find the right one for you. Unfortunately, it's not so easy. However, we have found it matters little whether your host is in the same city or even the same state (provided you use a separate service for dial-up).

CHAPTER five

Besides the cost of an occasional long distance phone call (though many offer toll-free support), there is really no difference. So, let's begin the process of finding a suitable virtual host.

COMPARING VIRTUAL DOMAIN HOSTS—WHAT TO ASK

How do you know which virtual host is right for you? Well, you will need some information to make that decision. In fact, we assume that you don't even know the questions to ask, much less the answers to them. In order to speed you through the process, we've put together a basic list of your potential needs and have incorporated them in a checklist format for sending out a questionnaire via e-mail.

Here are some questions that you may want to ask each potential ISP (your own priorities may differ):

1. **Do you offer virtual hosting of my domain name?**

Obviously, this is why you're looking in the first place. However, we've run into providers that have tried to talk us out of using our own domain, and there is simply no good reason for this.

The biggest reason providers would try to do this is that it gives them control over how you handle your online business. If you perform business under a provider's domain, the provider has the control. For

instance, if you keep your pages at www.provider.com/~yourname/, you won't be able to move to another server without changing your address. In short, don't fall for this ploy.

Another situation occurs when the provider's WWW (HTTPD) server is not sophisticated enough to properly handle aliasing. The server should be set up so that it recognizes your domain as something unique, and not just an alias of its own domain name. The address www.yourname.com should lead directly to your own index (home) page. If your provider candidate says that your address will have to look like www.yourname.com/yourname, or www.yourname.com/home.htm, you'll want to keep looking.

2. **Do you provide a high-speed, redundant connection to the Internet?**

There are many different connection possibilities to the Internet. It's possible to host a WWW system on a computer that's hooked up to the Net through a modem, but, of course, it's very slow. For commercial purposes, you'll want a T1 or faster connection.

Most modems access the Internet at a rate of at least 14.4Kbps (fourteen point four thousand bits per second). A single-channel ISDN line connects at 64Kbps, and there are other types of connections that range in speed from 56Kbps on up.

A full T1 connects to the Net at a rate of 1.54Mbps (one point five four *million* bits per second). In other words, it can access the Net 100 times faster than a 14.4Kbps modem, or it can transfer enough information to keep 100 14.4 modems working at full speed (as in the case when 100 people are accessing the system at one time).

> **Note:**
> A T1 may not be fast enough if your service provider is using this line to service many accounts. This is dealt with later in the chapter, when you test your server's speed. Just keep in mind that anything less than a full T1 is probably not going to work well for you.

We say "full" T1 because it is possible to have a T1 connection, but only use (and pay for) part of the possible bandwidth. This is called a *fractional* T1 (or FT1). If a provider says they use a T1, always make sure they are running a *full* T1.

Your next option is a T3, which transfers at a rate of more than 44Mbps. (Don't get into the habit of thinking that a T3 is three times faster than a T1—it's actually nearly 30 times faster.) The next evolution in high-speed data transfer are optical connections (as in fiber-optics) that start at about the same speed as the T1, and may soon begin offering speeds that will make the T1 look like two tin cans and a piece of string. It's good that you know things will be getting faster, but just keep in mind for now that a full T1 is minimal.

3. **Do you provide access logs?**

Access logs contain information on your site hits: who accessed your system and when, any errors that occurred, and so on. They are kept in a file on the server. There are three main ways hosts offer access logs to clients. Online access log summaries are very easy to use and generally offer the most graphical interface to view your access logs. Many hosts send their clients the summaries of their access logs via e-mail (on a weekly or monthly basis). While these summaries certainly involve the least amount of your time, they are often quite limited in the information they provide. Some hosts only offer access to their raw logs, which look like a huge mess unless you use software to decipher them. This is by far the most difficult way to view your hit information, but it can also be the most informative. (For more information on access logs, see Chapter 25, "Maintaining Your System.")

4. **Do you have a secure commerce server?**

A commerce server uses encryption methods to transfer secure information (such as a credit card number) over the Internet. It literally puts your information in a very hard-to-break code, so that it can be sent over the network, away from peeping eyes. Even though current encryption methods create codes that are so hard to break the U.S. Department of Defense and National Security Administration regulate them, there's no way to make an unbreakable code. This has been a big issue on the Net.

The problem stems from the fact that the Net is a public network. Remember in the first chapter of this book, where we talked about how information is transferred over a network? We said that the machines are given addresses, and that they ignore messages that aren't addressed to them.

Well, for the most part, you can consider that everything you send over the Net is available to everyone else. If they wanted to, people could read your e-mail, or anything else you send or receive. The only way to secure it is to encrypt the files in a way that makes the files useless gibberish to anyone who doesn't have the code *key*.

Commerce servers use what is called Public Key Encryption. This is a method whereby an encryption key is sent out as public information. This key enables people to write to you in a code that only you can decrypt. It also allows for ways to verify who sent the file/message. It's way beyond the scope of this book to get any further than this into the details of encryption methods (there are good books on the subject), so suffice it to say that it gets very elaborate and is relatively secure.

We say relatively secure because, even with all the hubbub you may have heard with respect to sending your credit card information in cyberspace, it's probably the safest way to use your credit card. Think about it. Every time you use your credit card, you're giving people access to your number. Whether you're ordering something over the phone, giving your card to a restaurant server, or handing it to a cashier, this person can copy the number and use it. People can even dig through the garbage for your imprinted carbon paper and get the number there.

So what we're really talking about is perceived security. In reality, a good encryption system that is worthy of national security (as most are) is a heck of a lot better than entrusting your card number to a telephone operator. Unfortunately, there has been so much press about online security that people are scared to use their credit cards for purchasing. To help overcome this, you'll want to offer ordering options (phone, fax, and mail), and you'll want to use a smooth, highly user-friendly commerce server that sets people's minds at ease.

Netscape has made security a main focus, and the Netscape browser has security functions built in (it even warns you when a transfer is about to be made to an unsecured server). Since Netscape is a name recognized by most users, it also plays a big role in perceived security—a potential customer might feel better using a Netscape Enterprise server than they would using "Billy Joe Bob's secure server." This is why we specifically requested a Netscape Commerce Server on our e-mail questionnaire, although we give a prospective provider the opportunity to offer an alternative.

Note:

The Netscape Enterprise server is the newer release of the Secure Commerce server. However, it was not released prior to our writing this section of the book.

5. Is your server hardware on site?

Some companies selling Web space have no actual hardware on site. They act as resellers for the server space on other people's systems and serve as middlemen for technical problems and setup. There is absolutely no reason to use this type of service; they often charge more than an on-site service and can end up being a pain when you have a problem. After all, when looking for efficiency, involving more middlemen seldom does the trick.

6. How much storage space do you provide?

A big misconception when it comes to Web sites is storage space needed. People often overestimate the amount of space their system will need. Many providers will package storage in sizes of 5, 10, 20 megabytes on up. In reality, most systems will use less than a megabyte of storage space. (We've produced highly graphical WWW systems that take up less than 250KB total.)

Unless you are planning a system with hundreds of pages, or plan to post very large files online, 5MB should be ample space for most commercial sites (unless people are uploading information that you plan to store). A good provider will tell you this.

7. How do you provide for CGI services?

CGI stands for Common Gateway Interface—and also, Computer Graphics Interface, which we mention so that you'll know that to some computer people, the term CGI might mean something else. This is covered in more detail in Chapter 11, "Integrating HTML with CGI," but it's important that we address it now, because you will almost definitely want to run CGI scripts.

CGI makes it possible to run an external application (or gateway) under a Web server. (Actually, it's designed for other uses as well, but those are not our concern at this point.) A CGI-BIN is the place where the CGI scripts are held. These scripts enable the WWW server and browser to run external programs, without the need to launch another application.

If one CGI script were able to do the same thing on every computer, scripting would be easy. Unfortunately, the CGI script relies on the operating system of the server, so a Perl (UNIX) script might look like garbage to a non-UNIX server, and so on. You'll need to have a custom setup of your CGI scripts.

Most servers have CGI-BIN directories, which you are able to make use of. This is a good start, but not good enough. You should be able to have your own CGI-BIN so that you can run your own scripts (rather than adapting your system to work with the scripts that already reside on the system). Furthermore, your provider should be willing to set up the CGI-BIN, and should also help you in writing the scripts. This stuff is a cake-walk for a decent programmer, and your provider should be willing to offer this service at little or no charge.

8. **Do you provide e-mail boxes under my domain?**

> **Note:**
> By no means do you have to have e-mail boxes through your access provider (the computer you dial up to access the WWW yourself). Your mail server can be anywhere on the Internet, and as long as you have a decent dial-up provider, you should never notice a difference. You might even ask for a discount, since your dial-up provider will not be providing mail service (unless your access and WWW hosting provider are one and the same).

Since you can only register your domain name under a single server address, your ISP should be able to provide you with several e-mail addresses under your domain. If you've surfed the WWW much, you may have come across pages that have an address such as `www.somename.com`, but the webmaster's address is something like `joe@someothername.com`. This might occur if the person who owns the page has someone else acting as webmaster, but it's more likely that the server hosting the Web site doesn't have a mail server.

A virtual host should be able to set up multiple e-mail boxes for you, so that you can have e-mail for everyone working for the company, as well as aliased mailboxes such as `sales@`, `support@`, `webmaster@`, and so on—even if you're the only person in the company. Any provider who can't do this is not for you.

Furthermore, an e-mail address has eight characters before the @. There are, however, ways of aliasing this address, so as to allow for more than eight characters. In some cases, you might want to have an e-mail address such as `William.Shakespeare@domainname.com`, rather than `wshakesp@domainname.com`. This won't pose any problems to a service provider worth his/her salt.

9. **Do you have an autoresponder e-mail system?**

These are used to send automatic responses to people requesting information. For example, people wanting pricing information from you can simply e-mail `price@your_company.com`. They are then sent an automatic reply with the information. Although we can set these up without the host's help, we have found it much easier to go with a host who has already set up an autoresponder. Remember, no need to reinvent the wheel—you have more important things to concentrate on now.

10. **Do you provide any mailing list services?**

If you want to run a large discussion group, or send an electronic newsletter, you will need a mailing program. There are other options available to you (see Chapter 15, "Customer Service Online"), but it's just so much easier to have that resource available to you, and there's really no excuse for your ISP to not provide this service.

11. **How do you handle file transfers?**

You'll need to have direct access to your HTML files, so that you can update them and fix errors immediately. Most providers are able to put the files in a secure directory, where you can access your pages via an FTP (File Transfer Protocol) client. Obviously, these files should be secured by a password, so that only you can add, delete, or make changes. (Note that for the WWW to work, *anyone* must be able to *read* your files, but only you should be able to mess with them.) This is usually accomplished by having the WWW server *mirror* certain directories on the FTP server.

Some providers have firewalls set up between the directories where you place your files and the directories where they are stored for WWW retrieval. A firewall is a protocol that protects one part of a network from another by controlling the access between the two parts. In some cases, there may be a time delay in posting the pages that you've changed. The provider may have a time lock that won't post pages until the next day, and so on. This is rare, but you might run into it.

Sometimes, a provider has set up no protocol for using FTP to access your files on the WWW server, and says that you can just e-mail the files to them and they will post them. Forget it! If the provider hasn't made the arrangements to handle this automatically, they're not the company you should be dealing with.

Another problem occurs when the provider uses your FTP directory as the WWW directory itself, with no security measures to keep others from gaining access. In other words, your competition could easily access your directory and delete your pages—or put their own up! Obviously, you don't want this.

12. **How do you provide technical support?**

You want to be able to get on the telephone with a real person. If a provider tells you that its technical support communicates only by e-mail, forget them. While e-mail works great for some questions, many problems require the back and forth communication that e-mail simply doesn't provide (such as figuring out software problems). As a bonus, a few hosts now offer toll-free numbers for technical support.

13. **Are there any discounts on setup fees?**

If you already have your domain name, you will have to modify your information with InterNIC. If you do this yourself, many hosts will discount their setup fees. They should be willing to do the same if you are registering your domain name yourself (that is, a new domain), since the work involved on their part is identical.

COMPARING VIRTUAL DOMAIN HOSTS CHECKLIST

The following is a checklist to aid in your search for the perfect host. Each aspect of this checklist is addressed in more detail later in this chapter.

1. Find a list of host candidates and begin your virtual host study. E-mail them inquiring about your special needs and specific pricing. (Do this even if you have no special needs.) Here is where you'll cut your list dramatically—consider only those who respond within a day, and in a user-friendly manner.

2. Visit their sites, looking for information on their companies. Note the speed of their servers. (Many things can affect speed, such as your own dial-up connection, so check a few times, during different times of the day to make sure it is running smoothly; if possible, have others check the server from their systems as well.) If a server is slow, or is down, chuck it off your list now!

3. Find their client lists and visit some of their sites, noting the speed of the server to make sure they don't run their own sites high speed, and run their clients on bogged-down servers.

> **Note:**
> You want your pages to appear as if you are running your own server, and so will a good service provider. Therefore, a provider should be hesitant to give you a list of clients. However, many small companies like to be listed on a provider's client list (since they see that as additional traffic), and any good businessperson will have at least a couple of clients who don't mind acting as professional references.

4. E-mail a few of their clients, asking them if they are pleased with their host. Oh goody, we've eliminated a few more.

5. Now, think of an annoying question and give the remaining candidates a call on their technical support phone numbers—use 800 numbers if possible. Choose a question to which you already know the answer, but act as if you're absolutely clueless ("If I turn my computer off, can people still see my pages?"), or read through the next chapter, and ask a technical question about software, hardware, and so on. This is, of course, the main reason you're using a provider. Note how long you are left waiting on hold. If you have to leave a message, do not tell them you are a new customer; just leave your annoying question and wait to see how long until you get your reply. How friendly and helpful are they?

6. Pick your favorite. Ask whether you should register your domain name or if the host will do it. It's easier to have them do it, but it could cost extra. Chapter 3, "Your Domain," has more information on this.

If this all seems like too much trouble, consider the trouble of having your system go down once a week, or missing an important deadline because your inhospitable host won't answer your phone calls, or finding out that every time you turn around there's some added charge. When we started with our first small site, we simply used our dial-up access provider as our host—let's just say it didn't turn out very well. So take our advice, spend the couple of days now, and save yourself endless amounts of frustration.

WHERE TO LOOK

If you use an ISP to dial up to the Internet, the ISP is a good place to start. Many offer reduced hosting rates to dial-up customers. Beware though, as a general rule we usually steer clear of hosts who offer dial-up access, because their dial-up customers demand too much of their server's resources. Another problem is that many people have gotten into the ISP dial-up business without much forethought. After paying for the hardware, software, and bandwidth necessary for a decent server, there's not a whole lot of profit. In order to keep a decent margin, and keep prices competitive, dial-up providers often have to push their equipment to the limit. This causes slow speeds and frequent system crashes.

There are exceptions to this rule, however. If the provider runs its dial-up and WWW hosting services on separate servers, or if it has massive resources that can handle the load on its system, it should be fine. The best-case scenario would be to use the same ISP for all of your needs, but it's often too difficult to find a company capable of doing this.

Local computer magazines can be a good resource if you are interested in using a local host. You will generally find these in supermarkets, libraries, and coffee shops. Even national publications can be a good place to look for a provider. Again, it doesn't matter if they're out of your area, although the threat of "coming down to the office to straighten things out" doesn't hold much water when your provider is a thousand miles away.

> **Note:**
> Beware of deals that sound too good to be true. You may see ads for WWW hosting that offer huge amounts of storage and bandwidth for a small price (especially in national magazines). These people are generally counting on high volume, which will lead to very slow speeds.

If you've had no luck so far, or would like to expand your search, your next stop should be the Internet. A couple of great resources are `http://www.yahoo.com/Business_and_Economy/Companies/Internet_Access_Providers/` and `http://www.thelist.com`.

HOW TO CONTACT THEM

In the case of virtual hosts, it is not only important what you ask, but how you ask it. Your concern is not only with what hardware and services they offer, but how they will deal with you on an ongoing basis. Remember, this is a service, and you are a customer—make sure anyone you think of dealing with appreciates this.

Being in the Internet business, we have the opportunity of dealing with hosts all over the country—many good, and some downright awful. They sound great when you are signing up and sometimes turn out to care less after you're on their service. Though there is no absolute way to avoid this, there are some steps you can take to reduce your chances of signing up with an inhospitable host. This is one of the most important decisions you have to face in developing your site. After all, it doesn't really matter how fabulous your design is if nobody can access it.

We have developed a way to deal with this challenge. Through a six-step process, we eliminate the bad apples and, hopefully, end up with a winner.

> **Note:**
> This small study is by no means meant to be applicable to the population of ISPs as a whole, or as a referral to any specific provider. This is only as a guide on how to conduct your own virtual host study.

Round 1: For our study, we visited the USA Nationwide as well as the California listing at `http:www.thelist.com` (see Figure 5.1).

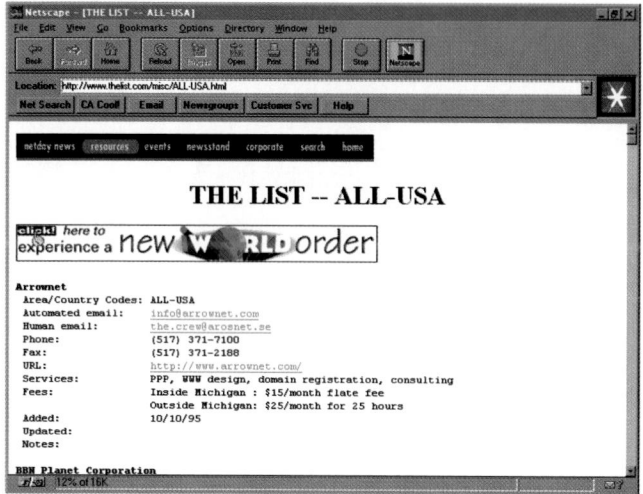

Figure 5.1.
ISP resources at `http://www.thelist.com/misc/ALL-USA.html`.

We chose 60 ISPs at random from the two listings, and fired off an e-mail to each of their "human" e-mail boxes. We didn't ask all of the questions we pointed out earlier in this chapter because we didn't foresee the need for all of the services we mentioned. Our e-mail looked something like this:

```
Hello-
We are comparing Web Hosting services. It would be
very helpful if you would take a moment to answer the
following questions. This will enable us to determine
if your services will fit our needs as well as our
budget.
Do you offer the following, and if so how much do you
charge:
1. Virtual hosting of my existing domain name:
2. High-speed (T1 or faster), redundant connection to
the Internet:
3. Access logs (online, via e-mail, other):
4. Netscape Secure Commerce Server (if not, do you
have an alternative?):
5. Server hardware on site (you are not a reseller):
6. 5 megabytes (MB) of storage space:
7. Unique CGI-BIN directory:
If applicable give more details of your CGI system
(support, free scripting, etc.):
```

```
8. 5 e-mail addresses under my domain:
9. Autoresponder e-mail system (please
comment):
10. Mailing list program (such as
majordomo or listserv):
11. FTP access (direct, secure access
to WWW directory):
12. Technical support (by telephone
with a real person):
13. 800# technical support (this is a
bonus):
14. Discount set-up fees for having an
existing domain name and doing the
InterNIC domain name modification
ourselves:
Do you have a package which includes
all of these services?
Anything else you feel is unique about
your service:

Additional comments?

Your name:
Your e-mail:
Company name:
URL:
Phone:
Street Address:
City, State, ZIP:
Thank you for your cooperation, we
look forward to hearing from you,
Kim and Brad Hampton
```

What we got back was alarming! We received seven form letters (they either did not even attempt to answer our specific questions, or had their "human" mail routed to an autoresponder), six e-mail error messages, five replies that either had the wrong information or did not answer our questions fully, and one that did not arrive until seven days later. We received only 11 responses out of the 60 that even answered our questionnaire correctly, and 50 percent of our questionnaires went totally unanswered. Wow! Now you can see why we're putting you through all this.

Out of the eleven acceptable responses, five were very expensive, and two did not have the services we required, so we tossed them off our list. Luckily, four respondents fit our

price range and needs. Although two respondents did not offer a Netscape Secure
Commerce Server, we kept them on our list,
since they appeared to have an alternative.
We crossed our fingers that our four possibilities would pass the test, so we wouldn't
have to send out another mailing. Here is a
sample of a response we found acceptable:

To: Hampton & Associates
<hampton@ha.net>
From: "Martin G. Bayerle"
<bayerle@imagixx.net>
Subject: Re: Web Hosting Services
>Hello-
>
>We are comparing Web Hosting ser-
vices. It would be very helpful if you
>would take a moment to answer the
following questions. This will enable
>us to determine if your services will
fit our needs as well as our >budget.
>
>Do you offer the following, and if so
how much do you charge:
>
>1. Virtual hosting of my existing
domain name: Yes, $150 first year,
$85/year thereafter. (If we process
your request for an original domain:
$250 first year), with monthly charges
of $35/month, 5mb storage.
>2. High-speed (T1 or faster),
redundant connection to the Internet:
Yes, one step removed from backbone.
>3. Access logs (online, via email,
other): Real-time on-demand customized
demographic analysis of your web site.
For an actual example, try our "Some
Data for our Advertisers/Customers"
button from our home page http://
www.imagixx.net. See also our on-line
info kit at
http://www.isiah.com.
>4. Netscape Secure Commerce Server
(if not, do you have an >alterna-
tive?): Yes, with Enterprise Server.
$20/month additional for order page
within our secure directory.

>5. Server hardware on site (you are not a reseller):
We run BSDI 2.01
and NT on several hardware platforms.
>6. 5 megabytes (MB) of storage space: Included.
>7. Unique CGI-BIN: Yes, but self-developed CGI is
first reviewed by our staff.
>If applicable give more details of your CGI system
(support, free >scripting, etc.): We offer several
stock scripts which we can modify for your personal
requirements. Any CGI scripting outside of our stock
scripts comes at an extra charge of $45/hour.
>8. 5 e-mail addresses under my domain: Four aliases
are included. They filter into your actual mailbox.
Additional private mailboxes are at $10/month.
>9. Autoresponder e-mail system (please comment): One
included.
Additional are at $10/month.
>10. Mailing list program (such as majordomo or
listserv):
$35/month
>11. FTP access (direct, secure access to WWW direc-
tory):
Included.
>12. Technical support (by telephone with a real
person):
10a - 8 p M-F, By web pager access at other times.
One-hour response if
after normal hours.
>13. 800# technical support (this is a bonus):
Yes, as well as e-mail.
>14. Discount set-up fees for having an existing
domain name and doing >the Internic domain name
modification ourselves:
See above.

>Do you have a package which includes all these
services?
Visit our web site. For more info, and to see how an
autoresponder works, send an e-mail to
info@imagixx.net.

>Anything else you feel is unique about your service:
We are flexible and innovative. Just e-mail any of
our other customers for their opinions!

>Your e-mail: docdet@imagixx.net
>Company name:Imagine Communications Corporation
("Imagixx")
>URL: http://www.imagixx.net, http://www.isiah.com
>Phone:800 562-4499
>Street Address: Network Operations Center, 2567
University Avenue
>City, State, ZIP: Morgantown, WV 26505

Round 2: We visited the prospective ISPs over a period of time, noting their access speeds. We were sure to visit during different times of the day (especially during peak usage times, like the lunch hour), and from different dial-up accounts (so that it wasn't our own dial-up server we were testing). Knowing that different factors affect access speed, we used another site, which we know runs consistently, as our benchmark. We did these things to make sure our prospective hosts' servers were *consistently* fast. They all passed the test.

Round 3: We found our prospective hosts' client list and visited some of their sites.

Note:

One of our prospective ISPs did not list any of its clients at its site, so we e-mailed asking for references. The ISP stated that for the privacy of their clients, they did not give out this information. We told them we respected their point of view (which we do) and asked them to please forward our questionnaire (Round 4) on to five of their clients for us. They told us they would try, but we never received any questionnaires back, so we crossed them off our list.

We noted the speed of the server (we were making sure they didn't run their own site high speed and run their clients on bogged-down servers). They all passed this test as well.

Round 4: We e-mailed a random selection (five each) of our ISPs' clients, asking them for comments regarding their host.

Our e-mail looked something like this:

```
Hello-

My name is Kim Hampton, I am considering using host_name as
a Web Site host. Before committing myself to their ser-
vices, I wanted to get an idea of what some of their
clients think of them (yes, your honest opinion :). If you
could, please help me by replying to these questions:

1. How long have you had host_name hosting your Web Site?
2. Is host_name's technical support accessible and helpful
if you have a problem?
3. How many times do think your WWW service has been
"down"?
Have you had any complaints from people accessing your
system?
Do you consider your Web Site host reliable?
Have you ever needed a programming service which your host
could not provide?
Any other comments?

Thank you very much for your time. Any help is truly
appreciated.
```

We lost two more prospective ISPs at this point and were now down to two.

Round 5: We thought of an annoying question and gave the finalists a call on their technical support phone numbers. We chose a question to which we already knew the answer, but we acted absolutely clueless. It's a question we get from time to time: "If I turn off my computer, will people still be able to access my Web site?" We noted how long we were left waiting on hold, which was not long. They were both friendly and helpful and treated us with respect.

Round 6: We picked our favorite. At this point they asked us for our billing information and a password. We needed information from them as well, such as

- ◆ The necessary server and technical contact information, so we could modify our domain registration with InterNIC ourselves. (See Chapter 3.)
- ◆ Their mail server information, to set up our mail program. (See Chapter 14, "Mail Delivery Systems.")
- ◆ Where our FTP directory would be located.
- ◆ Where to access our logs.

We let them know which mailbox names we wanted under our domain and wished them a good day, and that was it.

> **Note:**
> At this time we told them that we were writing a book on Web development, and that the site we were discussing would provide updates for our readers.

CONNECTIONS TO THE INTERNET

You will need access to the Internet in order to transfer your pages and test them on your server, as well as to keep abreast of the WWW. The minimum type of account you want is a PPP (Point-to-Point Protocol) or SLIP (Serial Line Internet Protocol), and not a Shell account, which limits you to text-only access.

DIAL-UP ACCOUNTS?

Ultimately, you'd want to have a dedicated T3 connection to the Net, but this is too expensive for most people to consider. Because price is a consideration for all (well, most) of us, you'll probably settle for a modem connection, or maybe an ISDN (Integrated Services Digital Network) line.

Although some companies offer dedicated modem line service (meaning you are *always* connected to the Net), there really isn't much advantage to this. You probably don't want to spend the whole day online, and if

you do, you'd want to be accessing the Net at faster speeds than a telephone line allows. The dial-up services we've seen that offer "unlimited hours" are generally as slow as molasses.

If you can afford about $150 (current market price at the time of this writing), you'll definitely want to get a 28.8Kbps modem (as opposed to a 14.4Kbps, the minimum). Almost any access provider will now support 28.8Kbps for the same price as 14.4Kbps, so you're getting twice as much service for the same cost (to say nothing of waiting half as long to transfer anything). While there are now faster modems, even a 28.8Kbps modem will start to experience errors on a standard U.S. phone line, and it's probably best to go for an ISDN connection if you want to increase your speed.

HOW TO USE FTP TO POST AND UPDATE

So, how do you set up your system to post and update your site? For a while now, we have used an FTP client, called CuteFTP (CUTFTP), which is very simple and intuitive. Remember that we are not posting any files yet (since we haven't even started them); we are just going to set the connection between you and your virtual host so it is ready when the time comes. (See Figure 5.2.)

1. If you don't have your FTP software, install CUTFTP from your CD now. (Installation instructions are in Appendix I.)
2. Open the FTP program.
3. Open the site manager from within the program (in CUTFTP it's in the FTP drop-down menu).
4. Choose Add site.
5. Enter the required information. Don't forget to enter your password.
6. That's it!

Figure 5.2.
Setting up your
FTP connection.

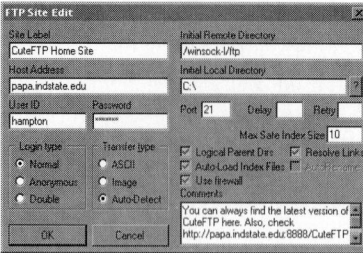

Note:
This site does not actually require a
password; we have included it for
instructional purposes only.

SETTING UP YOUR MAILBOXES

You will probably want several mailboxes,
even if you're the only one in your company.
Not only does this make you look bigger, it
also lets you track responses more easily. A
few mail aliases you should consider are
`webmaster`, for questions and problems relat-
ing to your WWW system; `sales`, for purchase requests; `office`, for administrative
e-mail; `support`, for customer support; and so
on. Your ISP will help you set these up in a
way that is most convenient to you (or else
they won't be your ISP!).

QUICK & DIRTY GUIDE
Testing Your Server

There is a new service called WebGauge (run by the Internet Resources Group) that
monitors Web hosting services. It works by pinging (a program used to test reachability of
a site by sending them an ICMP echo request and waiting for a reply) the main Web page
of each designated site, then generates a ranking of most-to-least available locations. It is the
first in what we hope becomes many of these types of services. Of course, pinging a site is only
one part of judging the adequacy of its server, but it is an important part, and if you're in a
big hurry, it's awfully handy.

SUMMARY

In this chapter, we've discussed some of the issues you will need to address when deciding on
a server. Take our advice, spend the couple days now, and save yourself endless amounts of
frustration. There are hundreds of people who want your business, and only a few who are
worthy of it.

In the next chapter, we discuss the option of using your very own server and the associated
issues.

Your Very Own Server

If we haven't scared you away from setting up your own server yet, the complexity of this chapter may do the trick. As we have mentioned, server setup and maintenance are not projects for the novice; if you have any doubts of your ability to handle this task, you would be well-advised to seek the assistance of a qualified network administrator before proceeding any further.

CHAPTER six

The topic of setting up your own server is far too complex to cover completely in this book. There are many books available on just this subject, and we suggest you read one if you plan to tackle this project by yourself. We would, however, like to provide you with some basic information to get you started, as well as to enable you to make good purchasing decisions.

A simple server is pictured in Figure 6.1.

Figure 6.1.
A simple Internet server.

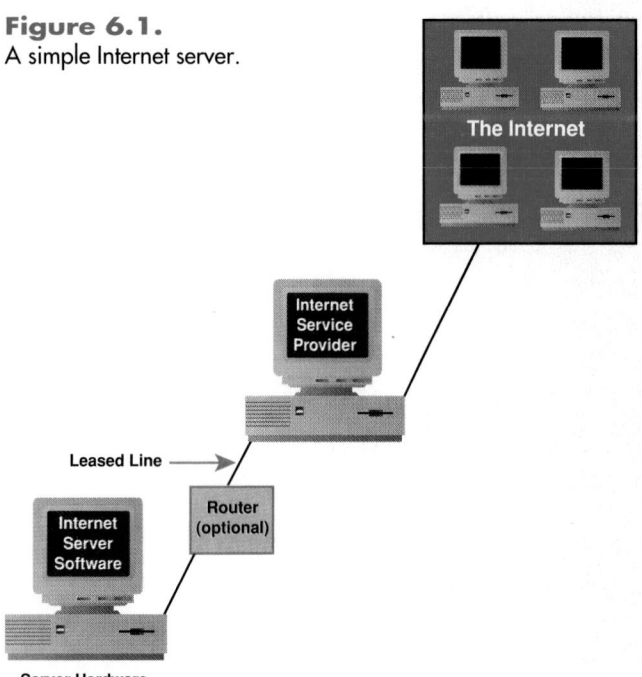

COMPARISON OF THE MAJOR SERVER SYSTEMS

There are several issues that need to be addressed with regard to server systems. The hardware and software configurations of a server can vary widely, and there are a number of combinations that will result in a good server system. In order to give you the best overall picture of your options, we cover these issues separately.

HARDWARE

Servers can be run off anything from small under-powered machines to massive network systems. The system you choose will mostly depend on your budget. You can choose to develop your own server or use a company that specializes in turn-key server packages (preconfigured hardware/software solutions). No matter what system you decide on, make sure that it is able to grow as your site expands. Your server hardware is one of the most difficult parts of your system to change, so make sure you choose wisely, and don't cut corners here.

> **Note:**
> If you are planning to connect your LAN (Local Area Network) to the Net, there are a variety of commercial solutions available. You can either choose to install client software as well as a server on each workstation (yuck), or choose a complete server-based system (yeah). System integration services are available from computer companies like IBM (http://www.ibm.com/) and Digital Equipment Corporation (http://www.digital.com/). There are also a growing number of services (such as PSINet or UUNet) that offer connectivity services. These are usually partnerships between LAN providers and ISPs.

Web servers run on so many types of systems, it is impossible to explore each in this limited space; however, the next sections give a quick overview of the systems we see used most often.

SUN WORKSTATIONS

Sun (http://www.sun.com/) owners are generally quite happy with their technology, and go so far as to say that you'll have the least trouble if you go with one of these systems, as we hope you would at that price. Some claimed advantages are the system's stability, the quality hardware installed, and that public domain UNIX software is easier to compile than on another platform. Sun components, however, are more difficult to locate than PC components, and it is more expensive than most other systems.

SILICON GRAPHICS WORKSTATIONS

SGI (Silicon Graphics Incorporated, see Figure 6.2) is considered the Rolls Royce of workstations. Those who use SGI workstations generally fall in love with them. Graphic designers as well as Web server administrators find SGI out of this world.

Figure 6.2.
Silicon Graphics' high bandwidth Web site.

So why doesn't everyone use them? Two main reasons: the high cost and the difficult security setup. If security is a concern, be prepared to spend lots of time making your host secure. In fact, many feel it is not a good idea to use an SGI box as your shell machine at all! Apparently, the default SGI configuration disregards security almost

completely. Therefore, you may not want to run credit card numbers through an SGI system. If you are interested in this system, check out the SGI Administration Frequently Asked Questions (FAQ) section; it has a comprehensive list of known SGI security holes and how to fix them.

Basically, if you want to buy a really neat workstation, you are prepared to deal with the security issues, and money is not a major concern, an SGI machine may be right for you. Visit Silicon Graphics' slick Web site (http://www.sgi.com), which has lots of useful information and a great FAQ to answer all your questions.

PENTIUM-BASED SYSTEMS

Pentium-based server systems (like Intel's, see Figure 6.3) are becoming more and more popular, especially with the decreasing cost of Pentium Pro and PCI chip sets. Everyone seems to agree they are taking over the market. Not only is the set-up cost inexpensive, but so are the add-on components. This has led to an explosion of software solutions geared toward these systems. Another added bonus is that you can exchange parts with your existing PC or build a whole PC network using Windows NT. Some say that setting up these systems to use as a Web server can be difficult. If you are planning on going this way, we think it is a good idea to invest in one of the pre-configured, complete server packages (more on these later in this chapter).

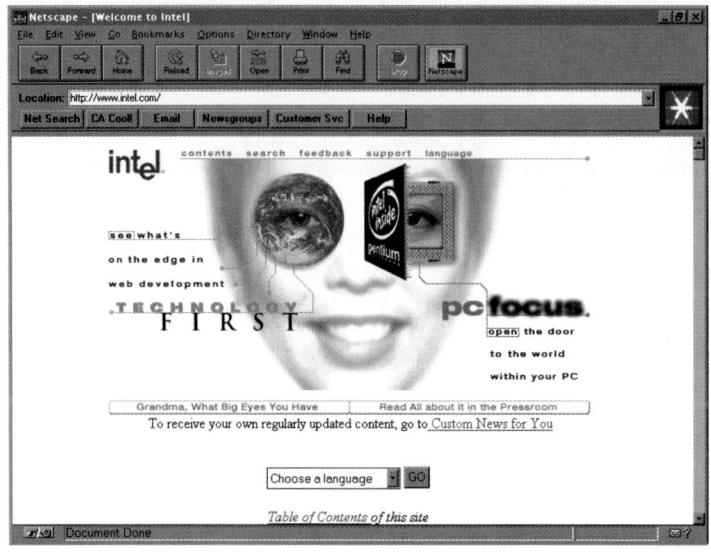

Figure 6.3.
Intel's Web site.

If you want to build your server from scratch, there are literally thousands of sites on the Net with information on buying and setting up a PC. These will get you started:

Intel	`http://www.intel.com`
Compaq Online	`http://www.compaq.com`
Dell	`http://www.dell.com`
Epson	`http://www.epson.com`
Hewlett-Packard	`http://www.hp.com`
IBM	`http://www.ibm.com`

MACINTOSH-BASED SYSTEMS

The best source of information on the Macintosh server is available straight from the horse's mouth at `http://www.apple.com`. Apple has made some great strides lately and is gaining popularity quickly. If you want a preconfigured Web server, Apple sells a range of packages called the Apple Internet Server Solution.

PRECONFIGURED SERVER PACKAGES

A growing number of companies are selling complete server packages; many of these are inexpensive and use Pentium chip sets. Some companies also sell "complete" Internet servers.

These companies are a good place to begin your search for hardware and investigate your hardware needs if you don't know much about setting up systems. A few we have found are

WebCube	`http://www.pacnet.com/pacnet/wcube/home.html`
Computer Data Networks	`http://www.kuwait.net/~cdn/servers.html`
Intergraph	`http://129.135.1.3/webserver`

The real advantage to these types of systems is that they come preconfigured with your server hardware and software, which could end up saving you days of setup.

ROUTERS

If you are purchasing a server package, your router may be included in this system. If not, your ISP may be able to provide you with one. If this is not the case, you may need to purchase a router. What is a router, you say?

A router looks at packets in your internal network, finds the ones that are destined for the Internet, and sends them out. This has to be done at extremely high speed, and the consequences of errors can be horrendous. Because of this, you may need a high-quality router for your system. Routers can also be configured to allow only certain packets between networks, a process called packet filtering. Packet filtering can be used to prevent users from seeing or connecting to internal computers and resources. (See "Firewalls," later in this chapter.)

The standard is the Cisco (`http://www.cisco.com`) 2500 series. They are a little expensive at around $1,900 each, but well worth the cost. You can theoretically program a PC (using special software, such as BSDI) as a router, but the configuration is best left to true experts only.

Depending on your specific Internet sevice provider, you may need to provide the router at your own site only, or at both your site and their site. Look for connections, called full service, which will provide the equipment and maintenance at both sites.

SOFTWARE

The following sections list some of the more popular software options. If you want the most up-to-date information about what the most popular server is, check out `http://www.netcraft.co.uk/Survey/Reports`. (See Figure 6.4.)

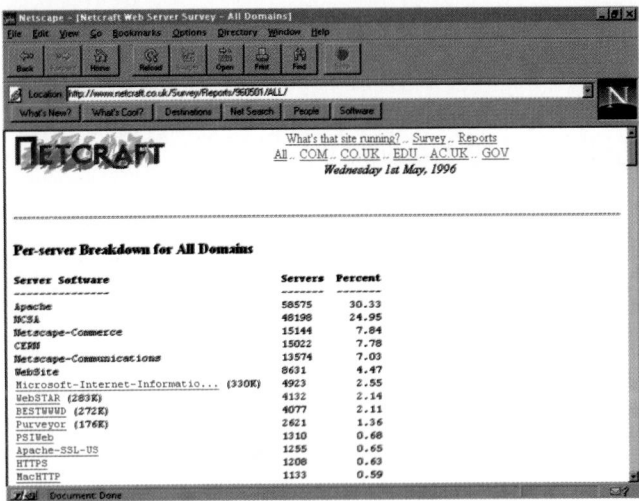

Figure 6.4.
Netcraft's Web site, listing the most popular servers.

SERVERS FOR WINDOWS

Although it is possible to run a server off all Windows systems, most of the good software available is geared toward Windows NT machines.

Netscape FastTrack Server

The Netscape (http://www.netscape.com) FastTrack Server (for Windows NT and UNIX platforms) is Netscape's basic Web server.

Some of its features are

- Set-up wizard (to simplify installation)
- Java and JavaScript support
- Netscape Navigator Gold client software for authoring Web pages
- Access authorization, which enables users to specify a username and password to gain access
- Support of the Secure Sockets Layer (SSL) protocol, providing client-side certificate authentication and Internet-ready access control
- Server Manager, a task-oriented server administration tool

- Dynamically scaling capability to handle heavy loads or to be extended to include the many features that can be added by Netscape's API
- Easily upgradable to the Enterprise server
- Competitive price

Netscape Enterprise Server

Netscape Enterprise Server (now available for Windows NT and UNIX machines) is an "industrial strength" Web server with many advanced features, including

- All the security features offered by the SSL protocol
- Netscape Navigator Gold client software
- Netscape LiveWire integrated visual development environment, which provides visual site management, hyperlink integrity management, and database connectivity to Informix, Oracle, Sybase, Illustra, CA-OpenIngres, Microsoft SQL Server, and ODBC-compatible databases
- Transparent multiple domain support, remote monitoring, and configuration rollback
- Verity Topic search engine technology with full text-search facilities
- Read/write document level access control
- Document cataloging in conjunction with the vendor's Catalog Server software
- Java and JavaScript support

Microsoft Internet Information Server

Microsoft Internet Information Server (http://www.microsoft.com/infoserv, see Figure 6.5) runs on all Windows NT Advanced Server hardware platforms (Pentium, x86, MIPS, Alpha, PowerPC). It is designed to be scalable from single-processor to multiprocessor architectures.

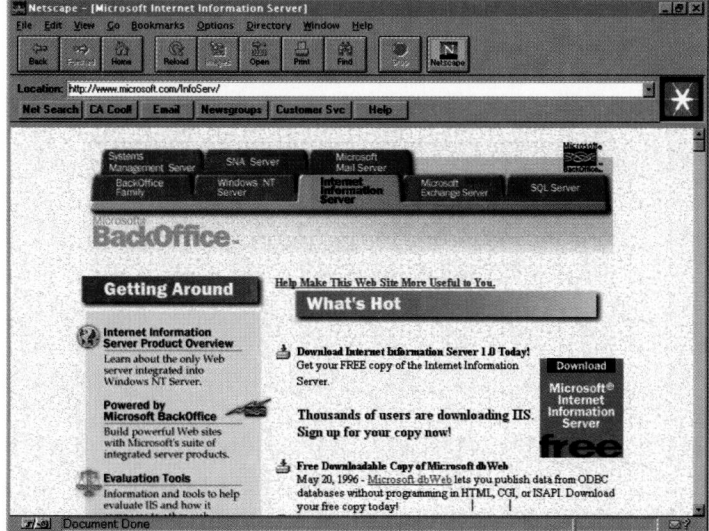

Figure 6.5.
The Microsoft Web site.

Some of its key features are

- FTP support of DOS- or UNIX-style directory listings
- User-level and object-level security integrated into the Windows NT Advanced Server directory service
- SSL for encrypted communications
- Logging for all services; includes basic text file format with auto rollover and extended logging to any ODBC data source such as the Microsoft SQL Server
- Centralized administration from single location for multiple servers, including secure administration over the Internet with or without SSL
- Configurable service, including TCP/IP port and time-outs; multiple virtual roots, including roots located on other computers over the network; home page location; and default name
- Multiple virtual Web servers running with only one administrative unit and one operating system process
- Per-user default directories support
- Configurable logon, logoff, and per-directory welcome text
- Capability to develop database applications using the World Wide Web and any ODBC data source
- Gopher+ support

Microsoft's Internet Information Server is up to four times faster than competitive Web server products, including the Web servers from Netscape, Process Software, O'Reilly & Associates, and Novell. This is according to a study conducted for Microsoft by independent testing services.

WinHTTPD

WinHTTPD (http://www.city.net/win-httpd) is also a popular system for Windows-based and Windows for Workgroups-based (16-bit) systems. This software is based on NCSA's HTTPD and provides the CGI capabilities through a DOS or Visual Basic interface. While this system is inexpensive (around $99), it's much less user-friendly than other available systems.

WebSite

O'Reilly and Associates offers a 32-bit version of WinHTTPD called WebSite (`http://website.ora.com/`). It is a commercial offering that costs $379 and is available as a 60-day demo.

SERVERS FOR APPLE MACINTOSH

Apple (see Figure 6.6) has made some great strides lately with regard to its Internet server software and is gaining popularity quickly. The people who use and love these systems always mention their ease of use.

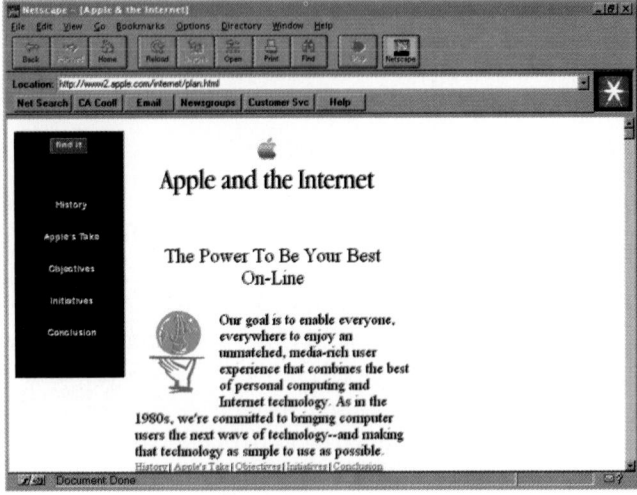

Figure 6.6.
Apple and the Internet Web site.

MacHTTP

For Macintosh, there is an inexpensive (and we hear, user-friendly) HTTP server called MacHTTP (`http://www.starnine.com/machttp/machttpsoft.html`). You can try out MacHTTP for 30 days free. It provides its CGI capabilities through Applescript. There are some problems with trying to apply Macintosh rules to the Internet environment, but with some care, most of these can be overcome (more on this in Chapter 12, "Working with Graphics"). For more information, visit the FAQ posting dedicated to MacHTTP (`http://arpp1.carleton.ca/machttp/doc/`).

WebSTAR

WebSTAR (`http://www.starnine.com/`) is StarNine's industrial-strength commercial World Wide Web server. It is faster than many Web servers running on UNIX, and three times faster than MacHTTP. It is also apparently much more secure than UNIX, and evidently does not need a firewall. (Famous last words?)

WebSTAR supports all browsers, forms, and clickable maps (ISMAPs) and integrates with both Mac and SQL databases. It supports thousands of connections per hour, can be administered from anywhere on the Net, has an integrated search engine for fast data retrieval, and enables control of multiple servers from one Mac. It also has optional security (SSL and S-HTTP authentication and encryption) and commerce toolkits (which support commercial transactions via the First Virtual Internet payment system).

SERVERS FOR UNIX

The Internet began on UNIX-based systems, so much of the server software is developed for this environment. Not only are there more tools available for UNIX servers, often they are available as freeware.

NCSA's HTTPD and CERN's HTTPD

Both NCSA's (`http://www.ncsa.uiuc.edu/InformationServers/`) HTTPD and CERN's (`http://www.w3.org/hypertext/WWW/Daemon/Status.html`) HTTPD are widely available on the Net. They are both very popular and seem to work equally well. They are, however, not for the faint of heart. These systems require an experienced UNIX systems administrator, with much more server knowledge than your average geek.

Of the two systems, NCSA's server is the most widely used and best supported. NCSA's server also has the capability to include documents within documents, so that they can be customized when a reader requests them. It is available at `ftp://ftp.ncsa.uiuc.edu/Web/httpd`.

CERN's server, on the other hand, is often used as a firewall to control Internet connections (see more on this in the section titled "Security Issues," later in this chapter). This is called a proxy server, and not only is used as a security measure, but can also aid in increasing the speed of the system by keeping commonly requested information in its cache rather than having to retrieve it from within the firewall on every request.

Apache HTTPD Server

The Apache HTTPD server (`http://www.apache.org`, see Figure 6.7) is a plug-in replacement for NCSA 1.3. A few of the features Apache claims are

◆ It fixes numerous bugs and security holes seen in NCSA 1.3 and 1.4.

◆ It's free.

◆ It's much faster than NCSA 1.3, and more efficient and faster than 1.4/1.5 as well.

◆ It offers better compliance with existing HTTP specs.

◆ DBM databases for authentication enable you to easily set up password-protected pages with enormous numbers of authorized users without bogging down the server.

◆ Customized responses to errors and problems are possible.

◆ The server enables you to set up files, or even CGI scripts, which are returned by the server in response to errors and problems. For example, you can set up a script to intercept 500 server errors and perform on-the-fly diagnostics for both users and yourself.

◆ Multiple Directory Index directives are possible.

◆ Apache has no fixed limit on the numbers of aliases and redirects that may be declared in the configuration files.

◆ Content negotiation—the ability to automatically serve clients of varying sophistication and HTML level compliance, with documents which offer the best representation of information that the client is capable of accepting—is supported.

◆ It has the capability to handle multihomed servers.

◆ It can distinguish between requests made to different IP addresses (mapped to the same machine).

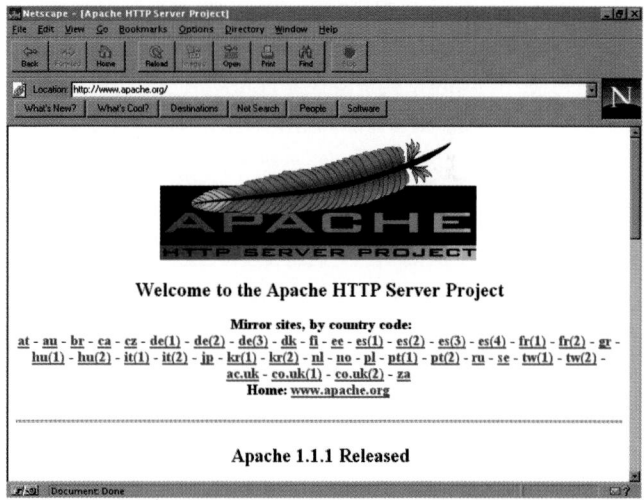

Figure 6.7.
The Apache Web site.

Netscape

Netscape (`http://www.netscape.com`) offers two commercial options for UNIX platforms: the FastTrack server ($295) and the Enterprise server ($995). If you can afford it, upgrade to the

Netscape Enterprise server; it offers all the features of the FastTrack server as well as encryption software, which enables secure transactions over the Internet. Not only is Netscape leading the way in secure transactions, it is perceived by users as the most secure way to send credit card numbers over the Web. For more information about these two Netscape servers, see the previous section, "Servers for Windows."

CONNECTIONS TO THE INTERNET

There are two separate entities to consider when you connect to the Internet: your ISP and your telephone company. Although we must deal with them each separately, the costs involved are directly related. With both your ISP and your phone company, there will be setup charges as well as recurring charges. The first step in determining these costs is deciding on the speed you need. The more speed you want, the more money you will spend (both for setup and on an ongoing basis).

YOUR SPEED—FROM ISDN TO T1 AND BEYOND

You have several choices when deciding on which type of line you'll use to connect your server to the Internet. For most purposes, a point-to-point dedicated T1 is the best decision, but there are other options, as you will see here.

Both your server configuration and Internet bandwidth will determine how fast data is transferred and how many requests can be serviced simultaneously (see Table 6.1). As the number of requests increases, delays or failures are more likely to occur unless you have sufficient bandwidth.

Table 6.1. Typical levels of service for full Internet connections.

Connection	Maximum BPS	Simultaneous Users Supported
ISDN	128,000	10–50
Fractional T1	Varies as needed	Varies
T1	1,544,000	100–500
T3	about 45,000,000	5000+

A very light-duty server could get away with using ISDN. ISDN is fast on its way to becoming the universal standard for switched digital access. While it is great for accessing the Internet, it is usually too limited for all but the smallest Internet servers. However, if you expect very few visitors at a time and want the smallest investment, but insist on your own server, ISDN is an acceptable choice. ISDN is also more readily available than higher speed connections and is now available in most metropolitan areas within the United States.

A server with average traffic might have a T1 or a Fractional T1 (which is a fraction of a T1) line installed. A T1 supports transfer speeds up to 1.544 megabits per second, and is the most frequently used option for point-to-point dedicated lines. Many telephone companies have also begun offering Fractional T1 (FT1) services, which are configured as a number of 56Kbps channels. This is designed for companies that don't require as much throughput as the T1 provides.

Big businesses who expect heavy Internet traffic may need multiple T1 lines, or even T3 service, if they want to be able to serve thousands of users. A T3 is the emerging high-end option for a point-to-point dedicated connection and supports a 45Mbps connection. A T3 is way beyond what most sites require (or can afford), but it does run awfully fast, enabling you to run all the high bandwidth applications (like video and sound) your little heart desires.

GETTING YOUR LEASED LINE INSTALLED

After you have decided on the speed you want, and before you commit to any hardware or software, you'll need to contact your local phone company regarding services available in your area and to set up your line installation.

Depending on your location, you will either find them helpful or clueless. In the area where we live, our phone company is putting together more and more services for the Internet. They have now assigned special departments for Internet-related issues and have many people qualified to lead businesses through the whole setup process. This was not always the case, however. When we first started investigating high-speed connections, we had trouble reaching anyone at our local phone company who even knew what an ISDN line was. If you find this to be the case in your area, begin by making friends with a local ISP. Ask them how they went about setting up their service and whom you should contact.

YOUR ON RAMP TO THE SUPERHIGHWAY: ISPS

Okay, so you're connected to the phone line, but how do you connect to the Internet itself? Well, for that you need a direct connection to the Internet. A direct connection means you are connected to the backbone (a term used for the highest level of a network).

The Internet consists of high-speed circuits connecting routers, which transmit data in the form of IP packets. The circuits are maintained by huge telecommunications companies (MCI, Sprint, Worldcomm); the routers, on the other hand, are owned by ISPs. National ISPs like SprintNet, MCI, UUNet, AGIS, and EUNet lease circuits from the telecommunications companies to connect their routers at their various Points Of Presence (POPs). Local ISPs then purchase connections from these national ISPs. The national ISPs have connections to the Network Access Points (NAPs), where they exchange routes and traffic. So you see, the Internet backbone is in actuality many backbones owned by the National ISPs that come together at the various NAPs (...is connected to the knee bone, and the knee bone's connected to the...).

Your connection to the Internet will generally be leased from an ISP. Where you will find one will depend on what is available in your area. Now that the large communications companies (SprintNet, AGIS, AlterNet, and others) are becoming involved in the Internet, they would be a good place to start looking. If you don't find what you're looking for there, start calling around. Your phone company or a local ISP may be able to help you out. A couple other places to check out are Yahoo!'s listing (`http://www.yahoo.com/Business/Corpora-tions/Internet_Access_Providers/`) or the DLIST (send mail to `dlist@ora.com` to ask for an updated version).

You now have two choices of T1 line: standard or frame relay.

A standard leased line connects you directly to your provider. It's the easiest and fastest solution. In contrast, a frame-relay leased line connects you to a network operated by the phone company. This network can connect you to your provider, even if it's located in another region of the country. So, why do we recommend against it? Frame relay is not nearly as efficient as a standard leased line; as a result, a frame-relayed T1 will not give you anything near T1 throughput.

IP ADDRESSES AND DNS

The Internet is a worldwide collection of individual Transmission Control Protocol/Internet Protocol (TCP/IP) networks. Every computer on the Internet has a unique address (IP address). Information is transmitted on the Internet in data packets.

Each packet is addressed to a specific computer's IP address, such as `206.170.169.42`.

Since IP addresses are so difficult to use and remember, the Domain Name System (DNS) was created to pair a specific IP address, such as `206.170.169.42`, with a friendly domain name, like `ha.net`. When you enter a domain name into your browser, the browser first must contact a DNS server to resolve the domain name to an IP address, and then contact the computer with that address.

So, you must have at least one permanent IP address assigned to your server on the Internet, then you need to register a domain name (see Chapter 3, "Your Domain") in the DNS for your permanent IP address. These services can be provided to you by your ISP.

SECURITY ISSUES

OK, writing this section scares the britches off us, so we want to start with a warning: There are many security measures you can (and should) take when setting up your own server. However, the only way to make your server truly secure is to never connect it to the Internet in the first place. Of course, if you want to reach the public, this is not an option. We will also put ourselves on the line here by saying: No matter what precautions you take, there is *always* the possibility that a hacker will find a way into your system. Keep this in the forefront of your mind when connecting your server to *any* of your internal systems. Though it is very handy to make certain up-to-date information available from your mainframe, it can leave you wide open to security breaches. If you are planning this route, and have sensitive information you wish to protect, we suggest you enlist the aid of a top-notch network security specialist.

We discuss more security issues in Chapter 17, "For Your Eyes Only: Site Security," but there is some information you should know now, while setting up your server, which we discuss here. Keep in mind that in dealing with site security, you are not only trying to guard your system from hackers, but also from innocent users *accidentally* messing with your system.

FIREWALLS

A *firewall* is a damage prevention and security system usually used by companies connecting to the Internet and Wide Area Networks (WANs). A firewall consists of code that aliases, blocks, or hides the firewalled computer from being identified by any other computer on the network. Well-constructed firewalls discourage hackers and help to prevent industrial espionage and sabotage. Firewalls are also used to prevent novice users from accessing commands and services that could jeopardize the integrity of the system.

There are basically three distinct firewall strategies: embedded systems, router-based packet filtering, and proxy servers.

EMBEDDED SYSTEMS

This is a real-time firewall that supplies the security of a proxy server while at the same time delivering the added bonus of high-performance packet filtering. This means a real-time firewall system can provide the performance to support up to 100 times more users than a proxy server. In addition, it has no operating system or disk for hackers to mess with, requires no maintenance, and can be very simple to install. The downside is that these systems can be very expensive and serve only this very specific function.

ROUTER-BASED PACKET FILTERING

Most commercial routers (such as the Cisco we mentioned earlier) have packet-filtering capabilities. Based on rules defined by the administrator, packet filtering enables the router to permit and deny traffic. After a packet is passed through the router, the packet filter forgets the information, as well as the connection associated with it. Think of them as traffic cops with Alzheimer's. These systems are usually the least expensive; they are also high-performance and transparent. Some people do, however, say that they can be very complex and difficult to work with.

PROXY SERVERS

A proxy server is a single point of contact for Internet access for the client. The proxy server generally resides on a specific port, waiting for connections from clients on the network. When a client sends a message to the proxy server indicating where he or she wishes to connect, the proxy proceeds by making the connection to the specified destination. Since the proxy uses the proxy host's TCP/IP, it is aware of every connection in process and will drop packets that don't meet its high standards. You see, a proxy spends its life doing the very basic job of reading from one side and writing to the other. Think of it as a voyeur with an attitude. A proxy server is also multifunctional, since it runs on a general-purpose operating system, so it can provide many additional services to your internal network. The main disadvantages of these systems are that they're difficult to set up, and that the speed of the system suffers under heavy usage.

SEPARATING YOUR SYSTEMS

The simplest way to deal with these security issues is to use separate servers for your internal and external communications, and to never connect the two. You will lose the advantage of interconnecting your systems, but this challenge can often be overcome by manually updating the external server on a regular basis. Consider doing this if security is a major concern.

QUICK & DIRTY GUIDE
Turn-Key Server Packages

Knowing the confusion many face in setting up servers, some astute companies offer "complete" server packages. One such product is WebCube (http://www.pacnet.com/pacnet/wcube/home.html). WebCube (see Figure 6.8) includes most of what you need for your own server (besides the actual connections). There are also companies that offer turn-key server packages and promise total setup of your server. If you are looking to set up a server under a time constraint, and your budget is not a major concern, one of these solutions may be your answer. Some of these are listed at http://www.yahoo.com/Business_and_Economy/Companies/Computers/Networking/Consulting/.

Figure 6.8.
WebCube, just one of the complete server packages available.

SUMMARY

In this chapter we have discussed various server issues and how you can choose to develop your own server or purchase a turn-key server package. We have also covered some of the different software, hardware, and connection choices you will need to make, as well as the security issues involved in running your very own server.

Now it's time to move on to Part II of this book, "Designing a Site that Succeeds." Roll up your shirt sleeves, and let's get started!

Designing a Site that Succeeds

PART II

http://www.mcp.com

Laying the Foundation

It's natural to want to start designing HTML documents as soon as possible, but before you jump head first into Web design, it is important to lay the foundation of your Web site. In developing a site—just as in developing any marketing material—you don't just start pounding out materials in the hope that you'll eventually end up with something that works; you must first decide on the complete design, and then work step by step to ensure that your overall message comes through. Designing a Web site differs in many ways from designing traditional print (interactivity and updateability being only two key differences), but it still requires that you establish some type of organization before you start.

After you've had some experience designing Web sites, you will develop your own way of laying the foundation for a new project. You'll know what you can expect to achieve with the tools at hand, how to organize information for different audiences, how to optimize for navigation and multiple platforms, and other issues. Once you've become a seasoned pro, you may just want to barrel through the following subjects, keeping them in mind but not bothering to write down anything more than a simple site diagram. That's OK, but at this point, we hope that you will take the time to consider the issues discussed in this chapter up front, before you actually start designing pages.

In this chapter you will

1. Determine what specific topics your site will cover
2. Determine the needs of your specific audience(s)
3. Organize your topics into main subject areas
4. Determine how your viewers would most easily navigate through your system
5. Determine the best way to guide viewers through your site
6. Develop your multiple platform strategy (so everyone can view your system)
7. Map out your site diagram

WHAT INFORMATION SHOULD I PUT ON MY SITE?

This question leads us first to targeting your audience. For a start-up business, it can be a difficult task figuring out what kind of people will be looking at your site and what they will want

to find there. For an established business, you'll have a better idea of what the residents of cyberspace might want because you can find out what has been requested in the real world. You can ask the salespeople, customer support, and so on, and get a good picture of what might belong on your site.

Regardless of the type of business you're dealing with, never forget that a Web site will always be evolving. New technology is moving at such a rapid pace that a year-old Web site is a dinosaur. While you are adapting a page to be up-to-date with the current information and technology, you will also have the opportunity to change the format of the site to meet viewer needs. By accessing logs and getting feedback, you'll be able to redesign your site to better fit the exact needs of your viewers (more about this in Chapters 25, "Maintaining Your System," and 26, "Marketing Your Newly Acquired Web Skills").

Regardless of what you're presenting on your site, you'll need to establish to whom you will be communicating. Communication requires two parties—you know who the first is, now you'll have to establish the second.

WHO'S LOOKING?

Unless your site will be private, you really won't be able to control exactly who may be viewing it. The best you can hope for is to establish whom you'd like to have perusing your masterpiece and to design it with this audience in mind—never discounting the fact that there will be others looking as well.

We can estimate who might access an average corporation's Web site:

◆ Existing customers

◆ Prospective customers

◆ Job hunters

◆ Shareholders

◆ Employees

◆ Competitors

◆ Web surfers

Although a single person may fit into several of these categories, it may be easiest for you to break viewers up into these types of manageable groups. Looking at the preceding list, you can predict that each of these groups will have different interests when visiting your site. For instance, a prospective customer will want product/service information and pricing, a job hunter will want to know about your employment opportunities and company information, shareholders will want up-to-date press releases and company forecasts, and so forth. Each of these potential uses for your site will help to dictate how you lay out your design.

Don't forget that in some instances the same page will be accessed by different viewers for different reasons. It's probably not your goal to create a different system for each individual group you anticipate visiting your site, but to organize the information in a way that enables individuals to view the maximum amount of information they want while keeping the information that they don't want (or that you want them to avoid) to a minimum.

For instance, in designing this book's Web site (hampton.org), we have determined our audience will fit into two main categories: those who have bought the book (existing customers) and those who have yet to buy the book (new customers). We will organize our site for these two markets. There are, of course, many other types of people who will be viewing our site (such as surfers and the press), but these two categories will be our main focus. Now we'll try to anticipate what these viewers will want to see.

WHAT INFORMATION ARE VIEWERS LOOKING FOR?

Again using hampton.org as an example, we must determine what specific information our two focus groups would like to find at our site. Existing customers will be interested in book updates, WWW development resources, and perhaps contacting the authors. We will also provide a place for customers to post their URLs. We hope this section of the site will expand as time progresses and will help give readers a sense of partnership and community within our Web site. New customers, on the other hand, will be interested in information about the book, may want to know how to purchase it, and may also be interested in the Web development resources. We'll focus first on existing customers—like you.

The amount of previous knowledge your viewers have in regard to your chosen subject will dictate how much background information you will need to provide, and to what extent you will have to define and explain specific terminology, concepts, and so on. It will also define the way you organize your information.

For instance, if your viewers will include previous customers, try to anticipate what their needs might be. Does a particular product generally need more customer support than others? If so, focus on that product. Now, what specific problem are they trying to solve? If you sell vacuum cleaners and the question you get on your support line most often is "How do I change my vacuum cleaner bag?," you should definitely include a tutorial on changing vacuum bags. Makes sense, right?

Think of it like this: In a customer support Web site (or section of a Web site), your goal is to have every potential customer question answered by your Web system. The only reason people will look to your Web site for answers is if they think they can find them there. Of course, it is very unlikely that you will actually succeed in answering every potential question, which is why you should always include an e-mail link on your pages for people to get more information. Even if your pages are for use only within your company, you should do a similar analysis of the potential readers of your pages.

In the case of this book's Web site, we can anticipate that most of the existing customer viewers will be pretty savvy in regard to HTML and WWW terminology. What we anticipate is that readers will be wanting up-to-date links to resources (since they can change regularly), that they will want updates and clarification on certain subjects of the book (hey, we're the first to tell you that we're not perfect), and that they will want to contact us in some way (kudos and condemnations). So we're designing the Web site with this in mind.

If your Web site is intended to gain new business, you'll be more careful in planning the depth of information you wish to present. Most potential customers are looking for a good representation of who you are, what you do, and what sets you apart from your competition. They're looking for something to make their decision process easier, not more difficult. The hierarchical structure of Web navigation lends itself well to this, as it enables a potential customer to retrieve information on the company to a level of their choice.

For `hampton.org`, we're not really looking to hard-sell our book. We do, however, want to give some overall background about the book, and some information on where it can be found. In the instance of a true commercial site, you may want to provide a company background, key sales points, specific product/service information, ordering information, and so on.

Were we to try to approach even more audiences, as in the previous list (shareholders, employees, and so on), we would need to anticipate their specific needs and see how we can apply them to the overall system. The more audiences you want to address, the more information you'll need to process, and the more you'll have to organize.

How to Organize Information

Now that we know what we will write about, we must arrange this information into main subject areas. As an example, the subject areas we anticipate for `hampton.org` are resources, about the book, feedback, hotlinks, and updates.

Be very careful not to go overboard on this one. Too many choices generally only confuse your viewers, so try to limit yourself to a few well-defined areas. Also, try to keep similar information in one area, rather than repeating it for each group. For instance, don't have one company background page for new customers, another for existing customers, and a third for stockholders. Instead, use the same page of information for all three and apply the customization to the way you link to this information. Failing to do this will cause problems in that viewers will get the impression that they aren't getting the whole picture when they view your system, and may attribute this to your failure to be either organized or honest.

CREATING A SYSTEM DIAGRAM WITH THE CUSTOMER IN MIND

After you have determined what your main subject areas will be, you must determine how your viewers would like to view this information. To do this effectively, you need to design a site diagram. You have a couple of choices here. You can design a Web presentation (leading them through the sales argument or step-by-step instructions) or design a site with many different ways to navigate. The best way to determine which strategy is best for you is to first look at your main subject areas. Do your subject areas follow a timeline? In other words, will your viewers be lost if they view your site in no particular order? Is your audience very narrow, do you expect all your viewers to be seeking the same type of information? A good example of a site that fits into this format is a site such as an instructional guide. For example, a Web site focused on how to brew your own beer would fit into this sequential format nicely.

Home Page: How to brew your own beer

  Step 1: What you will need
  Step 2: Your yeast
  Step 3: The brewing process
  Step 4: Fermentation
  Step 5: Bottling or kegging
  Step 6: Sweet rewards

The diagram for this site is shown in Figure 7.1.

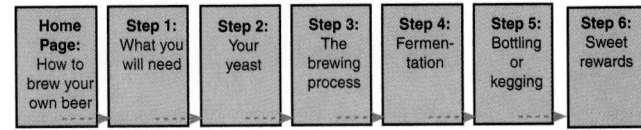

Figure 7.1.
A sequential Web site.

Another option for organizing your site is to use a basic hierarchical structure. (See Figure 7.2.) This is the way most Web sites are arranged. Main subject areas on the home page lead to more specific information within. This way, viewers can have as little or as much information as they wish.

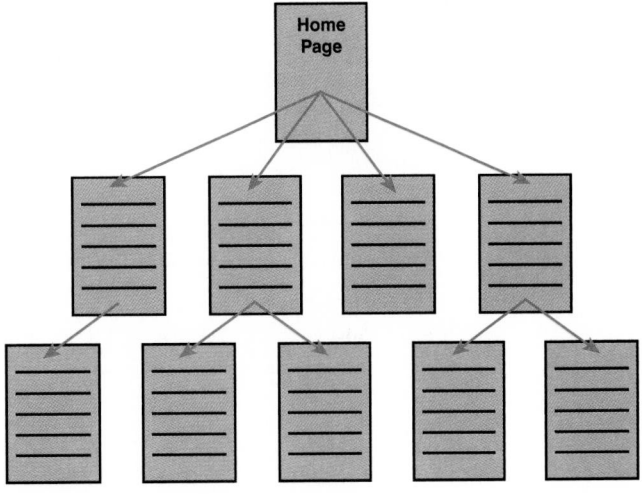

Figure 7.2.
A hierarchical Web site diagram.

For example, Yahoo!'s Web site uses a hierarchical structure in addition to a search engine. This makes it simple to find a subject even if you do not know exactly what you are looking for. So, let's see how it works.

For this example, say you are seeking information on hiking. Starting at Yahoo!'s home page (see Figure 7.3), you select "Recreation and Sports." This links you "down" in the hierarchy to that listing. Here you find another listing with more choices. (See Figure 7.4.)

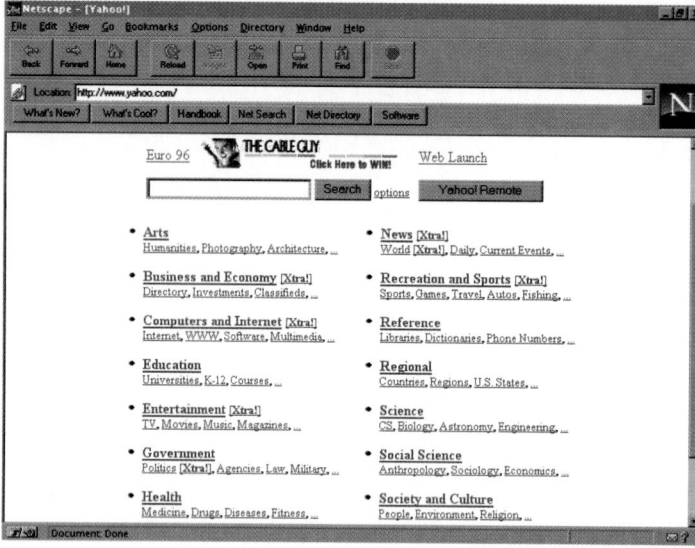

Figure 7.3.
Yahoo!'s home page.

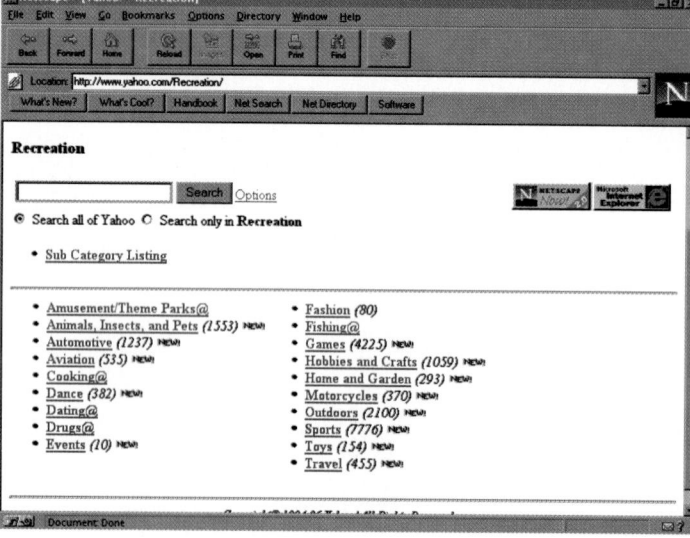

Figure 7.4.
Yahoo!'s second tier.

Because hiking is an outdoor sport, you click on this, which links you down the hierarchy yet another step. (See Figure 7.5.)

Now you're cooking. Selecting hiking brings you further yet into Yahoo!'s hierarchy (See Figure 7.6.)

There it is, that elusive information you seek, and it only took four clicks of the mouse to get there. Not bad for a site as huge as Yahoo!.

For hampton.org, we will be using a hierarchy structure much more limited than that of Yahoo!. We'll be setting things up so that the main subject areas will link to subsets, which may continue down the line to further subsets.

For instance, we will assume that the first stop at our site for someone unfamiliar with this book will be the About the Book section, so rather than having How to Order the Book as a main subject area, we will make it a small subtopic under About the Book, which brings us to five main subject areas (a very good number for an average site).

Our main subject areas will be

◆ Resources

◆ About the Book

◆ Feedback

◆ Hotlinks (reader's pages)

◆ Updates

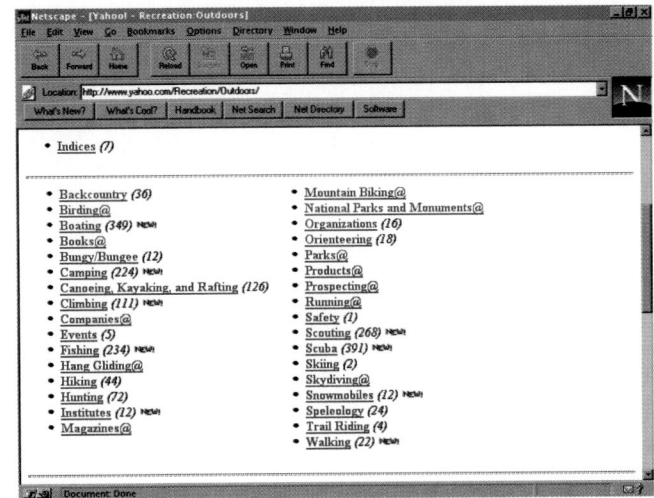

Figure 7.5.
Yahoo!'s third tier.

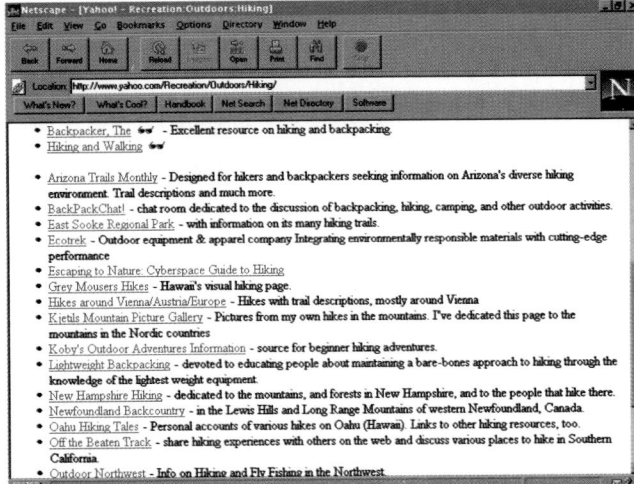

Figure 7.6.
Yahoo!'s fourth tier.

Our bare-bones site diagram is shown in Figure 7.7.

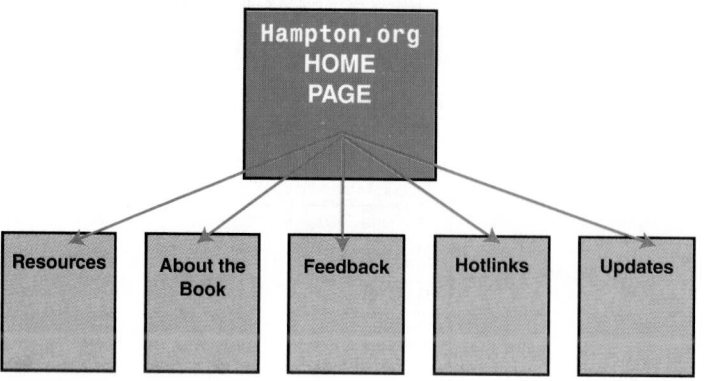

Figure 7.7.
hampton.org's bare-bones site diagram.

Optimizing a Web site for your viewers is important— you want them to be able to find what they're looking for. Another consideration is to design the site so that people will see what you want them to see. Your purpose is not just to provide information, but to provide it in a way that will benefit your business.

LEADING VIEWERS THROUGH THE SALES ARGUMENT

You have an opportunity when designing your site diagram to use it not only for organization, but to enhance your sales argument. This is an opportunity most novice Web designers fail to exploit. But it is by far one of the most engaging reasons to use the Web in the first place.

Assuming that you are designing a system for commercial applications, you will want to do more than just provide information. While designers often describe WWW systems as "online brochures," it might be best to think of things in broader terms. Imagine that your company's Web site is actually a location, and that the home (index) page is the entrance.

So, potential customers found your place either by search (the phone book), referral, or surfing (driving around aimlessly). They've stopped and have walked in the front door. What do they see? Well, what do you want them to see?

First of all, the layout of your home page is going to tell them a little or a lot about you. Do you have a little storefront in a low-rent strip mall, or a high-end professional office? Do you keep your whole stock right at the front counter, or do you have different sections of the store? Do you have a customer service desk, company history display, and so on? Do you want people to walk through one department to get to another?

As we hope you're starting to see, designing a site goes beyond the restrictions of print layout. In fact, it's more than a little like architecture. You're not only deciding on what people will see, but how they will see it, and in what order. In this way, you're not just providing information, you are giving a presentation.

Of course, we'll be going into more depth in Chapter 8, "Make the Site Appealing," but it's important at this point to avoid underestimating the potential of your site. At the same time, you won't want to make your site so complex that people have a hard time finding what they want.

SIMPLICITY IS THE KEY

If at all possible, we try to use a "three clicks" rule, which means that no information should be more than three clicks away. If someone wants information on your widget #1234, they should be able to start getting that information within three clicks of your home page. For instance, say your first page has a link to a *products* page, which has a link to a *widgets* page, which has a link to the *widget #1234* main page. Three clicks, and the viewer is beginning to get information on the product. While you may have more in-depth information on the particular product that will require the use of additional links (product tests, applications, testimonials, and so on), the viewer knows he/she is on the right track within three clicks.

A common mistake is to make your Web structure too deep (see Figure 7.8.), ignoring the three clicks rule, thereby burying your valuable information beneath layer upon layer of menus. This causes the viewer to become frustrated and move to someone else's site (click, click, click, click, click, forget it).

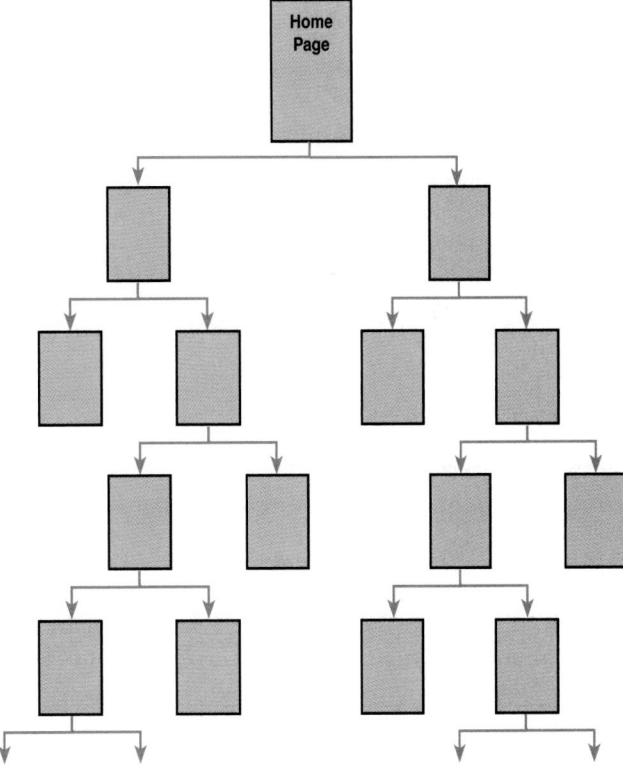

Figure 7.8.
This Web site has way too deep a hierarchy.

Of course, there's another Catch-22 situation here. While you may be able to keep everything just one click away by making a home page with lists of direct links to each individual subpage (see Figure 7.9), this is not a good idea. You'll see this on the Web sometimes, and this is generally because of two things: poor organization and pricing loopholes.

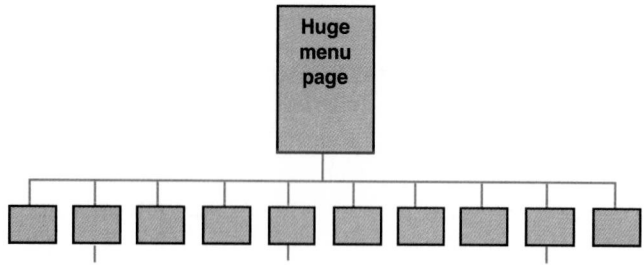

Figure 7.9.
This Web site has way too shallow a hierarchy.

The poor organization problem is self-evident—the designer did the equivalent of throwing a bunch of pieces of print collateral in a binder and calling it a brochure—and we know you're smarter than that.

The pricing loophole problem stems from the fact that many designers and ISPs have charged "by the page" for developing and posting WWW documents. Many unsophisticated advertisers thought they were pulling a fast one by putting everything they wanted to say on just one (or just a few) pages. Compare it to printing a flyer in 6-point type rather than a multipage, readable brochure. It doesn't do anything but make you look cheap, inexperienced, and small.

So, try to keep your choices to a minimum, as anything too complex will only confuse the viewer. Keep in mind your audience, and what specific choices they would want for the first step in your hierarchy (your home page). Then do the same thing for each additional step. This will separate the different types of viewers right away, avoid unnecessary choices, and will also aid in interpreting your site statistics (as we discuss in Chapter 24, "Tracking Page Success"). For example, people seeking product information probably don't need to have a link to shareholder information, and if they do, they can easily return to your home page and follow that path.

CONTENT ISSUES

Here's a hard and fast rule for you: no external links! You wouldn't invite customers into your store and then walk them right out the back door without even showing them your products, so why would you do this on the WWW? Hotlinks (or hot lists) only serve as an exit from your system, your company, and your sales argument. This isn't to say that you can't link out to other companies when it is strategic; just make sure that you've finished with the viewer before you invite them to leave. Never have a *hotlinks* page of *cool sites* unless it is somehow connected to your business.

Keep this in mind if you are selling a product that incorporates other products or services. If widget #1234 is designed for use on another manufacturer's product, don't take the easy route and just link out to the other manufacturer's page system. If you must do this, at least put the links at the bottom of the page, so that the viewer will have to read through your pages before leaving. The better alternative is to provide information on the other product yourself, and then *maybe* put a small link at the end of this for more detailed information. When you do this, try to link to the exact page that contains the information, and not the other manufacturer's home page (this makes it easier for the viewer to back up).

Also, don't think that your viewers will link out from your page in the middle of a paragraph, read the content of a page on another system, and then work their way back to the same paragraph to finish reading. Surfing is about jumping from link to link in order to explore—most surfers don't even try to remember where they've been. And always check your external links regularly, to make sure that they are up-to-date and that they don't list your competition.

KEEPING YOUR PRIORITIES STRAIGHT

We may sound a little cold in what we just said, and commercial designers like us have gotten some flak about "closing off" the interactivity of the WWW. Some people go as far as to say that offering hotlinks is almost a duty, as if it's some kind of dues you should pay for using the Web.

For the most part, neither we nor our clients give a rat's posterior about providing Web surfers with cheap entertainment. The business of business is making money, and we've seen nothing that would lead us to believe that paying homage to the Web god by providing hotlinks does anything for sales. Nor do many other "cool" things people

design into their systems, like external search-engine front ends. ("Here's the phone book, why don't you see if you can find somewhere else to spend your money?")

Furthermore, if you are designing a commercial Web site, you want to sell something, and you don't want people on your site who will never buy, or help convince others to buy, your products or services—just as you wouldn't want a bunch of people hanging around inside your store with no intention of buying anything. All these people do is slow down the process for real customers. You're not looking for hits, you're looking for sales.

STRATEGIES FOR MULTIPLE PLATFORMS

When you sit down to develop your basic site diagram, you will want it to be accessible to many different browsers. Don't ignore this step! Not everyone has a Pentium Pro Windows 95 machine running Netscape's browser. If you only design for this one group, many of your viewers may get less than acceptable results. Fortunately, there are many ways to make everyone happy and make your site look good in the process.

First, we need to discuss the differences in HTML. When we first started designing HTML documents, our job was pretty simple. HTML 2.0 was being used, and most browsers presented our documents in relatively similar ways. We didn't have all the great features that we now have, but at least we didn't have to worry about our page looking like garbage on someone's system.

Well, things have changed; in fact, the HTML language is changing and evolving every day. HTML 2.0 is the old standard and can be viewed by most Web browsers, but does not include many of the coolest features of HTML (such as backgrounds). The proposed HTML 3.2 can be viewed by many of the nicer browsers (such as those from Netscape and Microsoft), and, to make things even more complicated, Netscape and other browsers also have their own HTML extensions that work only with their systems (such as frames did until very recently). It gets even more complex—different browsers can also *interpret* HTML code differently and will give you undesired results if this is not taken into account.

> **Note:**
> The extensions on HTML (like 3.0, 3.2, and so on) are based on the idea that there will someday be some agreement about what is allowable in HTML code. HTML 2 was the last agreed-upon standard, and we don't really think that there will be another. There are just too many people involved to make a decision, which is why the proposed HTML 3 standard was bypassed to make room for the proposed HTML 3.2. In sales situations, we each use the term HTML+, and then go into a discussion of the different browsers, market shares, and so on.

So, what should you do about this? Well, that depends on who you expect your viewers to be, and how much time you have to ensure cross-compatibility.

The easiest way to deal with this problem is to simply use HTML 2.0 without graphics. This will ensure that everyone will be able to view your system. Of course, your system will probably look bland, and people will not be drawn back again to see your site. If you are interested in this route, visit `http://www.w3.org/pub/WWW/MarkUp/html-spec/`; there you will find the HTML 2.0 specifications. We would only use this option in cases where we are simply presenting non-sales information (like technical papers).

The next option is to use HTML 2.0 with a little advanced HTML to spice it up a bit. If you are careful, you can make your site viewable by all, while adding graphics and backgrounds for visual impact. In this case, use as few advanced HTML extensions as possible and make your images GIFs, to enable the widest audience to view them. Advanced HTML specifications can be found at `http://www.w3.org/pub/WWW/MarkUp/` and browser vendor sites such as Netscape and Microsoft. This option takes a lot of testing to get right. Before coding your entire system, be sure to start with a page as your template, and test it extensively with other browsers. Your pages may not look exactly the same on all browsers, but that's OK, as long as it's always readable.

The option we almost always use is to design with Netscape extensions. Although this doesn't cover all your bases, it will include the vast majority of the viewers on the Net. Estimates are that 70–90 percent of people on the WWW are using the Netscape browser. However, you should consider your audience thoroughly—with older browsers, many of the extensions will simply not work. If you know that a significant portion of your intended audience will not be using the Netscape browser, you'll need to take that into account.

Note:
Both Mosaic and Internet Explorer should support frames by the time you are reading this book, and the original problems with Netscape's frames navigation (you couldn't use the BACK button within a frames system) have been overcome. Frames are now a viable option in designing for even the broadest audiences.

The frames system allows for a fallback to HTML for other browsers. By using this, you can design a state-of-the-art frames page without ignoring people using other browsers. Here's how it works.

We designed a Web site using frames (see Figure 7.10).

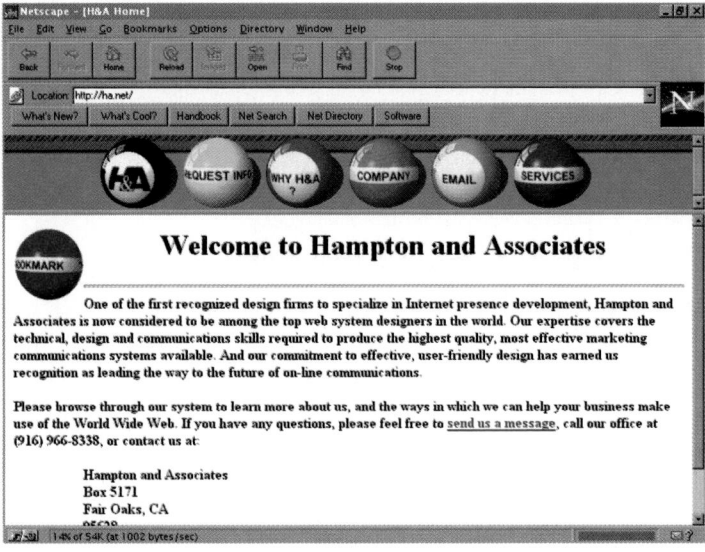

Figure 7.10.
A frames Web site.

HTML frames protocol has a <NOFRAMES> extension that will be used if the viewer does not have a frames-compatible browser. (This type of browser will ignore the <FRAMESET> tags and read only the straight HTML, while a frames-capable browser will ignore the content within the <NOFRAMES> tags.) Within this tag we include an entire HTML 2.0 page. (See Figure 7.11.)

This page reminds the viewers that they are using a browser that is not frames-compatible and gives them a choice to either download a frames browser (to view our cool frames site) or continue viewing our basic system. (See Figure 7.12.) Here's the good part: Instead of having to code two separate systems, we link to the same content pages as our frames system. To do this, make sure that your information pages use standard HTML 2.0 code and include any gee-whiz advanced HTML extensions in other frames. You will need to also include text links on each separate page of your system. If you're interested in this option, see more about frames in Chapter 10, "Taking Advantage of HTML."

One more option is to cover all your bases with separate sites for different browsers. While this is the most effective way of ensuring that everyone will be able to view your system while still allowing you to include the newest features of HTML, it is obviously very time-consuming. You can do this by separating your site into three categories: text only, GIF images, and advanced (or proprietary) HTML. If you want to get really complicated, you could also include separate sites for the newest Netscape browser and Java-capable systems (see Figure 7.13), or even for high- and low bandwidth connections. Keep in mind if planning on this strategy: Every time you want to update a page, you must update each page individually.

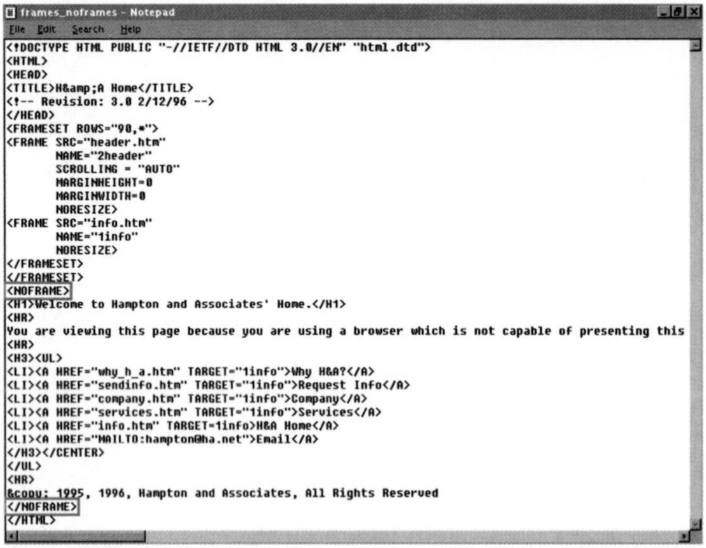

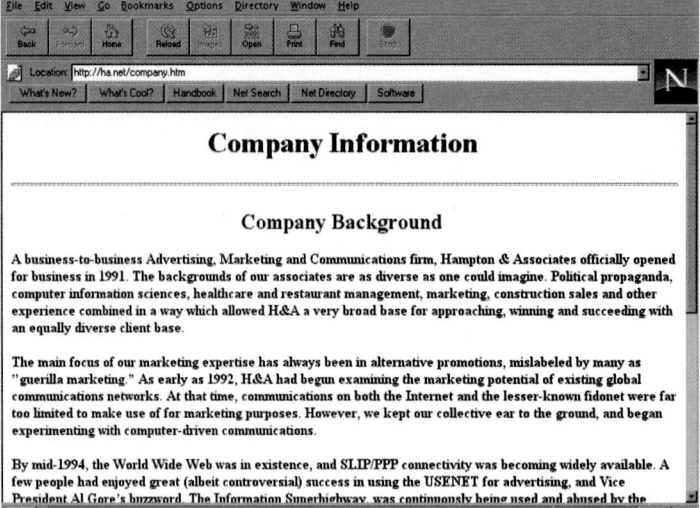

Figure 7.11.
The code of a frames/noframes Web site.

Company Information

Company Background

A business-to-business Advertising, Marketing and Communications firm, Hampton & Associates officially opened for business in 1991. The backgrounds of our associates are as diverse as one could imagine. Political propaganda, computer information sciences, healthcare and restaurant management, marketing, construction sales and other experience combined in a way which allowed H&A a very broad base for approaching, winning and succeeding with an equally diverse client base.

The main focus of our marketing expertise has always been in alternative promotions, mislabeled by many as "guerilla marketing." As early as 1992, H&A had begun examining the marketing potential of existing global communications networks. At that time, communications on both the Internet and the lesser-known fidonet were far too limited to make use of for marketing purposes. However, we kept our collective ear to the ground, and began experimenting with computer-driven communications.

By mid-1994, the World Wide Web was in existence, and SLIP/PPP connectivity was becoming widely available. A few people had enjoyed great (albeit controversial) success in using the USENET for advertising, and Vice President Al Gore's buzzword, The Information Superhighway, was continuously being used and abused by the

Figure 7.12.
The noframes Web site.

Now it's time to lay out a diagram of your own system. Please keep in mind that, because of the complexity allowed by hyperlinks, a two-dimensional diagram can only hope to be a representation of a system. Even a three-dimensional model, which incorporates all of the links on each page, looks like a tangled mess. The purpose of the diagram is to make things simpler for you and your team (and perhaps your client), but don't go overboard.

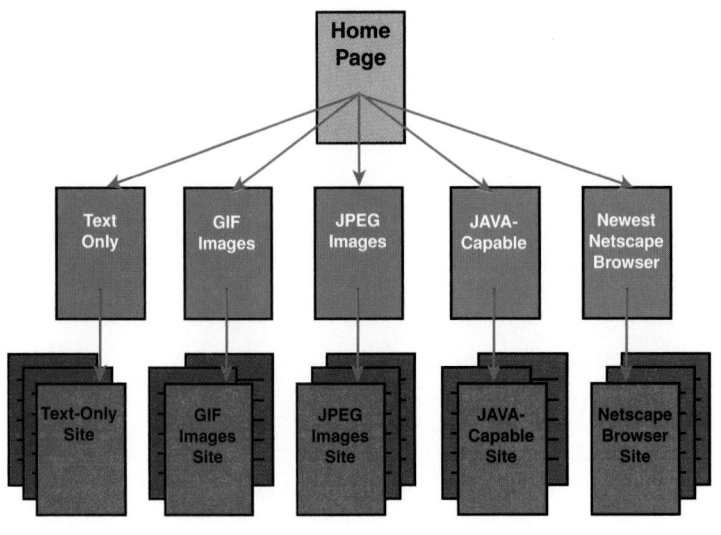

Figure 7.13.
The covering-all-your-bases Web site diagram.

QUICK & DIRTY GUIDE
Real-Life Examples

Figures 7.14–7.18 present some examples of real-life site diagrams, which we hope will help you in developing your own.

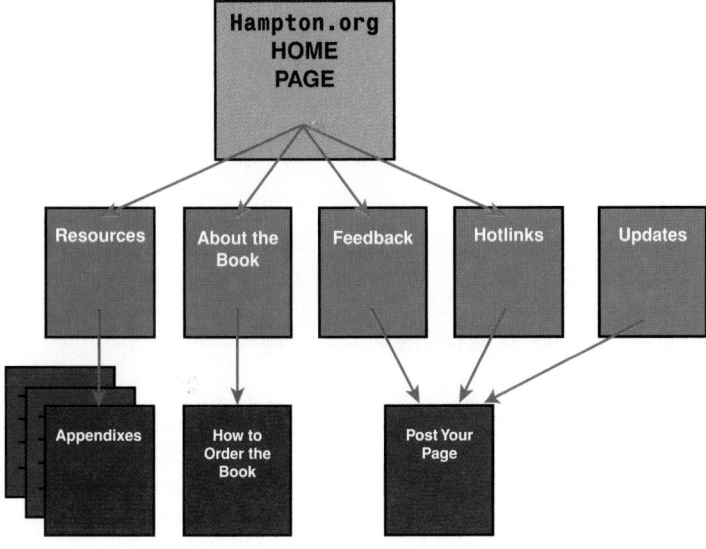

Figure 7.14.
The hampton.org Web site diagram.

Q&D Real-Life Examples

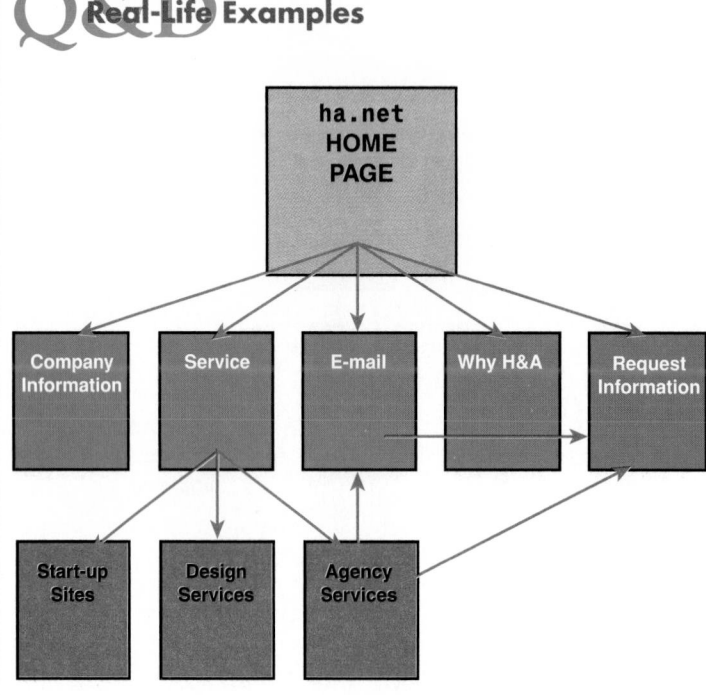

Figure 7.15.
The Hampton &
Associates Web site
diagram.

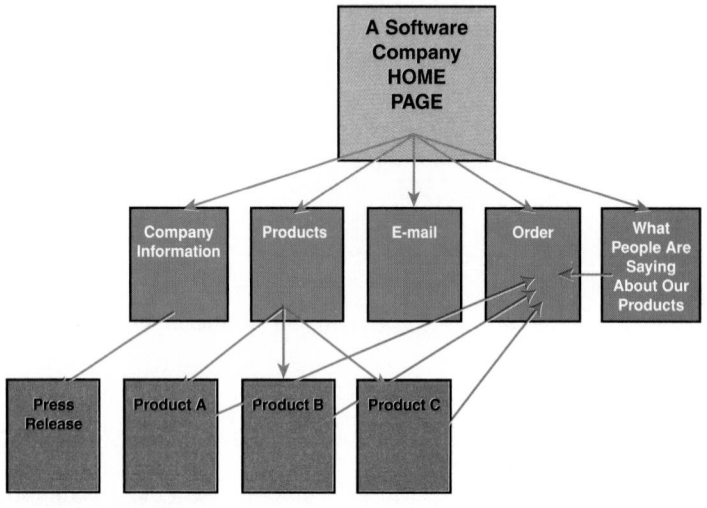

Figure 7.16.
A software
company's Web site
diagram.

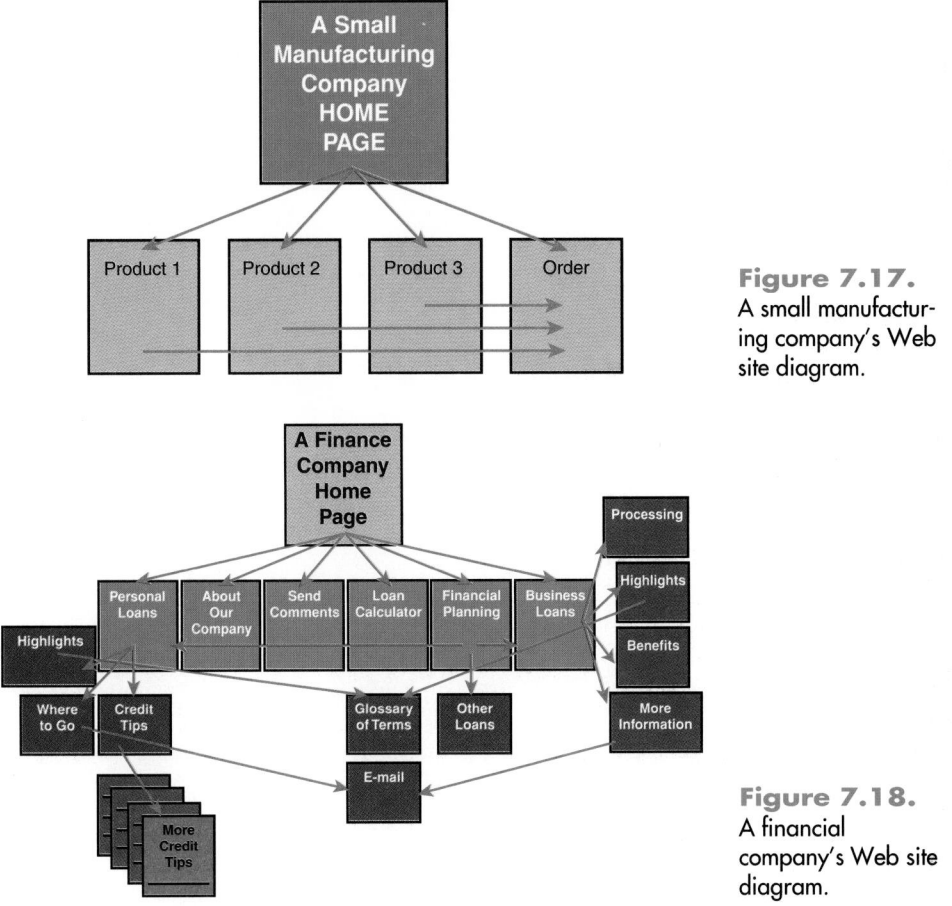

Figure 7.17.
A small manufacturing company's Web site diagram.

Figure 7.18.
A financial company's Web site diagram.

SUMMARY

Designing a Web site diagram can be a complicated process, but it is vital to the overall "friendliness" of your site. Diagramming will also help you tremendously in the long run by keeping you focused. Just as contractors must know what type of house they are building before laying the foundation, you should know the basics of your site before designing the actual pages.

In this chapter you have

- ◆ Determined the needs of your specific audience
- ◆ Determined what specific topics your site will cover
- ◆ Organized your topics into main subject areas
- ◆ Determined how your viewers would like to navigate your system

◆ Determined the best way to guide viewers through your site

◆ Developed your multiple platform strategy (so everyone can view your system)

◆ Sketched out your site diagram

Now that you have developed the foundation for your site, you are ready to learn how to make your pages appealing.

Make the Site Appealing

We hate to pigeonhole
communications, but there
seems to be a trend among
WWW design that lends itself
to categorization. We can break
many pages and systems into
three categories:

◆ **Information**
◆ **Entertainment**
◆ **Sales**

CHAPTER eight

As you've surfed the WWW, you've probably seen pages and systems that fit into the above categories. You've probably seen systems that give way too much information on a product (and do so in a dry, technical manner), systems that are all bells and whistles with no content, and systems whose only focus is on getting you to order the product *right now*.

Our focus in designing commercial sites is to combine these three types of systems into one, and thus create a complete marketing tool. As we have already said, marketing is a combination of things that lead to commercial advancement, and not a single entity. What we are seeking is a balance of information, entertainment, and sales communications that will provide a complete communications package.

To put things into perspective, here's a story about the three little business people. The first was an informer. When she was asked to send a client information about a product, she would gather everything she could get her hands on, bind it all together in one big book, and send it to the client saying that everything they could possibly want to know was in there.

The second person was strictly an entertainer. He would go to a client's office, tell jokes, show interesting slides, do magic tricks, and so on.

The third person was strictly focused on getting the client to order. She would walk into the client's office with a contract in one hand and a pen in the other.

Separately, these three people did very poorly. They would either confuse, distract, or irritate the clients. Together, however, they were unstoppable. They were able to engage the clients, provide them with the information they needed, and close the deal.

Your pages should keep the same balance. You want to provide enough information for your potential clients to make an informed decision (and to support them after the purchase), you want to provide this information in an engaging manner, and you want to make the sale. By balancing this carefully, you will make your system appealing to the broadest audience.

ORGANIZING YOUR PAGE TO YOUR COMMERCIAL BENEFIT

So, how do you go about making a system that provides all three elements in perfect balance? The key is in organization, both at the page and system levels. To make the site appealing to the broadest audience, you will need to design your work so that it provides effective communications to several different types of people (shoppers looking for a quick overview, people wanting in-depth detail, and so on). We'll start with the basics.

BASIC ELEMENTS OF A WEB DOCUMENT

These items should appear on every commercial WWW document:

- Company name
- Link to information on contacting company or company e-mail address
- Page title
- Author or contact person's e-mail address
- Content
- Link to home page
- Date of creation or latest revision (on time-sensitive materials)
- Statement of copyright
- Hypertext link(s) to other related local pages
- Company logo

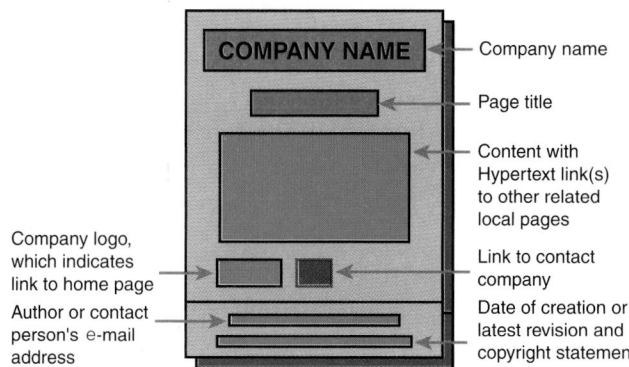

Figure 8.1.
The basic items in a commercial Web document.

Your company name and logo should appear on each page, so that it is clear to everyone, regardless of how they entered the system, who owns it. This also ties the Web system into any printed collateral.

Providing a link to information on contacting the company, or a company e-mail address, is crucial. Remember, this is two-way communication we're dealing with here. If the viewer can't get ahold of someone for ordering, further information, and so on, the system doesn't serve much of a purpose other than letting people know the company exists…somewhere.

> **Note:**
> Many of these elements can be addressed in different ways. The company name and logo can be a graphic on each page, a banner in a frames system, or something else. You should address all of these items in some way, but the exact way you do it is your choice.

The page title should exist on two levels: first, it should be included within the HTML <TITLE> tags, so that a browser will display it outside of the page (usually on the browser's top border). Second, the title of the page should appear clearly within the body of the page, so that it can be viewed within the first screen (without scrolling) on a 640×480 pixel monitor.

The author or contact person, often called the webmaster, should present an e-mail address, and a link to his/her e-mail, on every page if possible. This enables people to report problems with your pages. This sometimes becomes a nuisance, as there are people out there with way too much time on their hands who will fill your e-mail box with annoying observations. On high-traffic sites, you may want to drop the webmaster link after you're sure that most of the bugs have been worked out of the system.

A link to the system home page offers primitive navigation to people who may be unfamiliar with your other navigation tools, and it enables people to start over from the beginning. It's also useful if someone is accessing your system from anywhere other than the home page.

Press releases, technical updates, and other time-sensitive materials can include the date of creation and/or latest revision. If this is not something you want to make public (and there's really no reason to), you can include it in the code as a comment tag, or you can encode the date, revision and any other information on the bottom of the page (as in `080896r4`).

Copyright law states that you needn't claim a document as having a copyright for it to be valid and legally yours, but it will help if you are ripped-off and need to take it to court. Your statement of copyright should look something like this: `© Copyright 1996, Hampton and Associates, All Rights Reserved.`

Hypertext link(s) to other related local pages should be included for obvious reasons, but how and how many are a matter of style and application. For instance, don't link out in the middle of a paragraph if you want that paragraph to be read; instead, add a `more information` link at the end of the text.

PAGE LENGTH CONSIDERATIONS

When arranging your pages, be aware that novice viewers can be easily disoriented by long, scrolling Web documents. They seem unable to find links when they disappear off-screen as they move through very long pages. Though there are ways to keep your novice viewers oriented, it's a good idea to limit your documents to two screens worth of information. If you must use long documents, be sure to feature navigational links at the beginning, end, and even the middle (if your document is very large) of the Web document. A frames system helps to eliminate this problem by enabling you to keep your navigation bars on-screen while the content is scrolling (more on this in Chapter 10, "Taking Advantage of HTML").

Another disadvantage of very long Web documents is that the viewer must rely on the vertical scroll bar to navigate through the page. In many graphic interfaces the scroll bar slider is a fixed size and gives the viewer no real indication of the length of the document relative to what is currently visible on the screen, so users have no idea how long your Web document is, or when they will reach the end of it. In extremely long Web pages, very small movements of the scroll bar can completely change the contents of the screen, leaving the viewer no familiar landmarks on-screen (where am I?). This forces the viewer to creep slowly downward with the scroll bar arrows (often line by line), or risk missing sections of the page.

All this would seem a good argument for always limiting your Web documents to two page lengths, but of course, as with all rules, there are exceptions. For instance, it makes sense to keep very closely related information within the confines of a single Web document, especially when you are providing information which you anticipate the viewer will want to print or save to text. By keeping the content within one document, you make printing and saving much easier. When designing long Web documents such as these, always provide internal links within the document. The best way to do this is to arrange your Web document like a book, with the information split into separate sections (chapters). You can then make a table of contents at the beginning and end of the document so viewers can jump to a particular section without having to scan through the whole page. (Figure 8.2 shows a good example of this.)

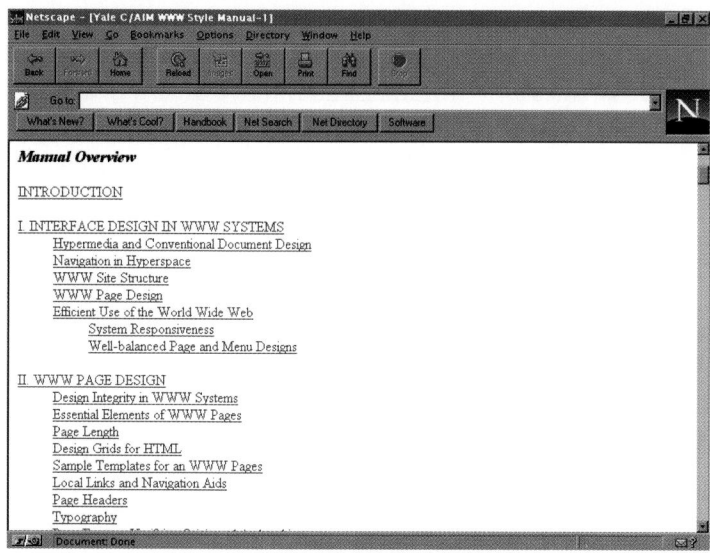

Figure 8.2.
A navigational table of contents.

Page length tips:

- Attempt to make the majority of your pages no longer than two screen lengths.

- If you must use long documents, feature internal navigation links at the beginning, end, and even the middle (if your document is very large) of the Web document.

- When a page is intended to grab people's attention, don't make the page longer than the average screen length.

- If your document is more than one screen "page," try to present some content on the first screen telling the user that there's more to be seen below the horizon.

- If your pages include text that viewers will want to read at length, it's all right to use lengthy, scrolling pages—just be sure to warn viewers that a big file is coming.

- If dividing information into separate segments, provide a separate link to a complete document. This will make it easier for viewers to print or save your document.

- If you have a page with only a small bit of information, try to combine it with related information. It's very annoying for the viewer to have to wait to download a page that only contains two links or one paragraph of text.

DESIGNING YOUR LOOK

The cardinal rule of design: Your design should enhance and not detract from the information you are trying to provide. This sounds like kid's stuff, but if you take a look at many of the sites on the Web today, you will see that a great number of them break this very simple rule. But not you....

The goal in designing for the WWW is to communicate your point. How do you do this? By getting and keeping your customers' attention.

Note:
The purpose of commercial art is to help communicate an idea. A graphic may be beautiful, striking, and appealing in and of itself, but if it doesn't assist in communicating the message, it has no place on the document.

Good Web design, just as good graphic design, always seeks the perfect balance between visual impact and the graphical and textual information you are providing. Without the visual impact of contrast, shape, and color, Web documents will be graphically uninteresting and may not inspire the viewer to investigate their contents. In addition, pages filled with solid text, ignoring the visual contrast and optical relief offered by graphics and a well-structured page layout, are more difficult to read. Nonetheless, without the content of the text, highly graphical pages run the risk of disappointing the viewer by offering a poor balance between visual sensation, textual content, and hypertext links, as well as providing little reward for the time spent downloading the graphics. So, your goal is to find this ideal balance, within the graphical constraints of the HTML language and the bandwidth limitations of the average viewer.

The six basic elements of good Web design, as we see them, are

- ◆ Simplicity
- ◆ Visual balance
- ◆ Proportion
- ◆ Contrast
- ◆ Flow
- ◆ Harmony

SIMPLICITY

Simplicity is the most important principle of Web design; after all, the WWW is supposed to make things easier and information more accessible to the public. While viewers are entertained by high-end graphics and kick-butt bells and whistles, they will only come back if your content is easily accessible and worthy of their time.

Viewers generally won't struggle too hard to get to your content, and if they do it makes them angry and frustrated and turns them off of your site. So your Web design has to be not only interesting, attractive, and informative, but simple and efficient as well.

VISUAL BALANCE

Each element in Web design (graphics, type, white space) has its own optical weight. In print work we call this their ink density. Graphics are weighty when compared to a block of type, which is relatively light. So, in attempting to achieve visual balance, keep in mind it takes a lot of type to balance even a small graphic.

Visual balance must be assessed top to bottom, as well as left to right. The left to right part can be really tricky, considering you never know how wide your page will be when viewed (the center point is unknown). Therefore, you should take full advantage of HTML alignment tags (`<CENTER>`, `<ALIGN=RIGHT>`, and so on), for text as well as images whenever possible (much more on this in Chapter 10). For example, say you have an informational page with lots of text aligned to the left (default); to achieve visual balance you need to add some weight on the right. You could do this in many ways—for example, by placing the majority of your graphics on the right, or by using graphics with brighter or bolder colors on the right.

To achieve top-to-bottom balance, each Web document should have a header and footer section; this creates visual bookends for your page. These should contain some similar elements (at the very least, keep your header and footer in the same color scheme). This is not to say that you should add unnecessary graphics at the end of your pages, but you should provide a good bookend, even if it is just a horizontal line with your copyright information.

Also, never underestimate the value of white space. Many inexperienced designers feel a need to fill every pixel with information, and this simply isn't the best way to communicate. Refine your pages to the point that the messages are concise, and use design elements that break the information up into manageable chunks.

PROPORTION

For some reason the human eye tends to favor particular horizontal:vertical relationships in the sizes of elements. A proportion of about .6 to 1 (roughly twice as long as high, or vice versa) is the most pleasing to the eye, while perfect squares are less pleasing. It is easy to do this with your individual graphics, but it is much more difficult to implement in your Web page (since there are so many variables in how someone will be viewing your site). Nonetheless, be aware of the proportions of your page elements: graphic dimensions, blocks of text, white-space area, and so on.

CONTRAST

Contrast is a very important part of Web design, as it is in all other design. Contrast is easy to explain; if you shout all the time, people will stop listening, but if you whisper and all of a sudden shout at the top of your lungs, you'll be sure to get people's attention.

An example of how this works in Web design comes from some novice HTML programmers. Because heading tags are the easiest to learn, novices often begin designing Web documents by making nearly all the text a heading, as if for some reason they think the bigger the better (we wish we could show you how awful this looks in a real example, but we can't very well ask people if we could use their page as an example of bad design). The result of this is the whole document looks as if it is shouting. Nothing stands out, and the viewer becomes disinterested and tunes out. Another common mistake is to load every document with dense text, ignoring the important inclusion of white space (empty space on your page); this causes viewers to see a wall of gray and their brains instinctively reject the lack of visual contrast. Yet another common mistake is to ignore the contrast between the background color (or image) and the text. If you have ever tried to read yellow type on a white background you know exactly what we mean. So remember, your type must stand out very clearly from its background to be read easily.

Good Web typography depends on the contrast between one font and another, as well as the contrast between blocks of text and the surrounding white space. Web pages with lots of dense type, small or no headlines, and low-contrast graphics tend to look dull and lifeless on a Web page. Strong visual contrast and unique patterns attract the viewers' attention and make/keep them interested.

Use heading tags very sparingly, in other words, only if you want to really emphasize the text (less is more). Otherwise use bold, italics, or font size to contrast segments of type you consider important details. In other words, you can use contrast of your fonts to portray what you want the viewer to see as important, in addition to adding visual interest.

> **Note:**
> A good typographer's rule is to use only one type of font treatment at a time. For instance, either *italicize* or **bold** a word, but avoid doing ***both*** if at all possible (*sometimes you may **need** to do this in a caption*).

Keep visual contrast in mind for your entire document. Remember: People see contrast and pattern before they notice anything else, so edit your design just as tightly as you edit your copy. Take the time to erase the unnecessary and accentuate the essential.

FLOW

Viewers tend to quickly scan and then read, making many passes through information, not just one. Their first scan looks at the overall shape and patterns, while further scans begin to examine the content more deeply.

A good Web page design leads the viewer to the starting point, and then distinctly through the page in the best order for maximal understanding. Keep in mind that viewers see big, colorful, or bright elements of the page first, and then follow the normal left-to-right and top-to-bottom pattern.

HARMONY

Your Web site should be harmonious; in other words, your individual Web pages should look as if they belong together. You can do this by making your individual elements (graphics, type, white space) sized, colored, placed, and used the same way on each page on your site. You should also employ the same overall structure for each document on your site.

This consistency helps guide viewers through your information and gives them a sense of where they are on the Web (they know they are on your site and haven't jumped to New Guinea accidentally). There is also an issue of the harmony between the graphics and the text. Try to match the art to the copy, and vice versa. The purpose for both is to send a message (more on this in Chapter 12, "Working with Graphics").

MOCKING UP

The first step in mocking up your Web site is to establish the basic layout map for your pages. Do this by gathering representative samples of your text (if you have any; if not, just guesstimate your average text length with nonsense text, often called "greeking"), along with your logo art and any additional graphics you will be using (if you have none, estimate the average size of your graphics). Think of each of these elements of your page as blocks—your goal is to arrange these blocks in the way that is most pleasing to the viewer. Experiment with various arrangements. We do this on a white board with tape on the back of our blocks so we can rearrange them, but you can use any method you like. You are trying to arrange a basic map that will apply to your entire Web site. Of course some pages are larger than others, or require more graphics, but the basic placement of your blocks should stay consistent throughout your site.

Determine where the graphics and text blocks will be placed on your documents, and decide upon the position and font style (size, treatment, and color) for page titles, subtitles, and navigation links. Once you've done this, you'll have a starting point for each of your pages.

Keeping Continuity

Consistency and predictability are essential characteristics of any well-designed Web site. They are key elements in helping users identify the origin of Web documents, providing predictable access to the interactive elements of the site, and giving the viewers a harmonious graphic design scheme as they move about your system.

Navigation Strategies

The amazing capabilities of the WWW and other highly graphical, interactive media (such as multimedia presentations) have led many "information experts" to completely reject print standards as a guideline in designing Web systems. As we've said earlier, you should not limit yourself to traditional media constraints in designing for the

WWW, but we heartily disagree with anyone who believes they can chuck out thousands of years of communication refinement just because something is new and unfettered.

The fact of the matter is, you are trying to communicate something. To do this, you have to speak in the language of your intended recipient. Hypermedia and interactive design are, without a doubt, much more powerful than simple text in presenting information. However, your audience is far more used to getting information from print than in any other form except the spoken word (which includes television and radio), and several lifetimes of experience have gone into refining this medium.

> **Note:**
> There's a personal information system that takes handwritten input, stores it indefinitely without the need for external power, retrieves the information instantly, and fits in your pocket. It's called a piece of paper.

It is part of your job to educate your readers in the use of hypermedia, and to do this, you must reference their existing knowledge of information technology (which will vary from audience to audience, and reader to reader). If you completely disregard communications standards, your chances of confusing and thereby losing a viewer increase exponentially. This is certainly not to say that you shouldn't make use of the capabilities of the WWW, but that you should understand that many of your viewers will be novices to the medium, and that you need to take this into account in designing your pages.

The biggest problem in hypermedia is that the sheer complexity of the links and navigation are extremely difficult to put into a conceptual model. As you've seen, we like to diagram our page structure as hierarchical (with different levels and sublevels). The truth is, however, a diagram that truly reflects all of the possible links and paths through even a simple WWW system looks incredibly complex and often is impossible to diagram in two dimensions. What we are dealing with is perception.

We design our systems in hierarchical diagrams because we need to work with something that both our clients and ourselves can understand. This is very important, obviously, but there's more. We also need to view things from the Web site visitor's perspective, and if *we* have a hard time conceptualizing a Web system's structure, we can be pretty sure that it will be more difficult for the viewer.

You want your viewer to perceive your system as being straightforward and simple, regardless of how complex it really is. This is a double-edged sword in that you want your viewers to have the idea that they are working their way through your system and information in an orderly fashion, but you don't want to limit them to a structure that makes them miss key points of the message.

This is, perhaps, your most difficult task in designing a system, in that you want your viewers to perceive their trip through your system as being a linear progression from one page to the next, when actually they are bouncing all over the place as they move from page to page to page.

The best way to accomplish this is to provide clear navigation throughout your page systems and to have at least a Home link on each page (never, never leave viewers at a dead end, where they will have to work their way back through your system in order to go ahead). If possible, provide navigation on each page that includes the key

elements and areas of your message—even if this means that the viewer will have the ability to jump around without viewing each section in its entirety. It's better for viewers to get a partial view of the overall message than to get a full view of the partial message, and then leave thinking they've seen it all.

HEADERS

The use of headers, either textual, graphical or (best) both, tell your viewers where they are within your system. The best way to do this is often to go back to the hierarchical model and label the page by set and subset. For instance, if a viewer is reading about a certain product, you might represent this textually on a page by using headings such as

XYZ MANUFACTURING

PRODUCTS
WIDGET #1234

Any or all of these headings can be graphical, as in the illustration in Figure 8.3, where the heading can also be a navigation link.

Figure 8.3.
A graphical heading.

"PREVIOUS" AND "NEXT" NAVIGATION

It would be nice to use "previous page" and "next page" navigation in order to preserve your viewer's simple, linear navigation concept, but it really doesn't lend itself well to the power of the WWW. This type of navigation should only be used when there is one and only one way to go through the system, or when the linear navigation is relevant to a prechosen path through the system (as in a guided tour). In the latter case, the forward and back navigation should be an option, not the primary from of navigation (think of it as a bonehead way through your system). If you do choose to provide Back and Next links, always tell the viewers where they will be going if they choose the link (for example, Back to Customer Service, and Next: Ordering).

SITE MAPS

There has recently been a move toward providing a large, linked graphic or raw HTML page that shows your system in a map form. (See Figure 8.4.) Again, the format is usually hierarchical (either a tree, or a series of concentric circles). It's not a bad idea to provide this off of your home page, or as an alternate navigational system listed within a header or footer, but it really shouldn't be relied upon as the primary form of navigation.

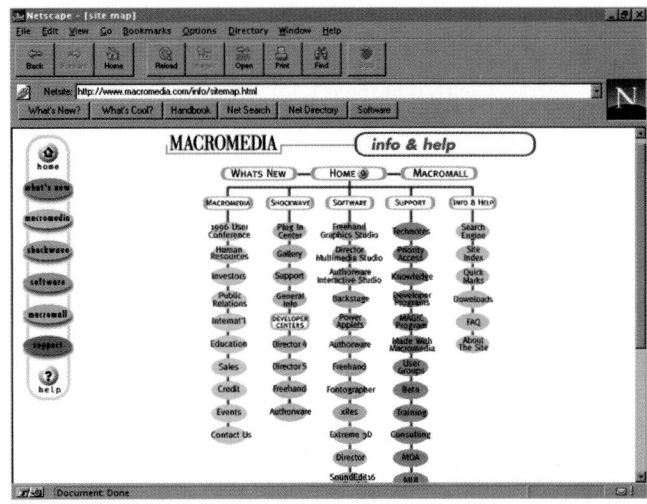

Figure 8.4.
An online site map.

Here are some problems with relying on a site map:

◆ You lose your sales argument—the order in which you'd like potential clients to receive information for the best effect, or the way you'd like to lead viewers through your system. (For example, company, quality, product, and price might be a better order than price, company, product, quality.)

◆ You lose the ability to rely upon main pages for general information (so that you may have to repeat it on each page).

◆ You must update the map constantly, rather than simply changing relevant links transparently.

Alternately, here are some strong points for providing a site map within your system:

◆ It provides rapid navigation within large and/or complex sites.

◆ It gives people an overview of your system content and design.

◆ It provides a reference point for repeat visitors.

Overall, we feel that site maps are often used as an easy way out of carefully planning site navigation. They are best used for sites that deal strictly with technical information and documentation, rather than those designed for overall marketing. In the case of a site that presents both a marketing section and technical documentation, you may opt to provide a map that only lists the pages you would wish a viewer to access directly. If you do this, you should make it clear that the site map is only a list of key areas, and not a complete page structure diagram.

SOME NAVIGATION TIPS

Following are some key tips for designing navigational tools. These will help make navigation simpler for the viewer, and will also help you approach the broadest audience.

- If you're using graphic navigation buttons or image maps, use redundant text links as well, to make things clear.

- Make the clickable regions in an image map easily identified when information is the main focus of the site. (You can make things more esoteric if you want people to spend time "discovering" your site.)

- Always supply alternate text (in the image tag) for graphic navigation buttons.

- In a long document, provide a brief table of contents with internal links at the top (and possibly the bottom) of the document.

- Select a title that accurately summarizes the content within that document and matches the header.

- Always use a header on the top of each page, indicating the viewer's location within the site (this can be graphical, text, or both).

- Provide a site map if your site is large or sprawling, or if your main focus is on providing easily accessible, specific information.

- Consider duplicating navigational tools at the top and bottom of your pages.

- Avoid using Next and Back buttons and links without saying where the links are going.

COOL VERSUS EFFECTIVE MARKETING

Because we're in "Advertising," friends and family often want to tell us about some great TV commercial they've recently seen. It usually goes like this:

> THEM: "Hey, have you seen that beer commercial, where the guy walks into a bar, and everyone in the bar is a goat, and then the guy has a beer, and all the goats turn into beautiful women in bikinis?"
>
> US: "Uh, no. I haven't seen that one, what beer is it advertising?"
>
> THEM: "I dunno, but that's a great commercial!"

Well, it might be a funny commercial; it might be a cool or entertaining commercial, but it obviously isn't a great commercial. If it were a good commercial, they'd have remembered the name of the beer, and if it were a great commercial, they'd have been drinking one when they told us about it.

In Web design, it's easy to get caught up in the latest technology—providing cool graphics, bells and whistles, and all of the nifty things that the WWW allows—but you've got to remember your focus. You've got to prioritize what it is you want to accomplish, and not just try to be cool.

There is certainly a place for cool. Ultimately, everything on your site should be cool—even the way you present uncool things. But you should use the cool factor only as far as it assists in the effectiveness of presenting your message, not as an end in itself. The coolest thing is accomplishing your objective.

> **Note:**
>
> Cool is especially useful if you have little to say. For instance, you'll notice that many of the most entertaining beer commercials you see are from brands that vary little from their competition. Their beer tastes pretty much like the next, so they focus on something that has absolutely nothing to do with which beer you buy—like bikini-clad goats.

EFFECTIVELY COOL

So where does this leave you? What's cool and what's not? Well, we can't hope to address every option you have in WWW design, and many are addressed in detail within their respective chapters, but we can talk about a few right now.

QUALITY OF INFORMATION

Obviously this is key. You not only want to present quality information—answering the questions your viewers may have—but you want to do so in a way that gives you some control over the communication. This is especially the case when you are marketing a product or service.

Unless you are trying to sell something relatively inexpensive, your potential customers will probably be better serviced by a salesperson than any kind of multimedia presentation. In this case, the Web site acts as the first step (or one of the first steps) in the selling process. What you are trying to

accomplish is to get someone on the phone, with the true interactivity only allowed by speaking with another human being. Therefore, you're not going to want to do more than pique your viewer's curiosity, or overcome what you anticipate might be their initial objections.

EFFECTIVE ORGANIZATION

We've probably spent enough time talking about organization, but that won't stop us from stressing the point yet again. Organization is perceived as being the fundamental aspect to good design—as many companies have found out. Great graphics, well-balanced pages, and even quality content don't impress people if they can't find what they're looking for.

WELL-PLANNED NAVIGATION

Your navigation doesn't need to be clearly defined text links, nor does it have to be a series of shadow buttons, but it does have to give the viewer the impression that they have a complete tool for getting around your site.

We've both made pages that have purposefully unmarked navigation tools—buttons that have only an icon, for example—and we've gotten some powerful responses, both pro and con. Surprisingly, many of the responses that were against our use of cryptic navigation were the most heartening. Here's a typical letter we might receive:

> **Webmaster:**
>
> I'm writing to tell you that I don't think your Web site is as effective as it could be.
>
> Your navigation buttons weren't clearly marked, and I had to go through each one of them before I saw all of the information. I also felt that I had to move my cursor over every graphic to see if it might be linked to something.
>
> I think that you should clearly label your navigation icons, so that people can jump on the site, find the information they need, and then leave.
>
> I really do think your site is good, I just think it could be better.
>
> Regards,

So, the viewer logged on to the system, went through every page meticulously, and then felt compelled to write a letter. Do you think this would have happened if the navigation buttons were clearly marked? It's more likely that the viewer would have logged on, looked at a page or two, and logged off.

When we design pages like this, we do so very carefully. We wouldn't design this way for a client who has a clear-cut, buy-something-now objective. The type of business that benefits from a system such as this is one who is hoping to achieve mindshare, not an immediate sale. The fact that viewers are willing to spend time going through each page, and even write us a letter, shows that we have achieved mindshare.

We're not saying that you should plan pages this way. In fact, we'll say that you probably shouldn't, at least not until you've had quite a bit of experience. There's a fine line between balancing enough mystery to compel people without going so far as to truly confuse them.

When we design a system like this, we always make sure it's clear that there is navigation (that the buttons are buttons, and not just graphics, and that they are the same size and in the same location), and we check the statistics regularly, to make sure that people are hitting the content pages, and not just leaving after the opening page. We never use cryptic ISMAPS (like a street scene where you click on different people, buildings, or objects) because we've found that ISMAPS are already confusing to some people, and they're useless if the areas aren't defined.

The reason we're bringing this up at all is that you should know there is more than one way to go about planning your navigation, and that completely "clear" navigation isn't always the best route to take.

ORIGINAL CONTENT

There are sites on the WWW with tons and tons of icons, horizontal rules (bars), background graphics, and banners. There are also backgrounds, clip art, and effects packaged with many software packages. These things can really speed up the process of getting a page published, and you're really going to hate that we're telling you not to use them, but we are…sorry.

In a case where you need to get a page up fast, you might want to use something as a temporary placeholder (like bullets you plan on replacing), but it's best to avoid this completely if at all possible. Graphics shape your system's look and feel, and using cookie-cutter graphics will give you a cookie-cutter effect. There's also the fact that you have no ownership over the graphics, and people might see them all over the Net—which will not help you set yourself apart.

Make sure that your graphics are designed for your page, and that all of the text content is original. You should also, where possible, identify your graphics. Design them so that they work within your page, but not elsewhere—you can do this by working in a logo or company name, or by balancing two or more graphics so that they work together, but not separately. This helps to keep snooping surfers from grabbing your graphics for their own use (which happens all the time).

EFFECTIVE GRAPHICS

Many sites overuse graphics. This is often caused by graphic artists who are used to print media (and don't understand the bandwidth issue), but is more often attributable to bad design. A few well-placed graphics will spice up a page, while too many (or too large) will bog it down.

We try to use JPEGs when possible (if we don't have to worry about transparent backgrounds), and we use graphics sparingly, employing some special tricks to add color and depth (see Chapter 12). JPEGs offer high (16 million) color, small size, and fast loading. On the other hand, some old browsers won't read them. These types of browsers are pretty much dinosaurs, and you can almost discount the people who would use them as being poor prospects anyway. (If they don't have the time to download an up-to-date browser, or the money to update their system or dial-up account, they're probably not great consumers.)

With GIFs, we try to stick to the rule of 51, which is a way of dither-proofing your art (more on this in Chapter 12). GIFs are always 256 or fewer colors.

Here's a rule we break all the time: State the size of your graphic within the image tag. We break this rule because we often want to be able to update graphics without updating the HTML of the page that contains them. But, don't do as we do, do as we say, and state the size:

```
<IMG SRC="graphic.jpg" HEIGHT=80
WIDTH=300>
```

This enables browsers to place the text on the page before adding the graphics, so that your viewers can start reading before the graphics are loaded. Otherwise, the browser won't show the text until it has begun to decode the graphic elements (so that it knows how and where to place the text).

INTERACTIVITY

A high degree of interactivity (extensive use of CGI, server push/client pull, and so on) engages the user and makes your site memorable. The WWW is an interactive, communications medium, and your site should reflect the potential of that medium. By allowing viewers to interact, you can also get valuable feedback on how to make your site more appealing.

There is, of course, a drawback to a highly interactive site, that being the issue of bandwidth. The Net can be like viewing the world through a drinking straw. A 14.4Kbps modem (which you will probably have to accept as the lowest common denominator for at least a while) will take a very long time to load even moderately graphical pages. Add to this the fact that there is often a taxed server on the other end, and gridlock within the Net itself, and the concept of high-interactivity, with its constant back and forth communications, loses much of its appeal.

So, as with all things, you want to find an acceptable compromise. Use interactivity sparingly, and rely on some other things for animation and the like (such as GIF animations). Every link is interactive—it's the viewer saying "I want this," and the system responding by providing whatever "this" is. Other interactivity, like Shockwave or Lingo applications, are rarely worth the download time and are usually pretty slipshod.

Java applets (little applications, like cigarettes are little cigars) are, in our opinion, rarely a good option. While we agree that they will someday increase the horsepower of the WWW, most current applications are pretty barbaric. "Oooh, look! There's a little message scrolling across the screen! Over and over and over again! And a little calculator! It works about as well as the one on my old Commodore 64!" Suffice it to say that Java should be used to accentuate your system, with searching capabilities and the like, and not for its limited abilities as a gee-whiz toy.

CUSTOM WEB SITES

Some large companies are providing viewers with custom Web sites. These sites are dynamically created to meet the needs of each individual viewer and to direct advertising to their personal demographic profile. There's no way that it's within the scope of this book to describe how this is done, as it requires some very heavy programming.

There are test sites on the WWW now using this system and good results are being reported (albeit with bugs galore, and slow downloads). Some people say that this is the future of the Web—but some people say that about everything.

AVOID SILLY FEATURES

We had to include this because of our feelings. We see many pages and sites that make poor use of CGI, HTML, Java and the like, for no apparent purpose except that it's possible. Good examples are the <BLINK> tag, overuse of headings (we're mentioning this again because it's very prevalent), and page counters.

We'll just come out and say it: Page counters are stupid. What could anyone possibly hope to accomplish by telling people they're the 27,343rd person to view a page? Who started this whole thing? You wouldn't tell everyone how many brochures you sent out last year, or how many phone calls you've had ("Hello, this is ACME Inc., you are our 132rd caller this week!"), so why would you want to publish it on the WWW?

We're mentioning features like this in the hopes that we will overcome any ideas you may have that such elements are part of a good Web site. Even though you may run into these things all the time (even on the pages of very large companies), don't think that they're in some way cool or expected.

SUMMARY

In this chapter, we've kept you from getting your hands dirty by dealing with the issues of making a site both effective and appealing, as well as issues of style and common sense. By now, you're probably champing at the bit to get into the actual HTML design of your page—it won't be long now.

The next chapter briefly beats the concepts of organization even deeper into your skull and will help to get you organized before you dive into HTML.

Keeping Organized

Organization is one of the (by now you've noticed many) keys to building an effective Web site. This organization takes place on several levels—page structure, site structure, directories, and even the way in which you organize your tools. We're not saying that you must be a completely detail-oriented person to build effective Web sites. In fact, it often seems that the goal-oriented person who can see the big picture has the type of personality best suited to developing commercial systems. Getting stuck in the details can be counterproductive, and often the result is Web sites that are never quite finished.

This chapter deals with two areas of organization. The first has to do with how you organize your tools, and the second confronts the issue of directory structure on WWW servers—you've already dealt with site and page organization. While it may seem that this chapter is out of order, and this topic should actually have been addressed earlier on, we assure you that there is a method to our madness. Up to this point, we hope that you have been thinking about what you want to create, and now we begin discussing how you're going to create it.

The next chapter, "Taking Advantage of HTML," is the first step in diving into the blood-and-guts of WWW design, in that you will be taking your ideas and applying them to a real, working system. Before you do this, we want you to get everything organized so that the immense and confusing job of organizing your entire system won't overwhelm you. HTML can be confusing at its best, and making some simple preparations now can save you headaches in the future.

HOW TO ORGANIZE YOUR TOOLS

You'll be using several tools to design your pages, many of which you can find on the CD-ROM. You really only need a few tools to design, test, and place HTML documents, and you may find that you prefer applications other than those we are supplying—which is fine. Four tools you will absolutely need are

1. **An ASCII text editor**. This can be any kind of text editor, including one that probably came with your computer. There are also editors such as HTML Notepad and WebMania (both included on the CD-ROM), which can help you by giving you buttons and hot keys that will place some of the tags for you, and thus release you from some of the mundane, repetitive typing required in HTML coding. Another option is to use a WYSIWYG (What You See Is What You Get) editor such as Netscape Navigator Gold,

which enables you to place your text and graphics as if you were using a printed page layout program.

> **Note:**
> If you decide to use a WYSIWYG editor, you will still need a text editor to check the code and a browser to test the pages. While WYSIWYG editors are becoming better and better, there's no substitute for crunching the code yourself. This gives you complete control over the content of your code and enables you to eliminate the odd formatting many WYSIWYG editors incorporate to make things easier for the author. To tell the truth, we never use this type of editor, and we advise against it.

2. **A bitmap graphics manipulation program**. Even if you are outsourcing your graphics work, you will almost definitely need to do some tweaking yourself. We've included Paint Shop Pro on the CD-ROM, as we consider it to be the best shareware program of its kind. If you choose to use a different application, make sure that it has the capability to read and convert JPEG and GIF 89a graphics, and that it enables you to resize high-color graphics with antialiasing, set a transparency value for GIF 89a graphics, and control both pixel resolution and JPEG quality.

3. **A collection of browsers for testing your pages.** You want to get your hands on as many browsers as possible—not just the one you intend to design your pages for.

These are available from Netscape, Microsoft, and others, and will make it possible for you to test your pages in a variety of ways so that you'll have control over how your pages will be viewed by the broadest audience. Of course, if you've been surfing the Web as we've suggested, you'll already have at least one browser.

4. **An FTP client.** Unless you are on a local network with your server, you will need an FTP client to post your pages to your host. We've included CuteFTP (and it *is* cute) on the CD-ROM because we've found it easy to use. If you choose another FTP client, try to find one that automatically switches between 7- and 8-bit transfer protocols, as your graphics are 8-bit (binary) and your HTML is 7-bit (ASCII). Manually switching back and forth is a pain.

Once you've decided on your tools, try to put them into a directory/ folder where you can quickly access them. If you are able to keep them on your desktop, do so. You'll be jumping back and forth between them constantly as you design your pages, and the less time it takes to do this, the less likely you are to lose your train of thought. The same thing applies to any reference files you may wish to use—keep them at hand so that you can remember what it was you were looking for.

If you are converting files from print editing applications (MS Word, Aldus PageMaker, for example), you may need to get that software, though with many "viewers" (applications that are generally available for free and enable you to read but not write the files) you can select text for cutting and pasting.

> **Note:**
> Most print editing applications use representative links (OLE, EPS, CGM, WMF headers, and so on) to signify graphic placement. The true graphic is only represented on the screen and isn't presented in full detail until the file goes to print. If you are using print layout files as your design basis, you will want to get and convert the original image files for use on your WWW pages. Cutting and pasting the graphic elements of a print layout document usually results in poor-quality graphics.

DIRECTORY STRUCTURE

If you're at all familiar with DOS, you'll have a good overall picture of UNIX directory structure. Like DOS, UNIX uses a hierarchical tree structure for organizing directories and files. Where DOS uses *drivename:\directory1\ directory2\directory3\file* (C:\programs\graphics\tools\psp.exe), the WWW and UNIX use *machine name/directory1/directory2/file* (www.domain.com/photos/animals/ hoppy.gif). As you can see, the most obvious difference is simply which way the slash goes—DOS uses a backslash (\), while UNIX uses a forward slash (/).

Whether you use a virtual host or have your own Web server, you will use a directory structure to organize your Web system. If you are using a virtual host, you may access your virtual server directories by many means. A common way this is done is that your files will be accessed via FTP as a substructure of your host's main system. This means that although your WWW system is accessed as www.yourname.com, you will actually be placing your files somewhere that looks like hostname.com/ users/you/WWW. Your host server is set up so that files placed within the WWW subdirectory of your FTP account are aliased to your domain name and virtual server. This can be set up in different ways and is something on which your provider will have to instruct you.

USING DIRECTORIES TO YOUR ADVANTAGE

Unless your WWW system is quite large, you will probably opt to place all of your files in one directory—at least initially. A good argument for doing this is that many FTP clients do not upload subdirectories; therefore, you must upload files one directory at a time. If your WWW system is in one directory, you can simply upload or download everything at once. This works well when you redesign your system because you can easily keep track of uploads by moving the entire directory at once, thus updating all of the files in one big chunk.

After your system becomes larger, as it inevitably will, you will want to start making use of directories to keep things organized. This way you won't have to search through dozens and dozens of files to find the one you'd like to replace, and you'll also have more control over different sections of the system when and if there comes a time that you will allow other authors to update the system.

For instance, say that you plan on allowing the sales force to upload an up-to-date chart graphic each month. You can allow them access to a single directory without giving them access to the core of the Web system. In a case like this, the page containing the graphic might reside in the main directory, while the graphic resides on a subdirectory—the one you have allowed the sales team to access. The image tag on the page may look like this: `<IMG SRC="sales/chart.jpg">`, which refers to a subdirectory called `sales`. If you've allowed the sales team access to only that directory, that's all that they can screw up.

Now, say that the sales team is responsible for several pages on the system and that you want them to have control over sections of the pages, but still want to keep continuity throughout the system. This will be like the reverse of the above example, in that the pages will reside on the sales directory and the graphic elements will reside in another, secure directory. So, the page address may look like this: `www.yourname.com/sales/page1.htm`, and the image tags might look something like this: `<IMG SRC="/graphics/header.gif">`.

> **Note:**
> If a directory name has a slash in front of it, as in `...SRC="/graphics...`, this means that the directory is a root—higher up the hierarchical structure than the page accessing it. If a directory has no slash in front, as in `...SRC="sales/...`, this means that the directory is a subdirectory of the one containing the page. This is very important in testing your pages on a local system because many browsers and operating systems will not discern between the two—`/graphics/` and `graphics/` will both be treated as subdirectories on a DOS PC, for example. Thus, things that run great on your PC may not work on a server if the directory structure isn't correctly assigned within the HTML code. For testing on a system such as this, you will need to make all directories subdirectories and sort them out when you upload.

If you're planning on having multiple authors updating the system (and this is also addressed in Chapter 25, "Maintaining Your System") and you want to have page continuity throughout the system (matching headers, footers, background, and so on), you should set up a root directory that contains the elements common to the entire system. For instance, as in the preceding examples, say you have a header that you want included in each page. To make things more confusing, say that the sales department wants to have a subdirectory for placing graphic images, so that they are not included within the same directory as their HTML files. Therefore, a section of one of their pages might look something like this:

```
<HTML>
<HEAD>
<TITLE>
```

```
Winning with Widget #1234
</TITLE>
</HEAD>

<!-- Begin corporate header -->
<BODY BACKGROUND="/graphics/bground.jpg">
<A HREF="/header.map">
<IMG SRC="/graphics/header.gif"
BORDER=0
ISMAP
ALT="[Navigation Header]">
</A>
<!-- end corporate header -->

<IMG SRC="graphics/1234.jpg" ALIGN=RIGHT>
<H1>
Winning with Widget #1234
</H1>
```

This page would load a navigation graphic (`ISMAP`) from a root directory called `graphics`, as well as a picture from a subdirectory also called `graphics` (see preceding Note). Obviously, it would be better to call the subdirectory by a different name to avoid confusion, but this illustrates that you don't have to.

Even if you will be the only author and don't have to worry about others accessing the system, you may still want to use a directory structure to keep things straight—this is a matter of choice. In either case, it's best to design a basic page that includes all of the common elements in the system and to use this page as the starting point for each subsequent page you or any other authors design. This is called a *template*.

QUICK & DIRTY GUIDE
Developing Your Own Templates

When you design a template, it's best that you keep the code in a line-by-line structure that's clear and concise, labeling exactly what must be changed on each page and clumping things together that will remain standard. Here is an example of a basic template, based on the previous example code:

```
<HTML>
<HEAD>
<TITLE>

PUT THE TITLE HERE

</TITLE>
<!-- Page design by webmaster -->
</HEAD>

<!-- Begin corporate header -->
<BODY BACKGROUND="/graphics/bground.jpg">
<A HREF="/header.map">
```

Q&D Developing Your Own Templates

```
<IMG SRC="/graphics/header.gif"
BORDER=0
ISMAP
ALT="[Navigation Header]">
</A>
<!-- end corporate header -->
<IMG SRC="

PLACE MAIN PAGE GRAPHIC HERE

" ALIGN=RIGHT>
<H1>

REPEAT PAGE TITLE HERE

</H1>
<HR>

BEGIN TEXT HERE

<!-- Begin corporate footer -->
<A HREF="/footer.map">
<IMG SRC="/graphics/footer.gif"
BORDER=0
ISMAP
ALT="[Navigation footer]">
</A>
<HR>
&copy; Copyright 1996, My Company, All Rights Reserved<P>
Problems viewing this page? Contact the
<A HREF="mailto:webmaster@yourdomain.com">
Webmaster
</A>.
</BODY>
</HTML>
```

In the interest of time, you may wish to make more specific templates based on your main template. For instance, you may want to make product page templates, business information templates, forms templates, and so on. Templates can be as specific as you'd like and can be laid out in any way that makes you (and your other authors, if any) comfortable and efficient.

To get you up and running, we've included some basic templates on the CD-ROM, which you can use to develop your own system. (See Chapter 10, "Taking Advantage of HTML.")

SUMMARY

By now, you should have some idea of what you want to say and how you'll go about preparing yourself to leap into page design. Roll up your sleeves, clear your desk, and get ready. The next chapter is about raw HTML code.

Taking Advantage of HTML

All right, now that you've designed the Mona Lisa, you get to paint her—with both hands tied behind your back. HTML is a horribly limiting media, and full of bugs. However, those bugs can usually be avoided through the use of clear HTML programming, which is what this chapter discusses.

Note:

A comparative list of HTML tags is
included in Appendix H, "Comparative HTML Reference Guide."

The first thing you should take into
consideration when designing HTML
documents is that HTML describes the
content and structure of the page, and
not the appearance. If you are used to
working with WYSIWYG (What You
See Is What You Get) text editors like
PageMaker or even Microsoft Word,
you may be sadly disappointed with the
lack of control over the final output
that HTML provides.

Rather than describing exact page
placement (as in exact x,y coordinates),
HTML describes the structure of the
page by using HTML tags—it's almost
as if it's giving the browser hints instead of solid commands. For instance,
instead of enlarging the title text, you
enter the text with the tag <H1> before
the text, and </H1> after the text. This
tells the browser to display this text as
a large heading (which may look different on different browsers, but will always be larger and bolder than text
without these tags). This is one of the
main reasons it is so important to test
your pages on different browsers and
make sure they look good on all platforms (more on this in Chapter 19,
"Getting It Up and Running").

Many programmers see this lack of
control as a major hurdle when designing the layout of their pages; we have
found that there are ways around most of these layout limitations,
which we will describe to you as this book progresses.

Note:

It is one of your jobs to use as little HTML code as possible. This is
not to say that you should be creating simple, sparse pages and
sites, but that you should try to remove all unnecessary tags—they
are a constant problem with many "simple to use" Web page
creation software applications. The only way you'll be able to do
this is if you understand what each tag means.

A REFRESHER ON THE BASICS

HTML files are just ASCII text files with special commands (tags);
they look like this:

```
<!DOCTYPE HTML PUBLIC "-//IETF//DTD HTML 2.0//EN">
<HTML>
<HEAD>
<TITLE>Your title here</TITLE>
</HEAD>

<BODY>

<H1>Welcome to a basic HTML document</H1>

This is a basic HTML document.

</BODY>
</HTML>
```

The text within the brackets describes the structure of the regular
text (as in Figure 10.1).

For example, if the title of your page is My Home Page, and you want
that displayed as large, italicized text, your code for that would be
<H1><I>My Home Page</I></H1>. You'll notice that you not only must
define the text at the beginning, but in many cases you must also turn
that definition off with an ending tag. Ending tags are defined with
a slash (/) before the description; this tells the browser to discontinue
that format; otherwise, the rest of your entire page will be in that
style. An HTML element will include a tag name, may include some
attributes and some text or hypertext, and will appear in an HTML
document in one of three ways:

```
<tag_name> your text </tag_name>
<tag_name>
<tag_name attribute_name=argument> your text </tag_name>
```

So, the best way to start an HTML file is to write out all of your content in a text editor and then go back adding HTML tags.

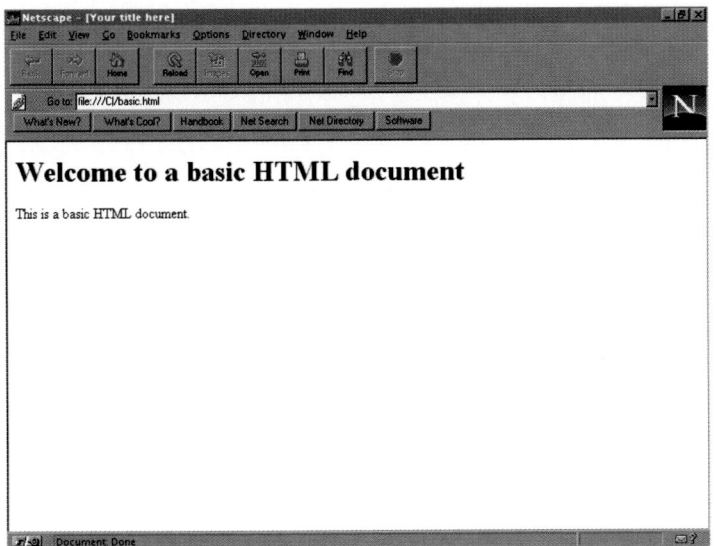

Figure 10.1.
A basic HTML document.

THE HTML VERSION DECLARATION TAG <!DOCTYPE>

This tag is the first to appear and is used to declare which HTML version your page is using:

◆ For HTML 2.0, use

```
<!DOCTYPE HTML PUBLIC "-//IETF//DTD HTML 2.0//EN">
```

◆ For HTML 3.0, use

```
<!DOCTYPE HTML PUBLIC "-//W3O//DTD W3 HTML 3.0//EN">
```

◆ For HTML 3.2, use

```
<!DOCTYPE HTML PUBLIC "-//W3C//DTD HTML 3.2//EN>
```

THE HTML ELEMENT <HTML> AND </HTML>

All of your text and HTML tags go within the <HTML> tags. This tag indicates that the file is an HTML document—it's telling your browser what to expect.

THE HEAD ELEMENT <HEAD> AND </HEAD>

These tags contain within them your document head elements, such as the following:

◆ <TITLE> and </TITLE> contain the document title. (Note: This is the title of your HTML page and appears within the browser, but not as text on your page.)

◆ <ISINDEX> (optional) is used for simple keyword searches. It specifies that the current document describes a database that can be searched using the index search method appropriate for whatever browser is being used to read the document.

◆ <BASE> (optional) specifies the name of the file in which the current document is stored. It is useful when link references within the document do not include full pathnames (that is, are only partially qualified).

◆ <LINK> (optional) is used to define the document's relationship with other documents.

◆ <META> (optional) is used to supply meta-information and is often used to associate keywords to your documents (readable by search engines). Meta-information is generally in name/value pair form.

◆ <!-- --> (optional) can be used anywhere in your document to place a comment within the HTML code. A comment affects the document in no way other than enabling you to place a comment within it. The most common use for this is within the <HEAD> tag for providing information about the document, such as

```
<!--Author: you -->
```

A common head element looks something like this:

```
<HEAD>
<TITLE>A common head element</TITLE>
<!-- Author: Kim and Brad Hampton -->
<!-- Revision: 2.0 08/08/96 -->
<META Name="description" Content="A common head element,
including the META tag!  Associate keywords to your Web documents!">

<META Name="keywords" Content="A common head element, HTML, HEAD, META,
TITLE, keywords, taking advantage of HTML, Website, Kim Hampton, Brad Hampton,
commercial web sites">
</HEAD>
```

THE BODY ELEMENT <BODY> AND </BODY>

These tags contain within them the contents of the document (tags and the text) and can be used to describe optional attributes of the document, such as the following:

◆ BACKGROUND="?"

(HTML 3) This attribute describes the name (if within the same directory) or URL of the graphic that will be tiled to create a background for the page. The viewer will not see this image if they are using a noncompliant browser, if they have chosen the option of overriding background images, or if their image loading is turned off. Never use in conjunction with the BGCOLOR attribute.

◆ BGCOLOR="?"

(HTML 3) This attribute defines the background color of the page, which is specified using a hexadecimal color code (for example, white = "#FFFFFF"). The color wizard included in the HTML library on the CD-ROM is a very useful tool for determining these codes. You can also use a few select color names for this attribute: blue, fuchsia, gray, green, lime, maroon, navy, purple, olive, aqua, black, silver, red, teal, white, and so on. Never use in conjunction with the BACKGROUND attribute.

◆ TEXT="?"

(HTML 3) This attribute describes the document's text color (in hexadecimal code or by name).

- `LINK="?"`

  (HTML 3) This attribute describes the color of textual links in hexadecimal code or by name.

- `VLINK="?"`

  (HTML 3) This attribute describes the color of previously visited textual links (in hexadecimal code or by name).

- `ALINK="?"`

  (HTML 3) This attribute describes the color of an active textual link (in hexadecimal code or by name). This is the color that appears while the user is selecting the link (for a split second).

A common `<BODY>` tag looks like this:

```
<BODY BACKGROUND="backrd.gif" LINK="#0000FF" VLINK="#0000A0" ALINK="#FF00FF">
```

BLOCK ELEMENTS

Block elements define the placement and treatment of text blocks. These can include paragraph structure, list structure, and other text formatting.

Note:
All of these elements cause paragraph breaks.

HEADINGS `<H1>` THROUGH `<H6>`

Headings are always closed with a closing tag (for example, `</H1>`). `H1` stands out the most (is the largest heading in most browsers), and `H6` stands out the least (the smallest heading). In HTML 3, you can set an alignment for your heading like this:

```
<H1 ALIGN=CENTER>This heading is centered</H1>
```

PARAGRAPHS `<P>`

This one is tricky. Different versions of HTML use paragraph tags differently. Originally, this tag was used as a one-sided tag and was placed at the end of a paragraph as a paragraph break (a double-return). HTML 2 and 3 indicate its use as a two-sided tag, with the `<P>` tag going at the beginning of the paragraph and the `</P>` tag being optional at the end. We never use this `</P>` tag; it doesn't seem to make a difference in how the paragraph is displayed and seems unnecessary work to us. We therefore use the `<P>` tag as a paragraph break at the end of a paragraph (as we always have) and leave it at that. Some people recommend getting into the habit of placing your `<P>` tags at the beginning of the paragraph because it may become a standard; we have just gotten used to using the tag at the end, and we have seen no reason (yet) to change. With this information in mind, use your own judgment regarding where to place your `<P>` tag.

LIST OPTIONS

List options create the automatic numbering, bulleting, and/or indentation of list items. Different list options treat the enclosed text differently and can be useful when presenting long lists or important items.

Unordered Lists <UL> and </UL>

An unordered bulleted list contains one or more <LI> elements, which represent individual list items. Netscape adds a type attribute to this, which can describe whether the bullet used is a circle, disk, or square, and is used like this: <UL TYPE=circle>. Here's an example:

```
<UL>
<LI> First item in the list
<LI> Last item in the list
</UL>
```

Ordered Lists <OL> and </OL>

An ordered list (1,2,3,…) contains one or more <LI> elements, which represent individual list items. Netscape adds a type attribute to this to specify whether the list items are marked with capital letters (TYPE=A), small letters (TYPE=a), large Roman numerals (TYPE=I), small Roman numerals (TYPE=i), or numbers (TYPE=1)—usually the default. Here's an example of code that will make a lettered list:

```
<OL  TYPE=A>
<LI> First item in the list
<LI> Last item in the list
</OL>
```

Definition Lists <DL> and </DL>

A definition or glossary list contains <DT> elements that give terms and <DD> elements that give the corresponding definitions. It is commonly used like this:

```
<DL>
<DT> Term to be defined #1
<DD> Definition of term #1
<DT> Term to be defined #2
<DD> Definition of term #2
</DL>
```

Menu Lists <MENU> and </MENU>

These tags define a menu list. A menu list contains one or more <LI> elements, which represent individual menu items. It is used just like <OL> and <UL>, and can also be used without <LI> to indent text.

PREFORMATTED TEXT <PRE> AND </PRE>

These elements are rendered with a monospace font and preserve the layout defined by spaces (like   this) and line break characters.

DOCUMENT DIVISIONS <DIV> AND </DIV>

These are used in HTML 3 to group related items together and can be used with the ALIGN attribute, as in <DIV ALIGN=LEFT>.

TEXT ALIGNMENT <CENTER> AND </CENTER>

This is used in HTML 3 to center text contained within the tags.

QUOTED PASSAGE <BLOCKQUOTE> AND </BLOCKQUOTE>

This is used for long quotes or citations and is usually rendered with indented margins.

FILL-OUT FORMS <FORM> AND </FORM>

This is used to define a fill-out form for processing by the HTTP server. Attributes include ACTION, METHOD, and ENCTYPE. More on forms is presented in Chapter 11, "Integrating HTML with CGI."

HORIZONTAL RULES <HR>

These place a line across your page and do not have an end tag. Attributes include ALIGN (HTML 3), NOSHADE (HTML 3), SIZE (HTML 3), and WIDTH (HTML 3).

TABLES <TABLE> AND </TABLE>

This is an HTML 3 tag. Every table can begin with an optional CAPTION followed by one or more <TR> elements, which define the table's rows. Every row has one or more cells that are defined by <TH> or <TD> elements. Common attributes include WIDTH, ALIGN, BORDER, CELLPADDING, and CELLSPACING. (More on tables later in this chapter.)

TEXT-LEVEL ELEMENTS

Text-level elements enable you to change the characteristics of the text contained within them. These can be very useful for distinguishing blocks of text or for emphasis.

Note:
These elements do not cause paragraph breaks.

FONT STYLE ELEMENTS

These elements all require starting and ending tags and include

<B>	Bold
<U>	(HTML 3) Underlined
<TT>	Monospaced text or teletype
<I>	Italics
<BIG>	(HTML 3) Large font
<SMALL>	(HTML 3) Small font
<SUB>	(HTML 3) Subscript
<SUP>	(HTML 3) Superscript
<S>	(HTML 3) Strike-through text
<BLINK>	(Netscape 1.0) Blinking text

THE FONT ELEMENT <FONT> AND </FONT>

This HTML 3 element enables you to change the font color, size, and face of the enclosed text. Colors are defined in hexadecimals or one of the understood color names. Attributes are COLOR (Netscape 2.0), SIZE, and FACE (MS IExplorer). Some examples of this tag's uses are

```
<FONT SIZE=+1>This font is bigger than the previous</FONT>
<FONT COLOR="#FF0000">This text is red</FONT>
<FONT FACE="Lucida Sans,Arial,Times Roman"> This text will be in either Lucida
Sans, Arial, or Times Roman, depending on which fonts are installed on the
viewers system, trying each in order.</FONT>
```

Phrase Elements

These all require starting and ending tags and include

`<STRONG>`	Strong emphasis, generally rendered in a bold font
`<DFN>`	Defining instance of the enclosed term
`<EM>`	The basic emphasis, normally rendered in an italic font
`<CODE>`	Used for extracts from program code
`<KBD>`	Keyboard, used for text to be typed by the viewer
`<SAMP>`	Used for sample output from scripts, programs, and so on
`<VAR>`	Used for variables or arguments to commands
`<CITE>`	Normally used for citations or references to other sources

Special Elements

Last, but not least, these special elements can also be included in an HTML document.

The Anchor Element <A> and </A>

This element defines hypertext links. Attributes include NAME, HREF, REL, REV, METHODS, URN, and TITLE.

NAME is used to associate a name with a part of a document that can be linked to, like this:

```
<A NAME="chapter1">Chapter 1</A>
```

You can create a link from within the page to this part of the document by using this code:

```
<A HREF="#chapter1">Jump to Chapter 1</A>
```

HREF is also used to define the URL of your linked image or document. A common usage looks like this:

```
<A HREF="http://www.hampton.org/index.html">Jump to hampton.org</A>
```

> **Note:**
> If you are linking to documents stored on the same machine, you can simply link to the directory rather than naming the entire URL:
> ```
> <A HREF="/products/widget.htm">This links to a page named widgets, which exists
> in the products directory</A>.
> ```

An anchor must include a NAME or HREF attribute, and may include both. REL, REV, TITLE, METHODS, and URN are attributes that are not commonly used.

THE LINE BREAK TAG

This tag is one-sided and is used to force a line break. Unlike the <P> tag, the <BR> tag can be used over and over, resulting in a carriage return with each use. (The <P> tag is usually ignored if there is no code between successive uses.)

THE IMAGE TAG <IMG>

This tag inserts images into the document and requires no ending tag. Common attributes include SRC, ALT, ALIGN (HTML 3), HEIGHT (HTML 3), WIDTH (HTML 3), BORDER (Netscape 1.0), VSPACE (HTML 3), HSPACE (HTML 3), USEMAP (HTML 3), ISMAP (HTML 3), and LOWSRC (Netscape 1.0). A common usage looks like this:

```
<IMG SRC="flower.gif" ALT="[A Flower]">.
```

More on the image tag in Chapter 12, "Working with Graphics."

THE APPLET TAG <APPLET>
AND </APPLET>

This tag is an HTML 3 specification and is supported by all Java-enabled browsers. It enables you to embed a Java applet into an HTML document. The contents of the element are used as a backup if the applet can't be loaded; it also uses associated PARAM elements to pass parameters to the applet. Attributes include CODE, CODEBASE, NAME, ALT, ALIGN, WIDTH, HEIGHT, VSPACE, and HSPACE. We discuss the applet tag more in Chapter 18, "Bells and Whistles."

THE IMAGE MAP TAG <MAP>
AND </MAP>

This HTML 3 tag enables the definition of client-side image maps and contains one or more AREA elements used to define the hot zones (linked areas) on the associated image and to bind the hot zones to specified URLs. We discuss image mapping much more in Chapter 12.

The best way we have found to learn and absorb how HTML works is to study others' code. Get on the Web, find cool pages, look at their source code (view source in Netscape), and see how it works. Compare the page on your browser to the source code. See how each tag affects the page.

Appendix H, "Comparative HTML Reference Guide," will be useful when you are designing your page from scratch or finding out what a particular tag does when investigating others' code. Another great tool for learning HTML is the shareware HTML Library included on your CD-ROM. It enables you to look up code in many different ways and can be invaluable to the beginner.

If you need more help with basic HTML coding, there are several good books on the market (our favorite being by fellow Sams.net author Laura Lemay, *Teach Yourself HTML in 14 Days, Premier Edition*).

GUIDE TO USING THE TEMPLATES ON THE CD-ROM

If you are trying to avoid a lot of HTML coding, you have a couple of options. The first is to use an HTML editor (such as HTML Notepad or WebMania, included on your CD-ROM); these are described in more detail in the preceding chapter, "Keeping Organized."

Another option is to begin with the templates included on your CD-ROM. There are three separate templates provided. The first is the home page template—a very simple page designed with the bare minimum of tags, just to get you started (D:\templat\home1.html).

The second is a tables template (D:\templat\tables.html). This template (see Figure 10.2) is designed for you to choose the table you need and then cut and paste it into your HTML document. (We have included this because many novice programmers have the hardest time with HTML tables.)

The last template is a frames/noframes template (as described in Chapter 7, "Laying the Foundation"). If you are interested in designing a frames Web site, you will find this template particularly useful. This template is actually a collection of several HTML files. The easiest way to work with it will be to copy the entire directory (D:\templat\frames) into a directory on your hard drive and alter each page individually. To make it easier on yourself, keep all the filenames intact (we have already linked the pages). We have put graphics on the pages to help explain what should be replaced and what to name the files.

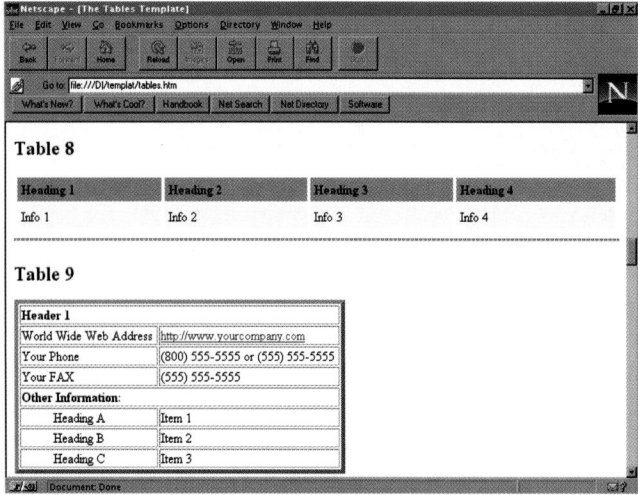

Figure 10.2.
The tables template.

When working with any of the frames layout templates, go over all the code in a text editor, changing all of the content text and appropriate links (and don't forget the mailto: links). These templates are designed not only to get you started, but as a learning aid, so don't just replace the tags. Investigate the HTML code, play with it, and see how small changes in the code can dramatically change the document.

USING FRAMES TO YOUR ADVANTAGE

You can use frames to show text and graphics in separate, partitioned, and scrollable regions simultaneously (see Figure 10.3). There is a lot of controversy over the use of the <FRAMES> tag, namely only Netscape and the newest Microsoft browsers can view frames properly (though this will change in the near future). The advantages of using frames are

- ◆ The ability to keep your company logo, name, and navigational aids visible the entire time someone views your site

- ◆ The <NOFRAME> option that enables you to use HTML 2.0 and newer HTML tags within the same screen, so you can make the document cool looking for viewers capable of reading frames and viewable by all others at the same time

- ◆ The ability to keep your design intact even when the viewer scrolls down your page

- ◆ The fact that hyperlinks in framed documents can update and control not just the contents of their own frames, but the contents of other frames as well, making it possible to build very sophisticated Web pages while maintaining an easy-to-navigate user interface

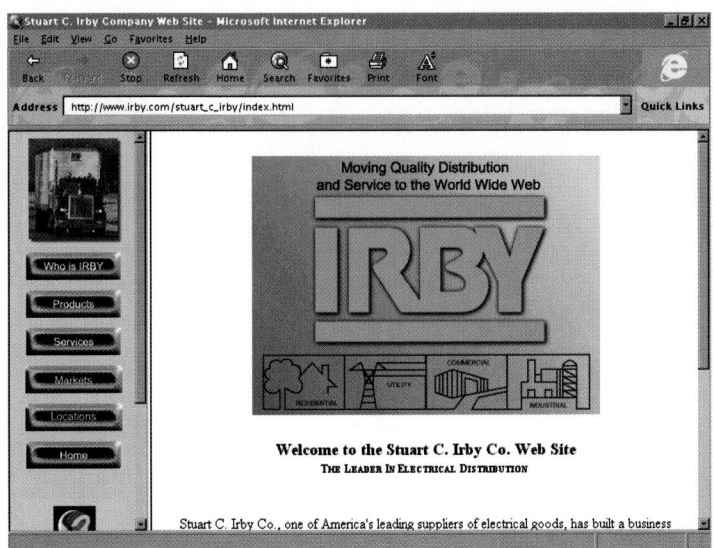

Figure 10.3.
A frames site.

FRAMES BASICS

The first thing you should understand when designing a frames site is that the home page of your site (usually `index.html`) does not actually contain your text (besides that which is within the `<NOFRAME>` tag). All the frames page does is tell the browser how to lay out your frames and which HTML files to place within each. Think of the frames HTML file as your layout file, and your HTML files contained within your frames as your content files.

The best way to learn how to use the `<FRAME>` tag is, of course, by example. For this example we are trying to create a frames site with layout, as shown in Figure 10.4.

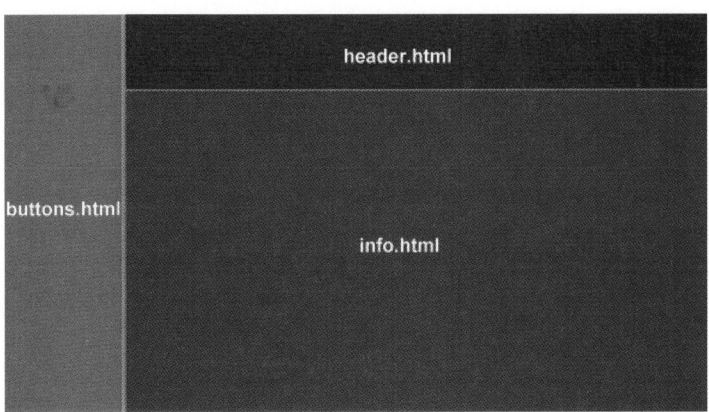

Figure 10.4.
The layout goal of our example frames site.

To accomplish this layout, we must first divide the browser window into left and right frames, and then further divide the right frame into upper and lower frames.

Listing 10.1 shows how this can be done.

Listing 10.1. An HTML frames example.

```
<!DOCTYPE HTML PUBLIC "-//IETF//DTD HTML 3.0//EN" "html.dtd">
<HTML>
<HEAD>
<TITLE>A Frames Web Site</TITLE>
<!-- Author: Kim and Brad Hampton -->
<!-- Revision: 3.0 8/08/96 -->
</HEAD>

<FRAMESET COLS="140,*">

<FRAME SRC="buttons.htm"
       NAME="1buttons"
       MARGINHEIGHT=0
       MARGINWIDTH=0
       SCROLLING="AUTO"
      FRAMEBORDER="YES"
       FRAMESPACING="1"
       NORESIZE>

<FRAMESET ROWS="65,*">

<FRAME SRC="header.htm"
       NAME="2header"
       SCROLLING = "no"
       MARGINHEIGHT=0
       MARGINWIDTH=0
       NORESIZE>

<FRAME SRC="info.htm"
       NAME="3info"
       NORESIZE>

</FRAMESET>
</FRAMESET>

<NOFRAME>
<H2>Welcome to our Home Page.</H2>
This is the NOFRAMES page, which is viewed by non-frames compatible browsers.
</NOFRAME>
</HTML>
```

Now we will explain what each of these tags and associated attributes does, and how it all comes together.

The first thing to notice is that the opening and closing <BODY> tags, which normally appear in HTML documents, have been replaced by <FRAMESET> tags. This is the tag that sets the layout for your frames page. This is also the container that hosts the FRAME, FRAMESET, and

NOFRAMES tags. The opening <FRAMESET> tag must include either a column list or a row list, taking the form "COLS=column_list" or "ROWS=row_list". Row or column lists are always separated by commas.

COLS= is the attribute of our first FRAMESET tag and is used to separate the frame document into two vertical columns. You can specify the column dimensions by pixels, percentage (%), or a relative size (*). In our example we used this description:

```
<FRAMESET COLS="140,*">
```

This means make the first column 140 pixels wide, and the other column as wide as the remainder of the browser screen.

The next section of code in our example is the <FRAME> tag. This tag is used to describe the individual frame, which in this case is the frame on the left. Unlike many tags, the <FRAME> tag does *not* occur with a closing </FRAME> counterpart:

```
<FRAME SRC="buttons.htm"
       NAME="1buttons"
       MARGINHEIGHT=0
       MARGINWIDTH=0
       SCROLLING="AUTO"
       FRAMEBORDER="YES"
       FRAMESPACING="1"
       BORDERCOLOR="0000FF"
       NORESIZE>
```

The attributes we used for the <FRAME> tag are

◆ SRC=

Describes the source file of the document contained within that frame (in this case buttons.htm). It is advisable to make your source files containing information (in our example, 3info.htm) HTML 2-compliant (containing no HTML 3,

Netscape, or Microsoft extensions). This will enable you to make your frames site compatible with non-frames-capable browsers.

◆ NAME=

Provides a target name for the frame (in this case 1buttons). Your name should always start with an alphanumeric character.

◆ MARGINHEIGHT=

Controls the margin height (in this case 0) of the frame in pixels.

◆ MARGINWIDTH=

Controls the margin width (in this case 0) of the frame in pixels.

◆ SCROLLING=

Enables you to choose the scrolling option for the frame (in this case AUTO). Choices are YES, NO, or AUTO (which automatically allows scrolling only if necessary).

◆ FRAMEBORDER=

Gives you the option to display or not display a border for a frame. This tag would create a frame with borders (which is the default). For now, this tag is only recognized by Microsoft Internet Explorer 3.

◆ FRAMESPACING=

Used to create additional space between frames (specified in pixels). For now, it is only recognized by Microsoft Internet Explorer 3.

◆ NORESIZE

Used to prevent the user from resizing the frame (as is usually allowable).

◆ `BORDERCOLOR=`

This is not used in this example, but when used, it defines the color of the frames border in hexadecimal or by name. It is only recognized by Netscape Navigator 3 (for now).

The next tag in our example is yet another `<FRAMESET>` tag, using a different attribute, `ROWS`. This creates a frame document with horizontal rows. You can specify the row dimensions by pixels, percentage (`%`), or a relative size (`*`).

In our example we use this code:

```
<FRAMESET ROWS="65,*">
```

which separates the remaining frames column into two different, horizontal frames.

This is followed by two `<FRAME>` tags describing those horizontal frames:

◆ `</FRAMESET>` is the ending tag for the `<FRAMESET>` tag and is simply turning off the frames formatting.

◆ `<NOFRAME>` and `</NOFRAME>` contain the page that viewers with non-frames-capable browsers will see. For best results, use only HTML 2 tags (for the widest audience) and have textual links to your contents pages.

Now that we have the frames HTML file set up, we add the three separate HTML content files to the same directory and end up with a page that looks like Figure 10.5.

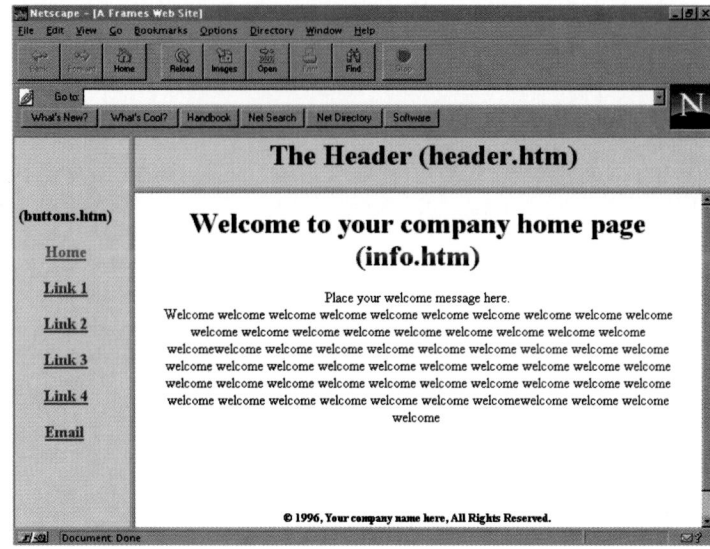

Figure 10.5.
Our example frames site.

Now that you know the basics of setting up a frames page, you are ready to get down to the task of linking within your frames.

FRAMES LINKS

When a viewer browsing a nonframes document selects a hyperlink to another document, the current page disappears from the browser window and is replaced by the requested page. When selected, each link instructs the browser to update the entire window with a new document. In frames, however, when hyperlinks are selected, the browser can update either the frame containing the hyperlink only, a separate frame, multiple frames, or even the entire screen. Which occurs all depends on the parameters specified in the hyperlink, specifically by using the `TARGET` attribute.

In frames, every hyperlink should specify where the new document should be displayed, using the TARGET attribute. The format used for specifying a target is

```
<A HREF="the_url" TARGET="target_name">The Hyperlinked Text</A>
```

The target name can be either the name assigned to frames in your frames HTML file (that is, NAME="*frame_name*"), such as 3info, 2header, or 1buttons in our example, or it can be an implicit name. The implicit name is determined by the frame's relationship to other frames. Implicit names are reserved words that all begin with an underscore (_). They are

◆ "_blank"

This specifies to load the link into a new browser window (your frames site will remain open as well). Example:

```
<A HREF="document.htm" TARGET="_blank">Clicking here will load this link
into a new blank browser window.</A>
```

◆ "_top"

Specifies to load the link into the full body of the window. Example:

```
<A HREF="document.htm" TARGET="_top">Clicking here will load the link into
the whole body of the window.</A>
```

Use "_top" for links outside your frames system.

◆ "_parent"

This specifies to load the link into the immediate parent of the document the link is in. Example:

```
<A HREF="document.htm" TARGET="_parent">Clicking here will load this link
into this page's parent window.</A>
```

◆ "_self"

Use this to load the link into the same window the link was clicked in. Example:

```
<A HREF="document.htm" TARGET="_self">Clicking here will load the link into
this same window.</A>
```

In our frames example, buttons.htm contains links to documents that we want to be placed within the right bottom window (3info). One of these links is to the welcome (home) page (info.htm). Therefore, our code (in buttons.htm) for this link looks like this:

```
<A HREF="info.htm" TARGET="3info">Home</A>
```

And that's it! We've just created a multiframe Web document, which updates selected frames on demand. Now that wasn't too hard, was it?

WHY USE TABLES?

Tables are very useful to organize information, condense text, or to lay out a complex page. They are an HTML 3 tag and are supported by most of the more popular browsers (Netscape Navigator, Microsoft IExplorer, Mosaic).

> **Note:**
> As with all newer HTML tags, it is very important to test your tables in different browsers before posting them on your site. Remember: All your table formatting will be lost in a non-tables-compatible browser.

As with any complex problem, the best way to learn tables is by example, and what do you know, we just happen to have one right here. First off, we should decide the goal (format) for our tables. In this case, we want our tables to look like the ones in Figure 10.6.

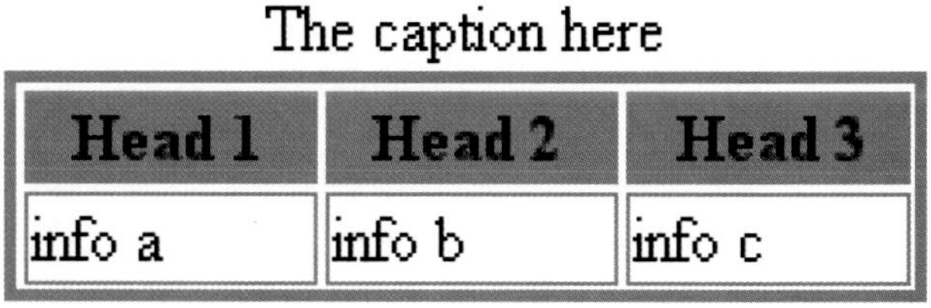

Figure 10.6.
The goal of our table example.

The caption here

Head 1	Head 2	Head 3
info a	info b	info c

To achieve this goal, we will use the code in Listing 10.2.

Listing 10.2. A simple table.

```
<TABLE ALIGN=RIGHT BORDER=3 BORDERCOLOR=#4682B4 WIDTH=30%>
<CAPTION ALIGN=TOP VALIGN=TOP>The caption here</CAPTION>
<TR>
<TH BGCOLOR=#4682B4>Head 1</TH>
<TH BGCOLOR=#4682B4>Head 2</TH>
<TH BGCOLOR=#4682B4>Head 3</TH>
</TR>
<TR>
<TD>info a</TD>
<TD>info b</TD>
<TD>info c</TD>
</TR>
</TABLE>
```

Now let's make sure you understand what this code means.

The first element in the table is the `<TABLE>` tag itself . This tag is just telling the Web browser that what follows is to be laid out as a table.

In our example we use the following attributes for our `<TABLE>` tag:

◆ `ALIGN=`

This specifies the alignment of the table, as in

`ALIGN=RIGHT`

Other possibilities for this attribute include `ALIGN=LEFT` and `ALIGN=CENTER`.

◆ `BORDER=`

This causes a border to be placed around the table, specified by a numerical value. In this case,

`BORDER=3`

causes a border to be placed around the table, 3 pixels wide.

◆ `BORDERCOLOR=`

This defines the color of the border (a Microsoft Internet Explorer 3.0 attribute), as in

`BORDERCOLOR=#4682B4`

You can either use a hexadecimal color (as in our example) or use one of Microsoft's specified color names (for example, `BORDERCOLOR=RED`). This attribute must be used in conjunction with `BORDER=`; otherwise, there is no border to color.

◆ `WIDTH=`

This specifies how wide the table will be, either in pixels or as a percentage, as in

`WIDTH=30%`

Other attributes you could use for the `<TABLE>` tag include `BACKGROUND`, `BGCOLOR`, `BORDERCOLORDARK`, `BORDERCOLORLIGHT`, `CELLSPACING`, `CELLPADDING`, `FRAME`, `HEIGHT`, `RULES`, and `VALIGN`.

See the HTML reference, Appendix H of this book, for a full explanation of these tags.

The next tag in our example table is the `<CAPTION>` tag, which can be used to put a label on your table.

In our example we use the following attributes for our `<CAPTION>` tag:

◆ `ALIGN=`

Used to align the caption, as in

`ALIGN=TOP`

Other possibilities for this attribute include `BOTTOM`, `LEFT`, `RIGHT`, or `CENTER`.

◆ `VALIGN=`

Instructs whether to place the caption on top or below the table, as in `VALIGN=TOP` or `VALIGN=BOTTOM`.

◆ `<TR>`

Stands for Table Row and contains a row of table cells. All tables must include at least one `<TR>` element. Attributes for `<TR>` can include `ALIGN`, `BACKGROUND`, `BGCOLOR`, `BORDERCOLOR`, `BORDERCOLORLIGHT`, `BORDERCOLORDARK`, `COLSPAN`, `NOWRAP`, `ROWSPAN`, and `VALIGN`.

◆ `<TH>`

Identifies a table heading cell. We used the `BGCOLOR` attribute, which can be defined as a hexadecimal value or by name as it appears in our example:

`<TH BGCOLOR=#4682B4>Head 1</TH>`

Other attributes for this tag include `ALIGN`, `BACKGROUND`, `BORDERCOLOR`, `BORDERCOLORLIGHT`, `BORDERCOLORDARK`, `COLSPAN`, `NOWRAP`, `ROWSPAN`, and `VALIGN`.

◆ `<TD>`

Used to define a table data cell, as in

`<TD>info a</TD>`

Attributes for this tag are the same as for the `<TH>` tag.

And that's about it for our tables code example! Figure 10.7 shows how it turned out. (Remember, testing is critically important, especially when using rare or new HTML tags and attributes.)

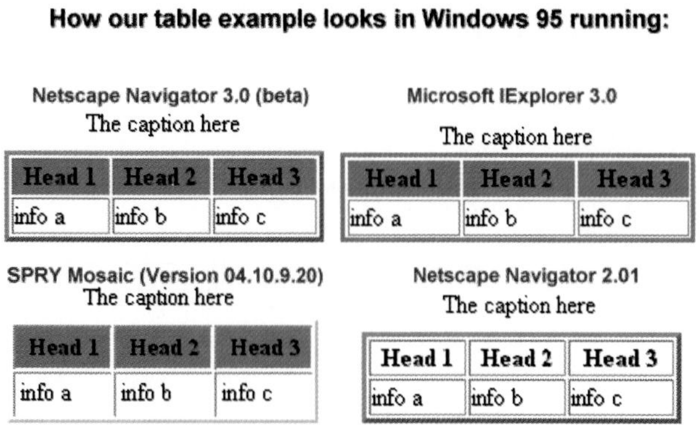

How our table example looks in Windows 95 running:

Figure 10.7.
How our table turned out.

The tables template on your CD-ROM will be your best tool in designing tables of your own. Find one which is close to your goal, and simply adapt it for your use. Appendix H lists additional tags that can be used for tables.

COOL TRICKS

We've mentioned some tricks throughout the book, and the point in discussing the attributes of HTML is so that you can figure out your own cool tricks, but there are a few techniques we want to mention that will help give your pages a polished look if you are in a rush.

USING BACKGROUND TILES

The `BACKGROUND ="filename.???"` attribute in a body tag enables you to place an image behind the page contents (which is why it's called a background). This can be a great tool if used wisely, and the downfall of a page if used poorly.

The browser will take your image and tile it—which means it will place it over and over again to fill the page. Obviously, you'll want to use a graphic that can be tiled so as to look like a complete image, as opposed to one that is obviously bordered. Here are some other tips:

◆ Don't use complex patterns—they will make the text of your page difficult to read.

◆ Don't use wild colors if you plan on placing text—again, it's difficult to read.

◆ If you are using a gradation or color change, make sure that your text will contrast with the area over which it will be placed.

◆ Make the tiles as small as possible—this will save bandwidth.

◆ Make any horizontal tiles at least 1,024 pixels wide to accommodate monitors set for this resolution.

◆ Don't use long vertical tiles unless you're absolutely positive that the page content won't reach the bottom of the tile on any window size.

USING TABLES TO LAY OUT A PAGE

You can use tables (usually with the border set to 0) to lay out your entire page. Since you will probably want to avoid placing text within the sidebar, this technique becomes especially useful if you want to use a background with a sidebar, as illustrated in Figure 10.8.

Figure 10.8.
Using background
tiles and tables.

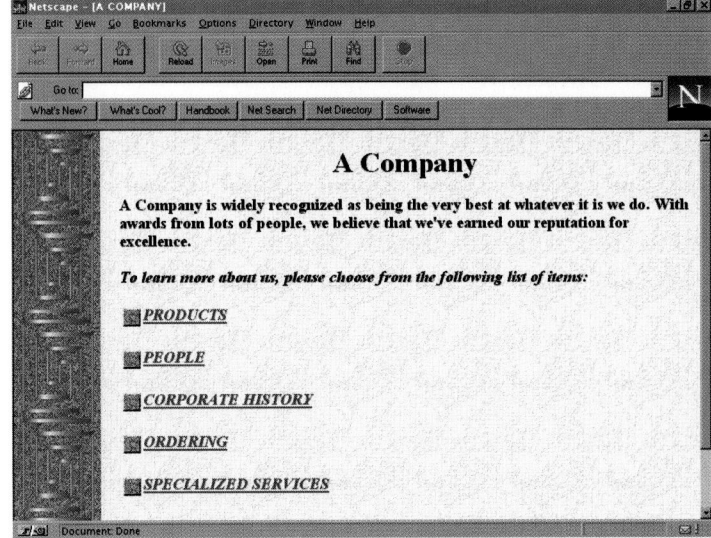

The example shown is Figure 10.8 is accomplished with the code in Listing 10.3.

Listing 10.3. Setting a table to work with a background tile.

```
<HTML>
<HEAD><TITLE>A COMPANY</TITLE>
</HEAD>

<BODY BACKGROUND="back3.jpg" LINK="#800000" VLINK="#000080" ALINK="#FF00FF">

<TABLE BORDER=0>
<TR>
<TD><IMG SRC="spacer.gif">
</TD>

<TD>
<CENTER>
<H1>A Company</H1>
</center>
<H3>A Company is widely recognized as being the very best at whatever it is
we do.  With awards from lots of people, we believe that we've earned our
reputation for excellence.

<P><I>To learn more about us, please choose from the following list of
items:<I><P>

<A HREF="1"><IMG SRC="icon.gif" border=0 align=top>PRODUCTS</a><P>
<A HREF="2"><IMG SRC="icon.gif" border=0 align=top>PEOPLE</A><P>
<A HREF="3"><IMG SRC="icon.gif" border=0 align=top>CORPORATE HISTORY</A><P>
<A HREF="4"><IMG SRC="icon.gif" border=0 align=top>ORDERING</A><P>
<A HREF="5"><IMG SRC="icon.gif" border=0 align=top>SPECIALIZED SERVICES</A><P>
<A HREF="6"><IMG SRC="icon.gif" border=0 align=top>CONTACTING US</A><P>
</H4>
```

continues

Listing 10.3. continued

```
<HR SIZE=5>
</TD>
</TR>
</TABLE>
</BODY>
</HTML>
```

As you can see, the left column of the table was sized using a transparent GIF. This kind of "spacer" GIF is also useful in placing graphics in relation to each other, as shown in Figure 10.9.

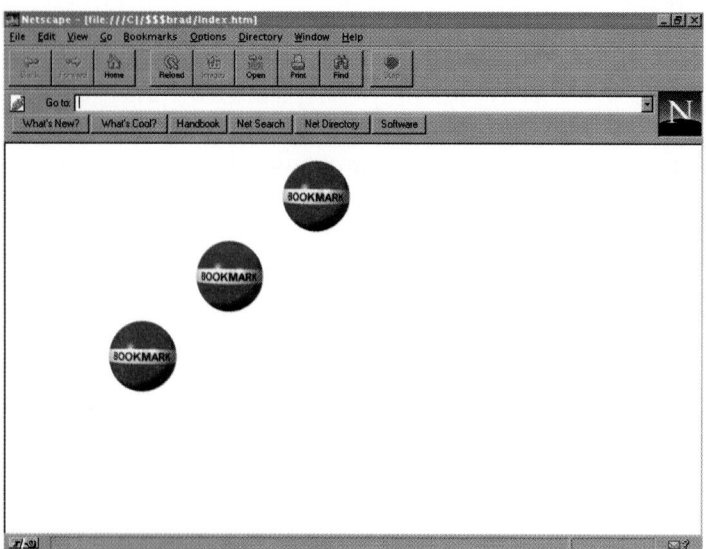

Figure 10.9.
Using spacer GIFs.

Figure 10.9 was achieved with the code in Listing 10.4.

Listing 10.4. Using tables to format graphics.

```
<TABLE BORDER=0>
<TR>
<TD><IMG SRC="spacer.gif">
</TD>

<TD><IMG SRC="spacer.gif"><IMG SRC="spacer.gif"><IMG SRC="ball.gif">
</TD>
</TR>

<TR>
<TD></TD>
<TD><IMG SRC="spacer.gif"><IMG SRC="ball.gif">
</TD>
</TR>
```

```
<TR>
<TD></TD>
<TD><IMG SRC="ball.gif">
</TD>
</TR>

</TABLE>
```

RESIZING IMAGES WITHIN THE CODE

You should always specify the image size in your code, as in

```
<IMG SRC="graphic.gif" HEIGHT=100 WIDTH=100>
```

This is done so that your browser will know where to place the text before it actually downloads the image. By doing this, your viewer will be able to begin reading your page as it's downloading.

You can also use the image size attributes to resize a graphic, thus enabling you to place a smaller version of the same graphic instead of loading a completely separate image file. All you have to do is change the attributes in the image tag:

```
<IMG SRC=" graphic.gif" HEIGHT=50 WIDTH=50>
```

Be careful in doing this, however, because the browser will stretch or shrink your image in whatever proportion you describe, as shown in Figure 10.10.

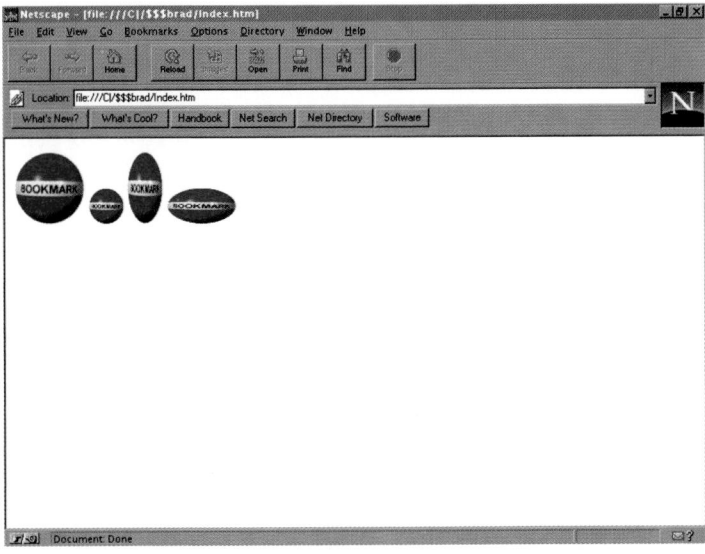

Figure 10.10.
Resizing graphics within HTML.

It's also important to note that browsers don't do the best job of resizing—they will often pixelate and alias the graphic (make it look choppy). The fewer colors in the graphic, the better the results will be.

Using Thumbnails

Sometimes you'll want to use a large graphic (like a map) that doesn't necessarily need to be viewed by everyone. It's usually best to keep this graphic as a separate file (`graphic.jpg`) and place a smaller version of the graphic within the page itself. Link the small "thumbnail" version to the larger, so that people who want to see the detail can download and view it. We discuss the creation of thumbnails in Chapter 12, "Working with Graphics."

Note:
Don't use the browser's resizing option (mentioned above) to make pseudo-thumbnails of the original graphic, as it still will require downloading the large file.

Summary

In this chapter, we've discussed some of the more useful tags and attributes of HTML and have offered some tricks for laying out pages. A comparative reference of HTML tags is included in Appendix H, and if you have absolutely no HTML experience, you may want to get a book that deals specifically with HTML code.

The next chapter moves on to CGI and discusses some aspects of interactivity in more detail. If you don't plan to use forms or CGI in your system, you may choose to skip ahead to Chapter 12.

Integrating HTML with CGI

CGI enables viewers to interact with your Web presentation, and that makes it one of the more powerful and complex aspects in Web design. If you have ever filled out an online form or used a search engine, you have used CGI, probably without even realizing it (which is exactly the point).

Because of security risks and strain on the server, CGI scripts should be used only when necessary, and should be integrated into your site seamlessly so the viewer doesn't even realize they are being used.

CGI is not for the beginner; it involves *much* more programming knowledge than basic HTML. If you are planning to tackle CGI, you should have not only a basic grasp of programming concepts, but also familiarity with the server system on which your script will reside. If you do not possess these requirements, we suggest you either pick up a book on CGI (preferably one that focuses on your system), visit some of the CGI resources listed in Appendix F, or move directly to the Quick & Dirty Guide, "Ways to Avoid CGI," at the end of this chapter.

This chapter explains how CGI works, describes some possible uses for CGI, details how to create HTML forms and their accompanying CGI decoders, and suggests some ways to avoid CGI. The subject of CGI is far too complex to cover fully within the constraints of this chapter; therefore, it is our intention to give you a basic understanding of the concepts of CGI and to teach its most popular use as an HTML form decoder.

Note:
We address specific uses of CGI in following chapters as they pertain to certain tasks.

Are you ready? Get yourself some caffeine, clear your desk, and let's dig into CGI!

WHAT IS CGI?

CGI stands for Common Gateway Interface (and also, Computer Graphics Interface, which we mention so that you'll know that to some "computer people," the term CGI might mean something else), and is a program run on a Web server that is triggered by input from the viewer (via the browser). CGI is an interface for running external programs (or gateways) under an HTTP server; it enables users on the Web to access programs of all types on remote systems as if they were actually using the remote computer themselves. The most common programming languages used with CGI are Perl (used mainly on the UNIX platform) and Visual Basic (used primarily with Windows). Other languages you can use to create a CGI script are C/C++, AppleScript, TCL, the Bourne shell, FORTRAN, and any UNIX shell. These scripts enable the WWW server and browser to run external programs launching another application.

CGI scripts work like this (see Figure 11.1):

1. The browser requests the URL of the CGI script (usually through an HTML form or a hyperlink).

2. The server receives that request (noticing that the URL points to a CGI script) and executes that script.

3. The script performs the action it is intended for (usually based on the input by the viewer). This action can calculate a value, query your database, or connect to another program on the server.

4. The CGI script formats its result into an understandable (for the Web server) document.

5. The server receiving the result passes it on to the browser, where it is then displayed to the viewer.

If one CGI script were able to do the same thing on every computer, scripting would be easy. Unfortunately, the CGI script relies on the operating system of the server, so a Perl (UNIX) script might look like garbage to a non-UNIX server, and so on.

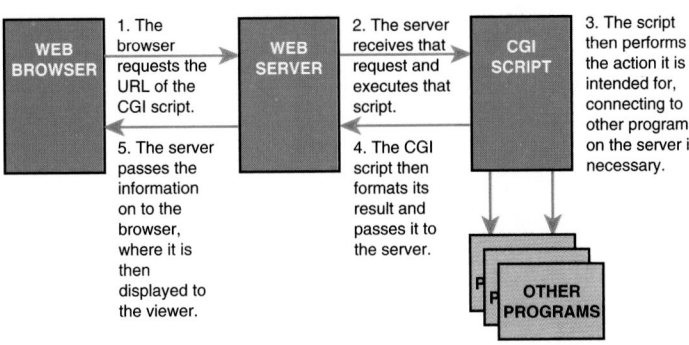

Figure 11.1.
How a CGI script works.

Note:
The CGI instructions and examples in this book focus primarily on UNIX Web servers. If your Web server is running on a system other than UNIX, these instructions may not apply, but will serve as an example of how CGI works. For CGI scripts specific to your platform, visit some of the CGI resource sites listed in Appendix F.

CGI scripts are generally held in a CGI-BIN. If you are using a virtual host, your ISP may have CGI-BIN directories, which you may be able to use. You should also be able to have your own CGI-BIN so that you can run your own scripts (rather than adapting your system to work with the scripts that already reside on the system). Your host will be the best source of information about how and where this is set up.

If your site is located on your own server, you will need to set up your CGI configuration yourself. Depending on your server and how it is set up, you will either need to create a CGI-BIN directory to store your scripts or name your scripts with a special extension (for example, .cgi). The best place to find information on how to set up your particular server will probably be the company who produced the software (usually located at the company's Web site).

USES FOR CGI

CGI has many uses, including

- ◆ To create a searchable database
- ◆ To create clickable image maps (though internal maps are often preferable)
- ◆ To convert pages into HTML on-the-fly and send the HTML result to the client (often called dynamic Web pages)
- ◆ To interface with databases, convert the results to HTML, and send the resulting page to the client
- ◆ To send a custom reply based on a completed HTML form
- ◆ To enable viewer feedback through an HTML form and an accompanying CGI decoder

This last use is the most popular, and the one we discuss next.

MAKING FORMS USER-FRIENDLY

Fill-out forms are used all over the Web for many different applications, but the use we see most often is to provide the viewers a place for feedback. This is most likely the first use you want to learn, so we are going to take you step-by-step through this process. By doing this, we intend to give you a general understanding of how forms work with HTML, as well as to help you to begin to understand the CGI scripts you will find available on the Web (some of which are listed in Appendix F). So here we go...

As with any complex project, we begin by assessing and sketching out our goal.

The goal of this project is to provide a feedback form for viewers' questions and comments. Once the viewers fill out the feedback form and click the Submit button, we want an HTML page to load, letting them know we received the form and thanking them for their time. We also want the information they provided to be sent to our e-mail box in a readable manner (which requires that we decode it; without decoding, the e-mail looks like a mess and is very difficult to work with).

Note:
If you wish to also send the viewer an e-mail in response to a form, check out Chapter 14, "Mail Delivery Systems," after reviewing this section.

So, there are three separate files we must create to develop the feedback form: the HTML form itself (as in Figure 11.2), the CGI script that will decode it, and the HTML redirect page (which lets the user know that the form has been submitted).

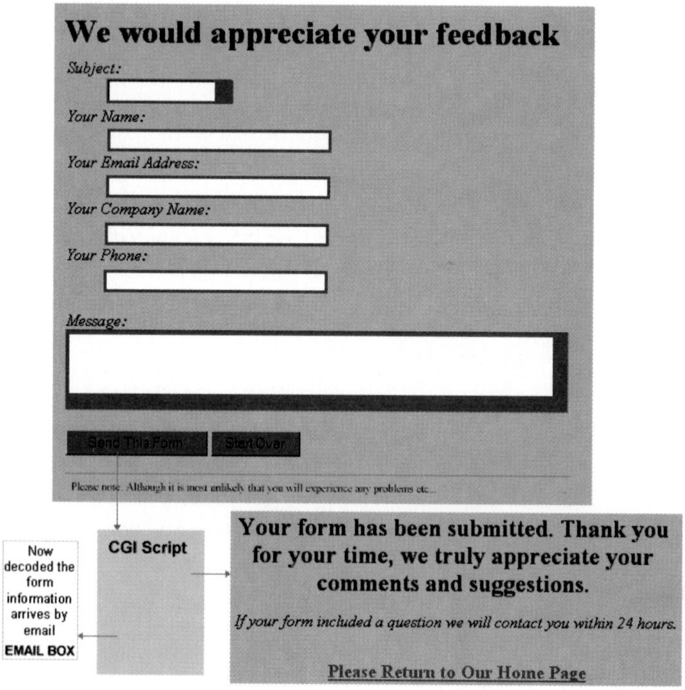

Figure 11.2.
The goal of our feedback form example.

Now that we know where we're headed, let's get started on the HTML form. For this very simple form, we will use the code in Listing 11.1.

Listing 11.1. Our feedback form code.

```
<!DOCTYPE HTML PUBLIC "-//IETF//DTD HTML 3.0//EN" "html.dtd">
<HTML>
<HEAD>
<TITLE>Feedback Form</TITLE>
<!-- Author:  Kim and Brad Hampton -->
</HEAD>

<BGCOLOR="FFFFFF" TEXT="000000" LINK="425AFF" VLINK="0018C4" ALINK="FFFFFF">


<H1>We would appreciate your feedback</H1>
<P>
<FONT FACE="Lucida Sans", "Arial", "Times Roman">

<FORM ACTION="/cgi-bin/formmail.pl" METHOD=POST>
<INPUT TYPE="hidden" name="recipient" value="hampton@ha.net">
<INPUT TYPE="hidden" NAME="redirect" VALUE="http://www.ha.net/thanks.htm">

<DL>
<DT><I>Subject:
    <DD><SELECT name="subject">
        <OPTION>My suggestions
        <OPTION>My comments
        <OPTION>I have a question
        <OPTION>Other
        </SELECT>
<DT>Your Name:
    <DD><input type=text name="realname" size=30>
<DT>Your Email Address:
    <DD><input type=text name="email" size=30>
<DT>Your Company Name:
    <DD><input type=text name="Company" size=30>
<DT>Your Phone:
    <DD><input type=text name="Phone" size=30>
<P>
<DT>Message:
<DT><TEXTAREA name="comments" cols=60 rows=3></TEXTAREA><p>
</DL></I>

<DT><input type=submit value="Send This Form">
<input type=reset value="Start Over">
<P>
</FONT>
</FORM>

<HR>

Please note: Although it is most unlikely that you will experience any problems
responding to this form, certain non-standard browsers will not respond
properly. If you experience any difficulties,(or if you are not using a
forms-capable browser) you may email your response to this form to:
<a href="mailto:hampton@ha.net">hampton@ha.net</A>.
</BODY>
</HTML>
```

Now, let's make sure you know what all this code means. Everything should look familiar until you get to the `<FORM>` tag, as in

```
<FORM ACTION="/cgi-bin/formmail.pl" METHOD=POST>
```

THE FORM TAGS `<FORM>` AND `</FORM>`

The `<FORM>` tags are used to define a fill-out form for processing by the HTTP server. All forms must be within these tags. You can include multiple forms within a document, but you cannot nest the forms (you cannot include a `<FORM>` tag within a `<FORM>` tag). Also, the `<FORM>` tag does not specify the layout of the form; you have to add regular HTML tags within the form to do that. Attributes for this tag are the following:

◆ `ACTION`

Describes the URL of the query server to which the form contents will be submitted in our example:

`/cgi-bin/formmail.pl`

◆ `ENCTYPE`

Specifies the encoding of the form contents. Only applies if the `METHOD` attribute is set to `POST`. We do not use this tag in our example.

◆ `METHOD`

Submits the form to the query server (which method you use depends mostly on your server). Options for this attribute are

`POST`　Used in our example, this option causes the form contents to be sent to the server in a data body (not as part of the URL).

`GET`　Causes the form contents to be appended to the URL as if it were a normal query. `GET` is the default, yet for most purposes `POST` is preferable.

`<INPUT>`

This is the next tag in our example and requires no ending tag. It is used to specify a form control. In our example, it looks like this:

```
<INPUT TYPE="hidden" name="recipient"
value="hampton@ha.net">
```

The first attribute we use for this tag is `TYPE`. This specifies the type of the control to use. In this case the type is `"hidden"`, which specifies that no field is seen by the viewer, but the content of the field is sent with the submitted form. This value is often used to transmit information about client/server interaction.

Other options for this attribute are

`CHECKBOX`　This is used for simple Boolean attributes or for attributes that can take multiple values at the same time. It is represented by a number of checkbox fields, each of which has the same name. Each selected checkbox generates a separate name/value pair in the submitted data, even if this results in duplicate names. The default value for checkboxes is `on`.

`IMAGE`　An image field that you can click, causing the form to be immediately submitted. The coordinates of the selected point are measured in pixel units from the upper-left corner of the image and are returned (along with the other contents of the form) in two name/value pairs. The x-coordinate is submitted under the name of the field with `.x` appended, and the y-coordinate is submitted under the name of the field with `.y` appended. Any `VALUE` attribute is ignored. The image itself is specified by the `SRC` attribute, exactly as for the `<IMG>` tag.

PASSWORD   The same as the TEXT attribute, except that the text is not displayed as it is entered.

RADIO   Used for attributes that accept a single value from a set of alternatives. Each radio-button field in the group should be given the same name. Only the selected radio button in the group generates a name/value pair in the submitted data. Radio buttons require an explicit VALUE attribute.

RESET   When clicked, this button resets the form's fields to their specified initial values. The label to be displayed on the button can be specified the same way as for the SUBMIT button. In our example it appears like this:

```
<input type=reset value="Start Over">
```

SUBMIT   When clicked, this button submits the form, like in our example:

```
<input type=submit value="Send This Form">
```

You may use the VALUE attribute to provide a noneditable label to be displayed on the button (in our example, "Send This Form"). If a SUBMIT button is pressed to submit the form, and that button has a NAME attribute specified, then that button contributes a name/value pair to the submitted data. If the button has no name, then a SUBMIT button makes no contribution to the submitted data.

TEXT   Specifies a single line text entry field, like in our example:

```
<input type=text name="realname" size=30>
```

This can be used in conjunction with the SIZE and MAXLENGTH attributes.

TEXTAREA   For multiple-line, text-entry fields— in our example, we use it for the message box like this:

```
Message:<TEXTAREA name="comments" cols=60 rows=3></TEXTAREA>
```

This can be used in conjunction with the SIZE and MAXLENGTH attributes.

FILE   This option (which is currently supported by Netscape) enables the inclusion of files with form information.

Other attributes we use for the <INPUT> tag are

◆ NAME

Specifies the name of the control, like this:

```
<input type=text name="realname" size=30>
```

◆ VALUE

This attribute is required for radio buttons and is used for numerical/textual controls. It specifies the initial displayed value of the field or the value to be returned when the field is selected. The value attribute generally appears like this:

```
<input type=submit value="Send This Form">
```

◆ ALIGN

Specifies the vertical alignment of the next line of text in relation to the image. For use only with TYPE=IMAGE. Possible values are the same as for the ALIGN attribute of the <IMG> element.

◆ CHECKED

This is used for checkboxes and radio buttons, and indicates that they are selected. The options are TRUE or FALSE; it is used like this:

```
<INPUT NAME="control2" TYPE=CHECKBOX CHECKED=TRUE>
```

◆ MAXLENGTH

This indicates the maximum number of characters that can be entered into a text control. It appears like this:

```
<INPUT NAME="control2" TYPE=TEXTBOX MAXLENGTH=20>
```

◆ **SIZE**

Used to specify the size of a control in characters (for TEXTAREA controls, both height and width can be specified) like this:

```
<INPUT NAME="control2"
TYPE=TEXTAREA SIZE="25,5">.
```

This would allow 5 lines of text, each 25 characters long.

◆ **SRC**

Used in conjunction with TYPE=IMAGE, specifies the source address of the image to be used.

The next line of code is

```
<INPUT TYPE="hidden"
NAME="redirect"
VALUE="http://www.ha.net/
thanks.htm">
```

This line means the following: This input is hidden, and once the form has been submitted, load the page http:// www.ha.net/thanks.htm, which will thank users for their input.

<DL>, <DT>, AND <DD>

These tags should look familiar to you; they have nothing to do with the form information itself, only the layout of it. Here we have used the <DL> tag, which is a definition or glossary list, containing <DT> elements that give terms and <DD> elements that give the corresponding definitions. We have included this

formatting here to encourage you to use your imagination with tags. They can be used for much more than their intended purpose. Note: <DT> and <DD> do not use closing tags.

<SELECT>

This indicates a listbox or drop-down list. In our example it appears like this:

```
<SELECT name="subject">
      <OPTION>My suggestions
      <OPTION>My comments
      <OPTION>I have a question
      <OPTION>Other
      </SELECT>
```

The NAME attribute gives the list a name. Here it is used for the subject of the message sent to us (the respondent's choice will appear in the subject line of our e-mail).

Two other possibilities for this tag are MULTIPLE, which specifies that multiple items can be selected; and SIZE, which is used to specify the size of the list control.

<OPTION>

This tag resides within our drop-down list, and each indicates one choice in a listbox.

And last but not least, our warning message:

```
<HR>
Please note: Although it is most unlikely that you will
experience any problems responding to this form, certain
non-standard browsers will not respond properly. If you
experience any difficulties, (or if you are not using a
forms-capable browser) you may email your response to this
form to: <a href="mailto:hampton@ha.net">hampton@ha.net</
A>.
```

It is a very good idea to include a message like this on your forms. It will not only aid viewers with nonstandard browsers, but will also be invaluable should there be a problem with your CGI script.

And that's it for the form itself! Figure 11.3 shows how it looks.

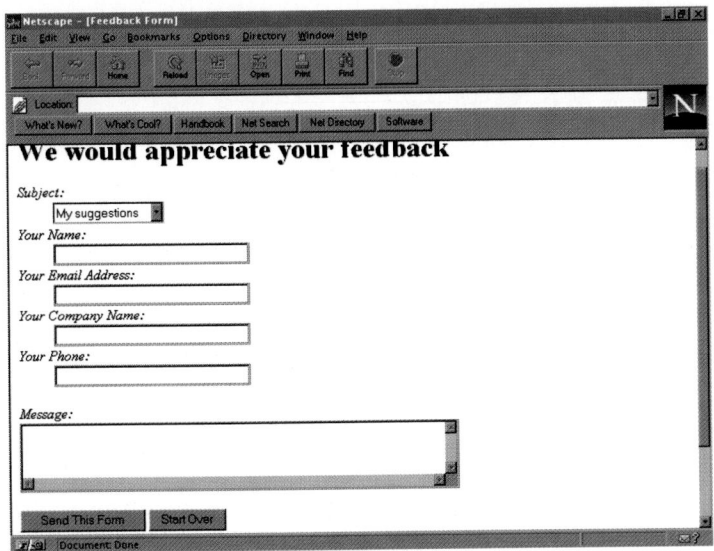

Figure 11.3.
How our HTML form example turned out.

The thank you page is next. This is just a standard HTML page (as described in Chapter 10, "Taking Advantage of HTML"). The code for our example is shown in Listing 11.2.

Listing 11.2. The thank you page.

```
<!DOCTYPE HTML PUBLIC "-//IETF//DTD HTML 3.0//EN" "html.dtd">
<HTML>
<HEAD>
<TITLE>Thank You</TITLE>
</HEAD>

<BGCOLOR="FFFFFF" TEXT="000000" LINK="425AFF"
VLINK="0018C4" ALINK="FFFFFF">

<CENTER><BR><H2>Your form has been submitted.  Thank you
for your time, we truly appreciate your comments and
suggestions.</H2><P>

<I>If your form included a question we will contact you
within 24 hours.</I><BR><BR><P>

<H3><A HREF="index.html">Please Return to Our Home Page
</H3>
</CENTER>
</BODY>
</HTML>
```

Now let's see what we can do with this baby!

DECODING FORMS WITH CGI

When you write a form, each of your input items has a NAME attribute associated with it (as we saw in the form example). Now, when a viewer places data in the fields on the form, that information is encoded into the form data. The response to each of the input items given by the user is called the value.

Form data is a stream of name=value pairs normally separated by the & character. Each name=value pair is URL encoded; that is, spaces are changed into plusses and some characters are changed. This makes the forms content very difficult to read and nearly impossible to import directly to a database. So, in order to use this valuable information, we need to unencode it. For this we will use CGI.

So, do you need to take a course in CGI programming and work around the clock to debug a script? Well, you could, but you have better things to do right? And, as we have said before, there is really no need to reinvent the wheel (especially in cases where there are experts who have spent their lives inventing it for you).

Now, we need the perfect script—one that will read our form, send the thank you page, and send us an easily readable e-mail. Well, we don't need to look very far—CGI scripts are all over the place on the Web (some are included on your CD-ROM as well), and many are free (provided you give the author or authors credit and are approved to use them commercially). But, before you go exploring the Web (and if you are using a virtual host), call to see if your ISP has any CGI scripts in the bin that could be used for your form. They will almost always have something that will work for this purpose. This is usually the easiest way to set up your form. Since the script is already on your server, you need only reference the directory it is in, and need not ever see the CGI script itself.

If you have no luck with your host (or you have no host), your next step is to visit some CGI resources. We found the script we were looking for at Matt's Script Archive: `http://www.worldwidemart.com/scripts/examples/formmail.shtml` (see Figure 11.4). There we found a CGI script called FormMail that is written in Perl and would work on our UNIX server. This CGI script is called `formmail.pl` and is included on your CD-ROM in the directory `D:\cgi\formmail` where D is your CD-ROM drive.

This is why our code reads

```
<FORM ACTION="/cgi-bin/
formmail.pl" METHOD=POST>.
```

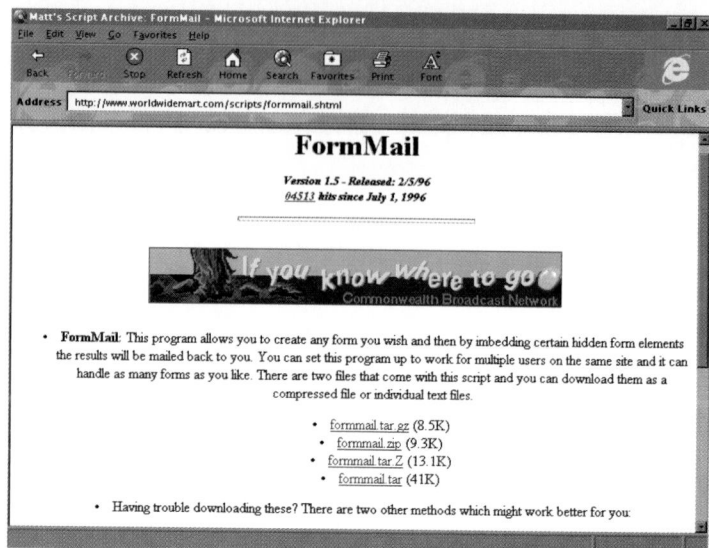

Figure 11.4.
Matt's Script Archive.

Now that you have found your script, you will need to configure it so it will work properly on your server. This configuration is generally pretty minor. You will usually find out how to do this by

1. Reading the author's notes within the code
2. Reading the `readme` file that was downloaded with your script (or in the case of `formmail.pl`, the `readme` file contained in the same directory on the CD-ROM)
3. Searching for the information at the site where you got the CGI script

After your script is configured properly, upload it to your server, and make sure it is referenced correctly in your HTML form. Now let's see if it works.

The viewer clicks on the feedback link from the home page and arrives at our HTML form. He/she fills out the form and clicks the Send This Form button (see Figure 11.5).

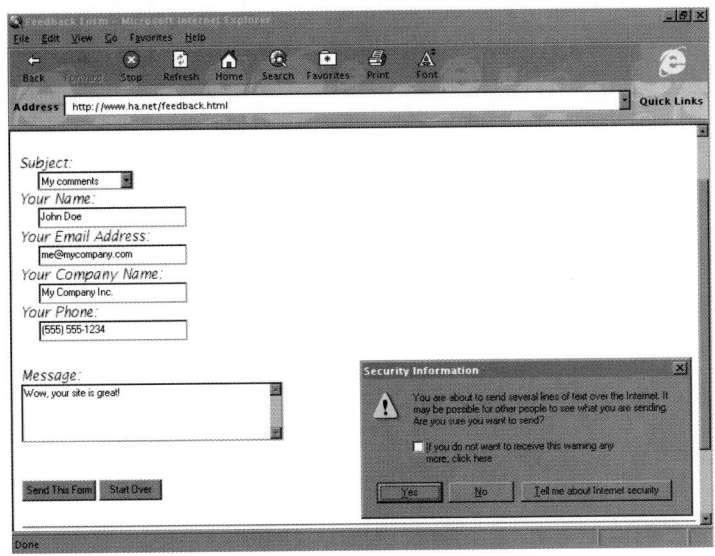

Figure 11.5.
How a viewer fills out the form example.

The form is then submitted, and the viewer jumps to the thank you page (see Figure 11.6).

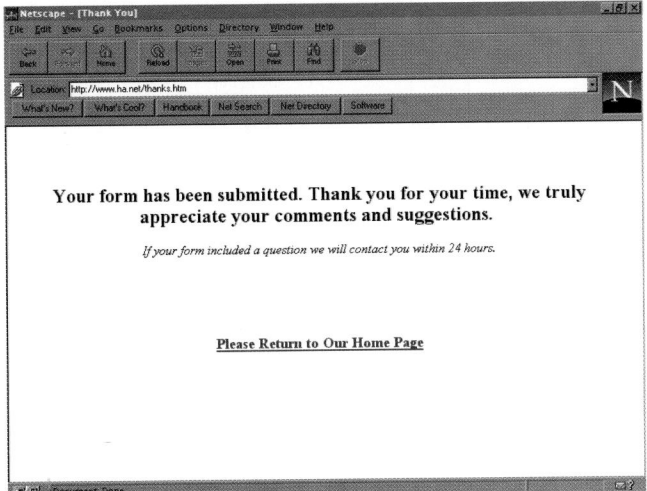

Figure 11.6.
The thank you page.

Our form contents then arrive in our e-mail box (see Figure 11.7).

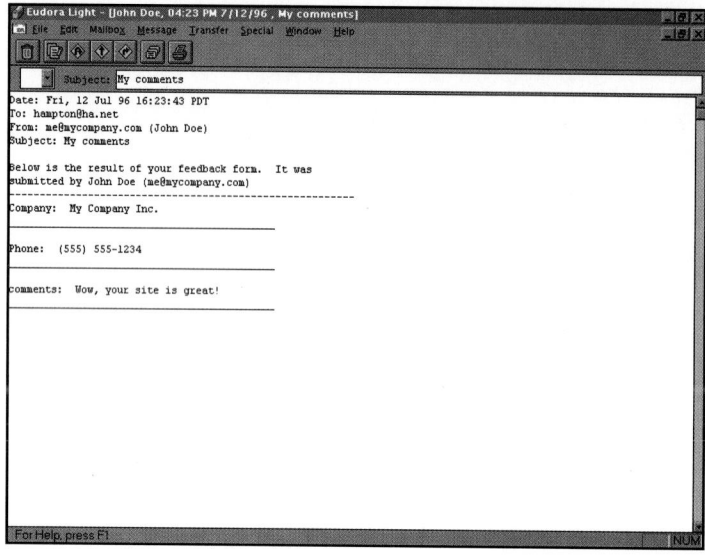

Figure 11.7.
How the form contents look when we get them via e-mail.

Hey, what do you know? It works!

QUICK & DIRTY GUIDE
Ways to Avoid CGI

The quick tip for CGI is simple: Don't use it. There are a variety of ways you can get around using CGI, and avoiding it has its advantages:

◆ **Your system is self-contained**. If you avoid using CGI-BIN applications, your system can be contained within its own directories.

◆ **Your system is mobile.** You don't have to rewrite the relative paths and links, change commands to meet those of different system's CGI-BIN files (some of which can be very quirky), and adapt everything to meet the demands of a different operating system if you're not relying on CGI apps. At least, that is, not as much.

◆ **You have control**. Most ISPs offering virtual hosting services are wary of CGI and will retain rights to delete any files that may risk site security. CGI applications are active programs—not simply files—and their use can put a system at risk. A poorly written CGI can make a mess out of a server system. If you avoid these applications, you're reducing that risk to little or nothing, and most administrators will leave you alone. Plus, you won't have to conform your site to meet your provider's CGI requirements.

Luckily, two of the most popular uses for CGI—image mapping and forms handling—can actually be accomplished using no CGI at all. In this Quick & Dirty Guide we show you how to use one of those programs on your CD-ROM, WebMania, to handle forms; we discuss quick image mapping in the next chapter, "Working with Graphics."

Form Handling with WebMania

WebMania is an HTML editor and forms generator that automatically creates HTML forms and reads their responses. Responses are automatically sent to your mailbox, then read by WebMania and collected in a response database. This means you can create your form, give the viewer a thank you (with the help of Java), and read your responses without the use of CGI—and it's so easy. Here's how it works:

1. Install WebMania. (See Appendix I.)

2. Open WebMania.

3. In the File drop-down menu, choose Forms New.

4. Fill out all the required fields, and any optional fields. (Click Forms Help… in the Help menu if you have any questions.)

5. Click the completion tag, refresh the controls, and place your fields in any order you like.

Using WebMania, we produced a form in 10 minutes. Aiming for our original layout sketch, we produced the form pictured in Figure 11.8.

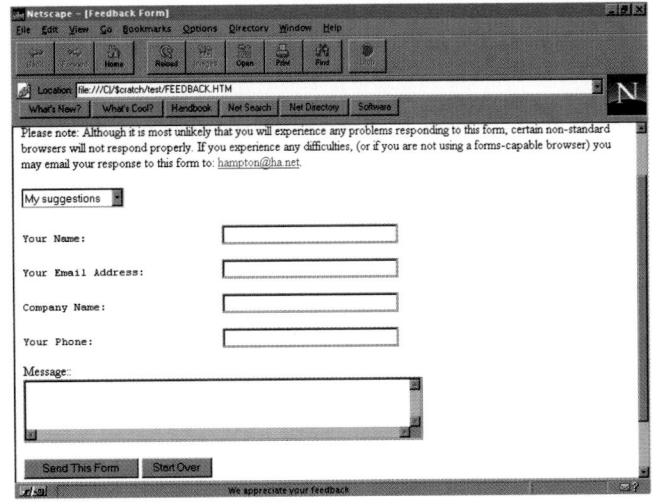

Figure 11.8.
How our form turned out using WebMania.

> **Note:**
> You can easily change the format of a WebMania form manually in an ASCII text editor to produce the desired layout. We could have spent an extra 10 minutes to make this form *look*, but not behave, just like the form we produced manually.

So, now how do you read the submitted information and import it for use into a database? We discuss that in Chapter 13, "Databases and Searches."

SUMMARY

The integration of HTML with CGI is a huge subject that is covered in more depth within this book as it pertains to different tasks. This chapter is simply intended to give you an overview of the subject. By now you should

- ◆ Understand how CGI works
- ◆ Have an idea of the uses and possibilities of CGI
- ◆ Know how to create an online form system to receive information from the viewer

Now that you have all the information you wanted from the viewer, what you do with it? Well, that is up to you, but we would like to suggest you keep this information in a database to use for sales leads. How do you do that? We discuss that in Chapter 13, but for now let's get creative as we move on to "Working with Graphics."

Working with Graphics

Electronic mail (e-mail)—
a system whereby a
computer user can exchange
messages and files with other
computer users (or groups of
users) via a communications
network—is one of the most
popular uses of the Internet.
This facet of the Net was one
of the first applied uses, and
continues to be a powerful
communications tool.

CHAPTER twelve

We've said it before, and we'll say it again: Graphics are what have made the WWW a realistic commercial option. Text alone is simply not an effective enough means of communication to be nearly as viable a marketing tool as text with graphics.

Graphic images give a document style and impact, yet they can also be counterproductive if used poorly. We address different issues of graphics earlier in the book, and we don't cover all of the possible topics again here. What we do cover here are the ways in which graphics should be used, as well as some of the tips and tricks we've learned in our work.

COMMUNICATING WITH GRAPHICS

Again, commercial art is more than pretty pictures. The purpose of commercial art is to not only decorate, but to communicate, motivate, and a bunch of other -ate words. One of the biggest problems with novice page designs are that the graphics have no purpose—they just sit there, gobbling up bandwidth.

Your graphics need to say something. They should at least reinforce things like the corporate identity (logos, font treatments, and so on) and should strive to do more. Graphic design is both an art and science. If you have no experience in this field, your best bet is to work with a designer. You may have the software to make very cool graphics, but a great tool set doesn't make you a mechanic.

If you already have print collateral, you have a resource. It's to your advantage to bring the look and feel of the print collateral (assuming it's well designed) to your Web documents for at least two reasons. First, it allows for a continuity in collateral, which will help to promote a company's image and identity. Second, it gives you a starting point.

GRAPHICS CONVERSION FOR THE WEB

Whether you are taking your graphics from master (print design) files or from paper, and whether or not you are working with a designer, you will want to have control over the conversion to Web graphics.

Most graphic designers are accustomed to designing art for print. There are differences between screen and print presentation, big and small, which drastically affect the quality and usefulness of artwork placed on the WWW. Most designers are still unaware of those differences, and it will be your job to either train them or make the adjustments yourself.

> **Note:**
> Regardless of your source, you will probably need to reduce the resolution of the image prior to publishing. Computer monitors usually have a resolution of either 72 or 96 dpi (dots per inch); any resolution higher than this is a waste of file space and bandwidth. We usually set the resolution to 96 dpi, so that it will be optimal for even the best systems—but to be quite honest, it's difficult to tell the difference.
>
> It's also important to note that many viewers will have their monitors set to a resolution of 640 pixels by 480 pixels, so graphics should have a maximum width of about 600 pixels or less. This way viewers can see your images without scrolling horizontally.

CONVERTING FROM HI-RES PRINT MASTERS (CMYK)

High-res (high-resolution) print masters come in several different file types, but can basically be broken down into two categories: bitmap and vector. Bitmap files (TIFF, GIF, JPEG, PCX, BMP, and so on) are actually a grid of pixels. The file tells the computer/printer to make one pixel one color, the next pixel another color, and so on. Vector images (Adobe Illustrator, CorelDRAW!, Aldus FreeHand, Windows and Computer Graphics Metafiles, and Encapsulated PostScript, to name a few) are based on mathematical calculations. The file tells the computer/printer to make (for instance) a curve from one point to another, to fill it in with a color, to lay another curve over the top, to fill it in with another color, and so on.

As it now stands, WWW browsers can only really work with bitmap images, and these are limited to the GIF and JPEG file types (there are plans to incorporate vector-type image formats in the future). So, whatever graphics you're working with will have to be converted into these file types for publishing. Sound simple? Well…

This becomes more complicated when you take into account the color palettes used in print. You see, screen graphics are made of three colors: red, green, and blue, or RGB (even 8-bit indexed colors are RGB). Print, on the other hand, is usually made up of four colors: cyan, magenta, yellow, and black, or CMYK. This is because four-color (CMYK) process printing uses these four inks to print full-color images (although some artwork specifies exact ink colors rather than process colors).

Most high-end graphics tools (such as Adobe Photoshop) allow for conversion between RGB and CMYK color palettes, so a CMYK TIFF image can be fairly easily converted to an RGB JPEG. Some bitmap graphics tools even read vector files and convert them to bitmaps—this can save a lot of headaches. Unfortunately, you may not have access to these tools, and you may have to convert the images another way.

If you can't automatically convert between CMYK and RGB, and from vector to bitmap, with your bitmap graphics tools, you will need to get creative. So, let's get creative!

PASS THE BUCK!

Let's say that you have a vector image created in a vector program. If you don't have the original software that created the image (or a package that can display it), you may not even be able to see what it looks like. Obviously, the file will be of little use to you. Your first option is to speak with the original designer (and you'll usually find that these people will be happy to help you). You'll want to ask this person to make you a bitmap copy of the image.

> **Note:**
> The licensing of graphics can take many forms, and just because a graphic has been purchased for certain applications does not mean that you (or your client) own it. You'll have to look into the use license to see whether there may be additional fees due the designer if you use his or her image on the WWW.

Your first choice is to get a hi-res RGB version of the image. Even though you'll be dropping the resolution of the image (hold on, we'll get to this), it's best to start with the most detail possible and to tear it apart yourself. This way, you'll be able to tweak things to meet your needs, and you'll always have a hi-res original to return to once you've screwed the whole thing up ☺.

You'll basically be limited to the storage medium available to both you and the original designer (unless you plan your graphic to be delivered by e-mail and don't mind receiving huge files). A hi-res image can be many megabytes (hundreds in some cases), and you will want to use a file that will fit on whatever medium you are using for transfer. For instance, if you're using 1.44MB PC floppy disks, you'll obviously need to tweak the file to fit on this size medium. If you are using Zip, MO, SyQuest, Tape, or CD-R formats, you'll obviously have more room to play.

You and the designer can cut down the size of the image in two ways. You can either reduce its physical size, or you can reduce its resolution (if working with JPEGs, avoid lowering the image *quality* at this point if possible). Dropping the resolution (DPI or dots-per-inch) to 96 will usually drop the file size dramatically, as this reduces the total number of pixels exponentially. If this doesn't do the trick, change the image's physical size to the largest that will fit on your storage device.

CHEAT A LITTLE

If you can view the image in one file type but have no way to convert it to a usable bitmap format, you may need to cheat. The simplest way to do this is via a screen capture. If there is another option, such as buying an application that will enable you to convert from the original file format or paying a service bureau to make the conversion, it is probably in your best interest to go that route. Screen captures generally produce only average results at best. Sometimes, however, you have no choice.

A screen capture simply takes a snapshot of your computer screen and saves it as a bitmap file. To perform a screen capture, you will need a screen capture application. (Windows systems have this built in—just hit your Print Screen button on the keyboard, and the screen image will be placed in your clipboard for pasting.) PSP, included on your CD-ROM, has this capability. Just choose the Full Screen option in the Capture drop-down menu. You will also need to take into account the quality of your graphics card and your graphics settings.

> **Note:**
> A screen capture can only present as many colors and pixels as your graphics settings allow. For instance, if you are running in 256-color mode at a resolution of 640×480, this is the best color depth and resolution you can get. Obviously, you may want to tweak your settings for an optimal screen capture.

CONVERTING FROM PRINT

If a graphic was originally computer-generated, you should try to get the file. In some cases, however, the file is unavailable, and you'll need to go from print. This will also be necessary if the artwork was not computer-generated, such as in the case of hand-drawn illustrations and photography.

In this case, you'll need to scan the paper (or film) and convert it to a digital bitmap format. There are many different levels of scanning, from hand-held grayscale scanners, to flat-bed (platen) scanners, to ultra-hi-res drum scanners. You'll probably want to avoid the scans from the hand-held types, as they are usually difficult to use and give poor results. Drum scanners produce more quality than you'll need, and the price is usually high for output (and way too high to consider purchasing your own). This leaves us with the flat-bed scanners.

Most flat-bed scanners can scan at a minimum resolution of 400 dpi, with a color depth of 24 bits per pixel (millions of colors). This will be more than adequate for our purposes. Simply adjust the scanner for optimal performance (according to your equipment and software instructions), scan the image, and save the digital file for later use. "Optimal performance" will depend on your original and your equipment, and you may need to tweak settings several times before you get the best quality.

If at all possible, avoid scanning four-color process printed pieces. For example, try to get a copy of the original photo or art rather than using a magazine ad. The little dots of ink that make up the four-color print can fool the human eye, but a scanner is looking much more closely than you, and the scanned results will look fuzzy and have poor color depth.

EFFECTIVE USE OF GRAPHICS

Now, how and where to place the graphics. There are no hard and fast rules we can give you on this subject. Creativity requires as few rules as possible, and far be it from us to try to chain you down to some type of ten commandments of "always" and "never." This said, here are some suggestions:

1. **Don't rely on graphics for your main message.**

   Many people are still accessing the WWW via low-speed (14.4Kbps) connections, and they set their browsers to ignore graphics. If all of your content is contained in the graphics, you're not communicating to these people.

   This is obviously a bandwidth issue and will probably be overcome in time, but it is still an issue. We've seen plenty of cases where a graphic contains most of the text on a page, and the only apparent reason is that it was easier for the designer to do this than to make use of the HTML layout tags. (Refer to the section "Graphics Without Graphics," later in this chapter.)

2. **Avoid stock graphics.**

   Stock graphics don't set you apart, nor do they assist in your creativity. Stock graphics make your pages look like other pages, and they force you to constrain your design. You should only use stock graphics as placeholders, as a starting point for your own graphics, and as parts of composite images.

   A composite image is created by using several images to make one. Imagine, for example, that you wanted to make an image map for navigation. You've found a very cool drawing of a mailbox, and you'd like to incorporate it into your image for the e-mail link. In this case, you might take the image, alter it to fit the style and color scheme of your composite (by cropping, filtering, applying effects, and so on), and drop it into your composite image in its altered form.

The final product may have only a vague resemblance to the original, but it now has a place within your system, and it was much easier to create than it would have been starting from scratch.

> **Note:**
> The uniqueness of your graphics will make them attractive to thieves. These people will rip you off and use your images (and code) on other people's pages—many so-called professional designers do this all the time. You can't really protect yourself from this, but you can make your images less appealing. This can be accomplished by making your graphics specific to your system by using logos (who would steal a bullet that has your name on it?) or by using graphic elements that would seem out of place on another page (either by using parts of larger graphics that would be meaningless when taken out of context, or by making the graphics specific to your subject).

3. **Try to keep your graphics, text, and empty space balanced.**

   Balance your page for optimal communication. Your graphics and text should look balanced, and there should be enough empty space that things make sense. A page-wide graphic, followed by dense text, followed by another page-wide graphic, will look crowded and confusing. On the other hand, separating your sections with some empty space, keeping your text blocks in bite-sized sections, and using left-, center-, and right-justified graphics can give your page a better flow. This will give your viewer a more enjoyable and easy-to-understand interface and will assist in your communication goal.

4. **Use the same styles and color schemes in all graphics (especially all graphics on a single page).**

First of all, this is just basic design. You probably wouldn't want to buy a house that was of Victorian design in one part, Mediterranean in another, Tudor on top, and Southwestern in the back. It would look like someone's nightmare. A page designed with no respect to continuity similarly looks bad.

Secondly, there's a technical issue. A GIF uses 256 colors, but two GIFs may not use the same 256 colors. Even if you have limited your palette to 256, placing graphics with different color schemes (palettes) will force a 256-color system to make its own adjustments in order to display your colors. Your lovely teal may come out looking like pea soup, and your perfect shapes and subtle colors may be dithered beyond recognition. See "The Rule of 51" later in this chapter, for more on dithering.

5. **Don't use graphics that are meaningless or seem out of place.**

Cute clip art doesn't cut it in professional design. Don't fall into the trap of placing images just because you have access to them. (This goes along with the previous suggestions about stock images.) What does a cute kitten with a bow around its neck have to do with real estate? What does a guy standing in front of a chart have to do with management? Don't use images that "kind of" fit the subject.

If your last name is Trout, having fish on your résumé might make both the résumé and your name more memorable to a prospective employer. If your name is Smith, however, a bunch of fish will make you look like a sucker, and your job search may flounder (sorry, couldn't avoid that one).

6. **Limit your total graphic files per page and recycle graphics when possible.**

This is more for technical and bandwidth reasons than for design. Limiting the total byte count of your graphics files will make things run faster (well, duh!), and will thus help you communicate your message faster. This is especially the case when people need to go through several pages to get to the information they want.

Your best tool to confront this issue is to recycle your graphics. After a browser has loaded a graphic, it usually keeps it in cache so that it can present the same graphic again without having to download it. If you use the same main graphic for each page, the viewer only has to wait once.

We often see that someone wants to highlight a certain area of an ISMAP in order to tell viewers where they are in the system. This requires that the browser download a different (often huge) file for each page, just so viewers can see that they are, in fact, where they wanted to be. A heading, smaller graphic, or use of a multiple file navigation graphic (that uses separate button graphics instead of one big ISMAP) can just as easily let viewers know where they are, without forcing them to wait nearly as long.

GRAPHIC FORMATS

There are two graphic formats that can be used in all three of the major current browsers without plug-ins: GIF and JPEG.

GRAPHICS INTERCHANGE FORMAT (GIF)

GIF was created by CompuServe as a way to compress and send image files. It presents a 256-color image in a fraction of the space required by uncompressed formats and is a very solid file, resistant to transfer errors. Although we feel it is in most ways inferior to JPEG, GIF 89a (a version of GIF) provides some very cool design options.

TRANSPARENCY

The transparency option tells the browser not to display a certain color. Applying this option to the background of an image makes the image appear to be floating on the page, rather than being a rectangle (make no mistake, however, it's still a rectangle). This is especially useful when you are using colored or tiled backgrounds.

This can be done in Paint Shop Pro (PSP) by making the color you wish to be transparent the selected background color (see Figure 12.1). Select the color you wish to make transparent with the dropper using the right-hand mouse button; this color will then appear in the background color box.

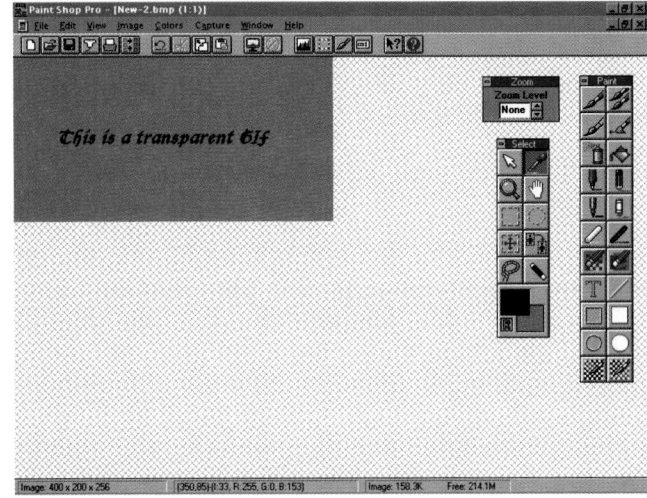

Figure 12.1.
Selecting the background color in PSP.

When saving this GIF image in PSP, first click the Options button to bring up the GIF Transparency Options window. Choose Set the Transparency Value to the Background Color, and click OK (see Figure 12.2). Type the name of your image and click OK (just as you normally would).

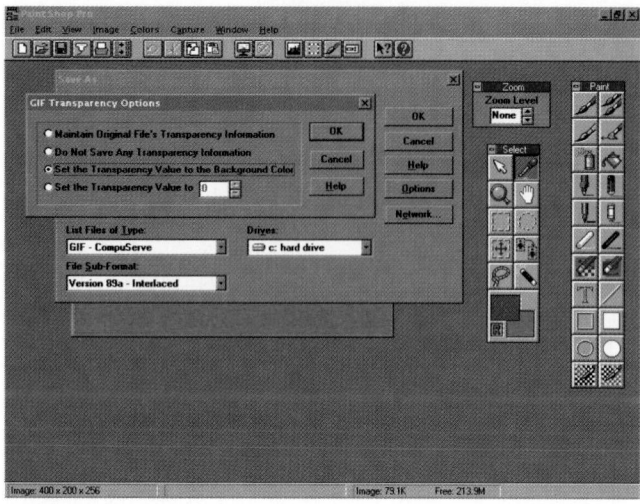

Figure 12.2.
Setting the transparency value in PSP.

You then simply place this GIF into your document with the <IMG> tag and—abracadabra!—you've created a transparent GIF (see Figure 12.3).

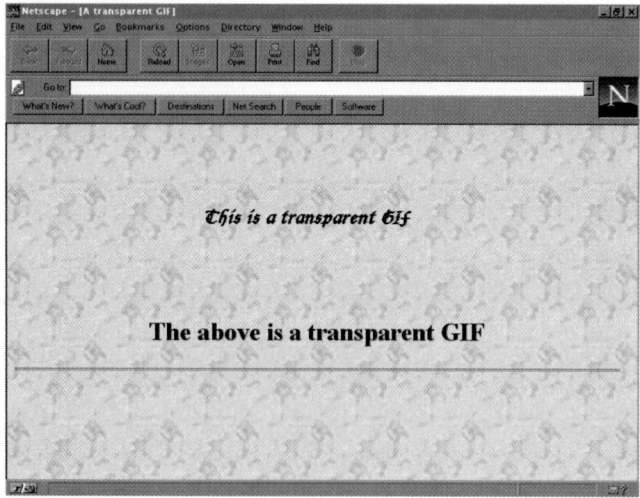

Figure 12.3.
How our transparent GIF looks on the Web page.

INTERLACED FILES

GIF files can be interlaced, which means that they can be made so that the file loads in a way that makes it appear to be coming into focus, rather than loading from top-to-bottom. What's really happening is that the browser is loading a line, skipping down a few, loading another line, skipping down a few, and so on. The browser is then filling in the empty spaces with colors based on the loaded lines. As more lines are loaded, the browser's "guesses" are corrected, and the image appears to be coming into focus. (JPEG has a similar option, called Progressive, which is not as widely supported—see the note in the following JPEG section.)

This is semi-cool, in that the viewer can see what's coming, but it's not really a big deal. The big deal comes from the fact that you can "trick" the browser by loading several images into one GIF file, and then use the interlacing code to make the browser load images on top of one another in a progression. Doing this makes an animation, and *that's* cool. To learn more about this, read the section on GIF 89a animations in Chapter 18, "Bells and Whistles."

JOINT PHOTOGRAPHIC EXPERTS GROUP (JPEG)

JPEG is a very aggressive compression format that tricks the eye by omitting useless information. It's been described as being a blueprint for an image rather than an actual image. This is to say that instead of drawing an image pixel by pixel, it paints with a broader brush, telling the reader (or browser) to "paint this area this color, and this one that color." This is a very simplistic way of looking at this very complex file format, and more in-depth discussions are available in print and on the Web for those who want to know more.

Suffice it to say that JPEG is in almost all ways superior to GIF. The color depth increases to 24-bit (16+ million colors), the file sizes are smaller, and the quality is close to that of uncompressed formats (such as TIFF and TARGA). The only times we don't use JPEGs are when the application requires a transparent background, or when we want to create a GIF 89a animation. (See the discussion of GIF in the preceding section and the Quick & Dirty Guide, "Get an Animation on Your Page in 30 Minutes," in Chapter 18.)

JPEG not only enables you to present more colors in a smaller file, but it also enables you to control file size with a Quality option. With the Quality option, you can control how much the JPEG will try to get away with, or how much it will try to trick the eye. A few points difference in the quality of a JPEG may reduce the file size by 50 percent with little or no apparent effect on the quality of the image. (This will vary from image to image, and you'll just have to play with it to get it right.)

> **Note:**
> There is something called a Progressive JPEG format that enables JPEGs to load in a way similar to interlaced GIFs (only more smoothly). The one problem with this is that very few bitmap manipulation tools enable you to open a JPEG that is in this format, and until recently, few browsers have recognized the format at all. Therefore, working with Progressive can be a pain. (On the other hand, it's a good theft-prevention measure—once we had a would-be thief actually write to complain that they couldn't open a JPEG we'd made!)

WHAT'S ON THE HORIZON?

The answer to this question depends on which way the WWW is turning. There seem to be two major camps here: one betting on higher bandwidth, and the other betting on more system-reliant file types.

The big-bandwidth folks believe that we'll all have a T1 in our home in the next year or so. This kind of connectivity will enable people to download huge, complex graphics, movies, high-quality sound, and so forth at such a rate that file size won't be as much a concern. Although we like the idea of this brave new world, the fact that many of the bottleneck problems occur within the Net itself lead us to believe that flawless throughput is a long way off, regardless of the speed of each individual terminal connection.

The system-reliant folks believe that we'll all continue to buy faster and faster systems, and that we'll be able to rely on these monster CPUs to process heavily compressed files. A good example of this is called FIF (Fractal Image Format). This format allows for incredible compression of graphics files because the file actually contains just the instructions for "painting" a picture. It's somewhat similar to a vector file in this respect. While it takes even a hot Pentium system a few seconds to decode an image, the final product is better than most bitmap files because the image does not pixelate.

What, you want our opinion? We feel that bandwidth will always be an issue, because everyone up the ladder (from you, to your ISP, to the telecommunications companies) will always try to get by with the least bandwidth possible. Because of this, we think that there will always be motivation for creating more and more effective means of compression. While it's not likely that everyone will run out to buy the Schmentium-based PC just because it will decompress files a few seconds faster, it is likely that people will continue to purchase systems on the leading edge (in order to run the latest applications), and that compression and transfer strategies that are reliant on these systems will be the most cost-effective solution to increasing content and interactivity in both the short and long term.

HINTS ON COLOR AND QUALITY

As you surf the WWW, you'll notice a difference in image quality from system to system. We're not talking about the actual content of the image, but the quality of the image's presentation. You'll notice that some graphics have jagged, pixelated edges, some have banding across color gradients and ugly blotches of colors, and other images appear to be photographic or at least print quality.

The poor images were not optimized for screen presentation. Screen presentation is different than print (as was stated earlier), and even the best graphic artists may not know how to adjust for this difference. We've found three specific areas which, when addressed properly, will help to make your images the best they can be. These are antialiasing, dithering, and color selection.

ANTIALIASING

When you resize a bitmap graphic, the graphic manipulation software calculates what pixels to keep, what to throw out, and how to make the smaller version look like the larger version with fewer pixels. Antialiasing is an option that enables the software to trick the human eye by blurring the edges of high-contrast areas. Figures 12.4 and 12.5 are examples of black text on a white background that has been resized with and without antialiasing, respectively.

R

Figure 12.4.
Aliased graphic text.

R

Figure 12.5.
Antialiased graphic text.

As you can see, the antialiased text looks slightly blurred, whereas the aliased text looks jagged (note that these two examples have been down- and up-sized to show extreme cases). Clearly, the antialiased text provides a cleaner effect.

Different graphics applications antialias differently, the quality of some being better than others. Some tools require you to convert a 256-color image to 24-bit RGB before it will antialias on resize. Others use the term "resample" to resize with antialiasing, and some tools won't offer antialiasing at all. Luckily, a shareware version of Paint Shop Pro is included on the CD-ROM, and offers antialiasing. (Isn't that thoughtful?)

If you are resizing graphics that will be used as transparent GIFs, it's important to note that the antialiasing effect will blur the edge between the object(s) and the background color. Always make the background color as close to the page background as possible before you resize with the antialias effect, so that the edges will blend. Failure to do this will result in graphics that have a strange-looking edge on them, as you can see in Figure 12.6, where the same text was antialiased against two different backgrounds before making the transparency.

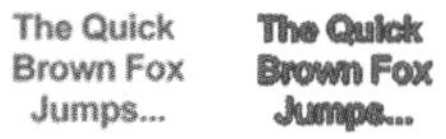

The Quick Brown Fox Jumps...　　*The Quick Brown Fox Jumps...*

Figure 12.6.
Antialiased GIF transparencies.

DITHERING

If you are taking a high-color image and reducing it to 256 colors, the computer obviously must reduce the number of colors used. This is done either by changing certain colors in the image, "blending" two or more colors to make one, or (most commonly) both. The "blending" of colors is called *dithering*.

Imagine that you were painting a house, and you wanted it to be light blue but you only had white paint and dark blue paint to work with. We'll push this analogy a little farther to say that, for some reason, you could not just mix the two paints together. You could, however, paint alternate white and blue dots on the house and, from a distance, the house would appear to be light blue. This is dithering—much like a mosaic.

Note:
Even if you're using high-color JPEGs in your Web site, many of the people viewing the site will be doing so with machines limited to 256 colors. Therefore, their graphics card and browser will do the dithering of any graphics that are delivered with more than 256 colors. Luckily, these people will be used to seeing dithered graphics.

Graphics manipulation applications will usually give you some dithering options when reducing the color depth of graphics. Exactly which options to choose will depend on both the software and the image, so we can't really give you exact settings for optimal performance. This is just another case where you'll need to play with things to get it right.

All in all, you want to limit dithering as much as possible. Dithered colors are poor in quality. They look grainy and give very poor detail. To help avoid dithering, follow the Rule of 51.

THE RULE OF 51

With most graphics applications, you can specify the RGB values of each color as an integer between 0 and 255. For example, (r=255, g=255, b=255) is pure white, and (r=0, g=0, b=0) is black. The Rule of 51 applies to this color scheme.

If each integer is divisible by the number 51 (as in [r=51, g=102, b=153]), the colors will not be dithered in most 256-color displays. This means that these colors will always be represented truly. The color palette for this is sometimes called *uniform colors*.

If you do the math, you'll see that there are 216 "51" colors. If you are creating graphics, try to use these colors whenever possible—especially in places where dithering will be obvious. If you are converting existing graphics, you can either manually change colors in the original (high-color) file, or force the graphics application to convert the image to this palette without dithering. (This almost never works satisfactorily—but wouldn't it be nice?)

DIRECTORY STRUCTURE

A good directory structure can help you keep things straight—especially in a large system. One good application of this is in the creation of graphics directories.

We usually set up two different types of graphics directories when working with large systems (on small systems, we generally keep everything in one directory when possible). The first is the root graphics directory, like `/graphics/`. This directory is used for global elements like logos, page headers, navigation graphics, and so on. Placing these types of files in a root directory assures that you can reference these graphics via a global template. Regardless of where the resulting page is placed on the system, it can always access the root directory without typing out the complete URL (`/graphics/image.gif` instead of `http://www.machine.com/graphics/image.gif`).

The second graphics directory type is a subdirectory. This is used to place page-specific graphics such as product photos. This directory is accessed just as simply as the root (`images/image.gif`—note that there is no `"/"` before the name, signifying that this is a subdirectory), but is not global. As long as the graphic is moved with the page, however, and all page directories use the same name for their graphics subdirectories, the code need not change as the page is moved. This is especially useful when archiving dated material.

GRAPHICS WITHOUT GRAPHICS

It's tempting to use graphics as the mainstay of your Web design, but as we've said, bandwidth is always an issue. Luckily, there are ways to use HTML code to give a graphical impression, without the use of huge bitmap files.

BACKGROUNDS

Backgrounds (both solid colors and image tiles) can make a gigantic difference in the appearance of a page without adding much in the way of total page size (the byte-count of the HTML files and all associated images). It's important to point out, however, that backgrounds are often poorly used on the Web, and that care must be taken in using these in your Web publishing.

The first and foremost problem with backgrounds is that all but the most subtle patterns and colors will make your text more difficult to read. All too often we've seen someone use very cool backgrounds with little apparent concern over the fact that the text on the page was impossible to read. Make sure that you don't make the same mistake.

One technique that adds impact and color without overpowering the text is to use a channel. The following example shows how this is accomplished.

First, a GIF or JPEG image tile is made, such as the small image in Figure 12.7, with a minimum width of 1,024 pixels.

Next, this image is used as a background, and the text is offset using a `<TABLE>` with a spacer GIF.

The code for this would be as follows:

```
<HTML>
<HEAD>
<TITLE>
Sample Channel
</TITLE>
</HEAD>

<BODY BACKGROUND="background.jpg">
<TABLE BORDER=0>
<TR valign=top><TD><IMG
SRC="space.gif"></TD><TD>
TEXT
</TD>
</TR>
</TABLE>

</BODY>
</HTML>
```

This results in a page like the one shown in Figure 12.8.

Figure 12.7.
A channel background.

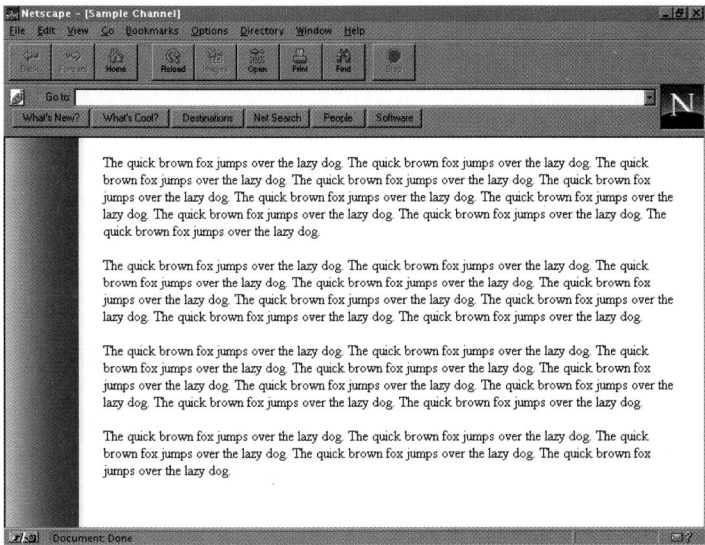

Figure 12.8.
A page with a channel background.

It's really as simple as that. For added effect, the first column of the table can include images or even text (as long as the text color contrasts that section of the background). It's important to note that you can use nonbulleted list formats (<MENU> or <DD>) to indent the type outside of the channel, but this often proves unreliable across platforms.

> **Note:**
> A similar effect can be achieved using frames. For more information on using frames, see Chapter 10, "Taking Advantage of HTML."

CASCADING STYLE SHEETS

Wouldn't it be great if you could lay out a Web page just like a print document? Imagine being able to specify indents and margins, font styles, sizes (in points, finally) and colors, leading, track widths, and even allow for overlapping text globally across all your HTML documents. Cascading style sheets provide this type of control.

Cascading style sheets are now not supported by any released browsers, though Microsoft and Netscape both say they will support the function (Microsoft Explorer 3.0 and Netscape 4.0). Since the format of these style sheets is not yet agreed upon, we are hesitant to give you any syntax for their use (and for that we apologize). We can, however, give you some idea how they will work.

The style sheets will be a separate file, which can be referred to by each Web document (meaning that one style sheet can be used for all of your pages). The style sheet will not be HTML, that much seems clear, but the prototypes we've seen look pretty simple—to the point that if you can learn HTML, the style sheets should be a breeze.

The style sheets will be able to specify how different items in your page will be displayed. For instance, you may choose to make all <H1> items a purple, Arial, 24-point typeface with a certain background—no problem! This will enable you to make Web pages look like print, without the need for using nearly as many graphics.

Of course, this will help with the bandwidth issue, in that many of the font treatments that now require specially placed images can be written as text. It will also help on the code side, in that you will not need to call out specific tags for each use of a font, style, or color. Obviously, we'll be looking forward to the time when the market share of style-sheet-capable browsers will justify their use.

CREATING THUMBNAILS

When browsing the Web, you will often see small graphics with instructions to click them to view the full-sized image. This technique is normally used to contain a large directory of graphics, or when the full-sized graphic is so large (that is, takes so long to download) that you should give the viewer a choice before downloading. This is most often used for product pictures in, say, an online catalog. By making the graphic much smaller, you can make it possible for your customers to get an idea of what the product looks like without downloading the entire graphic.

This technique is very simple. Instead of referencing your large graphic in the `<IMG>` tag, you simply reference your thumbnail and link the image to your large graphic. Here's an example.

The first step is to create the actual thumbnail itself. For this you can use just about any good graphics program—

there are even some programs that will automatically create these thumbnails for you (although we have yet to find one which produced the same level of quality as resizing manually). We would usually use Aldus Photoshop for this project, but this time we'll use Paint Shop Pro (PSP), since we know you have it on hand (it is included on the CD-ROM).

This resizing is done very simply in PSP by opening the graphic you wish to resize and choosing the Resample option in the Image drop-down menu (see Figure 12.9). The goal here is to make the image as small as possible while keeping the quality of the graphic intact. (You may need to play around with it quite a bit to achieve this.)

Figure 12.9.
Resizing the large graphic (woman.jpg) in PSP.

After this has been accomplished, save the image either as a GIF or JPEG. We generally name our thumbnails beginning with sm_, signifying a small image of the original. Our large image is named woman.jpg, so we will name our thumbnail sm_woman.jpg. (See Figure 12.10.)

Figure 12.10.
How our thumbnail
(sm_woman.jpg)
turned out.

Now all that is left is to insert this thumbnail into your page and link it to your original graphic. For our example, we will insert this code:

```
<A HREF="woman.jpg"><IMG
SRC="sm_woman.jpg" border=0>Click here
to see this image full size</A>
```

It's that simple. The viewer clicks this small image or the hypertext link, and the large image is downloaded (see Figure 12.11).

Figure 12.11.
The large image is downloaded when the viewer clicks the small image or the hyperlinked text.

QUICK & DIRTY GUIDE
Easy Image Mapping

Client-side (or embedded) image maps offer many advantages over the NCSA and CERN types of CGI image map applications and scripts. First and foremost, client-side maps need no external references outside of the page links. This means that they're easily portable not only to other servers, but for offline use as well. Secondly, the actual URL link is displayed on many browsers (rather than just the coordinates), just as it is when you place your cursor over linked text and graphics. Many viewers like to see the URL, so that they know where they're going if they choose that link.

Just as in an ISMAP MAP file, you define the areas of a client-side map with area shapes and x,y coordinates. However, rather than keeping this information on another file,

and instead of relying on a CGI application to translate the hot zones (hyperlinked areas) to links, you embed the link information within the HTML code and rely on the viewer's browser to make the calculations and translations.

So, how do you figure out the coordinates? Well, a very easy way is to use an application like MapThis! (included on your CD-ROM). MapThis! enables you to "draw" your areas over a copy of your image, and then writes those coordinates, along with the links you specify, into a MAP file (which is then ready to be used for a CGI IMAGEMAP application).

To apply this information into an HTML document as an internal (client-side) map, you simply open the MAP file in a text editor and copy the coordinates into the HTML.

First you must define the area by selecting it with your cursor, as shown in Figure 12.12.

Next, double-click on that area to assign a link, as shown in Figure 12.13.

Easy Image Mapping

Figure 12.12.
Using MapThis! to define an area.

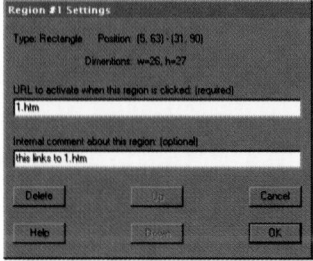

Figure 12.13.
Using MapThis! to define a link.

After you have done this for each area, you can generate a MAP or IMP file, which will contain text like this:

```
default sample.htm
# this links to 1.htm
rect 1.htm 5,64 31,94
# links to 2
rect 2.htm 42,64 68,94
# links to 3
rect 3.htm 76,64 107,94
# links to 4
rect 4.htm 114,64 144,94
# Links to 5
rect 5.htm 152,64 183,94
# links to 6
rect 6.htm 190,64 222,94
# links to 7
rect 7.htm 228,64 258,94
# links to 8
rect 8.htm 265,64 294,94
```

You now simply translate the information into the HTML client-side map and insert it into the code like this:

```
<MAP NAME="sample">
<!-- DEFAULT HREF="sample.htm" -->
<AREA SHAPE="RECT" HREF="1.htm" COORDS="5,64,31,94">
<AREA SHAPE="RECT" HREF="2.htm" COORDS="42,64,68,94">
<AREA SHAPE="RECT" HREF="3.htm" COORDS="76,64,107,94">
<AREA SHAPE="RECT" HREF="4.htm" COORDS="114,64,144,94">
<AREA SHAPE="RECT" HREF="5.htm" COORDS="152,64,183,94">
<AREA SHAPE="RECT" HREF="6.htm" COORDS="190,64,222,94">
<AREA SHAPE="RECT" HREF="7.htm" COORDS="228,64,258,94">
<AREA SHAPE="RECT" HREF="8.htm" COORDS="265,64,294,94">

</MAP>
<IMG SRC="sample.gif" BORDER=0 USEMAP="#sample">
```

Notice that the NCSA coordinates are set apart by a space (x,y x,y), whereas the HTML version requires that you replace the space with a comma (x,y,x,y). Other than that, the translation is pretty straightforward.

You can also just use a bitmap graphics tool (like Paint Shop Pro) to get your information—especially if you are just using the rectangle (`"RECT"`) shape. Simply use the application's selection tool and copy the coordinates of the selected area. This is often the fastest way to make a map.

SUMMARY

Used wisely, graphics can not only make your page more interesting to look at, but also can add power to the message you are trying to convey.

In this chapter we have covered the following topics:

◆ Communicating with graphics

◆ Graphics conversion for the Web

◆ Effective use of graphics

◆ Graphics formats

◆ Hints on color and quality

◆ Image placement

◆ Directory structure

◆ Graphics without graphics

◆ Creating thumbnails

◆ Easy image mapping

Now that you have an understanding of Web graphics, it's time to move on to a much more complicated topic: databases and searching.

Databases and Searches

Computers make it possible for you to organize huge amounts of data and recall that data quickly. When information is contained within databases, you can easily search, update, change, generate special-ized reports, and in general push, prod, or pull informa-tion from the system in any way you desire.

When you give WWW viewers the ability to search your databases, you are giving them a wealth of information.

CHAPTER
thirteen

You can easily separate the issue of databases and the Web into two distinct categories: from your database and onto the Web (presenting information contained within a database on the Web, a very complex project) and from the Web and onto your database (importing data from forms into a database, which is not so complex).

FROM YOUR DATABASE AND ONTO THE WEB

The use of databases with the Web is a new and complex issue; things seem to be changing on a daily basis in terms of the products available and the uses for those products.

A few uses for databases on the Web:

◆ Using the Internet for sales leads via an HTML form that is automatically entered into a "sales leads" database

◆ Creating customized Web sites (often called dynamic Web sites) that create HTML pages based on the viewers' specifications

◆ Providing "shopping cart" systems (online "stores" that enable the users to place items they wish to purchase in a virtual shopping cart until they are ready to "check out")

◆ Putting your up-to-date product information online

PUTTING YOUR PRODUCT INFORMATION ONLINE

When putting your product information online, you need to consider two points. First, your customers should be able to easily browse through or search for a product (and to have the product information up-to-date); and second, they need to be able to order that product online simply. (Payment issues are discussed in Chapter 16, "Taking Payment Online.")

The most challenging part will be keeping your information up-to-date. You could easily put your catalog online in HTML format within an easy-to-navigate Web site and accomplish this if you have a small inventory (see "Keeping It Simple," later in this chapter), but if you provide tons of different products or if your product information (such as pricing) changes often, keeping all this information up-to-date can soon turn into a time-consuming job. The solution? Providing this information in a database! We hope you are already using a database for keeping this information up-to-date, and if so, the solution is simply (or not so simply) a matter of connecting that database to the Web. This keeps the information all in one place, while allowing different ways to access and view it.

So, how do you hook up your database to the Web? Well, you'll need a program that queries the database and returns an HTML-formatted result. This is called a dynamic site. It offers ease of maintenance and administration for a large database system, and even enables dynamic, data-driven Web sites that use HTML documents which are generated on the fly (from information stored in databases and provided by users). Page content can be instantly customized based on user requests.

All this requires either a lot of programming skill or time learning a new commercial program designed for this purpose. It also requires that your information be in a certain database format or that you transpose all your product information into an acceptable format (what that acceptable format is depends on the program used to access it). This also requires certain things from your server that you may or may not have available. *In most cases, you will need your own server in order to do this.*

The programming involved in setting up and connecting a database to the Web is far too complex a subject to describe here, but we would like to give you a quick overview of some of the commercially available products for this purpose:

♦ Cold Fusion Professional 1.5

♦ Sapphire/Web 2.0

♦ NetDynamics 1.0 beta

COLD FUSION PROFESSIONAL 1.5

This is a self-contained Web database tool; about the only other things you need to put your database on the Web are your database and server. It can be used to create a wide variety of applications that integrate relational databases with the Web on the Internet (or on intranets).

Source: Allaire Corp. (`http://www.allaire.com/`); free demo available.

Databases supported:

♦ Any ODBC-compliant database

♦ Microsoft SQL Server

♦ Borland dBase III and dBase IV

♦ Microsoft Access 1.0, 2.0, and 7.0

♦ Informix with the vendor-supplied ODBC-UNIX drivers

♦ Microsoft FoxPro 2.0, 2.5, and 2.6

♦ Microsoft Excel 3.0, 4.0, and 5.0

♦ Sybase with the vendor-supplied ODBC-UNIX drivers

♦ Borland Paradox 3.*x* and 4.*x*

♦ Watcom SQL 4.0

♦ Oracle 7.0 with the vendor-supplied ODBC-UNIX drivers

♦ Plain text files

Platforms supported:

♦ Windows NT 3.51

♦ Windows 95

System requirements:

♦ 80386 or higher microprocessor; Pentium recommended

♦ 10MB free hard disk space

♦ 24MB RAM for Windows NT or 16MB RAM for Windows 95 (32MB recommended)

♦ TCP/IP networking software installed and running

♦ A Windows NT- or Windows 95-compatible World Wide Web server.

Web servers supported:

♦ O'Reilly Web site

♦ Netscape HTTPD

♦ Microsoft Internet server

♦ Process purveyor

♦ EMWAC HTTPS

♦ Internet factory system

♦ Spry Web server

♦ CSM Alibaba

If you are using one of these products, you can be assured that your server is fully supported. If, however, you are using another product, your server may still be supported. Your best bet is to check the support area of the Allaire Web site for information on your particular server.

Overview

Cold Fusion is a low-cost (under $500) Windows-based program that enables you to edit and enter information, create and read cookies, perform conditional queries, dynamically send mail, create thread-based discussion groups, create order forms, and even create "shopping cart" systems. Cold Fusion uses a template language called DBML (Database Markup Language) to create queries on your database and structure the results, so no CGI or C++ coding is required, and getting your database on the Web is fairly easy. (DBML tags are similar to HTML tags, which makes them easy to use and understand.)

With Cold Fusion, developers can build applications by combining standard HTML with high-level database commands stored in templates (which is theoretically faster and more flexible than first generation, code-intensive techniques). Using Cold Fusion, developers can create dynamic Web sites and full-scale Web applications.

The basic functions of Cold Fusion are

◆ To submit database queries that can then be used to dynamically generate Web pages. For example, you can use database query results to create menus (for product or other information), populate select boxes, and produce document lists.

◆ To intermix the results of queries with HTML tags and text for complete control over how data is displayed and formatted.

◆ To track users and customize their view of Web pages by using information about their browser, location, or other preferences.

◆ To insert and update records in database tables with HTML forms.

◆ To present the results of queries in attractively formatted tables.

◆ To send e-mail messages (SMTP) that use address and message content from database queries.

A Cold Fusion Web application uses templates instead of static HTML documents. A template is a text file that contains both HTML and Cold Fusion's Database Markup Language (DBML). Rather than being sent directly to the user's browser, templates are first processed by Cold Fusion, which generates a standard HTML page that is then sent to the viewer's browser. DBML contains a set of commands that tell Cold Fusion how to interact with the databases, validate form submissions, and process database output. (See Figure 13.1.)

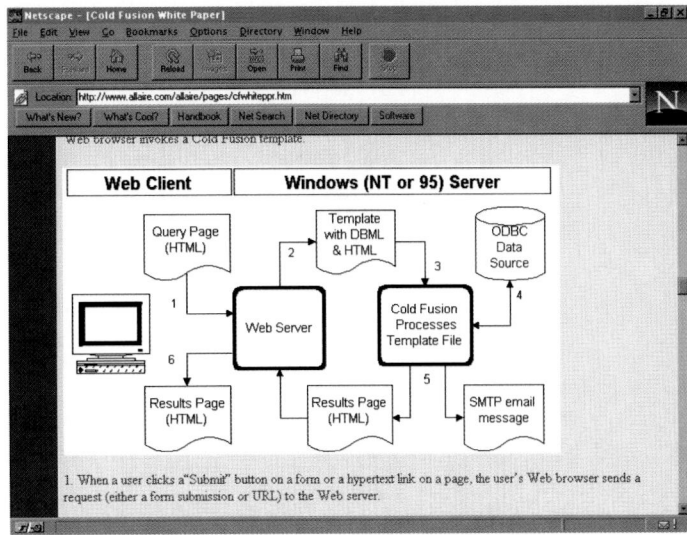

Figure 13.1.
How Cold Fusion works when a Web browser invokes a Cold Fusion template, straight from the horse's mouth.

Here's how it works:

1. The viewer clicks the Submit button on a form or a hypertext link on a page; the viewer's Web browser then sends a request to the Web server.

2. The server opens a Cold Fusion process, passing it the data submitted by the browser and pointing it to the appropriate template file.

3. Cold Fusion then reads the data from the client, in turn processing DBML commands used in the template, including the type of request to send to the database and the format that should be used to present information to the results page.

4. Using ODBC, Cold Fusion interacts with the database.

5. A dynamically generated HTML page, containing the results of the form submission or query, is returned by Cold Fusion to the Web server. (Cold Fusion can also dynamically generate e-mail messages containing the results of the query.)

6. The Web server sends the generated HTML page to the viewer's browser.

This system is very flexible because of the wide range of database interaction and data handling options available through DBML. Though Cold Fusion isn't the fastest program on the market, and is limited in the functions that are available, it is worthy of consideration.

Overall, Cold Fusion is simple to use, inexpensive (for a commercial product such as this), includes pretty good documentation, eliminates the need to learn complex CGI programming in order to provide crucial features (for example, customizing Web pages, tracking users, integrating databases), and is flexible enough to be used by small companies to create good live database applications. If you have to put your live database on the Web, but aren't ready to commit to a product that requires strong programming skills—or a large monetary investment—Cold Fusion could be just the ticket.

Sapphire/Web 2.0

This visual application builder is designed specifically for creating applications running on the Web (and for internal webs). Sapphire/Web has a "visual programming paradigm" that reportedly reduces the coding effort normally associated with developing applications.

Source: Bluestone Inc. (`http://www.bluestone.com`); free demo available.

Databases supported:

- Any ODBC-compliant database
- Oracle
- Sybase
- Informix
- Microsoft SQL Server

Platforms supported:

- Windows 95
- Windows NT
- HP
- Sun
- SGI
- IBM
- DECAlpha

Additional requirements: Microsoft Visual C++ 4.0 on the NT version; a C or C++ compiler on the UNIX version.

Web servers supported:

- NCSA
- Netscape
- Microsoft
- Open Market
- Any HTTP, SHTTP, or SSL server

Overview

This is a UNIX/Windows NT visual action builder enabling developers to create database applications for the Web. Sapphire/Web comes with documentation and uses CGI to interface with databases. Creating an application takes six steps:

1. Create your HTML forms (for data input and request) and HTML templates (that will hold data returned to the end-user from your application). These can be created in any HTML authoring tool.

2. Browse your application objects from Sapphire/Web. These can be

   - Database stored procedures
   - Dynamic SQL
   - Files
   - Executables
   - Functions
   - OLE

3. Select the appropriate object, and Sapphire/Web will bring up an Object Bind Editor with appropriate arguments, results, and special editors.

4. Drag and drop from your HTML documents and components onto the Object Bind Editor. This "binds" HTML elements such as a text input field or an option menu to arguments and results returning from your object to other HTML elements such as an ordered list or table. Sapphire/Web automatically populates the returned data into your HTML templates.

5. Add conditional processing code, or modify the default methods of populating data.

6. Generate code in pure C or C++. This generates a CGI program for immediate use. That's all there is to it! You can also test and load the CGI program in the specified HTTP server's CGI directory using Sapphire/Web.

Sapphire/Web is a versatile program. They say you can create anything with it that you can make with Cold Fusion and a lot more, and the program you end up with will purportedly be faster and more stable. Another bonus is that it supports the use of framed pages. Of course you'll pay for these advantages, not only monetarily, but with time (and possibly frustration). Although they say it is *possible* to use Sapphire/Web without being an expert C++ programmer, the potential of the product cannot be tapped without previous programming and database experience.

NetDynamics 1.0 Beta

The manufacturer says that NetDynamics integrates visual development, WAN-scalable database access, and a high-performance Java application server into a robust architecture for swift delivery of commercial grade Web/database applications.

Source: Spider Technologies, Inc. (http://www.w3spider.com); free demo available.

Databases supported:

- Any ODBC-compliant database
- Informix 6.0 +
- Oracle 7
- Sybase 10

Platforms supported:

- Microsoft Windows 95
- Windows NT

◆ UNIX application servers:

SGI Irix 5.3

Sun Solaris 2.3 +

HP-UX 9.05+

Other requirements: The current Sun Java Development Kit.

Web servers supported:

◆ Netscape NSAPI

◆ Microsoft ISAPI

◆ Any CGI-compliant Web server

Overview

NetDynamics provides an environment for utilizing Java in business applications. Development is promoted through the use of graphical wizards and palettes that automatically generate Java code, hiding the complexity of building Web/database applications and reducing the effort and cost of deployment.

It offers scalability within a single system or over multiple machines, and incorporates security features (like secure session ID, navigation controls, and access privileges) that enable it to interoperate with industry-standard Web and database security mechanisms. It is claimed to be an "open" solution in that it is supported by any Web server, forms-capable Web browser, HTML editor, and all major database systems and ODBC-compliant databases on both UNIX and PC platforms.

Many very useful sample applications are included with NetDynamics, including a shopping-cart project, a simple table-editing project, a three-tier project, and others.

The NetDynamics Studio is where most of the real work is done. It's a GUI that displays your current project in a nifty graphical hierarchy. It features tools, menus, palettes, and editors with which you create new items or make changes to items that already exist. The "palette" (which if you are accustomed to using Visual Basic or another graphical development tool you will find very easy to use) contains various tools such as Insert HREF, Insert Data Field, Insert Page, Insert Button, or Insert Security Object.

Wizards provided are a Security Wizard, a Page Template Wizard, a Data Object Wizard, and a Data Source Wizard. These allow for speedy development of applications by guiding you swiftly through the development process without burying you in details. After using the wizards to create your project, you compile the project and test it in your browser. If you wish to make any additional changes, you can use the Palette and Inspector and recompile.

Although NetDynamics doesn't require you to be a Java expert in order to create applications, making changes in the source code is a lot easier if you have some Java expertise, or C++ experience at the very least. NetDynamics should be easy to use (for someone with some programming knowledge), highly configurable, and should work with practically any database. The Java application server is said to speed up the use of SQL processes by as much as 10 percent over normal C++ CGI code. It's fast and very flexible, and uses Java—which some say is the future of Web application development.

KEEPING IT SIMPLE

The simplest way (provided you don't need to update your information very often) to provide your product information online is without the use of a database. Using just basic navigational aids and a good hierarchical web structure, you can create an easy-to-use product information site (see Figure 13.2).

If your product line is large, it would be a very good idea to provide an internal search engine within this site. The most important thing to remember when organizing a site such as this is the same as with any site: View your site as your viewers do. Special attention should be paid to separating your products into distinct areas. (For example, for a clothing manufacturer there would be separate areas for men's clothing, women's clothing, children's clothing, pants, shirts, and so on.)

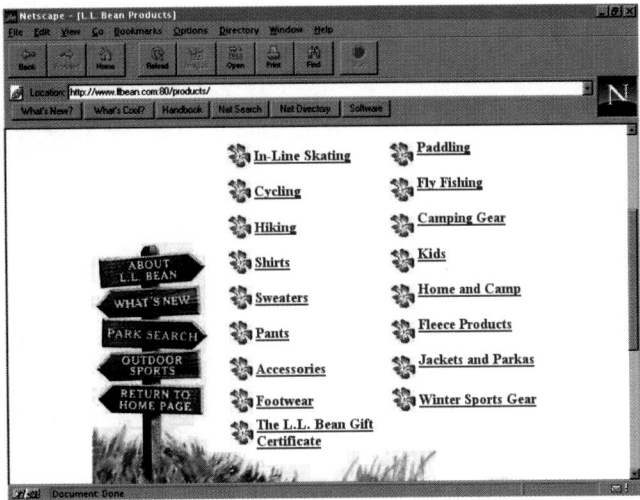

Figure 13.2.
L.L. Bean's well-organized (albeit slow to download) catalog site.

FROM THE WEB AND ONTO YOUR DATABASE— USING THE INTERNET FOR SALES LEADS

Using an HTML form and a CGI script, you can easily create a sales lead database on the Web. For this project we will modify the form from the last chapter to include spaces for the viewer's address. We will also have to modify a line of the CGI script (`formmail.pl`) to send us our e-mail in a different format (more easily read by a database).

The goal of this project is to provide a form for viewers to request a free informational brochure. After the viewers fill out the feedback form and click the Submit button, we want an HTML page to load, letting the viewers know we've received their form and thanking them for their time. In addition, we want our text brochure to be e-mailed to them automatically. We also want the information they provided to be sent to our e-mail box in a manner readable by the database (for instance, Microsoft Access).

So, there are four separate files we must create in developing this form system: the

HTML form itself (which will be discussed in detail in Chapter 14, "Mail Delivery Systems"); the CGI script with which to decode it (`formmail.pl`, as discussed in Chapter 11, "Integrating HTML with CGI," with a small modification); the "brochure" to be mailed to them (which is any e-mailable file); and the HTML redirect page (which is also discussed in Chapter 11).

Note:

The modification for the CGI script is very easy; simply change the code

```
[print MAIL "$name: $value\n"]
```

to read

```
[print MAIL "$name,$value,"]
```

This is saying to separate the fields by commas (comma-delimited text is easily read by most databases). That's it!

And here's how it works: The viewer clicks on the feedback link from the home page and arrives at our HTML form. They fill out the form (see Figure 13.3) and click the Send The Form button.

The form is then submitted and the viewer jumps to the thank you page. (See Figure 11.6 in Chapter 11.) At the same time, the informational brochure we promised is forwarded to the viewer's e-mail box.

Our form contents then arrive in our e-mail box, where we can save it as text (see Figure 13.4).

Entering this information in a database is truly simple, as most database applications allow simple importation of comma-delimited text. If your own database prefers a different layout for text input, you can make the adjustment in your CGI.

If you are running your own server, you can automate the input (which is obviously preferred) in several ways. The simplest way is to have dynamic input for your database, which will require a special CGI script/application. This configuration will depend on your database and server, and instructions may be included with your software. The second way to import directly is to give your database an e-mail box and have it import information from that.

Figure 13.3.
How a viewer fills out this form example.

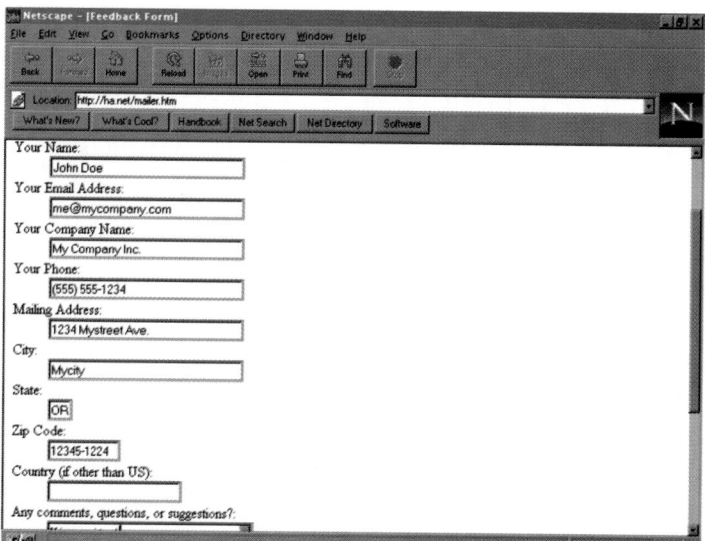

Figure 13.4.
How the form contents look when we get them via e-mail and save them as text.

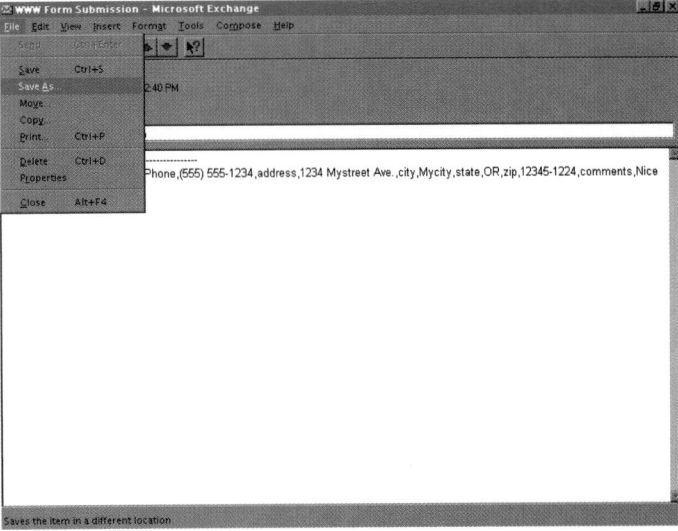

Figure 13.5.
Excite for Web Servers.

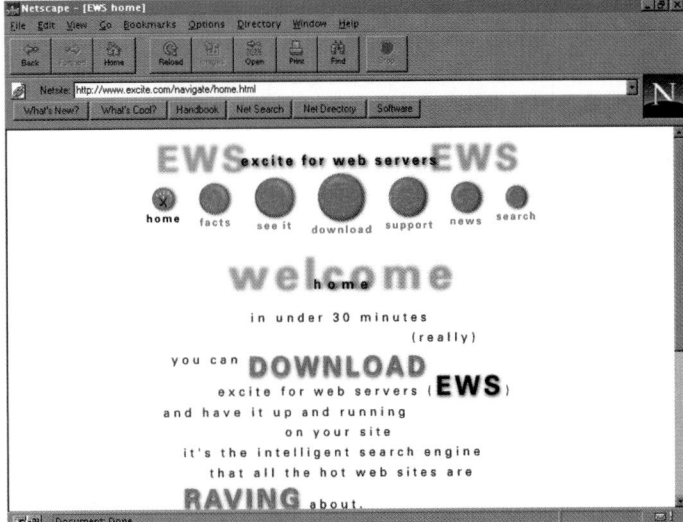

CAN CUSTOMERS FIND WHAT THEY ARE LOOKING FOR QUICKLY?

On a small site with good navigational aids and narrowly defined subject areas, customers should have no trouble finding what they are looking for. However, after a site grows more complex, a good internal search engine may be necessary to aid in the site's user friendliness. (After all, no matter how good your widgets are, they won't sell if no one can find them, right?)

A Cool Free Product: Excite for Web Servers

If you are running your site off your own server, there are some commercial "ready-made" products available for performing searches of your site, the most popular being Excite for Web Servers (Refer to Figure.13.5).

Excite for Web Servers (EWS) is a new generation of Web navigation software. It gives your Web site the same search capabilities used by the Excite service (as well as the sites hosted by Netscape, Sun, Info World Electric, HotWired, Chevron, United Airlines, and others).

EWS supports the following platforms:

- ◆ SunOS
- ◆ Solaris
- ◆ SGI Irix
- ◆ HP-UX
- ◆ IBM AIX
- ◆ BSDI
- ◆ Windows NT

To run the software, you need a minimum of 32MB of RAM and enough disk space for the following requirements:

- ◆ 5MB for the EWS search engine
- ◆ Sufficient disk space for your Web site document collection
- ◆ Additional disk space equal to approximately 40 percent of the size of your document collection for the indexing process

ETW uses the following searchable document formats:

- ◆ HTML
- ◆ ASCII

EWS's underlying concept-based architecture was developed specifically for the Internet by Excite. This architecture supports not only searching (which assumes the viewer knows exactly what they're looking for), but browsing and exploration as well. In other words, with Excite for Web Servers, viewers don't need to know the right keywords, they can simply describe what they're looking for in their own words.

EWS quickly returns a list of documents ranked by confidence (of keyword match), and is unique in its capability to let users sort the search results list by subject. This helps them understand what's on your site and how it's organized. Another unique feature is that when a viewer finds a document he or she likes, EWS's query-by-example (with a simple click) can hunt down more just like it. An additional feature is the EWS Notifier, which automatically updates the Excite search service's master index with information on your site when you add content.

Although Excite for Web Servers is free, the company currently sells maintenance agreements (which include upgrades, as well as e-mail and phone support) for $995 per year per installation. EWS contains all the functionality you need to add searching to your site—which means you do not need to purchase other products, such as a database, to use it.

Excite claims you can have EWS up and running in just 30 minutes since it writes all the CGI scripts and HTML pages for you (yeah, no programming!). You simply fill out a few forms and point EWS to your Web documents, and it creates a custom, concept-based index of the contents of your site in minutes.

Here is how the company says the installation process works, and how it can be done in under 30 minutes (times are approximate):

Step 1: Download your copy of Excite for Web Servers. (3 minutes 30 seconds)

The time varies, depending on your network connection.
You can download Excite for Web Servers free from
`http://www.excite.com/navigate/download.cgi`.

Step 2: Register EWS with Architext. (4 minutes)

Once you've agreed to the license terms, you will need to fill out their registration form.

Step 3: Configure your collection of documents. (4 minutes)

You will need to enter a name for the collection, and tell EWS which files you want included.

Step 4: Index your document collection. (3 minutes 30 seconds)

The exact amount of time needed depends on the size of your collection.

EWS is kind enough to send you an e-mail when it's done; 300MB can be indexed by EWS in about an hour on a single processor workstation.

Step 5: Add your search page to your site. (2 minutes)

You simply define how you want your search page to look by filling out a form, and after it's defined, EWS will create the search page, along with all the necessary CGI scripts. Link the search page to your site, and you're up and running!

That's all you need to do to make your site more searchable with Excite for Web Servers. It's a strong product and, considering the price, we recommend that you at least check it out.

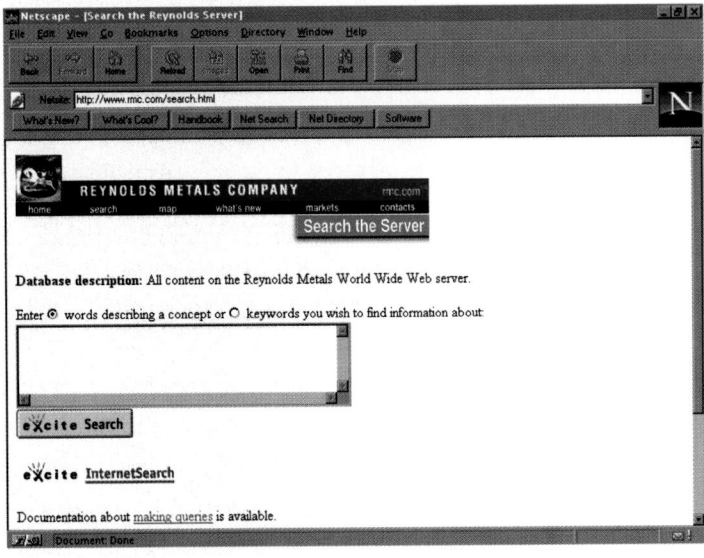

Figure 13.6.
Excite for Web Servers in action at the Reynolds Metals Company site.

QUICK & DIRTY GUIDE
Using WebMania for Sales Leads

In Chapter 11 we use WebMania to produce an HTML form. After reading that section, you were most likely left with the question: "OK, so how do I read the submitted form, and how can I import that information to a database?" Well, that's what we explain in this Quick & Dirty Guide.

After your viewer submits the WebMania form, an e-mail arrives. Now, there are a couple of ways you can get that information into WebMania (to enable you to read it). One way is to directly import it, which means you can check your e-mail from within WebMania—you can find out how to do this by reading the Importing (direct) subject in WebMania's help system. (We did not use this method, however, since this e-mail address gets standard e-mail as well.) The other (more indirect) way of retrieving the form information is by saving the e-mail (after receiving it) as text. After you have saved the e-mail as text, it is very simple to import this data. Here's how:

1. Open WebMania.

2. In the File drop-down menu, click Response | Import....

3. Find your text file and double-click on it; it will then appear in the import list.

4. Click the OK button.

5. To view the response, click Response | View... and select your form.

6. You can then browse through the information.

7. To export this information to an Access database, in the File menu choose Response | Export....

8. Select the form to export and click OK (note the name WebMania assigns to this Access file).

9. Open the Access file to view results and make any formatting changes necessary (see Figure 13.7).

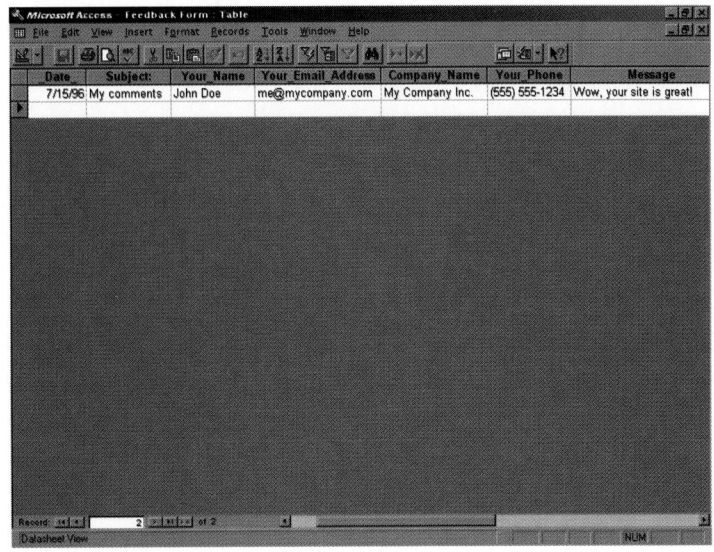

Figure 13.7.
How a viewer submits a WebMania form.

SUMMARY

In this chapter we have discussed an overview of databases and their use with Web sites. We have also presented brief overviews of several commercial products available for linking your server to a database.

There is ample information on this subject available on the Net, and you should research the subject carefully before investing in a single product. The purpose of this chapter is to provide an overview only, and not to recommend any specific product over another.

The next chapter deals with e-mail delivery systems and the use of e-mail in communication.

Mail Delivery Systems

Electronic mail (e-mail)—a system whereby a computer user can exchange messages and files with other computer users (or groups of users) via a communications network—is one of the most popular uses of the Internet. This facet of the Net was one of the first applied uses and continues to be a powerful communications tool.

USING E-MAIL TO YOUR ADVANTAGE

By collecting viewers' names and e-mail addresses (in addition to other information) at your site, you can develop an e-mail mailing list. You can also develop this list by requesting this information on service calls, product registration postcards, sales calls, via online forms, and so on. Basically, think of an e-mail address the same way you do a phone number—as necessary information.

Why would you want to do this? To save money and trees (among other things). How do you do that? By converting much of your existing direct mail and print campaigns to an e-mail campaign. There are many advantages to using e-mail over print, some of which are

◆ Saving on print, bindery, postage, fulfillment, and other costs

◆ Saving trees ☺

◆ Nearly instant delivery (as opposed to that of the postal service, which has become known as "snail mail")

◆ The ability to update information quickly and with minimal cost

DEVELOPING MAILING LISTS

So the first step in developing your own e-mail list is to get the viewer to fill out an online form. You could do this by simply asking viewers to fill out your online form to be added to your mailing list. But if you want to develop a large list, you need to entice the viewers a bit more. They may need some "What's in it for me?" incentive. Some options that work are

◆ Offering free information not available on your site

◆ Offering to answer questions (and really answering them)

◆ Having some kind of contest or free offer as Disney has done in Figure 14.1

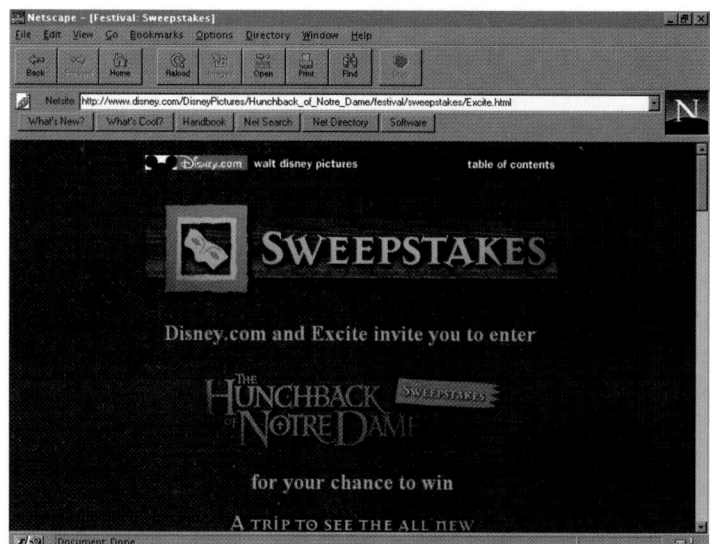

Figure 14.1.
The viewer needs a "What's in it for me?" incentive.

So, are you ready? Let's do it!

The goal of this project is to provide a form to collect information for use in our mailing list. For taking the time to do this, we will reward viewers with free information. After the viewers fill out the online form and click the Submit button, we want an HTML page to load, letting them know we received their form and thanking them for their time. In addition, we want our information to be e-mailed to them automatically. We also want the information they provide to be sent to our own e-mail box.

There are four separate files we must create for this form system:

- ◆ The HTML form itself
- ◆ The CGI script with which to decode it
- ◆ The text information to be mailed to the viewer
- ◆ The HTML redirect page

The code for the HTML form is shown in Listing 14.1.

Listing 14.1. The code for our HTML form.

```
<!DOCTYPE HTML PUBLIC "-//IETF//DTD HTML 3.0//EN" "html.dtd">
<HTML>
<HEAD>
<TITLE>Feedback Form</TITLE>
<!-- Author:  Kim and Brad Hampton -->
</HEAD>

<BGCOLOR="FFFFFF" TEXT="000000" LINK="425AFF" VLINK="0018C4" ALINK="FFFFFF">


<H1>Please fill out this form to receive your free information</H1>
<P>
<FORM ACTION="/cgi-bin/formmail.pl" METHOD=POST>
<INPUT TYPE="hidden" name="recipient" value="hampton@ha.net">
<INPUT TYPE="hidden" NAME="subject" VALUE="Free Information">
<INPUT TYPE="hidden" NAME="redirect" VALUE="http://www.ha.net/thanks.htm">
<INPUT TYPE="hidden" NAME="replyfile" VALUE="info.txt">


<DT>Your Name:
    <DD><input type=text name="realname" size=30>
<DT>Your E-mail Address:
    <DD><input type=text name="e-mail" size=30>
<DT>Your Company Name:
    <DD><input type=text name="Company" size=30>
<DT>Your Phone:
    <DD><input type=text name="Phone" size=30>
<DT>Mailing Address:
    <DD><INPUT TYPE="text" NAME="address" size=30>
<DT>City:
    <DD><INPUT TYPE="text" NAME="city" size=30>
<DT>State:
    <DD><INPUT TYPE="text" NAME="state" size=2>
<DT>Zip Code:
    <DD><INPUT TYPE="text" NAME="zip" size=10>
<DT>Country (if other than US):
    <DD><INPUT TYPE="text" NAME="country" size=20>
<DT>Any comments, questions, or suggestions?:
    <DD><TEXTAREA name="comments" cols=27 rows=4></TEXTAREA>
<P>
</DL></I>
```

continues

Listing 14.1. continued

```
<DT><DD><input type=submit value="Send This Form">
<input type=reset value="Start Over">
<P>
</FORM>

<HR>

Please note: Although it is most unlikely that you will experience any problems
responding to this form, certain non-standard browsers will not respond prop-
erly. If you experience any difficulties, (or if you are not using a forms-
capable browser) you may e-mail your response to this form to: <a
href="mailto:hampton@ha.net">hampton@ha.net</A>.
</BODY>
</HTML>
```

All of this code should look pretty familiar (if it doesn't, refer to Chapter 11, "Integrating HTML with CGI"). There are just a couple new commands.

The first is

```
<INPUT TYPE="hidden" NAME="subject" VALUE="Free Information">
```

This just means that the subject of the e-mail sent to us will read "Free Information."

The next,

```
<INPUT TYPE="hidden" NAME="replyfile" VALUE="info.txt">
```

is saying to send the file `"info.txt"` to the viewer as a reply to this form.

Now we need the CGI script that will decode this form. We'll again use `formmail.pl`, the same script discussed in Chapter 11 (included on your CD-ROM).

Next, we need the information that will be mailed to the viewer. Since our information is pretty small, we will make this an attached TXT file. If our file were large, we might need to offer the information in a different format (or several different formats), since files will often be divided (or even bounced) by an e-mail program or server when they are too large.

The HTML redirect page is just a simple HTML page thanking the viewer for filling out the form (refer to Chapter 11 to see the code for this page).

And here's how it works: The viewer clicks on the feedback link from the home page and arrives at our HTML form. They fill out the form (see Figure 14.2) and click the Send The Form button.

Figure 14.2.
How a viewer fills
out this form
example.

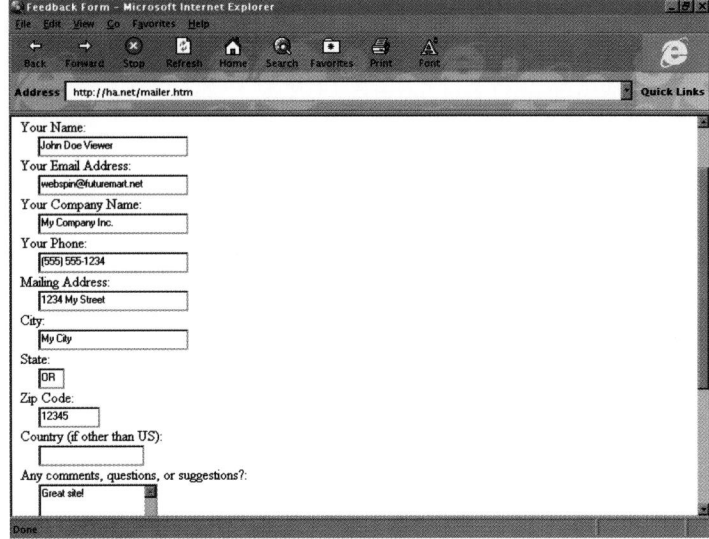

The form is submitted, and the viewer jumps to the thank you page. (See Figure 11.6 in Chapter 11.) At the same time, the informational text file we promised is forwarded to the viewer's e-mail box.

By now the form contents have arrived in our e-mail box. We can at this point manually cut and paste the information into a database (or some kind of text file), or we could import these responses directly into a database for use as sales leads. (For information on how to do this, see Chapter 13, "Databases and Searches.")

AUTORESPONDERS

In our form example we set up the system to automatically send the viewer a specific e-mail. This function can also be achieved by an autoresponder (often referred to as a mailbot). An autoresponder is a software program that distributes files or information in response to requests sent via e-mail.

AUTORESPONDER SERVICES

There are many ISP and specialized companies that provide autoresponder services (such as in Figure 14.3)—your ISP may be one of them. These services are usually inexpensive and will save you lots of time. A list of some of these companies is provided at http://www.yahoo.com/Business_and_Economy/Companies/Computers/Software/Communications_and_Networking/Electronic_Mail/Autoresponders/.

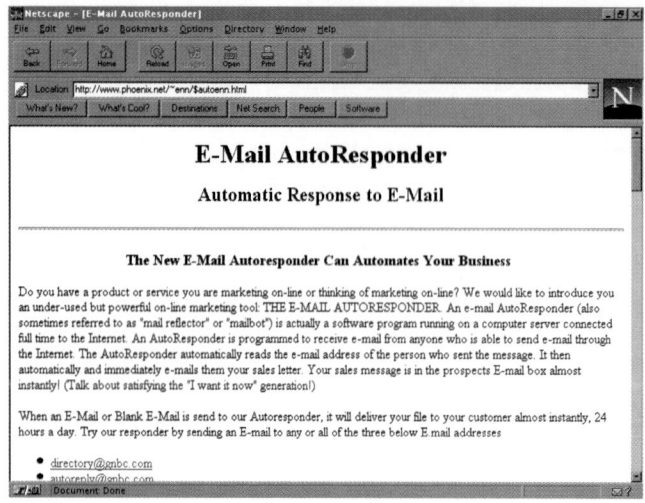

Figure 14.3.
An autoresponder service.

AVOIDING AUTORESPONDERS

Now, if you're thinking "All this autoresponding sounds neat, but I don't think I need it," you're probably right. If you only receive a small amount of e-mail requesting information, you could easily just send the information manually. This not only simplifies things (for a limited amount of requests), but it also forces you to read through your responses more thoroughly and quickly, which your viewers will appreciate, and allows you to add a personal touch.

It's this simple:

1. A viewer sends you a request for information via e-mail (it's a good idea to ask that they put the file or information they are requesting in the subject line), or through your online form.

2. You view the information and save it somewhere.

3. You find the file they requested.

4. You reply to the sender with your information in the body of the e-mail, or as an attached file.

Now you have all those e-mail addresses! What you do with them is up to you, but we suggest setting up a mass mailing. Some simple ways to do this are discussed in the next section.

EFFECTIVE MASS E-MAILING

You are probably familiar with mass mailing. This is when you send the same information to an entire list of people. Mass e-mailing does the same thing, but does so with the speed and efficiency of e-mail. One example of the advantage mass e-mail has over direct mail is in the case of a catalog.

Suppose you had a list of, oh, let's say widget users. Traditionally, you might send a business reply card to these people, offering them a free catalog (as sending each person a catalog right off would be too expensive). You incur the printing, mailing, and return mail costs for the cards, and then must print and ship the catalog to those that request it.

Now, if you do this all electronically, you can simply send an e-mail to each person on your list, giving them the URL of your new catalog site. You can probably imagine the cost savings.

> **Note:**
> Just as with regular mail, recipients are annoyed at having to sift through e-mail that is of no use to them. The first rule of e-mail mass mailing is *only send out useful information.* (Just because you have the e-mail addresses of people who bought your widgets, don't send them information on llama rearing—they'll start to delete e-mail from you without even reading it.)

How do you send a mass e-mailing? There are at least two options: a listserver and an ordinary e-mail program (Eudora, MS Mail, and so on). The option you choose depends mostly upon the size of your list. If you have a small distribution list, you can avoid using a listserver and can skip to the Quick & Dirty Guide in this chapter, "Cheapskate Mail Delivery." If your list is large, however, a listserver is your best bet.

The three main practical differences between these approaches are as follows:

1. When an e-mail program sends out a mass e-mailing, it sends to each e-mail address separately. If your list is large, or the file you are sending is large, this could mean the program spends hours online sending the mailing—although you can usually automate the process so that you can begin the process before you leave the office for the night, and it automatically disconnects when it's finished.

2. When an e-mail arrives that has been sent as a mass mailing from a plain old e-mail program, the To: line displays the addresses of everyone the mailing was sent to. However, when a mass e-mailing is sent from a listserver, the To: line only displays the individual's address.

3. Some listservers are set up so that a reply to the message will go back to the listserver. In some cases, this may mean that each person on your list will receive the response. Obviously, you'll want to make sure this isn't the case.

LISTSERV

Listserv is an automated mailing list distribution system originally designed for the BITNET/EARN network. Listserv sends a list of e-mail addresses to something called a *mail exploder* (part of an electronic mail delivery system that enables the delivery of a message to a list of addresses). The mail exploder works like this: You send messages to a single address, and the mail exploder takes care of delivering the message to each of the individual mailboxes in the list you've provided.

If you are interested in using a listserver, your first stop should be at your virtual host (if you have one). Many hosts offer use of their listserver, and provide this service free of charge or for a small additional fee. If you have no such luck, there are many companies, like the one shown in Figure 14.4, that offer this service for a fee—a couple that we have found are Internet Tools, Inc. (`http://www.internet-tools.com/it_html/mail_list.html`) and L-Soft International, Inc. (`http://www.lsoft.com/ease-head.html`).

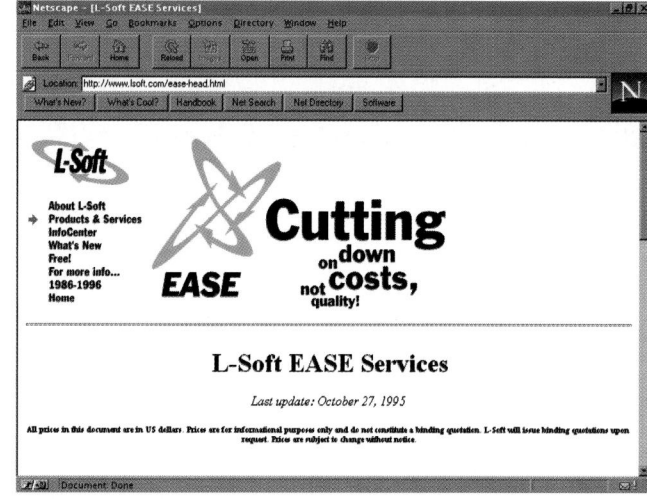

Figure 14.4.
A listserv service.

Setting up a mass mailing using a listserver can also be a do-it-yourself project, and there is already good information available at `http://www.earn.net/lug/notice.html`.

QUICK & DIRTY GUIDE
Cheapskate Mail Delivery

One option for sending out a mass e-mailing is to use the same e-mail program you always use. Many e-mail programs have this capability, two of the more popular being Eudora Light and Microsoft Exchange. This is a simple option if your mailing list is short.

So let's get started. The goal for this project is to send an e-mail to a list of 20 recipients, informing them that we are having a sale on an item for which they have previously requested information (widgets). First, you must choose the e-mail program you would like to use for this project. Read on if you plan to use Eudora Light; skip ahead to "Using MS Exchange for Mass E-Mailing" if you plan to use Microsoft Exchange.

Using Eudora Light for Mass E-Mailing

Eudora Light (freeware) is available at Eudora's home site (http://www.eudora.com) as well as various shareware software sites. Eudora also makes an advanced version called Eudora Pro, which is not freeware. For this project we employ Eudora Light because it is so widely used. Its home page is shown in Figure 14.5.

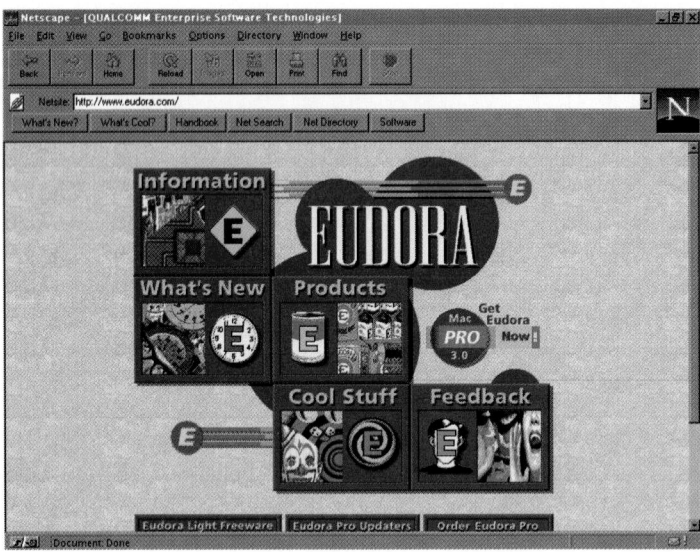

Figure 14.5.
The Eudora home site.

1. Open Eudora Light.

2. Hit Ctrl+L to open the Nicknames dialog box.

3. Click the New button to open the New Nickname dialog box.

4. Type the name of the mailing group you wish to create. (In our example we name this "widget" to signify that the mail group consists of viewers who have previously requested information on widgets—but you probably guessed that.) Select "Put it on the recipient list," and click OK.

5. Your nickname will appear in the Nickname box, and your cursor will appear in the Address(es) box.

6. Enter a recipient's real name (in quotes), and that person's e-mail address in brackets, like this: `"John Doe" <jdoe@mydomain.com>`. Repeat until all your addresses are entered (see Figure 14.6).

Figure 14.6.
The Nickname
dialog box.

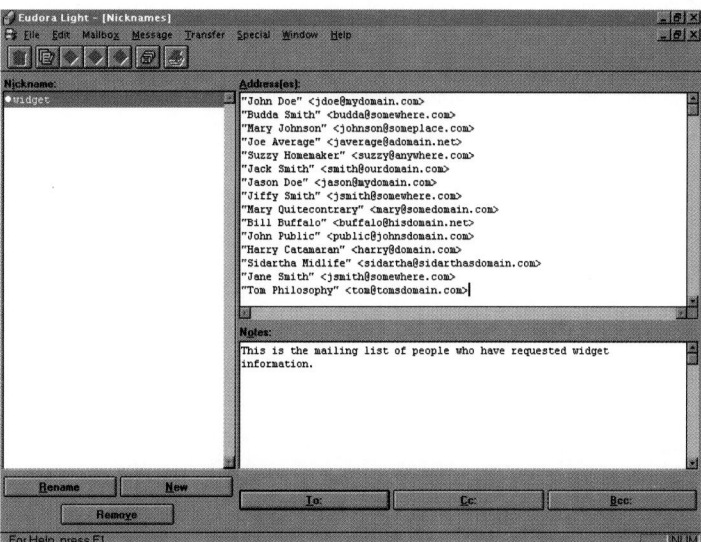

7. Once you have entered all your addresses, click To:, which will open a new message box addressed to your mailing list.

8. Type the subject of your message; in our example it's "sale on widgets."

9. If you want to attach a file to the e-mail, you can do this by pressing Ctrl+H and selecting the file to attach.

10. Type your e-mail message (see Figure 14.7).

Q&D Using Eudora Light for Mass E-Mailing

Figure 14.7.
Typing in a message.

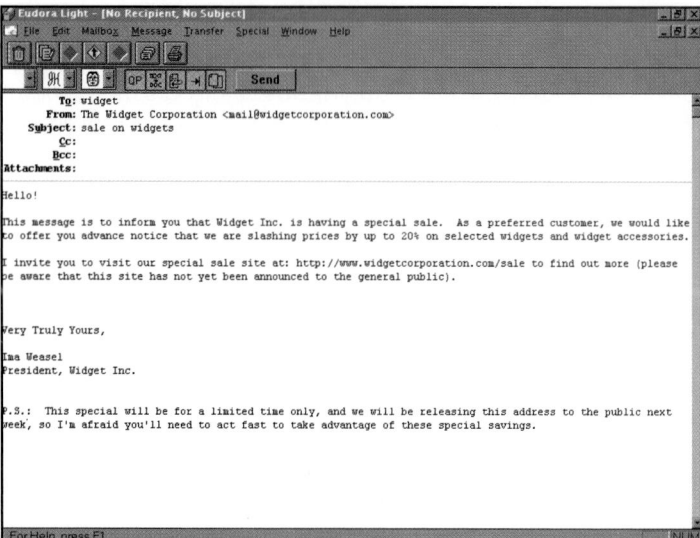

11. Connect to the Internet and click Send to send your mailing.

12. When the e-mail arrives at all those addresses, it will look something like Figure 14.8 (yes, we are viewing this through Notepad, and no, we didn't really send this mailing to all those fake addresses).

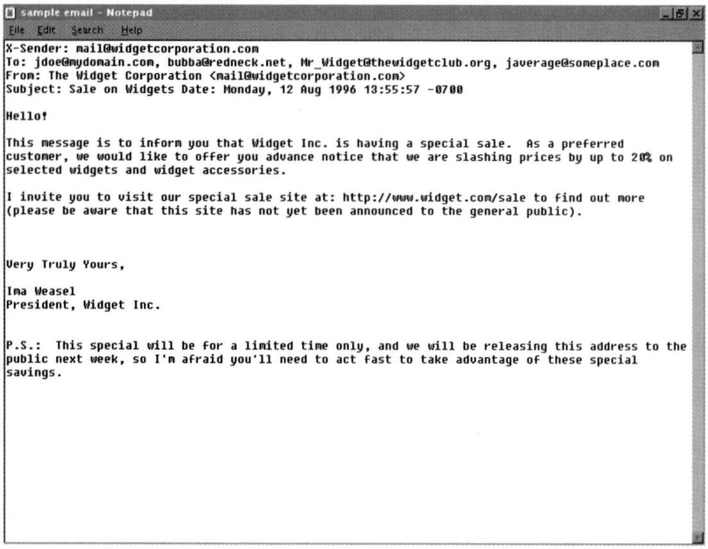

Figure 14.8.
A mockup of how this e-mail would arrive.

You'll notice that the To: line includes not only the address of this recipient, but of all the recipients on our mailing list. This is one of the reasons we don't recommend this method when sending to a large mailing list.

Using Microsoft Exchange for Mass E-Mailing

1. Open Microsoft Exchange.

2. Press Control+Shift+B to open the Address Book window.

3. In the File drop-down menu, choose New Entry… to open the New Entry dialog box.

4. Choose Internet Mail Address and click OK.

5. Fill in the display name (the person's real name) and e-mail address (you can also fill out the additional information if you would like to keep more contact information here), and click OK (see Figure 14.9).

Figure 14.9.
Filling in a real name and e-mail address.

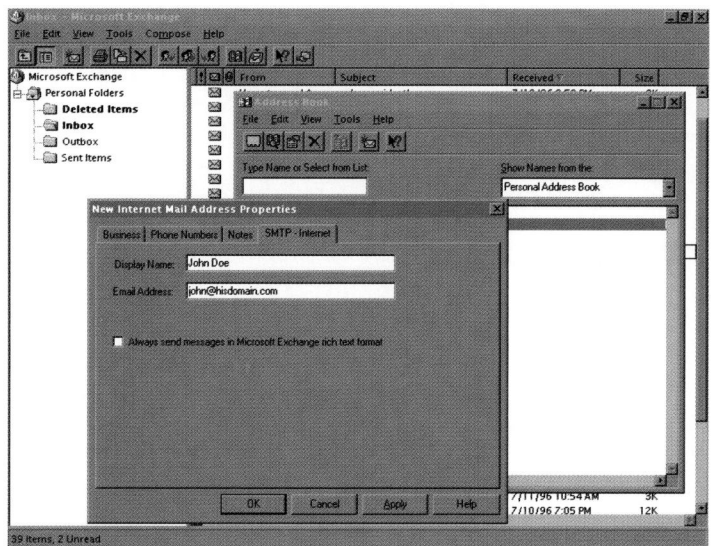

6. Repeat Steps 3 through 5 to enter all of your recipients.

7. Close the Address Book.

8. In the Microsoft Exchange Compose drop-down menu, choose New Message to compose a new message.

9. Type the subject of your message in the subject line (in our example, it's "Sale on widgets").

10. Type the body of your e-mail. (If you want to attach a file to this e-mailing, choose File… from the Insert drop-down menu, and select the file.) (See Figure 14.10.)

Q&D Using Microsoft Exchange for Mass E-Mailing

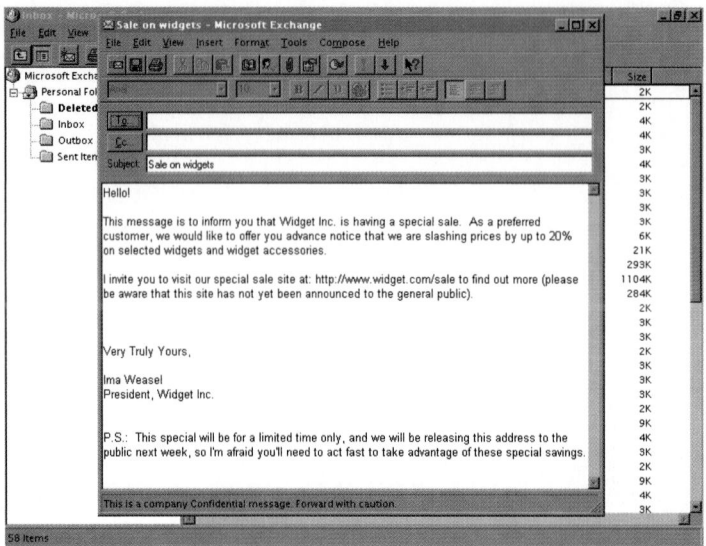

Figure 14.10.
Typing the e-mail
and clicking the To
button.

11. Click the To button, which will reopen your Address Book.

12. Select a recipient from the list and click the To button. This entry will then appear in the recipient list.

13. Repeat Step 12 until all the desired recipients appear in the recipient list, and click OK.

14. Click the Send button, which will place this message in your outbox.

15. When you're ready, go online and send.

16. The e-mail will then arrive at all those e-mail addresses. (Note: When the viewer receives this e-mail, the To line may display everyone on your recipient list—which is one of the reasons why we do not recommend this method for large mailing lists.)

SUMMARY

In this chapter you have

◆ Discovered how e-mail can be used to your advantage

◆ Learned how to develop an e-mail mailing list

◆ Learned about autoresponders

◆ Discussed mass e-mailing and how it can be achieved using Listserv, Eudora, or Microsoft Exchange.

In this chapter, we've addressed a way to open communication to new customers. In the next chapter, "Customer Service Online," we discuss communication with existing customers.

Customer Service Online

Many people have gotten the idea that whatever information they may have, whatever odd service or product they offer, whatever strange fetish or hobby they enjoy not only deserves to be on the WWW, but will be astronomically profitable once it is published online. The idea of "sell, sell, sell!" is bolstered by the almost constant Internet "symposiums" taking place, and the news media's superhype of the Information Superhighway.

Sales are certainly the primary goal of business, but it is often good customer service that generates sales—especially repeat sales. Many of the most successful companies on the Web have made customer service a primary goal of their sites, and for good reason. Poor customer service is often a great downfall of business.

Customer service is a main focus on Federal Express's excellent high-bandwidth site (see Figures 15.1 and 15.2).

Maybe it's the remnants of attitudes from the late '80s and early '90s. You know, the same ones that cut service to nothing, replaced real receptionists with voice-mail mazes, and replaced knowledgeable service reps with $5-per-hour "technicians" who do little more than read you your owner's manual. Whatever the reason, customer service (especially in the United States) has often become the sacrificial lamb when it comes time to cut budgets.

We're now starting to see a backlash, and we predict that this will continue. We won't go into the concepts of perceived value and other theories that might help to explain this trend because the reasons can be put fairly simply: People are getting sick of giving their money to companies who apparently could not care less.

Fortunately, the WWW and Internet are excellent tools for customer service. First of all, much of customer service is simply providing information. As you know, the Web provides

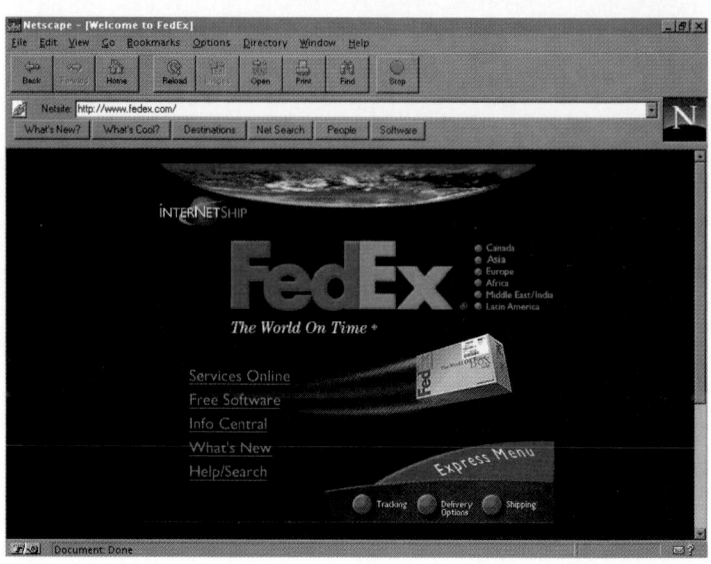

Figure 15.1.
Federal Express's home page.

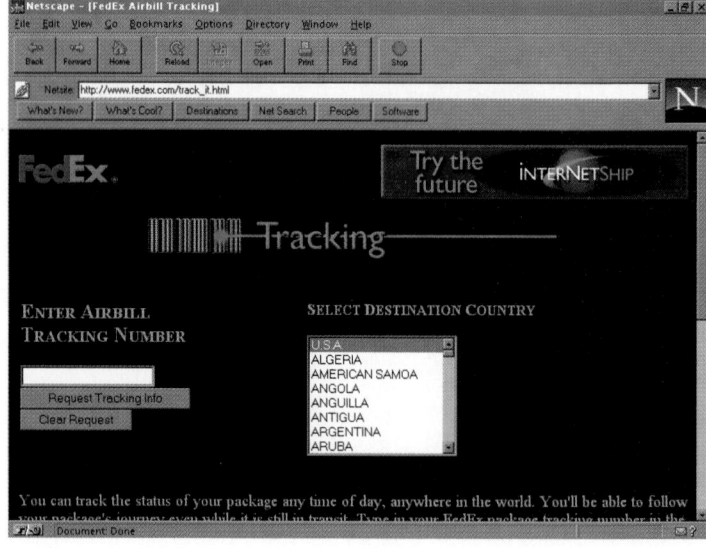

Figure 15.2.
Federal Express's tracking service page.

constantly updatable, cross-referencable (hyperlinked), graphical, interactive communications. Furthermore, the on-demand, 24-hour, 7-day nature of the Web lends itself well to answering customer needs immediately (think of how the ATM has changed the concept of customer service in banking).

Secondly, a good portion of customer service relates to peoples' need to belong. When people purchase a service or product, they've joined a club of sorts—they belong to a group of people who've bought something from company X. Have you ever seen someone who puts a $20 decal on their car to advertise the fact that they bought a pair of $100 sunglasses? The feeling that the WWW can promote, that whole cyberspace thing, the idea that you've entered some "realm" when you are viewing and navigating a site—all that really helps support the idea of belonging, the sense of community.

Thirdly—and this goes hand-in-hand with the other things—people like to have their purchasing decisions reinforced. They'll do whatever they can to facilitate this themselves, but anything you can do to help promote this will pay off ten-fold, as the least expensive and most effective form of advertising is word of mouth. Just showing that you care after the sale goes a long way to letting the customers feel that they've made the right purchasing decision, and good customer service communications help do this.

How Should I Do It?

We've touched on customer service in just about every chapter of this book. The concepts of clear communication, good site design, and user-friendliness all go hand-in-hand with providing customer service. In the following sections, we discuss some key communications goals you may wish to approach in your own customer service endeavors.

How you go about presenting an effective customer service site will depend on your company and the needs of your clients. Your best starting point is to find out what is and is not working in your current customer service efforts. What is it that clients want? What can be streamlined? What types of people are requesting customer service?

Providing Information

Suppose that your company makes vacuum cleaners, and you get a huge volume of calls asking how to replace the bags. Obviously, you'll want to include this information on your Web site. How you do this can make a huge difference, as you can see in the following examples of mock introductions to the vacuum bag page:

1. This bulletin is in response to customer reports of problems in the installation of X vacuum cleaner bags. The following steps should be followed to ensure proper installation of the X bag. Failure to follow these instructions may result in poor product performance.

2. Thank you for your purchase of the X vacuum—the most remarkable vacuum ever invented. Because of the revolutionary design of the X vacuum, the bag replacement procedure is somewhat different than that of old, ordinary vacuums. In order to assure full performance from your powerful brand X vacuum, please follow the step-by-step instructions below.

Now, which of these two introductions would have made you feel better about your vacuum? Which one would make you feel like the company cared, and that you made the right decision? While this has nothing to do with HTML design, it has a lot to do with communication. Customer service is communication, and for the most part, you should try to stay away from dry information like that shown in Figure 15.3.

BUILDING A COMMUNITY

Again, people like to belong. If you intend to include customer service information on your Web site, remember this point. In order to generate brand loyalty, repeat sales, and word-of-mouth advertising, it is in your best interest to foster a sense of community on your Web site. This also helps to promote your product/services to new customers, in that they can see what they're missing.

Your Web page design will already have given your system a personality. Most of the community (or exclusivity) your system promotes will be provided by your text and navigation. The previous example shows how text can be used to promote customer satisfaction. So, we'll now deal with navigation.

The best way to achieve a sense of belonging is to have a link right off of your main page. The link can lead to an "existing customer" site, which can have its own navigation, graphics, and so on. In this way, you will be building a subsite for existing customers. In some cases, where customer service is the main goal of the overall site, this step can be omitted.

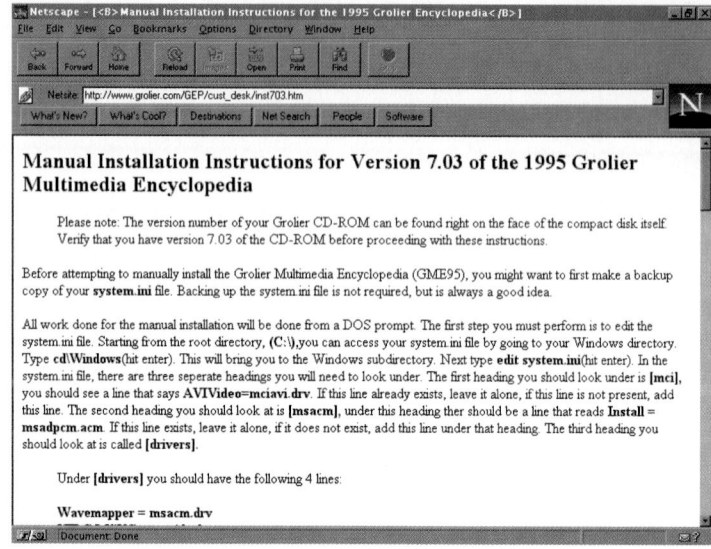

Figure 15.3.
This page gives dry, straight information. Good for an MIS person—not so good for a father who can't get his kid's new encyclopedia to work.

Note:
Some companies password-protect their existing customer sites. We avoid this when possible (obviously, if the company is selling information, this wouldn't work) for two main reasons. First, unless this is done very carefully, potential clients may get the impression that there are hidden problems being kept from them. Secondly, giving prospects a view of your customer relations activities, unless they're something to be ashamed of, is often a good idea.

The customer service site should be labeled in a way to give the impression of exclusivity, information, and interaction—not just recall notices. Labeling a link something like "Club X: The Brand X Owners' Site" will help promote the idea of community, as Pepsi has done on its site (see Figure 15.4). Furthermore—and this is a case in which we would break our hotlinks rule—including service-oriented features such as places of interest might be a good idea.

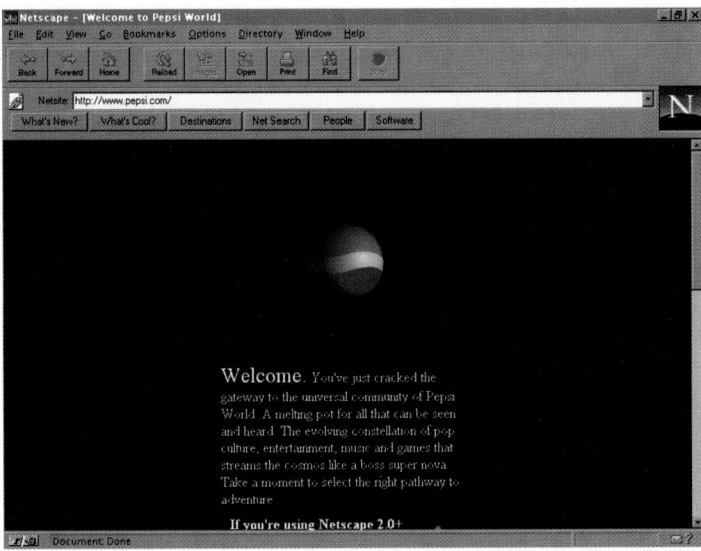

Figure 15.4.
The Pepsi site focuses on a sense of community and being "in the know."

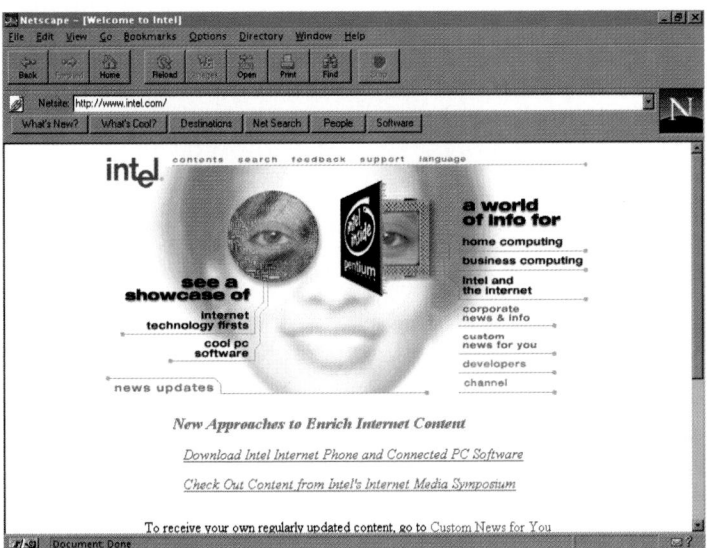

Figure 15.5.
Intel's sprawling site includes reams of information, as well as sample applications that make the most of the Pentium processor—thus reinforcing the buying decision.

Other headings you might include on your customer site would be Common Questions and Answers, Technical Information, Accessories, Service Locations, Feedback, and Contacting Customer Service.

REINFORCING THE PURCHASING DECISION

This is not really a separate aspect of customer service, but rather a thread that should be common throughout your site. Your pages should give existing clients the feeling that they made the right decision in purchasing your product, and should show them that you appreciate their business.

This is not to say that you should drool all over them, or fill every page with hype, but that you communicate to them that you appreciate their business. You may also wish to include examples of why your customer has made the right decision, as Intel has done (see Figure 15.5). How exactly you do these things will depend upon your clientele, your product/service, and the type of feedback you get from your customers.

KEEPING ON TOP OF THINGS

No matter how well you design your customer site (or customer portion of your site), you will probably not meet all of your clients' needs. Luckily, you'll be able to customize your design based on the feedback you get from your clients.

Obviously, this will require that you keep on top of things. You will have to provide your clients with ways to communicate with you—via e-mail, response forms, phone, telephony (chat phone or other digital voice communication), chat rooms, regular mail, and so on—and you will need to track those communications. If a significant number of people have a specific question or problem, or would like to see something on the site, it would obviously be a good idea for you to accommodate this group. There are two good reasons for doing so: You will be keeping your customers happy, and you will be decreasing the burden on customer service reps (who have to answer the same question over and over again).

QUICK & DIRTY GUIDE
Starting Small

If you are in a rush, designing a site for a start-up business, or designing for a business that doesn't really have a huge need for customer service, your best bet is to start small. The easiest way to accomplish this is to design a customer service page, and then simply provide a customer service e-mail link.

The page should say something about how committed the company is to its clients, how feedback is important in providing continued service, and then give a simple mailto: link. Your customer service section can then evolve in reaction to the feedback you receive from this page.

SUMMARY

Throughout this book, we have dealt with key issues of customer service. This chapter has gone into detail about key communication objectives in customer service, as well as the overall "feel" a customer service site should have. We have also discussed the need to adapt your site to meet your customer needs, and suggested a fast way to start out small.

We will now move on to discuss that green stuff (you know, the reason you work) in the next chapter, "Taking Payment Online."

Taking Payment Online

## CHAPTER sixteen

So, you want to sell something, do you? Oh, you
don't work just for the fun
of it? Well, we have been
discussing sales throughout
this book—not in the direct
sense, perhaps, but everything we have discussed
(making your site appeal-
ing, mass mailing, and so
on) comes down to working
for your sale. They now
know who you are and
what you do, and they want
your product. So now what?

Well, they can contact you via the e-mail address, phone number, or address listed on your Web site to order your product. But most likely you're now thinking, "Why can't they just order my product online?" Well, all right then, you can do that, too.

Although online ordering is still in its infancy, everyone seems to agree that this baby is growing, and fast. So, this is a great time to test the waters and work out your online ordering system. Don't despair if your sales are on the meager side in the beginning—this is very normal. The first step is getting the system to work and making it appealing; with *lots* of promotion, time, and great customer service the sales will follow (if done right). Just remember: As with a retail business, it will take time to develop a customer base; it doesn't happen overnight, and it may never happen if you don't aggressively promote and adapt your site on an ongoing basis.

CREATING A SUCCESSFUL ONLINE ORDERING SYSTEM

There are many facets to the creation of a successful online ordering system, and many more things to take into account aside from the obvious technical issues. Here are some guidelines you should consider, which will help you along the way:

1. **Promotion, promotion, promotion.**

If you build it, they will come. Not! This may have been true when there were only a handful of sites, but that is not the case anymore. If you want to attract crowds, you will need to promote your site vigilantly (more on this in Chapter 20, "Marketing Your Site Offline," and Chapter 21, "Marketing Your Site Online"), and you will need to pay close attention (as you always should) to your target markets when you do this. *You want to attract customers*, not surfers.

2. **Don't skimp out.**

Offer a fully representative product line. Don't just offer a few of your products online to save time. Customers will visit your site looking for one of your products—if it is not there, don't count on them sticking around to buy something else. (Not finding something also leads them to believe that your site is not useful, and for that reason they may never return.)

3. **Keep your pricing competitive.**

Don't get greedy! Yes, online shoppers are generally more well-off than the general public, but this does not mean they will pay a premium just for the convenience of ordering online. In fact, it would serve you well to discount your rates slightly for online customers (for example, five percent off of orders received via the Internet); this will encourage people to order from your site rather than using your (costly) traditional distribution channels.

4. **Establish a feeling of personal contact.**

In a regular retail outlet, a customer can examine products and have personal contact with a sales representative who can provide assistance. Unfortunately, this immediate personal contact is difficult to achieve via the Web. Although there are the means out there to provide it, like Internet telephone applications, most of your customers would not have the hardware/software needed to take advantage of those means. So, you're left with e-mail, which can still be a significant means of developing a personal relationship with a customer.

The only good way to establish a feeling of personal contact via e-mail is to answer your e-mail quickly (the faster the better). You should have a salesperson standing by at all times to answer e-mail questions as soon as they come in. This person should not only possess excellent writing skills; he or she should also be very personable and friendly. Just as in any sales situation, this salesperson (the customer's first contact) should remain the person through whom all contact with the customer comes. That way, the customer begins to know someone by name and knows a specific person to contact if he or she has further questions. This, in general, fosters a feeling of friendship between your company and this customer.

5. **Don't forget to close the deal.**

In other words, don't just answer prospects' questions and forget about them. Save their e-mail addresses, keep them informed (by adding their names to a mailing list), and close that deal.

6. **Simplify and secure the transaction.**

Usually the payment for goods is made by cash, check, or credit card. Until recently, the exchange of credit card information had to take place over the telephone or by mail (because of perceived security risks). This is no longer necessary since an increasing number of companies have introduced systems to enable secure credit card Internet transactions. Digital forms of currency are also emerging, offered by companies like CyberCash, DigiCash, and NetCash. The best course of action is to offer as many payment methods to the customers as possible and to let them choose (secure transaction over the Net, by fax, by phone, by mail, and so on).

7. **Please don't forget delivery of the goods.**

This is not just a matter of the shipping alone. You must consider how the billing and shipping information will arrive at their required destinations (your shipping and/or billing departments) quickly. Customers will not order from your online store if they know they will receive the product much faster if they order it via your 800 number.

There are some good Web sites that are enjoying successful online sales. You can learn a lot by browsing through these sites and noting how they are arranged. Here are a few:

◆ PC Flowers at `http://www.pcgifts.ibm.com` is one of the most successful online businesses.

◆ The Internet Shopping Network at `http://shop.internet.net` is an online mall.

◆ CDnow at `http://cdnow.com` claims to be the world's largest publicly accessible music information repository.

◆ Virtual Vineyards at `http://www.virtualvin.com/`—you guessed it, they sell wine. (See Figure 16.1.)

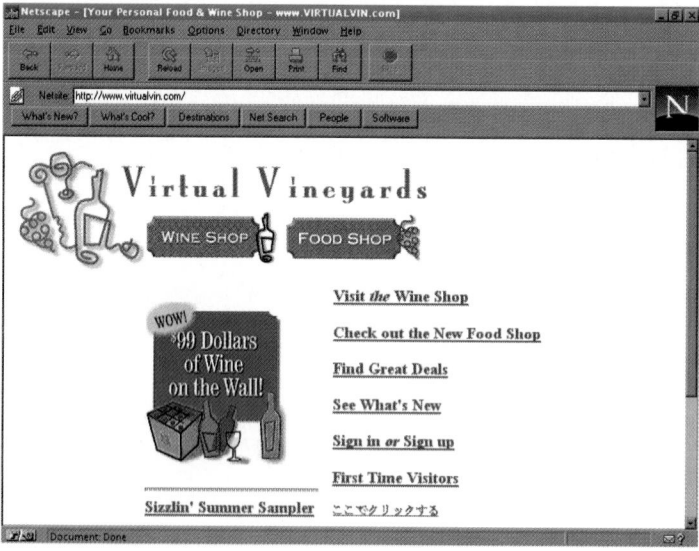

Figure 16.1.
Virtual Vineyards' site, which is enjoying success at selling online.

To develop an online ordering system, follow these steps:

1. Decide what type of payment you will accept. If you don't plan to take credit card orders, no sweat, you can skip the credit card section of this chapter and don't have to worry about the security of your customers' credit card numbers.

2. If you plan to take credit card orders, be prepared to make your site secure. (We talk about how in the section called "Security Issues.")

3. Program your online ordering system. This can be as simple as an online form (see the section called "A Simple Online Order Form" for information on this) or as complex as a full shopping cart application.

4. Validate your credit card orders (if you are taking them). (We discuss this in the section called "Credit Card Services.")

Are you ready? Let's do it!

CREDIT CARDS

"THIS TRANSACTION IS NOT SE-CURE!" If you have ordered a product via the Internet using your credit card, you have likely run into this message (or the message in Figure 16.2). Does this mean people can steal a customer's credit card number sent via the Net? Well, yes. Does it happen very often? Far from it. Is there anything you can do to prevent it from happening? Yes, which is what we discuss next.

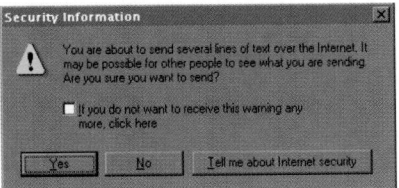

Figure 16.2.
A security message.

SECURITY ISSUES

Business-to-business commerce has used online transactions for years. Many large companies routinely move funds through automatic deposits, EDI systems, and EFTs (Electronic Funds Transfers). The difference between these methods and the Internet is that they ordinarily use point-to-point terminal connections or secure (private) networks via private communications lines. Someone would need to physically tap into that connection to monitor the transaction. On the other hand, the Internet is not private; it is susceptible to hackers wanting to intercept a stream of information (such as a credit card number) sent along the network.

Our belief is that sending credit card numbers via the Net is just as secure as using your credit card at your local gas station (where someone can just copy the imprint); in other words, we recommend using a credit card with a good protection policy. While credit card fraud is not uncommon in general, there has only been one case (that we have heard of) in which credit card numbers were stolen over the Internet—and he was caught. However, just because we can rationalize all this does not necessarily mean the buying public has (yet). You see, the media made quite a huge deal out of this occurrence, which served (as it often does) to scare the pants (or wallets) off the public. So, although many people carry on online transactions without worries, you will need to ease the public's fears if you intend to make selling directly on the Net a viable alternative to your other, more traditional distribution channels.

So, how do you ease the public's fears? By offering a secure network transaction. For a network transaction to be secure, you must provide the following:

1. **Privacy.** The private communications between two parties should be protected from eavesdropping at both ends, and at every step along the way. This is satisfied when the browser and server can exchange information in a secure manner.

2. **Party Authentication.** In other words, each person must know the other is who he says he is. So, if you are getting a file from Big Bank, Inc., you know it's actually from that bank, and vice versa.

3. **Message Integrity.** Once a message is written, it cannot be changed or duplicated.

4. **Transaction Agreement.** Neither party can deny the existence of the transaction once it has been accepted by both parties. This is generally achieved by both parties having certified keys. After an online agreement is made, knowledge of the key makes that agreement indisputable. Some legal experts have been quoted as saying that they believe this form of agreement is actually more binding than traditional paper and ink agreements.

Luckily, there's a protocol for meeting all of these needs: Public Key Encryption (PKE). With PKE, each transfer is encrypted by a verifiable key. If we want you to send us an encrypted message, we give you our key. When we receive the message, we will be able to verify your key, and the fact that the message came from you.

There are actually four keys involved—each party has both a public and private key. The public key enables someone to write you an encrypted message, but only your private key (which you *NEVER* send out) will allow you to open it.

IF YOU HAVE YOUR VERY OWN SERVER

Don't worry, most of the new popular servers (Netscape Enterprise Server, Microsoft Information Server, and so on) on the market come with capabilities to provide PKE. Some even have wizards or help systems that will save you a lot of time in developing an online ordering system.

Hopefully you are using one of these, in which case the process won't be too complex. Check the documentation (or online help system) that came with your software, or visit the company's Web site. This is one of the most requested features of a commercial server, and all the big guys have information on how to set things up.

> **Note:**
> Your merchant bank (the bank that handles your credit card collections) has a vested interest in your successful use of credit card ordering—it makes a percentage. Because of this, it is often an excellent source of free information, and even software.

IF YOU ARE USING A VIRTUAL HOST

We hope you read through our suggestions before making a decision and have chosen a host that provides a secure transaction channel. Call your host, tell them what you want to do, and ask what services they provide for this. They will let you know how and where to set up your secure site. If you are using a host without a secure server, you'll either need to switch servers, use an additional commercial service (some of the companies that offer credit card merchant services also offer hosting of your order system on their secure server), or skip the whole secure credit card transaction thing altogether. (Check out the Quick & Dirty Guide at the end of this chapter.)

CREDIT CARD SERVICES

Once a customer sends you credit card information requesting a product, you must of course process the sale through a merchant banking system (to make sure this is a valid card, and that the customer has credit available), just as you do through other distribution channels (unless you are using a system that automatically does this for you).

The best way to do this is through specialized software provided by service companies like Techcom, ICVerify (`http://www.webstar.net/tyner/ic.htm`), and VeriFone (`http://www.verifone.com`). A listing of these companies is available at `http://gnn.yahoo.com/gnn/Business_and_Economy/Products_and_Services/Financial_Services/Transaction_Clearing/`.

Many of these services will even host your order forms on their secure server; this can be a really simple solution if you are using a virtual host. Two we have found that offer this service are VersaNet International, Inc. (`http://www.versanet.net/secureorder/`—see Figure 16.3) and Techcom (`http://www.tech-comm.com/techcomm/imark/`). You could, of course, intercept the sale at this point and verify the card and process the sale manually (over the phone, or however you normally do it), but this will take time (which equals money, as we all know). Besides, automated processing can often result in lower processing fees by the banks, which can have a big effect on the profitability of your Web-based business.

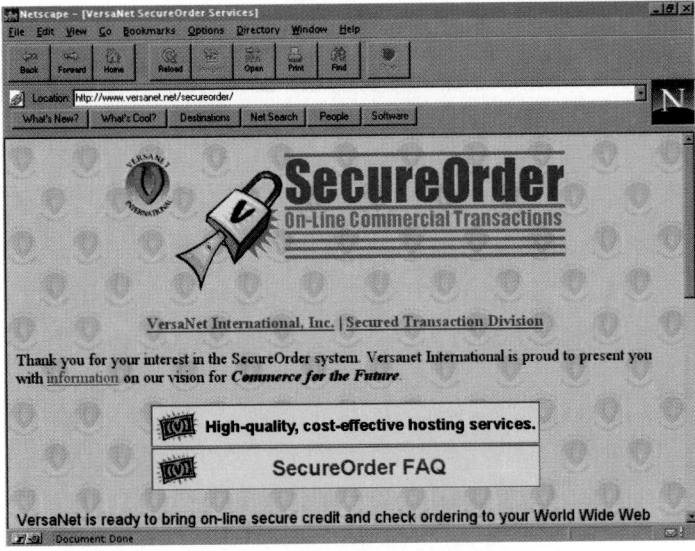

Figure 16.3.
VersaNet International, Inc.

CASH

Credit cards work great for companies selling products that cost more than $15, but what if you want to sell very low-cost items? Credit cards quickly turn into "too much trouble" for a customer wanting to purchase an item for, say, $2. Not only do credit customers find it a pain to fill out their card number and information for small items, some have another concern as well: privacy. They want protection against marketers, financial institutions, and the government tracking their buying habits through their credit. You remember Big Brother, The Net, Nowhere Man? The answer to this dilemma may be cash—virtual cash, that is. While virtual cash is far from a widely used commercial reality, people seem to be crying for it, and you know what that means…

DIGICASH

Ecash (provided by DigiCash at `http://www.digicash.com/ecash ecashhome.html`) was the first anonymous system of its kind. Only one U.S. bank (Mark Twain Bank) supports this anonymous method for small financial transactions. This St. Louis–based bank can be reached via its Web site at `http://www.marktwain.com/fee.html`. Ecash is similar to a traveler's check in that it provides finality (no chance for a user to renege on a transaction, as is possible with a check or credit card transaction), peer-to-peer transactions, anonymity (for both the payer and the payee), and "cash" that is refundable if lost or stolen.

CYBERCASH

This system uses CyberCash (representing secure checks or currency), and will soon also use CyberCoins (representing virtual coins). CyberCash (see Figure 16.4) uses an electronic "wallet" in addition to software that augments the Web browser. When customers are ready to buy, they pay out of the "wallet" via their credit cards or their virtual (CyberCash) checking accounts.

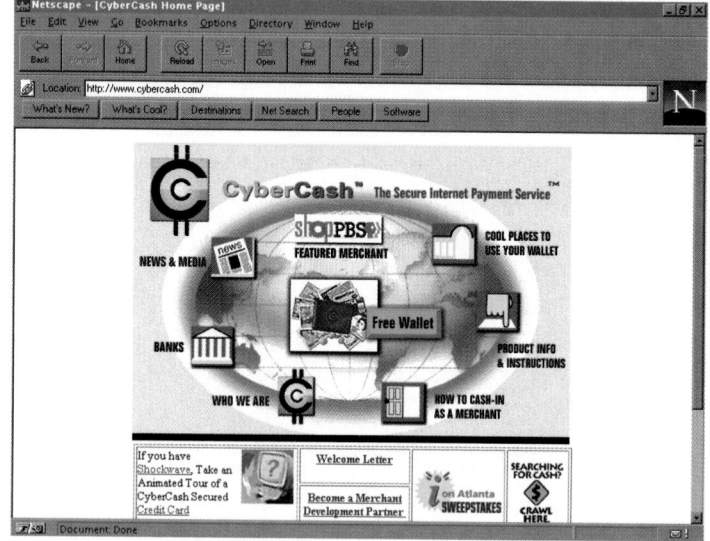

Figure 16.4.
The CyberCash Web site (`http://www.cybercash.com`).

CyberCoin will provide for very small transactions with or without a preexisting relationship between the customer and the merchant. Not only does CyberCash validate the transaction, it also does the record keeping at the end of the day, transferring the real cash to the merchant's checking account.

Customers will need the free client software that communicates with the CyberCash servers. As the merchant, you will need a CyberCash server (or the use of one) that is linked to the bank's own private networks. CyberCash's services also enable secure credit card transactions (see more about this under its listing for credit card systems at `http://www.cybercash.com/cybercash/merchants/getstarted.html`).

CHECKS

A number of Internet check services allow you to accept checks as payment online. It works like this: Rather than mailing a check to you via the mail, customers can provide their check information once to a check service (see Figure 16.5). This information generally includes the customer's name, e-mail address, phone number, mailing address, and the routing number from the bottom of the check. When your customer places an order by filling out your online order form, only the customer's username and password need to be entered (no check information is required). This information is then transmitted securely to the check service, which responds by sending an e-mail to both the customer and you containing a copy of the order. The check service then creates a check (just like the one in the customer's checkbook), and deposits that check into your account.

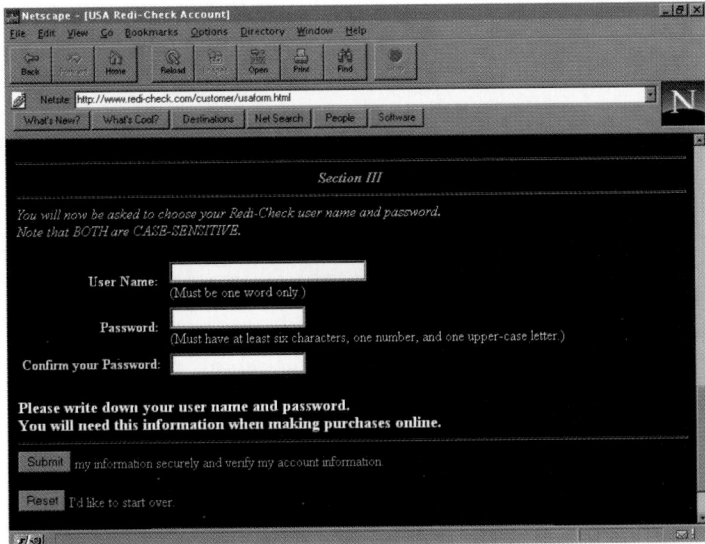

Figure 16.5.
The customer fill-out form for Redi-Check, one of the Internet check services.

That's it! If you're interested in this method of payment, check out the list of Internet check services at `http://gnn.yahoo.com/gnn/Business_and_Economy/Products_and_Services/` `Financial_Services/Transaction_Clearing/Check_Services/`.

A SIMPLE ONLINE ORDER FORM

Now that you're aware of the payment options, let's put this to practical use. To complete an order, you'll probably need not only the customer's payment information, but details about the products he or she is ordering, and where to send them. The easiest way to accomplish this is through the use of an online form.

> **Note:**
> You could get real fancy at this point and offer a full shopping cart application or some other neat way to order. For that we suggest you use your imagination, and check out some of the successful sites listed earlier in this chapter.

We've used online order forms a couple of times already in this book (in Chapter 11, "Integrating HTML with CGI," and Chapter 14, "Mail Delivery Systems"), so you should have a pretty good idea of what's involved. Here's a quick form to get you started on an online ordering system.

> **Note:**
> This example form totally ignores security, since the interface for different systems can vary dramatically. To make your own form secure, you will need to speak to your server's administrator.

Our goal is to create an online order form that will collect all the information necessary to fill the order and will allow the customer to make payment either by check or credit card. We will need a CGI script to decode the form, and will use `formmail.pl` (included on your CD-ROM). We would manually validate credit card orders after we received them via e-mail.

So, the first step is to create the online order form. This can be achieved with the HTML code in Listing 16.1.

Listing 16.1. An online order form.

```
<!DOCTYPE HTML PUBLIC "-//IETF//DTD HTML 3.0//EN" "html.dtd">
<HTML>
<HEAD>
<TITLE>Simple Online Order Form</TITLE>
</HEAD>

<BODY>
<BGCOLOR="FFFFFF" TEXT="000000" LINK="425AFF" VLINK="0018C4" ALINK="FFFFFF">
<FONT FACE="Lucida Sans", "Arial","Times Roman">
<CENTER>
<H2>Online Order Form</H2>
```

```
<FORM ACTION="/cgi-bin/formmail.pl" METHOD=POST>
<INPUT TYPE="hidden" name="recipient" value="hampton@ha.net">
<INPUT TYPE="hidden" NAME="redirect" VALUE="http://www.ha.net/thanks.htm">
<TABLE BORDER=2 BGCOLOR=GAINSBORO BORDERCOLORDARK=INDIGO
BORDERCOLORLIGHT=GAINSBORO>
<TR>
<TD>Your Name:</TD>
<TD COLSPAN=3><INPUT NAME="realname" TYPE=TEXT SIZE=35 MAXSIZE=40></TD>
</TR>
<TR>
<TD>Email Address:</TD>
<TD COLSPAN=3><INPUT NAME="email" TYPE=TEXT SIZE=35></TD>
</TR>
<TR>
<TD ROWSPAN=2>Shipping and<BR>Billing Address:</TD>
<TD>Street:</TD>
<TD COLSPAN=2><INPUT NAME="address" TYPE=TEXT SIZE=24 MAXSIZE=40></TD>
</TR>
<TR>
<TD>City:</TD>
<TD COLSPAN=2><INPUT NAME="city" TYPE=TEXT SIZE=24 MAXSIZE=40></TD>
</TR>
<TR>
<TD>State:</TD>
<TD><INPUT NAME="state" TYPE=TEXT SIZE=6 MAXSIZE40></TD>
<TD>Zip:</TD>
<TD><INPUT NAME="zip" TYPE=TEXT SIZE=12 MAXSIZE=15></TD>
</TR>
<TR>
<TH>Item #</TH>
<TH>Qty</TH>
<TH>Price</TH>
<TH>Total (Qty X Price)</TH>
</TR>
<TR>
<TD><INPUT NAME=ITEM1 TYPE=TEXT SIZE=22></TD>
<TD><INPUT NAME=QTY1 TYPE=TEXT SIZE=6></TD>
<TD><INPUT NAME=P1 TYPE=TEXT SIZE=6></TD>
<TD><INPUT NAME=EXT1 TYPE=TEXT SIZE=12></TD>
</TR>
<TR>
<TD><INPUT NAME=ITEM2 TYPE=TEXT SIZE=22></TD>
<TD><INPUT NAME=QTY2 TYPE=TEXT SIZE=6></TD>
<TD><INPUT NAME=P2 TYPE=TEXT SIZE=6></TD>
<TD><INPUT NAME=EXT2 TYPE=TEXT SIZE=12></TD>
</TR>
<TR>
<TD><INPUT NAME=ITEM3 TYPE=TEXT SIZE=22></TD>
<TD><INPUT NAME=QTY3 TYPE=TEXT SIZE=6></TD>
<TD><INPUT NAME=P3 TYPE=TEXT SIZE=6></TD>
<TD><INPUT NAME=EXT3 TYPE=TEXT SIZE=12></TD>
</TR>
<TR>
<TD><INPUT NAME=ITEM4 TYPE=TEXT SIZE=22></TD>
<TD><INPUT NAME=QTY4 TYPE=TEXT SIZE=6></TD>
<TD><INPUT NAME=P4 TYPE=TEXT SIZE=6></TD>
<TD><INPUT NAME=EXT4 TYPE=TEXT SIZE=12></TD>
</TR>
```

continues

Listing 16.1. continued

```
<TR>
<TD COLSPAN=3>Shipping and Handling (6%)</TD>
<TD><INPUT NAME=SH TYPE=TEXT SIZE=12 ></TD>
</TR>
<TR>
<TD COLSPAN=3>CA Residents Add 8% Sales Tax</TD>
<TD><INPUT NAME=TAX TYPE=TEXT SIZE=12></TD>
</TR>
<TR>
<TD COLSPAN=3>Total Of Order</TD>
<TD><INPUT NAME=TOTAL TYPE=TEXT SIZE=12 ></TD>
</TR>
</TABLE><BR>
<TABLE>
<TR><H3>Payment Method</H3></TR>
<TR><INPUT TYPE=RADIO NAME=PMTMETHOD VALUE=M>Check (Click <A
HREF="check.html">here</A> for remittance address.  Order will be shipped upon
reciept of order.</TR>
<TR><INPUT TYPE=RADIO NAME=PMTMETHOD VALUE=V>Credit Card</TR>
</TABLE>
<TABLE>
<TR>
<TD><H5>If Paying By Credit Card:</H5></TD><BR>
</TR>
<TD>Card Type:</TD>
<TD><SELECT NAME=CARD_TYPE >
<OPTION VALUE="MC">MasterCard
<OPTION VALUE="V">VISA
<OPTION VALUE="AX">American Express
<OPTION VALUE="D">Discover
</SELECT></TD>
</TR>
<TR>
<TD>Card Number:</TD>
<TD><INPUT NAME=CARD_NO TYPE=TEXT SIZE=19 MAXSIZE=19></TD>
</TR>
<TR>
<TD>Expiration Date (MM/DD):</TD>
<TD><INPUT NAME=CARD_EXP_DATE TYPE=TEXT SIZE=5 ></TD>
</TR>
<TR>
<TD>Name as it appears on card:</TD>
<TD><INPUT NAME=CC_NAME TYPE=TEXT SIZE=19 ></TD>
</TR>
</TABLE>
<BR>
<INPUT TYPE=SUBMIT VALUE="Submit My Order!">
<INPUT TYPE=RESET VALUE="Clear Order Form"><BR><BR>
</CENTER>
<INPUT TYPE=HIDDEN NAME=FORM_NAME VALUE=ORDER>
<HR>
</FORM>
</BODY>
</HTML>
```

The code in Listing 16.1 creates the page shown in Figure 16.6.

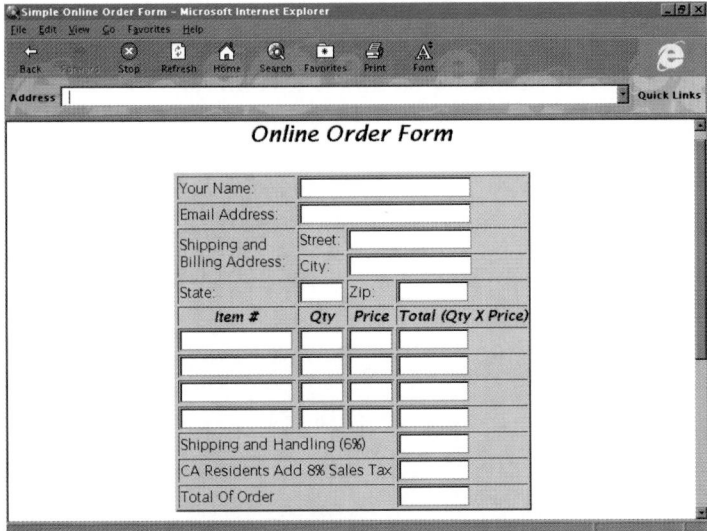

Figure 16.6.
How our order form
looks.

The customers simply fill in the required information on the form (we would have provided the item numbers in our product information site). They then move on to the second part of the form (see Figure 16.7), which requests payment information. After they have filled this out, they submit the form.

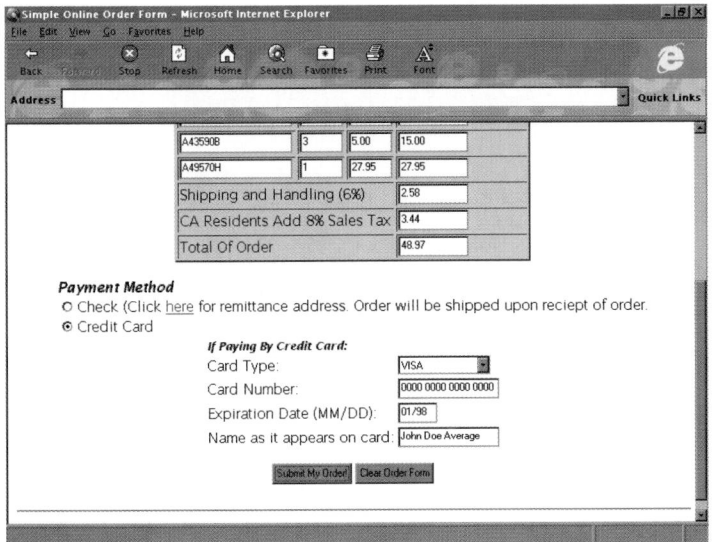

Figure 16.7.
The customer
submits the form,
having completed
the payment
information.

The customers then jump to the thank you page (`thanks.htm`, a standard HTML page thanking them for their order and letting them know when to expect their receipt), and we receive their order via e-mail. After we process the order, we send them their receipt and let them know when to expect their shipment. That's all there is to it.

CHARGING FOR ACCESS

Often new clients come to us with their grand idea to charge viewers for access to their site. Here's what we tell them: "Don't even think about it." Even if you plan to present information on your site that is truly unique, viewers will rarely pay to see it. Even the huge corporations who have dumped millions into marketing have had trouble in their efforts to charge for access.

An alternative to charging for access to your site would be to charge for "premium access," which usually means allowing everyone to view your general site but charging for access to specific files—usually through the use of a password, a subject we discuss in Chapter 17, "For Your Eyes Only: Site Security."

Another option is to allow full access to your site while offering special files to be downloaded for a fee. Some publishing companies, graphics houses, and software companies have had some success using this method. You could either set a system up like this yourself (by the use of a payment system integrated with a password-protected site) or use a company like InfoHaus (see Figure 16.8), which will help you sell text, graphics, and other forms of digital information for viewers to immediately download via payment by an Internet payment system. A good listing of companies such as this is located at `http://www.yahoo.com/Business_and_Economy/Companies/Financial_Services/Digital_Money/`.

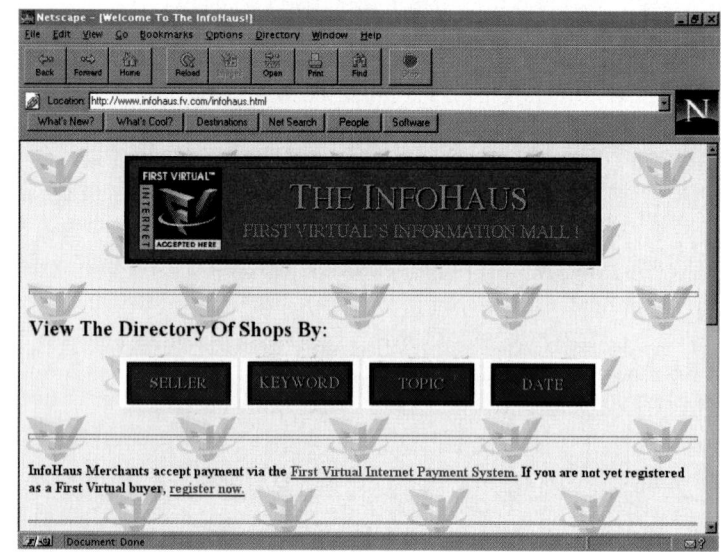

Figure 16.8.
The InfoHaus Web site.

QUICK & DIRTY GUIDE
The Easy Way Out—Avoiding Online Transactions

If you find all of the preceding methods too much trouble, there is a very simple solution.

Note:

Although the method we are about to describe works, you will most likely receive many more orders by *also* offering an online payment system. This method is a great alternative for customers leery of site security, and it would be in your best interest to offer both this and online payment methods.

This method simply involves adapting an existing order form (from your catalog) for use on the Web. By adapting your order form (or creating a new one) into HTML and ensuring that it can be printed, you can simply suggest to customers that they either print the order form, to be faxed or mailed to you, or that they have the required information handy when calling your phone number (an 800 number, preferably). Figures 16.9 and 16.10 provide a couple of real-life examples.

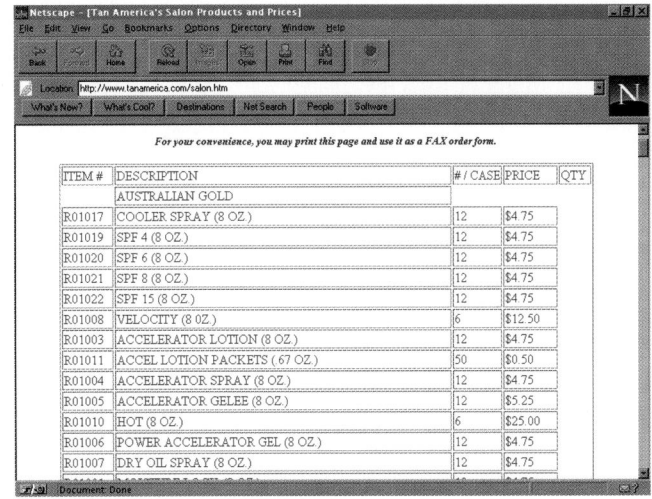

Figure 16.9.
The order form on Tan America's Web site.

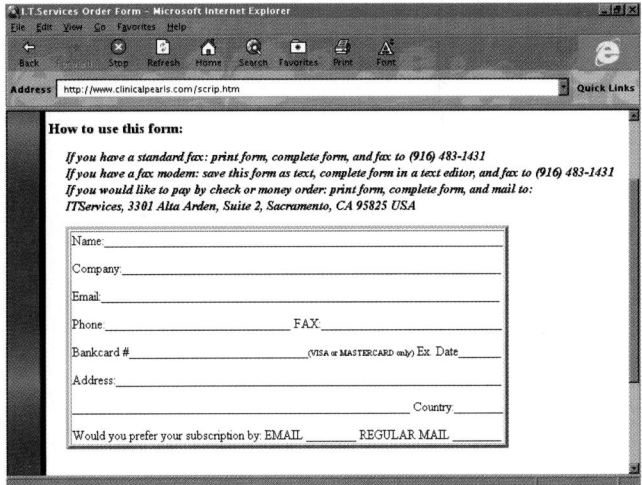

Figure 16.10.
The order form on ITService's Web site.

SUMMARY

In this chapter we have discussed:

- Tips for a successful online ordering system
- The steps involved in developing an online ordering system
- Different methods of payment, including credit cards and the security and service issues that surround them
- What's involved in providing a secure network transaction
- How to create a simple online ordering form
- Why not to charge for access
- Alternatives to online payment systems

Now that you know how to charge for your products, the next chapter will show you how to protect your site.

For Your Eyes Only: Site Security

Here's a good way to look at total site security: It's a myth. We always arrange our clients' sites with this point in mind: Anything you put on the Internet is not truly secure. Yes, there are things you can do to protect your information, or to let only certain viewers onto your site, but no matter what you do, there are ways to break in.

In fact, we have often unintentionally ended up at "secure" sites by following hypertext links or even just by hitting the wrong buttons—and we in no way consider ourselves hackers. Actually, the reason most security protocols are enacted is simply because many problems stem from inexperienced users inadvertently messing with systems. Which brings us to another good point: Everyone's not out to get you—really. There are probably very few hackers who will ever be interested in anything on your site.

This is not to say that you should ignore security, or write off any security efforts as futile. Skilled car thieves can easily disarm an alarm system, but it's likely they will move on to a car without an alarm. Providing some sort of site security will accomplish this same effect (though few car thieves break into a car just for the sense of accomplishment).

> **Note:**
> This chapter does not deal with encryption security. This is covered in the preceding chapter, "Taking Payment Online."

PUBLIC VERSUS PRIVATE SITES

In general, a *public* site can be accessed by any individual who knows the address. A *private* site, on the other hand, usually requires a Password Authentication Protocol (PAP). Most servers

and browsers have the capability to handle password authentication, and it is generally a case of either setting this up on the server yourself (if you are using your own server), or having your administrator set this up for you (if you are using a virtual host).

In most cases, the server will keep a database of the users and their passwords, and will check the input against the recorded file. Upon requesting information from a secure address (which can be the entire server, or just a directory), the viewer is confronted with a login/password interface. This can either be an input box generated as a function of the browser, or an HTML page that links out to a CGI file (see Figures 17.1 and 17.2).

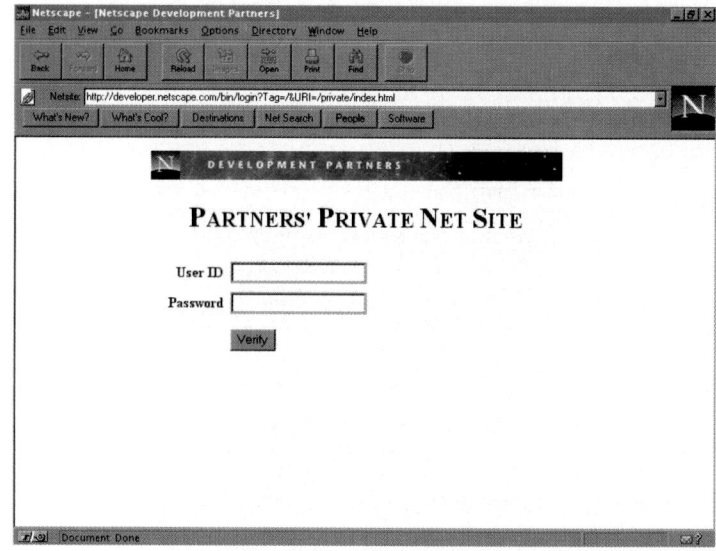

Figure 17.1.
An HTML PAP interface.

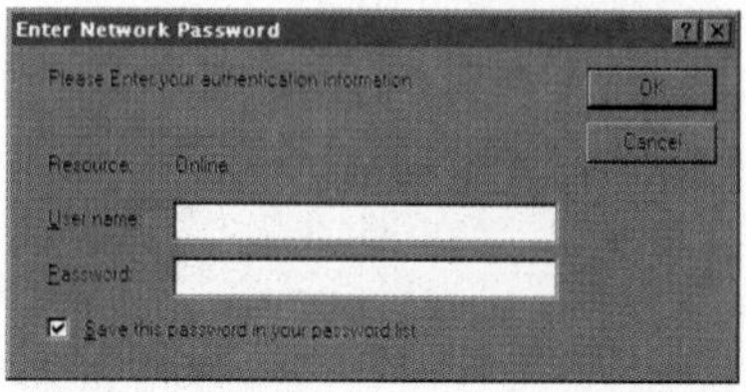

Figure 17.2.
A browser-generated PAP interface.

USES FOR PRIVATE SITES

Some uses for a private Web site are

◆ To provide a place for sensitive material (financial, proprietary, or medical records).

◆ To use in conjunction with a payment system on a "charge for access" site.

◆ To provide a premium site (a site that perhaps is only available to clients, past customers, sales staff, and so on).

◆ To build a sense of exclusivity.

◆ To track sales and marketing. By asking viewers to fill out information before receiving a password into the site (such as the popular HotWired site, Figure 17.3), you can track who is visiting and collect sales information at your virtual front door. (Be really careful of this—if not given enough incentive, viewers may never enter at all.)

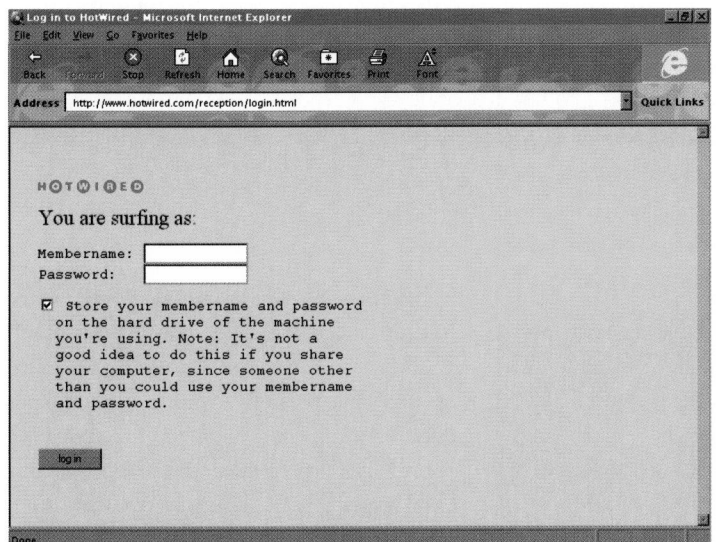

Figure 17.3.
HotWired's "free" site uses PAP and a rather lengthy registration form to collect demographic information.

SETTING UP A PRIVATE SITE

How you set up your PAP will depend on your individual server. This book does not go into the actual mechanics of setting up private sites, as most server documentation will give you detailed instructions. If you are deciding whether or not to make a site private, there are three major questions you need to ask yourself:

◆ What do I want to accomplish?

◆ Who do I want to keep out?

◆ What am I keeping secret?

WHAT IS THE POINT?

Previously, we listed some reasons for site security. Whatever reasons you have, consider the risks and benefits of putting any private information online. Putting private medical information online, for instance, can put you in a position of high liability. Putting your secret R&D files online may compromise your business future. Your question should be "Why?" If you can avoid compromising your security by keeping files offline, do so!

WHO WANTS TO KNOW?

If you are storing information that could be profitable to your competition, you have something to protect. If, however, you are designing a secure site just to track leads, or to restrict access to dirty pictures, or for some other noncrucial security issue, you can afford to be a bit more blasé about your security.

A good exercise (to feed your paranoia) is to sit down and think about the worst things that could happen if someone broke into your server. This will be your best tool in assessing your risks and benefits, and in deciding how to approach your security issues.

WHAT YA HIDING?

Obviously, this goes hand-in-hand with the other issues, but it's important to look at the raw information. To go back to the example of medical records, you could ask yourself if there might be a way to encrypt the records themselves, or to remove the most damaging information. In many cases, you can at least minimize your worst-case scenario by simply reducing the quantity or quality of information available.

DANGERS

There are at least four ways someone can break into your system. The first is to simply set up a program that will bang away at the front door, trying random usernames and/or passwords until a match is made. People who always use the same username and password are a great help to hackers, because once a username/password combination is found on one site, it will usually go to the top of the list to be tried at another site.

> **Note:**
> While not common, some PAP applications have a dummy login. This was usually set up so that either the programmer or the end user would have quick access. By all means, remove any username/password data that you have not entered yourself, prior to going online. A very common dummy login is to use "guest" as both the username and password.

The second way to break into a site is to access the server through a route other than HTTP (Telnet, Gopher, Finger, FTP, and so on). This is an operating system problem and must be dealt with as it pertains to each OS. This can usually be fixed by setting appropriate file permissions on the server system (as well as by just eliminating these other services, if unused).

The third way to gain access to a server is by getting shell access. This should not be possible on a Web server, but certain bugs can allow this to happen. Luckily, most companies who offer Web server software make protection from this a priority, and it's extremely rare for someone to break in this way.

The most likely (and dangerous) way for someone to break into a system is through CGI. Remember, the G stands for gateway. Sloppy CGI protocols can allow someone to walk right into your system. This is because of the power that CGI provides (it's a trade-off). There has also been concern expressed over scripting languages like Java. Always be aware that when you are running a script, you are providing a way for someone to get into your system. While the risk is very small, it does exist.

INTELLECTUAL PROPERTY

What do you do if a viewer copies something from your Web page to use as his or her own? Is there a legal remedy against this thief? Well, unfortunately that point is quite unclear. If the person did not use your work under a "fair use" provision, if the work copied was protected under copyright law, and if you find out about the thievery, then you may take action. Whether you can be successful in the litigation is where things become unclear. There have actually been cases where entire copyrighted books have been posted on the newsgroups, yet no action could be taken because the files were posted anonymously.

This subject is being hotly debated, and there are many issues involved. Hopefully, we soon will have foolproof protection measures against this (but don't hold your breath). In the meantime, there are steps you can take to protect yourself. Some we have used are

♦ Include copyright notices on each Web document.

♦ Make all your graphics as site-specific as possible (for example, incorporate your logo or something specific to your company into all graphics). They may steal your graphic, but they'll be advertising your company in the meantime. (Go ahead—make our day, punk.)

♦ Put sensitive information beneath a password-protected site, or don't post it at all.

♦ For information people may steal and claim as their own, you may want to use something like MD5 (freeware including documentation available at `ftp://ftp.cert.org/pub/tools/md5/`). MD5 shows that you had a certain file at a certain date. By using an MD5 hash code, and then publishing that code (in a newspaper, for example), you will have a record of your ownership. These hash codes cannot be inverted—meaning you can't start with a hash code and work backwards to create the text to produce that code. Furthermore, changing even one letter in a huge document will completely change the code.

SUMMARY

In this chapter, we have briefly discussed site security and Password Authentication Protocol. A few key things to remember are

♦ No site is ever completely secure, unless it's offline.

♦ When providing sensitive information, you must weigh the risks against the benefits.

♦ You can take steps to help protect your intellectual property.

The next chapter deals with bells and whistles—all those nifty, gee-whiz things that may or may not work for you.

Bells and Whistles

Communicate—don't decorate. This is the hallmark of commercial art, and even interactive art should heed this wisdom.

## CHAPTER eighteen

There are certainly reasons for using the latest whiz-bang features on a site. If you are presenting the site just for entertainment and brand recognition (like Pepsi), if you are trying to set your site apart from your competition's, or if your company image can be enhanced by the use of bells and whistles, by all means, consider their use.

There is, of course, a caveat: Bells and whistles annoy many people. We've talked with many folks who have very strong opinions about the use of features like Shockwave. As you know, many people turn plain old graphics off on their browsers. You can probably imagine how they feel about huge multimedia files.

DO I REALLY NEED ALL THE BELLS AND WHISTLES?

In short, no. Having an extremely accessorized site may increase traffic (exponentially), but the prevailing wisdom on the subject seems to point to one fact: Hits do not mean sales. If sales are the main goal of your site (as opposed to mindshare), and you are keeping an eye on time and/or expense, you will probably keep your bells and whistles to a minimum (but don't forget that graphics on the Web were once considered frivolous).

Having a clearly navigable, attractive, and informative site will give people a good impression of your company. Having a few special features may help put you ahead of your competition (all other things being equal). Overloading your site with bells and whistles, just for the sake of having them, will make you look cheesy.

Think of it this way: Have you ever seen a car that was way too accessorized? Did you think "Wow, that guy has class"? or was it more like "Jeez, what a goofball! Maybe he's a pimp." If you do choose to employ bells and whistles, do so tastefully. In many cases, your best bet may be to let people know if they are about to enter a feature-rich site, and to give them an alternative.

This is not to say that you should be aiming at producing plain, generic sites. What you should be doing, on a constant basis, is balancing bandwidth with communication value. You want to make the best presentation possible, and you want to do so using the least bandwidth. This is true even when you know that your site will be viewed by an audience with full T1 access—bandwidth is still a consideration.

So, what you should be thinking about is what communication value each component in your site will have, and whether it's worth the expense of bandwidth. Many authors try to keep each page under 40K total (HTML, graphics, and any other files). This is a difficult goal, and we don't necessarily adhere to it ourselves, but we always use it as a benchmark. When there comes a time to make a decision about including a component that will push our page size past this mark, we ask ourselves (and our client) whether this component is worth it. Sometimes it is, and sometimes it ain't.

ANIMATION

There are several ways to add animation to your site. Server push, client pull, applets (Java, ActiveX, and so on), embedded Shockwave, and GIF89a animation all provide movement on the screen. Each do so in a different way, and with different effects on the browser.

Server push and client pull generally reload images, one on top of the next, in order to achieve an "animation" of sorts. This is a real bandwidth hog, and the effect can be pretty untrustworthy (especially using low-speed connections). You will rarely see this on the Web anymore, not because of any specific fatal flaw, but because it was never well-hyped, and because of bandwidth issues.

A good example of server push animation is on the Armani Exchange Summer '96 site. The opening screen (see Figure 18.1) simply shows two people bundled up for winter.

After a series of slides (pages), in which the couple disrobes, the final slide (see Figure 18.2) shows the logo and tagline, "Summer is here."

It's a very cute use of this type of animation, though it's also very slow. The difference between server push and client pull is implied by the name. Server push sends the information (generally via a CGI script) without request, and the connection to the server stays open until the server is finished. Client pull requests each transfer individually (usually with the META/refresh tag), and generally necessitates the reopening of the connection each time a new page is loaded.

Client pull is generally the easiest to set up, as it requires only the addition of a tag in the <HEAD> of an HTML document. For example, adding the line <META HTTP-EQUIV="Refresh" CONTENT="10; URL=http://domain.com/feed2.htm"> will cause the page feed2.htm to load after 10 seconds. This page could have another "Refresh" command that would load a third page, and so on.

For the most part, client pull and server push types of animation can be replaced through the use of GIF89a animations, which have several distinct advantages.

GIF 89A ANIMATION

GIF animation is probably the best way to introduce animation to your pages. Both Netscape and Microsoft have expressed that they will support GIF animation in all future

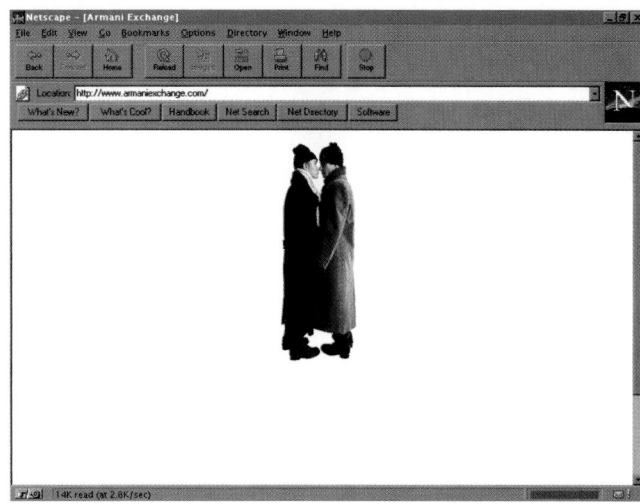

Figure 18.1.
The opening screen on the Armani Exchange Summer '96 site.

Figure 18.2.
The final screen of the Summer '96 site.

browsers, it requires no plug-ins, it is relatively small, and some nice effects can be achieved by its use.

The main advantages to GIF89a animations are that they are completely portable, do not require an open connection (like server push), and can work offline (unlike any connection-dependent animations). The downside is that they require a special tool to make (unless you want to get into the code yourself). Of course, we've included that tool on the CD-ROM (is there no end to our forethought and generosity?). Read the Quick & Dirty Guide at the end of this chapter for step-by-step instructions for creating GIF89a animations. Also refer to Chapter 12, "Working with Graphics," for more general information on this format.

SHOCKWAVE

Macromedia (see Figure 18.3) is the developer of the two major multimedia presentation applications on the market: Director and Authorware. Shockwave is a way to package movies and interactive applications from these programs.

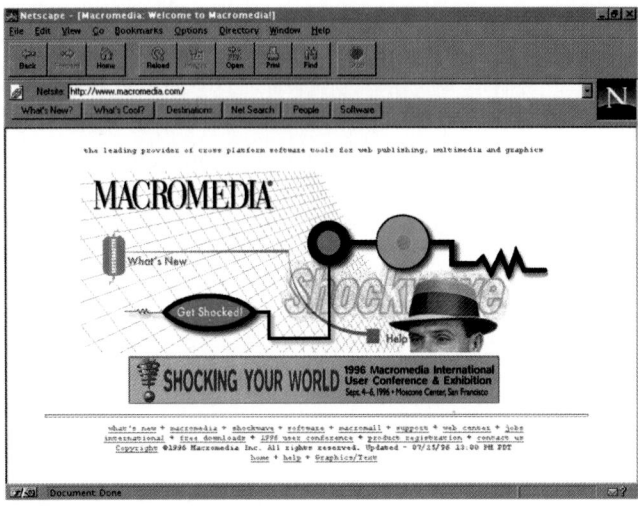

Figure 18.3.
Macromedia's home page.

Macromedia Shockwave for Director and Shockwave for Authorware are, without question, excellent interactive multimedia platforms. Unfortunately, the proprietary nature of

Shockwave, and the need to download plug-ins, makes it pretty unappealing for commercial use. Additionally, these are big files, and though the newest Shockwave for Authorware is supposed to stream (which means that you can view and interact with it while the file is downloading), there is still an issue of bandwidth.

For more information on Macromedia products, visit `www.macromedia.com`. If you are a multimedia developer, you'll find plenty of information on adapting and creating WWW/Shockwave applications.

> **Note:**
> We check all plug-in dependent applications through the BDWBWI (Better Damned Well Be Worth It) protocol. If you are expecting viewers to download and install a plug-in, then return to your page to download a large file, you'd better be sure that you're providing them with something that's worth the wait!

VIDEO

Everyone wants their $3,000+ computer to look like a $200 television. While you can link to (and even embed) AVI, QuickTime, and other video formats within your HTML pages, the files themselves are generally huge, of poor quality, and limited to 320×240 pixels. Although the technology for streaming video (video that is presented as it loads) is being improved constantly, the price for setting up the equipment and server required to run this type of application can be extraordinary, and the quality is questionable. These are the reasons why you don't see many video files on the WWW—yet.

MPEG (a proprietary algorithm-based compression, like JPEG) may soon change this, as MPEG allows for very aggressive compression, full-screen presentation, and high-quality sound and video. MPEG1 is often described as having similar quality to VHS video (again, the TV thing), while its big brother, MPEG2, has mastering digital quality.

Our advice on the use of video is to use MPEG (once it is fully supported). The WWW really isn't a proper vehicle for huge files, and current video formats require bandwidth beyond reason. MPEG encoders and decoders are constantly being improved upon, and your best bet is to continue to search the Net for up-to-date information.

SOUND

Adding sound to your pages is more difficult than you might expect. While you can always link to a sound file (of any type), this doesn't really present a very good effect. Your viewers will need to download the entire file before they can hear it—this isn't exactly what you think of when you want multimedia. Luckily, there are more and more options becoming available for sound.

ACTUAL CONTENT

If you want your page's sound to have actual content—which is to say you want more than just noise—you will want to go with a streaming application. A streaming application does not require a complete file download, but instead allows the viewer (listener) to hear a file as it downloads. One of the most exciting sound streaming applications is RealAudio (`www.realaudio.com`). RealAudio

has such an aggressive compression, and such an effective packet handling protocol, you can actually have a live feed. Visit the National Public Radio site off of the RealAudio home page (see Figure 18.4) for an example.

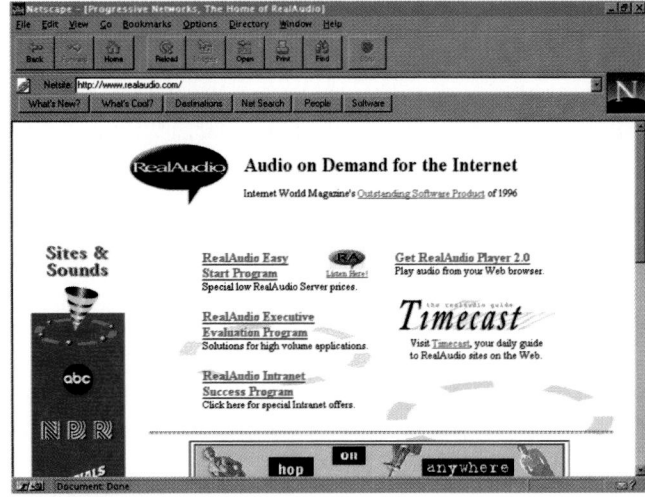

Figure 18.4.
The RealAudio home page.

Generally, the slower the access speed, the poorer the sound quality (because the sound file must be more highly compressed). On a 14.4 connection, RealAudio sounds like an AM radio that is not quite on the station. You can still make out the words, but it's not exactly great sound.

If you are considering adding a vocal sound file (such as a speech) to your site, RealAudio seems to be the best option. It will require vendor software for the server, encoding software for the designer, and decoding plug-ins for the viewers. Visit the RealAudio site for more information.

JUST PLAIN SOUND

If you are simply looking to create a background sound for your pages, you can avoid specialized server/client software in at least two ways. Microsoft Internet Explorer and the newest version of Spry Mosaic allow for the use of a "background sound" (in the body tag: `bgsound="sound.wav"`) within the code. The sound file will download, and then loop as many times as is specified or until the viewer leaves the page. This is, by far, the easiest way to apply sound to your page, and we anticipate that it may be included on other browsers very soon.

The second way to add sound is to use a Java applet. As with all things Java, using an applet for sound is not quite ready for prime time. The sound quality we've experienced on Java-enabled sites is comparable to that of old video games and low-quality MIDI players. Take heed, though, as this will likely change.

THE USE OF JAVA

Java was developed to be a platform-independent programming language. This is to say that it was designed to work under everything from UNIX, to MAC, to Windows. It's best to think of Java as a set of instructions for writing code. Upon loading the applet, your computer writes its own platform-specific code based on the applet, using what is called a runtime module.

The idea behind Java was that a single, small, powerful language that could be used by all platforms would find a perfect application on the Net. Unfortunately, despite the high investment made by many companies, and despite Sun Microsystems' efforts to keep the language pure, there is an almost constant battle being waged over how Java will be used.

Many of the people developing Java applets have found shortcomings in its application. This is to be expected from an entirely new language, as growing pains are par for the course. Unfortunately, some of these developers have bastardized the language to make it work with their specific applications (reducing its cross-platform compatibility and compromising security, among other things).

As we've alluded to before, we don't feel that Java's time has come quite yet. We do believe that the future of the Web may be paved (at least partially) with Java, but we can't quite see that future. There are simply too many problems to overcome, and too few good uses at this time.

This said, there is no doubt that Java is now available, and that there are clean, reliable applications where Java can be useful in presenting your message. Just the use of scrolling text may, in some cases, help you get your point across. In cases like this, by all means use Java. Sun offers a full development kit as well as instructions at its Web site, `http://java.sun.com/`. (See Figure 18.5.)

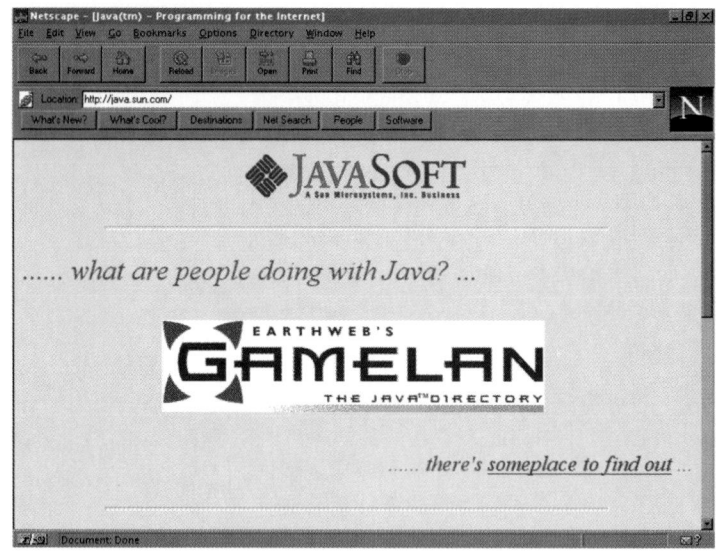

Figure 18.5.
Sun Microsystem's Java development site.

ACTIVEX

Microsoft didn't really jump on the Java bandwagon—it's more like they were dragged kicking and screaming. As an alternative, Microsoft developed ActiveX controls, which can be embedded into HTML to control a variety of objects (including Java).

ActiveX has several unique functions as a controller. One of the coolest is that it automatically downloads any specific software needed to run an object, and allows for digital authentication of these applications. In other words, the code contains the URL of the application (what would be a plug-in on Netscape), goes and gets this app, checks that the file has been digitally signed, and then presents you the verification (because applications can contain nasty things such as viruses, you wouldn't want them to download directly without knowing what might happen).

While ActiveX is clearly powerful, cross-platform, and compatible with many languages, the fact that Microsoft IE is the only browser currently supporting ActiveX (see Figure 18.6), and that IE only represents about 8 percent of the market, seems to make a case for taking a "wait and see" attitude. For information on ActiveX, check out the Microsoft site at www.microsoft.com.

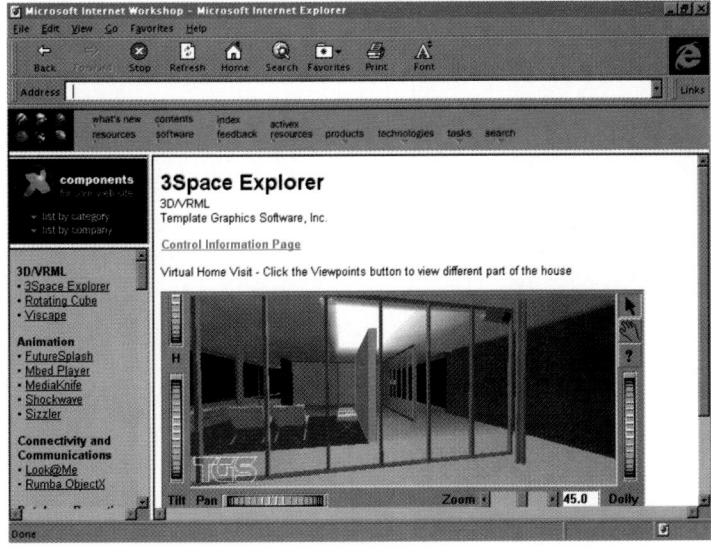

Figure 18.6.
Microsoft's ActiveX control with VRML.

VIRTUAL REALITY MODELING LANGUAGE (VRML)

VRML is, without doubt, the coolest bell or whistle in the works. Virtual Reality is a 3-D modeled "space" generated by the computer that enables the viewer to change perspectives and view objects as if they were "walking" through this space. You can see behind objects by "walking" around to the back. You can move closer and farther, look up and down, left and right. You can even interact with others in this virtual space.

Virtual reality may one day be the preferred method of GUI (Graphical User Interface). This is to say that you may one day interface with your computer via virtual reality—not only for entertainment and interaction, but for more mundane tasks as well. You want to open a file? Go to the file cabinet, open the drawer, and grab the file. Want to delete something? Crush it with your fist, or shoot it with a flame-thrower (it just doesn't get much cooler than that).

TV and films have pushed the idea that you'll be able to slip on a suit, put on some goggles, and "exist" within this virtual world. While this future is now residing as scattered components in many different labs (one place is working on a suit, another is developing goggles, and so on), it's certainly not outside the bounds of technology to believe that we will see consumer-priced virtual reality systems within the next few years.

As it stands now, virtual reality is pretty experimental, and VRML (the proposed standard for virtual reality on the Net) is a pale comparison to what we can soon hope for. The truth is, however, that VRML will probably be a big part of the Web within the next couple of years, and commercial designers should keep on top of the technology.

VRML applications currently enable you to "walk" through "worlds" that contain fairly simple shapes (called primitives) and give you navigational control for moving and viewing (like Intel's VRML in Figure 18.7). You can even create your own model (called an *Avatar*) to represent yourself as you move about a world. This model can be downloaded by others in the same world, so that they can see and even interact with you. This is kind of neat, but there really isn't much commercial application for it yet.

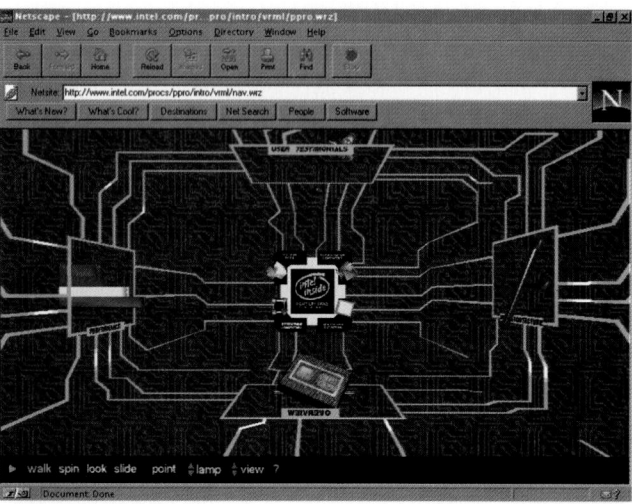

Figure 18.7.
Intel's example of VRML.

As with other cool things, it's the bandwidth bug that brings VRML to a crawl. Add to this the fact that the VRML standard is being pulled in every direction by proprietary concerns, and the conclusion is that VRML is not ready for prime time. Our advice: Wait for the dust to settle.

HYBRID APPLICATIONS

Hybrid applications provide the best solution for the bandwidth problem. A *hybrid application* is an application that contains most of its information on a local memory drive (like a CD-ROM), and uses data transfer only for updates. In this way, users can enjoy rich content and interactivity with only a minimal use of bandwidth.

DOOM was a great early example of a hybrid application. This 3-D shoot-em-up game enabled multiple users to play over a network (such as the Internet), without the need to transfer more than the minimum information. Each user's system had the entire game in memory, and all that needed to be transferred were the position and actions of the players. Compare this to current VRML worlds, where everything must be downloaded to each user's system, and you can imagine how much bandwidth can be saved.

Hybrid applications don't necessarily fit into this book, and it's certainly way beyond our scope to design a hybrid app, but you should know of their existence and rapid development. If you are developing a marketing CD-ROM catalog, for instance, and you want it to be updatable via the WWW (like downloading current pricing, or linking out to ordering), you are creating a hybrid application.

While hybrid applications may go against the "open" nature of the WWW (by requiring more than just a browser and plug-ins), they may provide the most realistic quick fix to the bandwidth problems faced by media developers. Keep an eye out, as this may be a big part of the future.

TRICKS OF THE TRADE

Here's what it comes down to: How much are you (or your clients) willing to pay for features that will only be seen or used by a small percentage of the market?

If a good Web site may take 100 hours to create, and a feature-rich Web site may take 1000 hours, you need to justify that 900 percent increase. If you'll be gaining 10 or more times the sales, or mindshare, or whatever is your goal with the feature-rich site, it's worth the expense (of time or money). Realistically, however, you probably won't be looking at this type of increase.

Clients will often say something like "we want Java." At that point we have to explain to them that Java is a programming language, not a feature. We then ask them what they want to accomplish with a Java application. Some people actually have a use for Java (such as some kind of interactivity), but 99 times out of 100, all the people want is animation.

As a commercial designer, you are looking to provide a good investment, and a good investment is rated by its returns. Your job is to provide the most effective Web site possible, under the constraints of time, money, technology, and bandwidth. The trick of the trade is to honestly assess the possible features of a site against their role in the site's overall effectiveness.

You don't have to be a downer, and just go in dashing everyone's dreams of an awe-inspiring site. What you should do is sit down with the client (or by yourself) and realistically examine your options. If option X will cost $Y, and will only be viewable by Z percent of the WWW community, is it a good expense? In some cases it will be, and in others it will not. You have to put these things in perspective—this is called being a professional.

QUICK & DIRTY GUIDE
Get an Animation on Your Page in 30 Minutes

In our opinion, GIF89a animation is unparalleled in function and simplicity. It adds motion to your page, requires comparatively little bandwidth, and gives a nice effect. Furthermore, these animations require no plug-ins, and either are or will be implemented in the major browsers. When asked to develop animation, GIF89a is almost always our first choice.

So, let's get animated! To continue our exciting generic streak, we've opted to use a 3-D-rendered globe for our example. We've used Asymetrix 3D-FX for our rendering engine, using a globe model supplied with the software. (Hey, we said 30 minutes.)

An animation requires several frames (images) to be used in succession. To do this, we create an animation path for the model (in this case, a spinning motion), and generate snapshots for each frame (see Figure 18.8).

Q&D Get an Animation on Your Page in 30 Minutes

Figure 18.8.
Rendering 3-D frames.

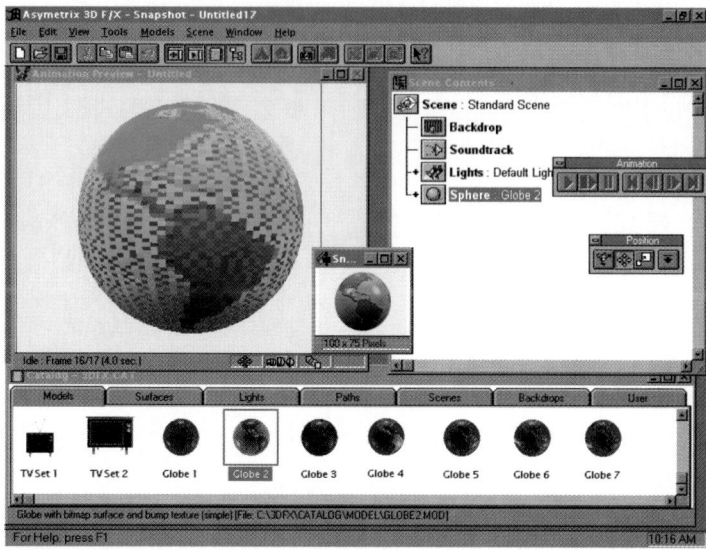

Note:

Most 3-D tools enable you to create animations automatically, using a variety of formats. We've found, however, that the compression and dithering these formats provide are inferior to static bitmaps. This is why we take a series of bitmap snapshots, rather than relying on animation tools.

For this globe, we decided to create a 16-frame rotation. This means that it requires 16 different GIFs to create the effect. The number of frames in an animation will affect the size of the final GIF file. In our sample, we used 16 files which, as individual GIFs, would be approximately 4K each. The resulting animation GIF is under 50K, which means that the size of the GIF animation is not equal to the cumulative size of all of the frames (64K).

Notice that we named the individual frames alphabetically (A,B,C...) rather than numerically (1,2,3...). This is to help us keep track of the sequence. If you are using more than 9 frames, you may want to name them as we've done, since a computer will put the number 10 before number 2 (1,10,11,12,2,3,4,...). Most applications list files in alphabetical order.

Now that we have our frames (see Figure 18.9), we can put them together with the GIF Construction Set (on the CD-ROM). This is a great tool, and we're not nearly using it to its potential in this example. Please note that you do not have to replace the entire GIF in each frame—only the area that you wish to change. The construction set will enable you to place smaller files over the top of larger ones. In this case, however, the entire image changes as the globe turns (though we could have cut the size down a little by reducing the white space).

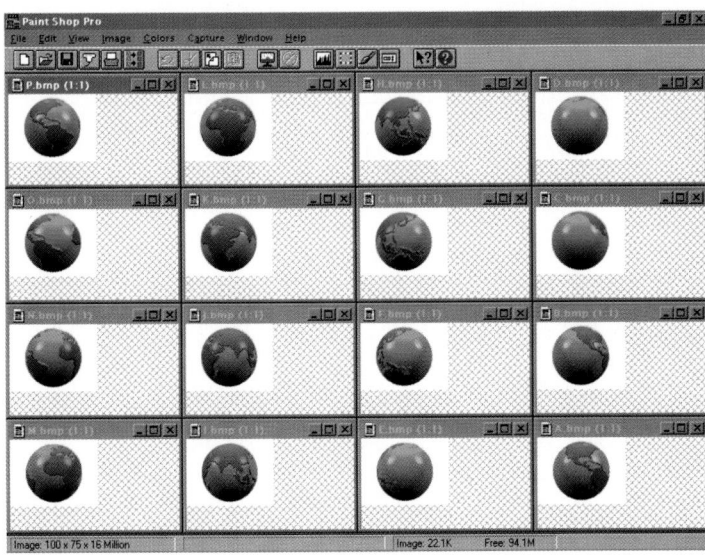

Figure 18.9.
Individual animation frames.

You'll notice in Figure 18.10 that we are adding commands within the construction set. LOOP does what it implies—once the GIF has reached the end, it starts over again. The CONTROL lines enable you to set the timing of the animation (how long each frame will stay on screen before the next loads), as well as how each frame will load in relation to the last. You may need to play with the CONTROL lines quite a bit to get the desired effect for each individual animation.

As you add each image, the construction set asks what palette you want applied. Here again, you will want to play around to see what gives the best effect. More often than not, you'll probably opt for the Use local palette selection.

Once you have created your animation GIF, you can simply place it as you would any other image. You can also resize the image within the code. In this way, one animation can be used for many applications within a site without the need for reloading. In creating a page to display our sample GIF animation, we've used the GIF twice at full size, and four more times as bullets. The effect is a lot of motion on the page (which you'll just have to imagine).

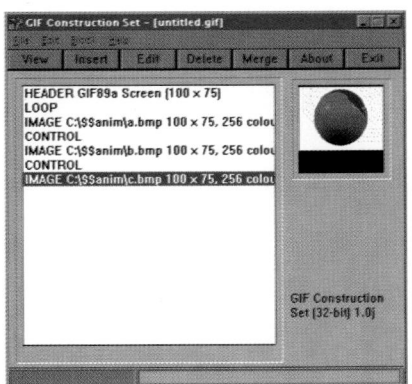

Figure 18.10.
Constructing a GIF animation.

Q&D Get an Animation on Your Page in 30 Minutes

Here's the code we used:

```
<HTML>
<BODY BGCOLOR="#FFFFFF">

<IMG SRC="zglobe.gif" HEIGHT=75 WIDTH=100 ALIGN=LEFT>
<IMG SRC="zglobe.gif" HEIGHT=75 WIDTH=100 ALIGN=RIGHT>
<center>
<h1>Welcome to the World!</h1>
</center><P><br><br><br>
<HR>
<h2><DD>Places to Visit:<P>
<IMG SRC="zglobe.gif" HEIGHT=25 WIDTH=33 ALIGN=LEFT>Forests<P>
<IMG SRC="zglobe.gif" HEIGHT=25 WIDTH=33 ALIGN=LEFT>Oceans<P>
<IMG SRC="zglobe.gif" HEIGHT=25 WIDTH=33 ALIGN=LEFT>Deserts<P>
<IMG SRC="zglobe.gif" HEIGHT=25 WIDTH=33 ALIGN=LEFT>Mountains<P></h2>

</BODY>
</HTML>
```

Figure 18.11 shows you the result.

Figure 18.11.
Our sample
animation page.

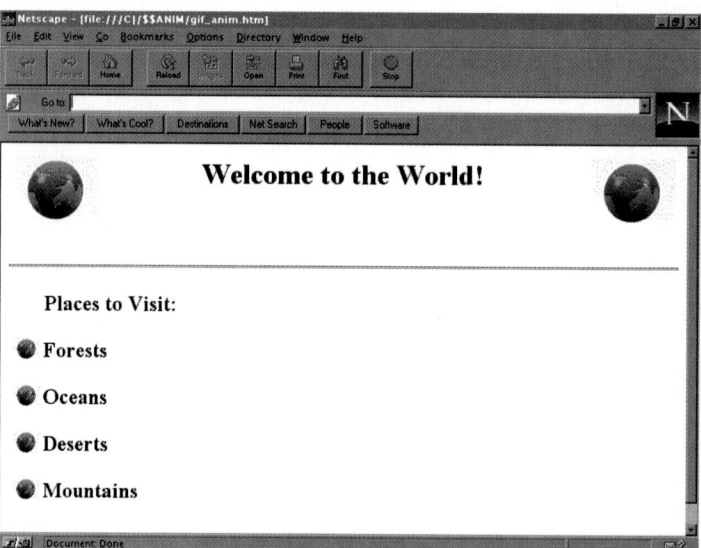

You'll notice that the browser's STOP button remains active (red) even though the document is loaded. When we first started using GIF animation, we received complaints that our pages weren't fully loading. This is not the case. Since most animations are set to LOOP, the browser is constantly reloading the image—but it's doing so from *local* memory. Even if you go offline, the image will continue to LOOP. Luckily, people have now become accustomed to this.

> **Note:**
> Browsers that are not capable of displaying GIF animations will only display a static "snapshot" of your GIF (as will most bitmap manipulation applications). This snapshot will generally be the first or the last frame in your animation, so make sure these frames look good on their own. Viewers using older browsers won't know what they're missing, which is preferable to them feeling like they're missing out.

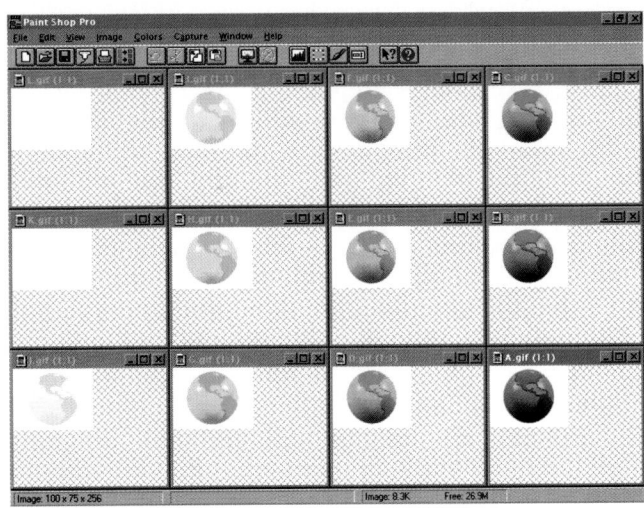

Figure 18.12.
A fade-in or fade-out animation's frames.

And there you have it! Even with the rendering, this took less than 30 minutes (though we must admit, we've done this before).

If you're not lucky enough to have 3-D rendering software, don't despair. A simple animation can be created using any graphics program, including Paint Shop Pro on your CD-ROM. For instance, you can create a simple animation by simply opening a graphic in PSP and lightening the image, little by little, using the Adjust Brightness tool and saving the image each time as a different GIF file (see Figure 18.12).

When put together in the GIF Construction Set (see Figure 18.13), this can create a fade-in or fade-out animation (depending on the order you place the GIF files in the animation). We created a fade-in animation in 10 minutes using this technique. Though this type of animation is very simple to create, the effects can be amazing. For instance, this fade-in animation (when timed correctly by

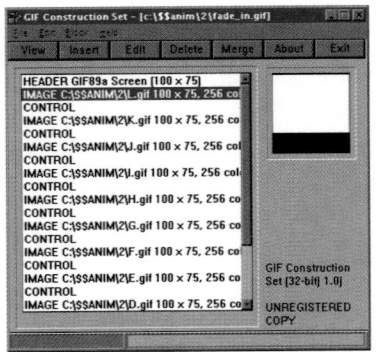

Figure 18.13.
Creating a fade-in animation.

editing the control) can make the graphic seem to appear out of thin air—or to slowly disappear.

See, it's easy—just use your imagination! Animation is just a series of slides. If you can make the slides, you can build the animation.

SUMMARY

Yes, we may have been a big downer throughout this chapter. You may have had grand ideas that we shot right out of the water—which is not really our intention. Our intention was to give you our *honest* opinions on the use of bells and whistles. You see, as Web developers (yes, you included), we are often inundated with software companies pushing their newest feature that will "revolutionize the Web."

We are not saying these companies are bad or lying (in fact the Web would not be what it is today without them). Far from it. They are producing a product that they believe in and we have the utmost respect for that. Our point is to bring all of this down to earth, and to give a more conservative view of things than that offered by sales hype.

In this chapter we have discussed

- ◆ Whether you really need all the bells and whistles
- ◆ Different ways to animate your pages
- ◆ Macromedia's Shockwave
- ◆ Video and the WWW
- ◆ How to incorporate sound into your Web site
- ◆ The use of Java
- ◆ Microsoft's new ActiveX
- ◆ Virtual reality and VRML
- ◆ Hybrid applications
- ◆ How to get an animation on your page quickly using GIF animation

Keep an eye on the development of these technologies, and begin learning how to use them. Don't rule them out, just keep the issues we have discussed in mind. We've said it before, but that won't stop us from saying it again: *Communicate—don't decorate.* Design by this philosophy and you'll be just fine.

Are you ready to get yourself up and running?

Getting It Up and Running

Now that you have developed all the pieces of your site, you're ready to make sure all of those pieces work together. In this chapter we start testing your site; we'll upload it, and we will discuss ways you can verify your code. Hold on, we're about to let the world view your work!

PREPARING FOR THE MASSES

The first step in preparing to go online is to test your site in all three major browsers—Microsoft Internet Explorer, Netscape Navigator, and Spyglass Mosaic—before you upload it. Start from your home page (usually `index.htm`), and check out each page one by one in your browser, making sure all your pages look good. Now, check your system twice more, using the two other major browsers. You are checking to make sure everything works and looks good, no matter what browser the viewer is using.

Tip:
During this testing process, you should resize your browsers' screens to various sizes. Although you may view the Web through your browser at full screen size (or through a large monitor), many viewers may not, and it is important to keep this in mind.

Note:
If you don't already have the three major browsers, you can download them for free from the following sites:

Microsoft Internet Explorer is available at `http://www.microsoft.com/ie/download/`.

Netscape Navigator is available at `http://www.netscape.com/comprod/mirror/client_download.html`.

Spyglass Mosaic is available at `http://spyglass.com/products/index.html`.

If you want to ensure total cross-compatibility, you would also test your pages with older browsers and on different machines (such as Macintosh, UNIX, and so on).

Figures 19.1–19.3 are screen shots of the same HTML file in different browsers.

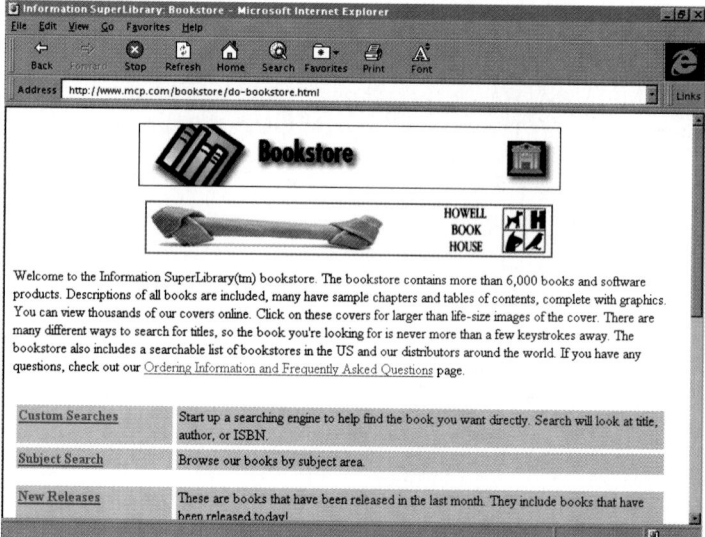

Figure 19.1.
The HTML file in Microsoft Internet Explorer 3.0 (Beta 2).

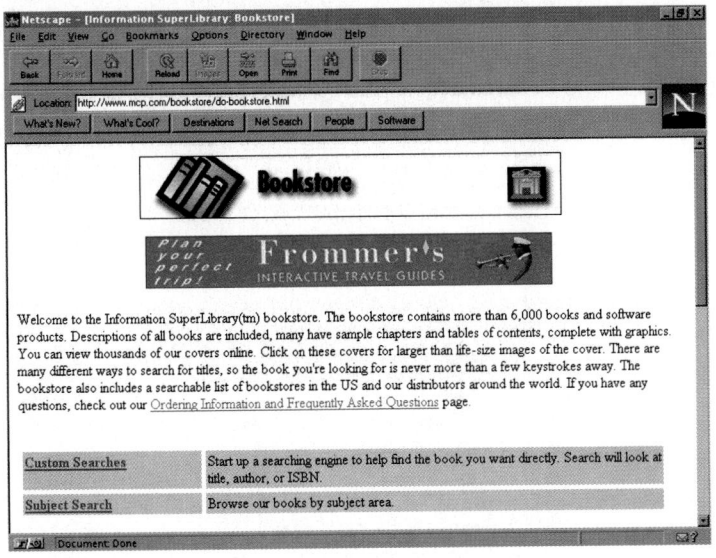

Figure 19.2.
The HTML file in Netscape Navigator 3.0 (Beta 5a).

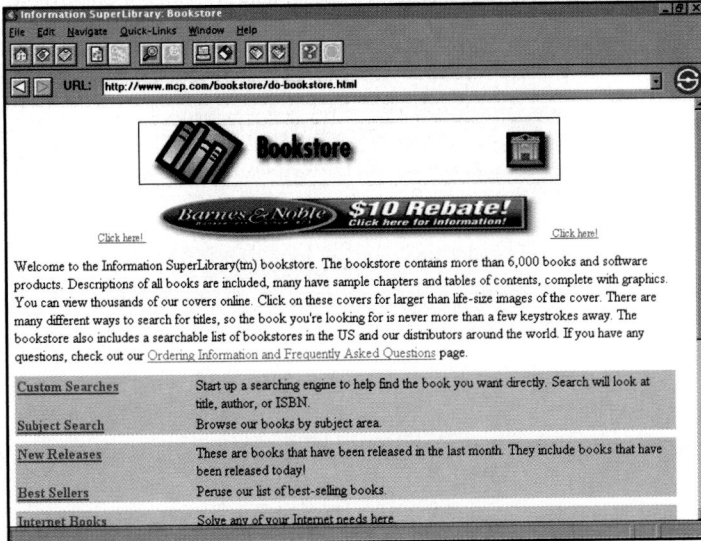

Figure 19.3.
The HTML file in Spyglass Mosaic 2.11.

You can see that this same HTML file looks very similar within the different browsers. This is difficult, but not impossible to achieve. If you have trouble with this, that's all right—just make sure that each page looks like a page you can be proud of, no matter what browser the viewer is using.

GOING LIVE

Before you can upload your files, you must set up your FTP program. (We discuss how to set up CUTFTP—which is on your CD-ROM—in Chapter 5, "Virtual Domain Hosts," in the section titled "How to Use FTP to Post and Update.")

Now, get online and upload your files (making sure you maintain your directory structure). If your site is contained within one directory, you can simply select all of your files within that directory and drag them over to your site. (See Figure 19.4.)

If you are using multiple directories for your site, you will first need to create that directory structure on your server. You do this in CUTFTP by pressing Control + M, typing the name of the directory (see Figure 19.5), and clicking OK. Then upload each file to the correct directory on your server.

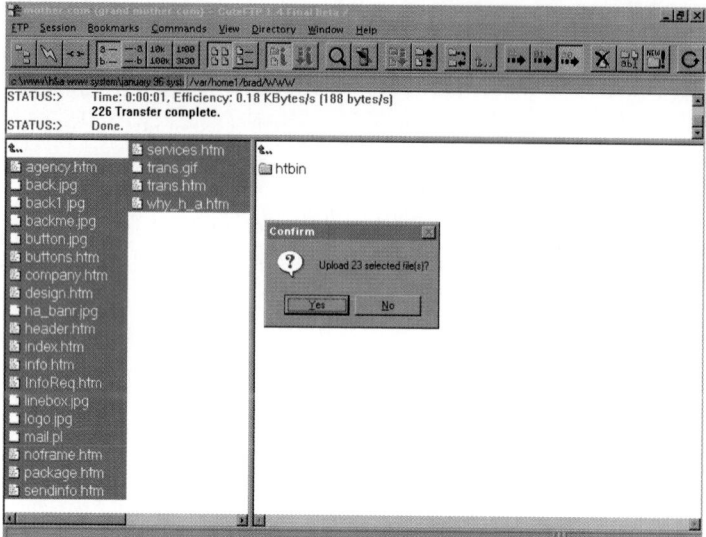

Figure 19.4.
Uploading your site via FTP.

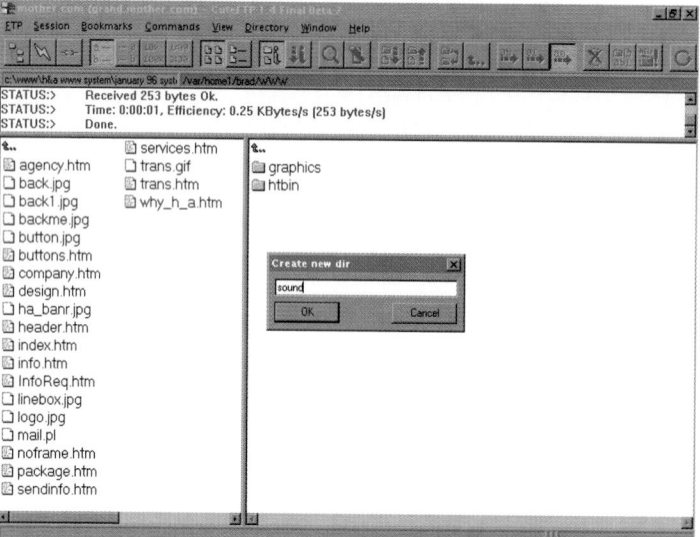

Figure 19.5.
Creating directories on your server via FTP.

TESTING 1,2,3...

Now that your site is uploaded, the next step is to see if it works. Connect to the Internet, open your browser, and enter your site's URL. Check to see if all the links on your site work now that they are online. Now, check with the other browsers. (This may seem repetitive, since you have just done this offline, but believe us, it's important.)

TROUBLESHOOTING

Here are a few of the most common problems you could encounter at this point.

1. **Graphics won't load.**

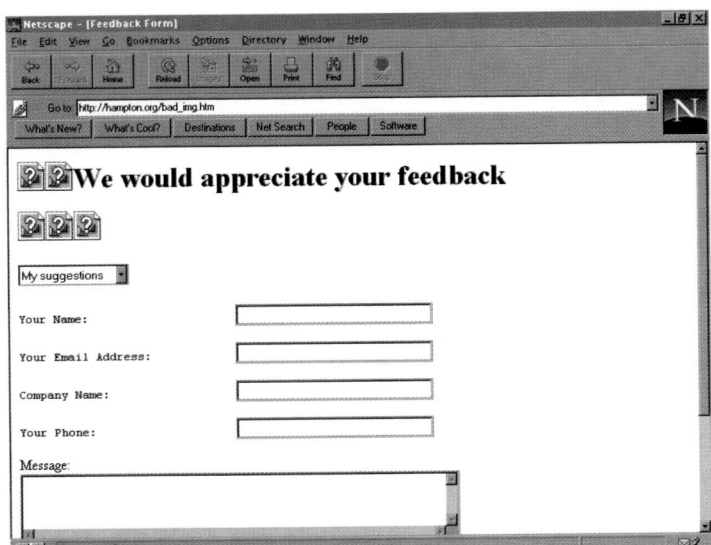

Figure 19.6.
Graphics won't load.

When your page appears but the graphics don't (refer to Figure 19.6), there could be a name problem or an upload problem. Make sure the graphics files are actually in the correct directory and that the filename (including the .gif or .jpg extension) matches the one in your HTML tag exactly, including the capitalization. (Windows machines, for instance, are not case-sensitive, whereas Web servers are.)

If the problem persists, you may have an uploading problem (that is, the files may have been uploaded incorrectly). This is very rare if you are using CUTFTP, which automatically switches between ASCII and binary transfers. In some other FTP software, however, you may need to manually select the transfer protocol. Graphics files use a binary transfer.

2. **File not found.**

When all you get is the message File Not found (see Figure 19.7), this most commonly means that you have misspelled the filename or that the file is not in the directory. Check to make sure that your file is actually where it should be (if not, move it or re-upload). If that doesn't do the trick, the problem is most likely your filename. Don't forget, filenames are case-sensitive, which is why it is a good idea to make all of your filenames lowercase.

A special note to Windows users: The problem may be that your server does not accept the `.htm` extension. Either configure your server to accept this extension (or ask your host to do this for you), or rename your files with the `.html` extension. This can be done from within CUTFTP by selecting the file, hitting Control + N, entering the correct filename (see Figure 19.8), and clicking OK.

3. **CGI problem: You get a 501 error when trying to submit a form.**

   This error message often says something like: "We are sorry to be unable to perform the method POST to non-script at this time." This means that the server did not recognize the referenced URL (the URL defined as the ACTION within the HTML Form) as a CGI script. Make sure that your script resides in the correct CGI-BIN directory and that it has the correct extension to be used on your server.

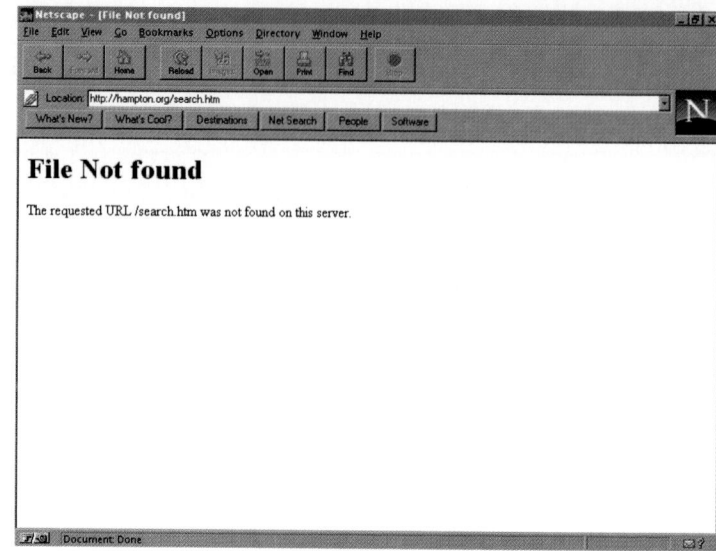

Figure 19.7.
File not found.

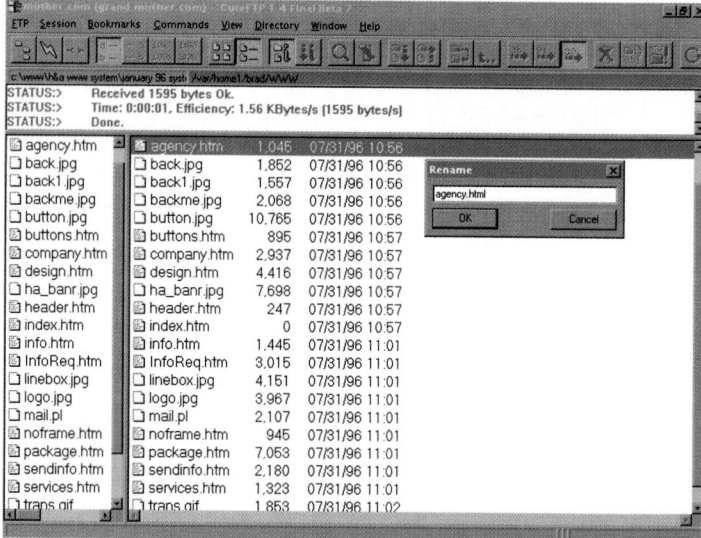

Figure 19.8.
Renaming files within CUTFTP.

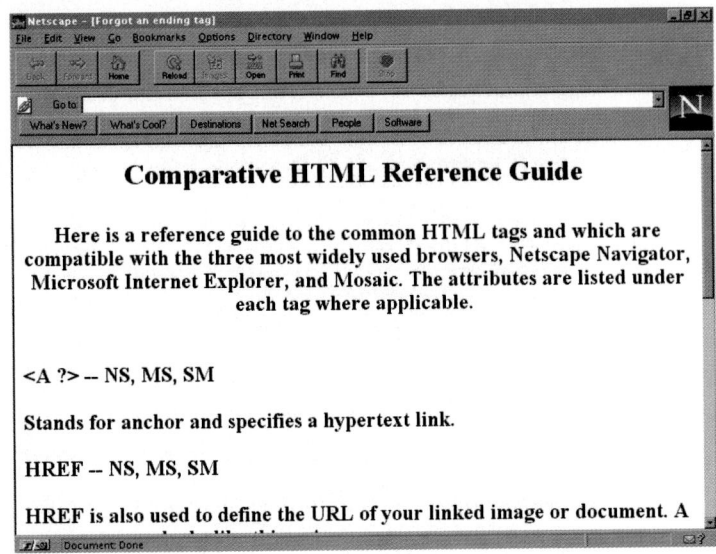

Figure 19.9.
An HTML formatting problem.

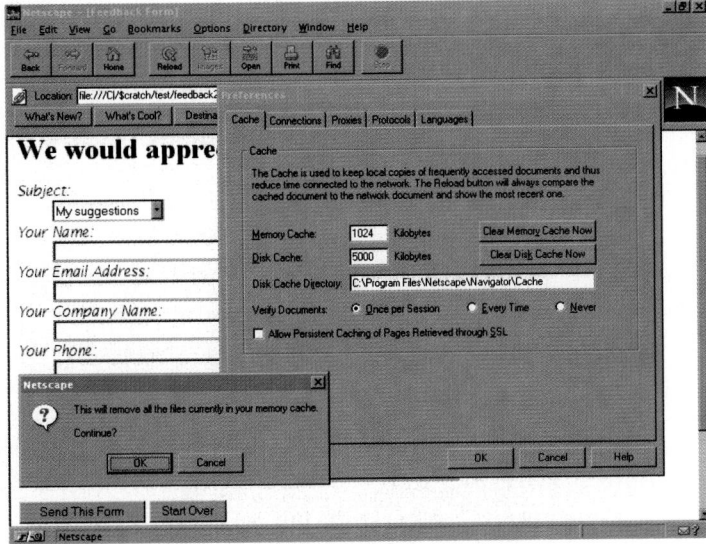

Figure 19.10.
Clearing your cache in Netscape Navigator.

4. **Tag formatting (such as BOLD or H1) goes on and on.**

   Figure 19.9 shows a very common formatting problem, which is generally caused by one of two things: You forgot to add an ending tag (as in </BOLD>), or the ending tag is improper—you forgot one of the brackets, for example (as in /BOLD>).

5. **You changed and reloaded the file, but it still looks the same.**

   We get calls about this all the time. You make corrections and reload the file, and the file is still not fixed. This is a simple problem that occurs when the browser keeps the file in local cache. (This most often occurs in older versions of Netscape Navigator.) The simple solution to this is to clear your cache. This is done in Netscape Navigator by choosing Network Preferences in the Options drop-down menu, and clearing both the disk and memory cache, as shown in Figure 19.10.

CHECKING YOUR HTML FOR UNSEEN ERRORS

So, now that you have checked out your site and have fixed any visible problems, you probably think you can sit back and enjoy a cold one. Well, not quite yet. The next step (if you want to be really thorough) is to check out your site's HTML through an online validation service, or with software developed for that purpose. These programs check your HTML code as only a machine can (in other words, much more thoroughly than we humans are capable of).

ONLINE HTML VALIDATION SERVICES

Tools to validate your HTML documents (check them for errors) are available. There are forms on the Web that hook up to specialized software and check your HTML documents for errors. Some of these services even allow you to specify the HTML version you are using. Here are some that we have found useful:

◆ Weblint (http:// www.khoral.com/staff/neilb/ weblint/lintform.html) hooks up to a Perl script that will check your HTML documents for errors.

◆ HTML checker (http:// www.ijs.si/cgi-bin/htmlchek) uses the Htmlchek software.

◆ WebTechs Validation Service (http://www.webtechs.com/ html-val-svc/) offers many levels of HTML specification conformance.

◆ Doctor HTML (http://imagiware.com/RxHTML/) spell checks a Web page, tests document and table structure, and performs additional tests. (See Figure 19.11.)

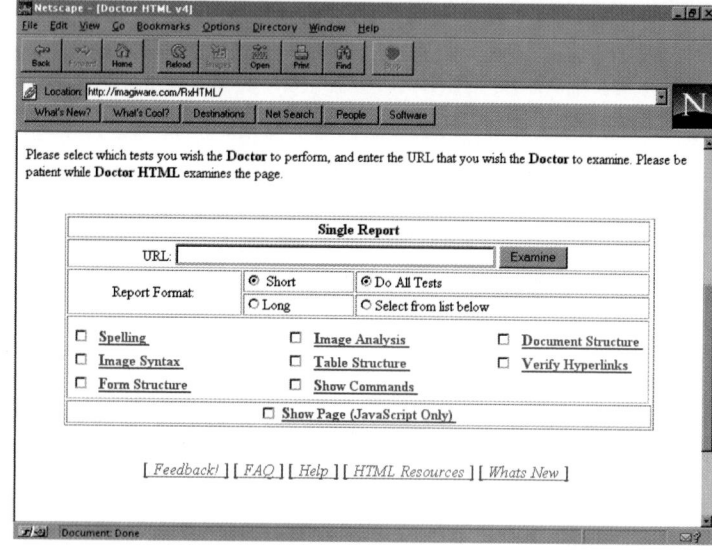

Figure 19.11.
Doctor HTML, an HTML validation service.

HTML VALIDATION SOFTWARE

If you would prefer to have the HTML checking software on your own system (for faster running), there is software available for this.

Some of the software programs we have found are

◆ HTML PowerAnalyzer (http://www.tali.com/) is a customizable HTML syntax checker for Windows that also validates links and scans all files in a Web site project with one click.

◆ Htmlchek (http://uts.cc.utexas.edu/~churchh/ htmlchek.html) is a program that runs under AWK or Perl and syntactically checks HTML 2.0 or 3.0 files for a number of possible errors.

◆ Incontext Spider (a demo version is provided on your CD-ROM) is not only an HTML editor, but also includes real-time HTML validation.

◆ If you're interested in other options, take a look at Yahoo!'s listing at `http://www.yahoo.com/ Computers_and_Internet/Software/ Data_Formats/HTML/ Validation_Checkers/`.

Then there are software programs that take another step in analyzing your site. Incontext WebAnalyzer (Figure 19.12) is a Windows program that identifies broken links or image references, as well as file information like size, modification date, URL, and so on. It then compiles a comprehensive report (see Figure 19.13) that is tailored to suit your own needs; a demo version of this is included on your CD-ROM. Although this program does not check your HTML syntax, it can be very useful for checking for broken links, as well as to give you an easily understood visual diagram of your site.

BACKING UP

After you have uploaded and tested your system, it's a very good idea to back it up. We generally do this by downloading the files we just uploaded and then saving them on a tape backup device. We then store this tape in a very safe place (like a safety deposit box). This ensures that you have an exact copy of your site, and also enables you to use your existing copies for experimentation without the risk of losing everything.

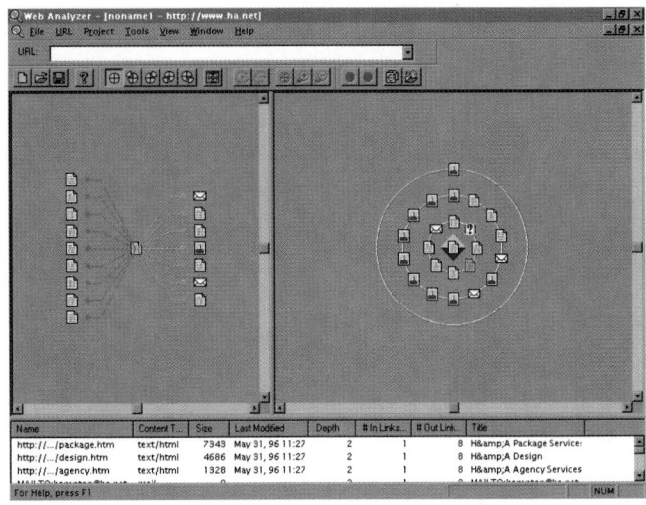

Figure 19.12.
Incontext WebAnalyzer.

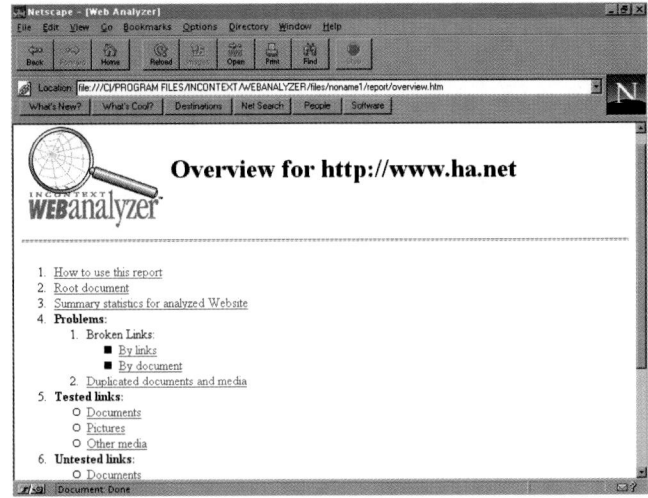

Figure 19.13.
An HTML report generated by Incontext WebAnalyzer.

MURPHY'S LAW OF WEB AUTHORING

If something can go wrong, it probably will (at least once). It is a really good idea to check your site personally at least once a week—better for you to find a problem than your customers, eh? Another option for keeping an eye on your server is to use an alert service like Red Alert (http://www.redalert.com/redalert/home.html), which will notify you—via e-mail or through your pager—if there is a server problem (such as server outage or a failed CGI script). (See Figure 19.14.)

Figure 19.14.
Red Alert, a server-checking service.

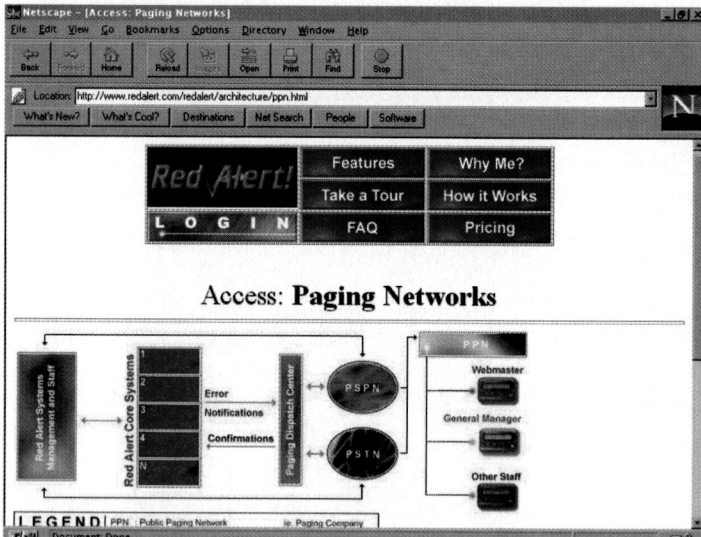

QUICK & DIRTY GUIDE
Site Checklist

1. If you haven't already done so, download all three major browsers now (Microsoft IE, Netscape Navigator, and Mosaic).

2. Test your site offline, ensuring that your pages look good and function properly, regardless of the browser used to view them.

3. Upload your files onto your server.

4. Check your site online (again with various browsers), checking links, appearance, and all special features (your HTML form, CGI script, Java script, frames/noframes system, and so on).

5. Check your site's HTML with an online checking service or your own software.

6. Make a backup of your site and put it in a very safe place.

7. Check your site personally on a regular basis to make sure everything is going OK.

SUMMARY

This chapter has covered the mechanics of getting your site online and running smoothly. We've discussed testing, FTP uploads, troubleshooting, and HTML verification. Welcome to the World Wide Web!

From here, we move on to explain the ways you can publicize your site. The next chapter addresses the issues of marketing in the real world and is followed by a chapter dealing with marketing online.

Marketing Your Site

PART III

Marketing Your Site Offline

Does it seem strange that we write a book on the power of Internet marketing, and our first chapter on publicizing your site deals with going offline? Well, it shouldn't. We've worked for years in traditional marketing communications, and while we now focus exclusively on digital communications, we still know a thing or two.

This chapter discusses the ways you can (and should) publicize your site offline, augment your existing advertising, and gain media publicity. Don't view the WWW as a stand-alone, view it as part of your overall marketing efforts—one tool in the tool chest.

> **Note:**
> The full name of your Web URL includes `http://`. You'll remember that this is telling the computer to treat the address as a Web site (hypertext transfer protocol). Most browsers will now accept an address without this prefix (applying it by default), and it's probably no longer necessary to include this as part of your address.
>
> In fact, most servers no longer need to identify a machine as www (as in `www.ha.net`) in order to pull up the pages, and this too can be omitted, though including this does make it clear that this is a Web address.

WHY OFFLINE?

Let's face facts: A computer screen can only hold a fraction of the information of a printed page, even the best online streaming sound is a pale comparison to radio in both quality and maximum audience size, and TV is still the entertainment medium of choice. It is the combination of text, graphics, and multimedia in an instant, interactive communications package that makes the WWW so powerful, not its strengths in any one facet. Therefore, you may want to look at other marketing tools to help make your WWW project a success—you aren't compromising anything by falling back on tried-and-true communications methods.

If you have the time and budget, even the smallest offline campaign can provide a great return on your investment, especially if you have an existing communications list that you'd like to convert to the WWW. Part of your job in online marketing is to help convert people to this new medium, and the way to reach these people is via traditional means.

One of the main ways to convert people is to augment your traditional advertising, and this is addressed later in this chapter. However, besides augmenting what you've already got, there are certainly some steps you can take to promote your site specifically.

JUMP ON THE BANDWAGON

The national and international news media have done quite a bit of selling for you already. You can hardly turn on the TV or read the paper without seeing something about "Cyberspace" or "The Information Superhighway," and this is certainly to your benefit.

Whether you are designing ads to specifically promote your Web site, augmenting existing ads and materials, or going after press publicity, the simple fact that you are now a member of the information revolution will go a long way toward promoting your site and company.

Furthermore, many professionals are starting to feel as though they're missing the boat when it comes to the WWW. A good information campaign about your own efforts will help your clients better understand this medium. If the clients are big enough, or if you are planning to streamline certain operations by handling them online, it may even be in your interest to help facilitate your clients' getting online themselves. (See "Be the Internet," later in this chapter.)

INVOLVE YOUR CLIENTELE

Perhaps one of the best things you can do is involve your clientele in the creation of the site. (See Chapter 15, "Customer Service Online.") By response mail, phone interview, or personal conversation, you can let your existing clientele in on the (secret) fact that you are creating a Web site, and ask them what they'd like to see on it.

Obviously, this may help you design at least the customer service section of your site, but it goes way beyond that. By requesting input from your clients, you are including them in the process and giving them some ownership of the outcome. Many will feel that they have contributed to your site and will like it that much more.

> **Warning:**
> This plan can sometimes backfire. If your biggest client gives you some input which you can't or don't choose to apply to your site, the client can feel a bit jilted. The best way to avoid this is to include what was requested if possible. Your second choice would be to plan on including the client's "design" in a future revision of the site, and to discuss this with the client.

If there is simply no way you are going to include a big client's input in your site design (like: "I think you should give hotlinks to your competitors' sites."), you should personally contact your client and discuss this decision. Of course, be diplomatic. Don't say it's the dumbest idea you've heard—say that it unfortunately conflicts with some of the goals of the site, and that you're working on a compromise that will meet both your needs.

Clearly, you won't be able to include everything your clients have requested, and that's OK. Fortunately, humans are pretty good at talking themselves into things, and if you include anything on your site that even remotely resembles their suggestion, they'll take credit for it. It may help, if you think

you've given clients the impression that they're unimportant, to put a spin on things. You can call them—before they call you—and tell them how their input "X" had a strong influence on the design of page "Y." Even if they can't see it, they'll often accept credit for it.

Finally, always thank people for their input—just as you have a thank you page after a form, and for the same reasons. First, it lets them know that their input has been received, and second, it lets them know they are appreciated.

SEND OUT A TEASER

A teaser can be a great way to get people interested in your site before it exists. This can help to achieve advanced mindshare, and even get people to bookmark your site before it has any information. Many companies do this all the time for other purposes ("On August 4th, the way you view widgets will change forever—stay tuned."), and the WWW can be well served by such an application.

It is often the case with this type of publicity that the less you say, the better—thus the name *teaser*. It's not teasing if you give full details on what it is you are planning. Your goal is to pique people's curiosity. It's best to use a permanent medium (print, direct mail, or distributed digital) for your teasers, as they can be kept by the individual for later reference. Here are some suggested steps and a sample teaser.

1. **Make a schedule.**

   Teasing relies largely on timing. You will want to nail down the exact date you will be putting your site online and work backwards from there. Therefore, you will need to set an absolute deadline for being up and running, and stick to it come hell or high water.

   Your direct mail piece should be scheduled for delivery within a window of time that is not too early (so as to keep it fresh), and not too late (where it will lose its effectiveness). In direct mail, you are lucky if you can expect a delivery window of one week. Generally, the lower the cost, the bigger the window. (If you are placing teaser ads in magazines, you will know the exact release date—but you'll often have to nail down your Web publishing date months ahead of time.) A window between one and two weeks prior to posting your site should be just about right.

2. Prepare a pre-site.

Since you will be giving your site address, you want to have something up that will reinforce the tease. Never, NEVER say "under construction." This is the sure sign of an amateur, and will give the impression that you haven't got it quite together.

What you want to put on your site is something that mirrors your direct mail piece (we'll be using a postcard as an example), and possibly gives just a crumb more information. This site will also serve to tease surfers that pass by, without their ever having seen the DM (direct mail) piece. You also want to remind and encourage people to bookmark the site, so that they will have it at hand when the day of reckoning arrives. The teaser site for our example is shown in Figure 20.1.

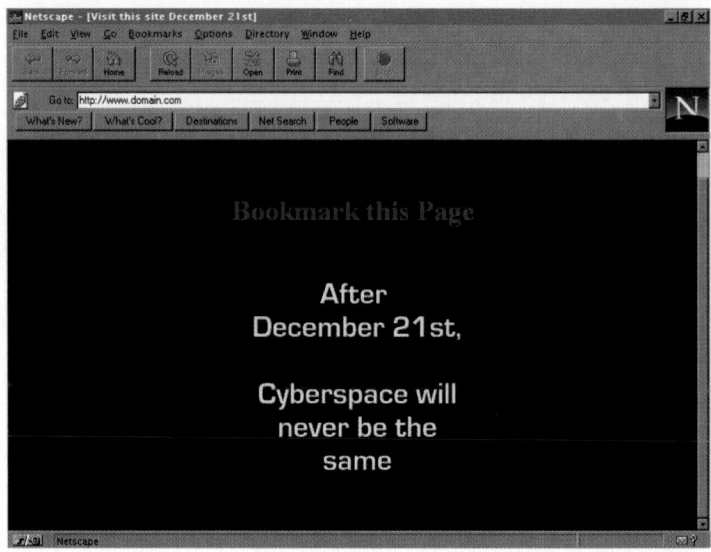

Figure 20.1.
A basic teaser site.

Note that the title of the page is "Visit this site December 21st." This will be the label for this site on a viewer's bookmark file, thus acting as a reminder to check it out on or after December 21st.

3. Prepare your DM piece.

Since we have little to say, a postcard suits our purposes just fine. We'll assume that we have a list of clients and prospects that we want to work off of (though we could also purchase a list from a list broker). So, now all we need to do is design it.

You will probably want to work with a professional designer when developing your piece, since its quality will have a direct effect on the tease. Remember, less is more in this case—all you want on the postcard is the URL, the release date, and perhaps a little teaser copy—don't try to combine the teaser with another promotion to save a few bucks.

In our example, we want to provide only the tiniest hint of information on what we're up to. (See Figure 20.2.) Don't forget that your URL will probably give the target viewers an idea of the company they're dealing with.

Figure 20.2.
A basic teaser postcard.

In this mockup, we went ahead and used some simple 3-D effects to create a door in space. You can certainly make a much simpler design that would be less expensive to reproduce (1- or 2-color).

4. Ship it out.

Remember your timing, and ship out your piece for delivery during your specified window. Also, remember to make sure that there will be something for the viewers to see before the specified date.

Be prepared to fend off some phone calls and e-mail. Even in our most cryptic teasers, a few people have put together the puzzle and have called us (or our clients) to see what was going on. Be vigilant, be vague, and continue to tease. Just don't let the cat out of the bag.

> **Note:**
> If you're going to whip your best clients and prospects into a frenzy, you'd better reward them with a useful (or at least cool) site. Don't apply this teaser technique to promote a vanilla site—it's like telling a kid that they'll get a "treat" if they do something, and then giving them "something healthy"—next time they won't listen.

AUGMENTING TRADITIONAL ADVERTISING

So, what's your current collateral? Do you have business cards and/or letterhead? Do you produce newsletters, product briefs, brochures, catalogs? Do you have T-shirts, key rings, pencils, or baseball caps? Do you advertise in print, or on radio or TV? Do you have outdoor signage, or sponsor events? Do you produce CD-ROMs or other non-Internet digital communication?

We said before that you can include your entire brochure on your business card by just adding your URL, and this same theory can be applied to almost everything else. Once you have a Web site, that URL can appear on everything you do.

> **Note:**
> An important point to make is that your personnel, and especially your sales and customer service staff, are probably your best line of communication. Make sure that they are fully versed in the details of your WWW project, and that they mention this information to as many people as possible. If you have a voicemail system that includes sales messages in its hold feature, insert a little message about your Web site.

PRINT COLLATERAL

Print collateral includes everything from business cards to direct mail promotions, to brochures, product information, and the like. It's basically everything you have printed that has to do with marketing your company—with the exception of specialty advertising. (See the section called "Trash and Trinkets" later in this chapter.)

Once you have a site address, you should include this address on everything (EVERYTHING) you print. Your letterhead, brochures, business cards—everything. It's one line of text, and there's almost nothing that doesn't have enough room for one line of text.

> **Note:**
> We hope you've taken our advice and have registered your own domain name. Doing this allows you to be sure that your address won't change, since you can move your domain name to any server. This way, your printed materials won't become outdated.

If you already have a warehouse full of printed material, and you aren't willing to trash thousands of dollars of printing just to add your address, you've got a couple of options. The first is to apply adhesive labels (stickers) or stamped text to your materials, which give the URL of your site. Unfortunately, applying a sticker or ink stamp to a well-designed four-color piece will often reduce its effectiveness. It's not in your interest to degrade your collateral just to add your URL.

Your second option is to design a special piece that can be included with any outgoing print communications. An insert that lists your URL and gives a little hype, if designed to work with the look and feel of your existing print, is probably the better option.

If you currently produce a newsletter for your clients (or even your personnel), the main story on your next issue should be your leap onto the Web. It should cover the background of the medium, your goals, and quotes from the top brass of your company (even if that's you).

PRINT ADVERTISING

Print advertising generally refers to the advertising space you purchase in newspapers and magazines. Adding "Visit us on the Web at…" to your display ads is usually a simple procedure. You may not even need to reproduce your pre-press art, depending on your layout, as most design departments will be able to strip in a line of text with no problem.

> **Note:**
> This applies to both print collateral and print advertising, and may also apply elsewhere. Many people in certain industries see the WWW as a threat, and may try to talk you out of including your WWW address. This is rare, and exceedingly unprofessional, but we've seen it. Obviously, ignore this "advice."

RADIO

If you are running radio ads, you may want to include your URL ("visit X company's Web site at…") in the voice-over copy. Though it's not likely that people are going to pull off of the freeway to write down your address, they're not likely to do this for a phone number either. Yet, somehow, giving out phone numbers on the radio seems to work.

> **Note:**
> As mentioned earlier, you can probably avoid the `http://` part of your address. In the case of radio and TV voice-overs, this should definitely be omitted—"AICH, TEE, TEE, PEE, COLON, FORWARD-SLASH, FORWARD-SLASH…"

TV

Television is multimedia—text, graphics, video, animation, and sound. If you are running TV ads, it should be no problem to add your URL in at least the titling (text), and perhaps the voice-over, of your existing production. Most post-production studios will be able to do this in a matter of minutes, and the rewards from this simple exercise can be dramatic.

Since TV is a visual medium, you can even include screen shots of your Web site. Of course, you can also do this in print, but TV can enable you to show the action on your site—something more likely to gain interest than a static shot. Clearly, a screen shot won't fit into most TV ads' themes, and you wouldn't want to cheapen your overall presentation just to make room for a screen shot, but it's something to keep in mind.

OUTDOOR ADVERTISING

If you have on-site signage or lease billboard space, and have room for your phone number, you also have room for your URL. People often forget this in their outdoor ads, and they shouldn't.

Furthermore, if you sponsor special events (like a golf tournament, for instance), your outdoor signage may have certain limitations. Many times, phone numbers cannot be included in certain recognition ads (like greens signs), yet there may be no such rules against listing a Web URL.

TRASH AND TRINKETS

Specialty advertising—like shirts, pens, Frisbees, refrigerator magnets, paperweights, and so on—can easily include a Web address. The easily recognizable format of a URL can often gain the attention of those "in the know," and a T-shirt, for instance, with a bold URL on the back, can gain a lot of attention from more than just the wearer.

As with all of the other things mentioned, there really isn't a reason to *not* include your WWW address, unless it somehow detracts from the overall effectiveness of the advertising effort. If you've got it, use it!

PUTTING IT ALL TOGETHER

If you are going to include the World Wide Web as an integral and important part of your complete marketing campaign, then it should have its place in your overall design efforts. This is to say that when you design future campaigns, the Web should be considered as part of those campaigns, and their overall design should take this into account.

◆ Try to give your traditional materials and your Web site the same graphical elements, and the same "look and feel."

◆ Within reason, avoid artwork that will be difficult to reproduce on the WWW.

◆ Orchestrate changes in your traditional efforts with those on the WWW (post your new Web site at the same time you send out your new brochure, or vice versa).

GAINING MEDIA PUBLICITY

The news media loves the Information Superhighway, and even the smallest mention of your site in a magazine, newspaper, or on radio or TV can do more to publicize your site than 20 full-page ads. Considering the negligible investment of a press release, you should think of publicizing your site in this way as a "must do."

Although you can send out your own news release, an experienced PR or ad firm that offers media relations services can be a great asset. This is not only because they will be able to put a "spin" on your story that can make it more attractive to reporters, but because they will have contacts in the industry who can help push that story through.

BE THE INTERNET

It may be both financially and logistically feasible to put your clients online yourself. Obviously, this will require that you assess the cost of sales to existing clients, and see if the numbers add up. Furthermore, you'll need to ascertain whether your clients will even want to go online. Think of it this way: Federal Express has been putting "shipping computers" in offices for years—there must be something in it for them. Using the Internet for your own WAN (Wide Area Network) can be both easier to sell and less expensive than trying to set up a bulletin board system or other non-Internet data transfer.

Suppose you provide some type of consumable, or some ongoing service (widget gaskets, or widget adjustment) that clients order on a continuing basis. You have 20 major clients spread across

the United States, and each client orders between $2,000 and $10,000 a month in goods or services. You accept both phone and fax orders, but those orders must be keyed in individually, which increases both the cost of the sale and the time to ship.

You discover that you can accept orders via the WWW and have them directly input to your database, thus streamlining the entire operation. Unfortunately, none (or only a fraction) of your clients are on the Net in any way. What do you do?

COUNT OPERATIONAL COSTS

Well, first you figure out the cost. You can contact some national dial-up ISPs and assess what it would cost on a monthly basis to provide Internet connectivity to your clients. Let them know that you want some sort of discount, and ask about any other specific features they might provide. Some ISPs can change their start-up software packages to include your company name and logo—making you appear to be the ISP yourself—which is sure to impress some clients.

Now, you probably don't want to get into the business of providing Internet access. So you need to make sure that whatever ISP you choose to work with will provide quality service and support—you don't want clients calling you continually to ask how to use their e-mail.

ASSESS INTEREST

Next, you'll want to talk to your clients and see if they're interested. Some people will jump at the chance to get online. Remember: Television, radio, and print continually present the WWW and Internet as *the future*, and the fact of the matter is that many (if not most) professionals feel that they are being left behind if they are not "Internet-ready."

Unfortunately (or, perhaps fortunately), it's rather difficult to get online. Good Internet service providers are difficult to find, and can be even more difficult when it comes time to ask for customer support. This has kept many people from joining the information revolution. By providing an easy solution, you can be the hero.

You may find that some of your clients are frightened of the Internet. This is not to say that they'll actually run screaming to the hills at its mention, but that they may strongly object to using this type of service, or completely reject the idea of their connectivity being to their own benefit. So you may have to offer incentives (which we address shortly).

COUNT START-UP COSTS

Did we already mention this? No, what we're talking about here is the actual equipment that your clients have on site. Once you've assessed your clients' interest in connecting, you'll need to find out what tools they have. If your clients already have decent systems on site, connecting them may simply be a matter of providing them with software and simple instructions.

If, on the other hand, your client's computer system is antiquated, or nonexistent, you may need to look into providing the client with both a computer and extensive training—which would clearly force the cost up quite a bit. For some clients and industries, this investment could be well spent; for others, it could be a waste.

> **Note:**
> The Internet Appliances ($500 stripped-down systems specifically made for Internet access) due out soon should help balance costs and provide an excellent alternative to placing a $3,000 computer in a client's office just for Internet access.

So, figure out both the equipment and training investments, as well as the software and service costs, and see whether it is in your interest to provide this type of service. In some cases, the clients may want to just stick to the status quo, seeing your efforts as an attempt to throw more work at their staffs for your benefit. In cases such as this, you may need to sweeten the pot.

OFFER INCENTIVES

Suppose you figure that after all is said and done (figuring software, training, connection charges, savings on your end, and so on), the first year cost-of-sale for a specific client will be reduced by four percent. So, on a $100,000 per year account, you'll be getting an extra $4,000. This will give you a little spending money.

The best incentive for a business might just be a discount. You may just wish to offer a two percent discount on all orders made via the Internet, pocket the other two percent, and everyone's happy. Sometimes, however, this won't cut it—especially if the decision to go online hinges on an office manager who will never see that two percent personally. You may need to hype things up a bit, and you have at least a couple of options:

> **Trash and trinkets**—"In appreciation for converting to our new ordering system, we'll send you this CD-player!" So you spend $100 on a boom box—big deal!

> **Prizes**—"Every time you send in an order, your name will be entered in a drawing to win an all-expense-paid Caribbean cruise for two!" This may really get the ball rolling—imagine an office fighting over who gets to send in an order!

Obviously, make sure that everything makes sense on the bottom line. You may find that it just doesn't make sense to bring your clients out of the dark ages. On the other hand, it may be the best investment you can make.

QUICK & DIRTY GUIDE

The Eight Most Important Things You Can Do to Market Your Site Offline

1. Involve your clientele in the creation of the site, to give them a sense of ownership.

2. If it's within the budget, plan a traditional media campaign to coincide with your Web site release.

3. Think of your URL the same way you do your phone number—include it everywhere from business cards, to brochures, to Frisbees and beyond.

4. Put your WWW address on all advertisements.

5. Take advantage of the hype surrounding the WWW, and issue press releases to get the media interested.

6. Treat the WWW as one part of the overall marketing effort, and not a stand-alone.

7. Orchestrate new print (or other media) campaigns with WWW campaigns, and vice versa.

8. If it makes sense, consider putting your clients online yourself.

SUMMARY

In this chapter, we have discussed several ways to provide offline support for your online ventures. We've gone over ways to incorporate WWW promotion with other media, the mechanics of a "teaser" promotion for a new site, and even ways to convert your clients to online sales.

In the next chapter, we get back online and show you how to promote your site around the world from the comfort of your own keyboard.

Marketing Your Site Online

So, there are tens of millions of Web viewers, millions of Web sites, and here's little ol' you just waiting for someone to happen upon your site. Well, wait you shall, unless you take action to draw some of those viewers in. Just being online is not enough—you've got to tell folks where you are.

CHAPTER
twenty-one

"Build a better mousetrap, and the world will beat a path to your door." "If you want someone to listen, whisper." Ever heard these before? Ever believe them? If you think that you can just sit and wait, and that the world will seek you out, you're going to be sitting a long, long time. The fact of the matter is that you need to make yourself available.

Luckily, there are several ways that you can promote your site and business online, and they are often the most effective and inexpensive promotions possible. To put things bluntly, you should consider online promotion as an integral part of your Web site implementation—there's no way to avoid it.

REGISTERING WITH SEARCH ENGINES

When you perform a search of the Web with a search service (such as Yahoo!, Lycos, Excite), the engine responds by returning a list of sites (see Figure 21.1). These Web sites didn't just pop out of nowhere—their administrators had to register them. This registration process is the most popular and simplest way to market your site online.

Figure 21.1.
The results of a search for "commercial web site development" using Lycos.

TELLING PEOPLE YOU'RE OUT THERE

Search engines are very widely used on the Web. When a viewer is looking for a specific piece of information, his/her first step will most likely be to use a search engine. If you hope to attract a large number of viewers to your site, you will need to register with these services.

While there have been some attempts to start search and indexing services that charge either the person requesting the search or the companies being indexed, the largest, most powerful and most widely recognized and used services are paid for through display ads and are free to both the listed and the viewer.

HOW THEY WORK

There are many popular search engines on the Web, using many different methods for their searches. Some (like EINet Galaxy) work mainly by categorizing the site into different topics (not actually a search engine) and returning a viewer's query based on the category and the description the company gave when it originally registered (using an indexer). Yahoo! (see Figure 21.2) adds a search engine, which enables viewers to find what they are looking for quickly (which may explain its popularity).

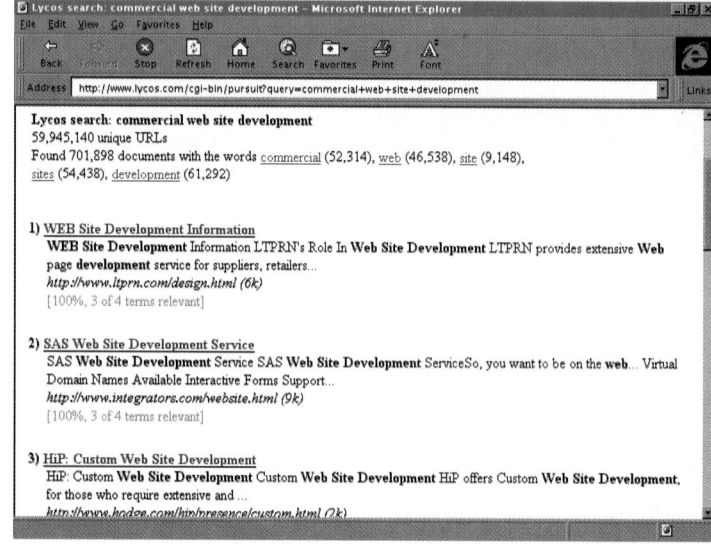

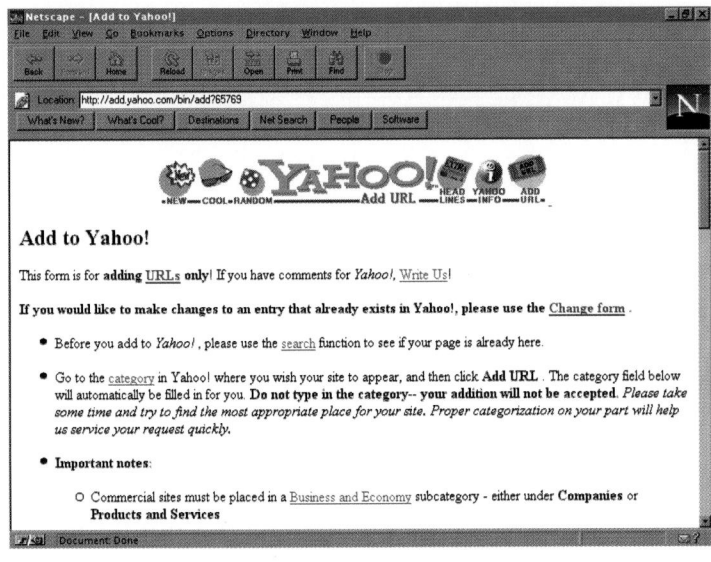

Figure 21.2.
Registering a site with
Yahoo!

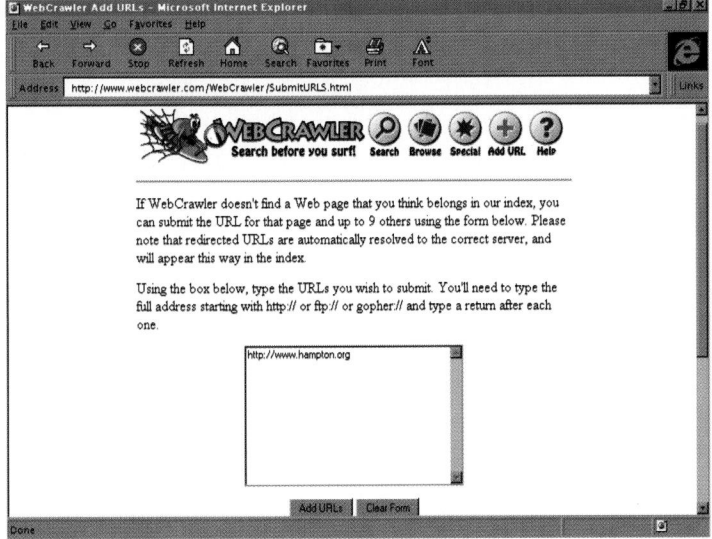

Figure 21.3.
Inviting WebCrawler to
take a look.

Others work by actually roaming through the Web using a "robot" or "spider" (like WebCrawler, Lycos, and AltaVista), searching for new or updated pages. When these search engines find a page, they search even more closely to see if that document is connected to any others. They will then roam those linked documents as well, indexing all they find in their search database. Now, in theory, these search engines will find your Web site whether or not you register with them. But in practice, it could take weeks or months for them to find you (if at all), so you're really better off submitting your site (usually by just entering your URL) and inviting their robot to take a look (see Figure 21.3).

You can assist these types of engines by providing meta-information (which we talk about later in the section called "Keywords and How to Use Them"), by making your page title descriptive, and by including as many keywords as possible.

Note:
In the Quick & Dirty Guide for this chapter, we tell you how to register with most of the following search engines quickly. However, to gain effectiveness in the registry process, it is wise to check these search engines out individually, to see how they work and how they are arranged, and to then register with them individually in order to better tailor your information to each particular engine.

WHERE TO GO

Most of the major search engines are set up to enable quick and easy submission of URLs. Here is a list of the submission pages for the major search engines:

AltaVista: http://www.altavista.digital.com

EINet Galaxy: http://galaxy.einet.net/cgi-bin/annotate?Other

Excite: http://www.excite.com/Search/add_url.html

Infoseek: http://www.infoseek.com:80/doc/FAQ/_How_do_I_get_my_Web_page_inde.html

Inktomi: http://inktomi.berkeley.edu/addurl.html

Lycos: http://www.lycos.com/lycos-register.html

NCSA's What's New page: http://www.ncsa.uiuc.edu/SDG/Software/Mosaic/Docs/whats-new.html

Open Text: http://www.opentext.com:8080/omw/f-omw-submit.html

Open Market: http://www.directory.net

Point: http://www.pointcom.com

WebCrawler: http://www.webcrawler.com/WebCrawler/SubmitURLS.html

World Wide Web Yellow Pages: http://www.mcp.com/newriders/wwwyp/submit.html

WWW Worm: http://wwwmcb.cs.colorado.edu/home/mcbryan/WWWadd.html

Yahoo!: http://www.yahoo.com/bin/top1?424,11

Simply go to these sites, follow the instructions, and submit your pages.

WHAT CATEGORY DO I FIT IN?

When registering with most of the search engines, you will need to decide the category your site should be listed under. (See Figure 21.4.) The category you choose should depend not only on the main focus of your business, but on your target audience as well. For instance, say your site is for an animation company that provides Web services for business. You could register your site under Web animation, but this category would be viewed mostly by people interested in creating Web animations. A better choice would be to list your site under a category like business or Web services, which is more likely to be viewed by your target audience. Makes sense, right?

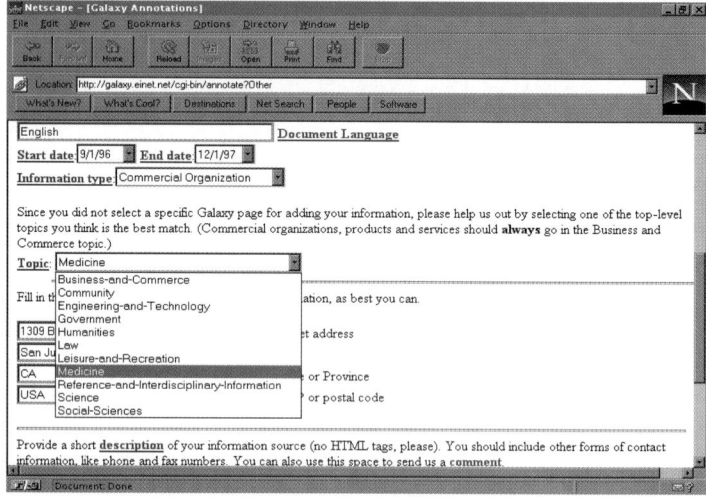

Figure 21.4.
Choosing your category for EINet Galaxy.

Different search engines categorize differently, so sketch out some ideas of good categories, and when registering, look for categories that fit your objective most closely.

THE IMPORTANCE OF YOUR COMPANY DESCRIPTION

Many search engine submission forms ask for a company description. The search engines use these descriptions in different ways, but almost all will access it for keyword searches. When writing yours, you should be aware of this and should attempt to include as many likely keywords as possible. (For example, if keywords such as clothing, designer, and discount are likely to be used for your clothing business, be sure to include these words in your description.)

This company description is also often used as a synopsis of your company and site (following your URL in the listing). For this reason, it is also important to make your company description appealing. Convince people to visit your site, and not the one listed beneath you. (See Figure 21.5.)

KEYWORDS AND HOW TO USE THEM

You can aid a "webcrawler" type search engine by giving it a clue to your Web page contents. This is done by providing meta-information, which specifies keywords or a description. (If this is not done, most often the description or keywords will be taken from the first 200 or so characters of your page.)

When choosing keywords, ask yourself, "What search string would viewers use if they were looking for my product or service?"

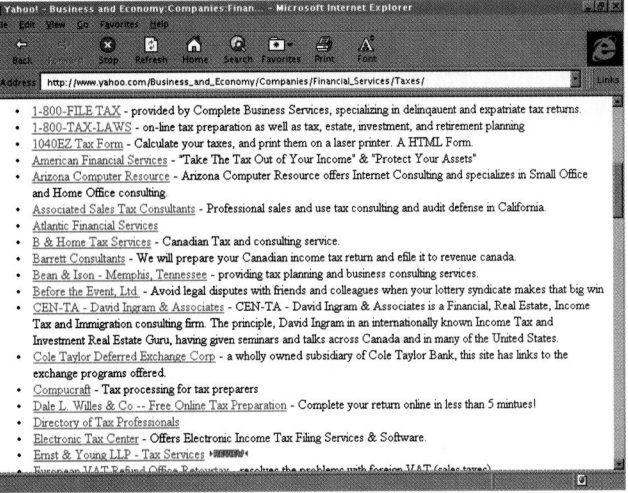

Figure 21.5.
How the company description appears in Yahoo!.

> **Note:**
> Providing this meta-information is particularly useful if your site uses frames because your frameset page may not contain an adequate description.

You can provide this meta-information by making use of the `<META>` tag in the `<HEAD>` element of your page. It should be provided like this:

```
<META Name="description" Content="Your description
goes here">
<META Name="keywords" Content="Your keywords go here">
```

Since the keywords and description are generally indexed in the same way as the rest of the text on your page, you should keep words which you want indexed together as a phrase close to each other. For example

```
<HEAD>
<TITLE>The Widget Home Page</TITLE>
<META Name="description" Content="Home page for the
Widget Corporation, providers of widgets and widget-
related products, discount widgets">
<META Name="keywords" Content="Widget Corporation,
widgets, retail widget products, search widget site,
find widget information, find widget retailers, browse
widget products, Joe Doe Average president of widget
corporation, get widget information, widget suppliers,
widget distributors, widget headquarters Alabama,
locate widget information">
</HEAD>
```

BUYING BANNERS, PAID LINKS, AND DIRECTORY LISTINGS

Taking advantage of another site's high hit count can be very effective, if you have the budget for it. Many companies (Yahoo!, Lycos, Playboy, and so on) offer paid links, banner advertising (see Figure 21.6), or special directory listings. Beware, though—costs can reach into the millions for these ads, and the effectiveness is often difficult to measure.

How do you determine how much you should pay for advertising on a Web site? This is quite a difficult question, since the market hasn't been around long enough to develop a good set of standards. You'll probably just have to wing it and use your own judgment.

The first question you'll want to ask yourself when considering buying a Web display ad is this: "What, exactly, am I paying for?" As with any advertising, you are paying to get your message out. Unfortunately, the measurements for Web advertising aren't as cut-and-dried as they are for, say, magazine ads.

The first issue is that of the reliability of the site and the server it resides on. Your ad won't do much good if the server is offline or under-powered. Think of this as the delivery of your message; slow or unreliable servers won't do a very good job of getting your message out (though they may be able to provide good-looking data, which we address shortly).

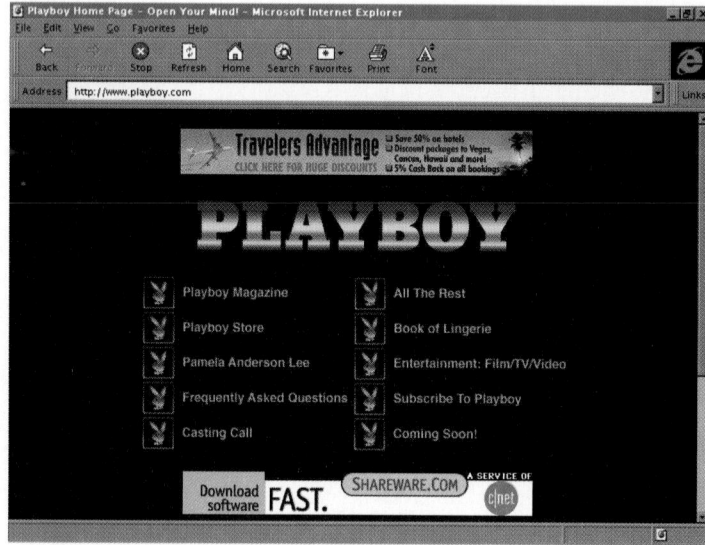

Figure 21.6.
Banner advertising on the Playboy Web site.

The next issue is the number of people who will be viewing your ad, the quality of those people, and the way in which this data is collected. If you are selling business equipment, for example, it won't matter a hill of beans how many hits there are on a page containing your ad if all of those hits are from 14-year-olds. Unfortunately, there aren't many good ways to assess this, and it's not yet in the seller's best interest to provide accurate information to its advertisers.

Most companies that provide paid links are using Web traffic analyses—based on the number of hits received by either the server itself, or by particular pages—in order to determine the amount of people viewing each ad.

Problems with using these hit counts include:

1. The number of Web hits on a document varies, depending on the number of graphics and other embedded links within it. (A page with five graphics might give you a hit count of six, when it actually only represents one viewer, for example.)

2. Determining the number of viewers with a server hit count is even more troublesome. A good example of this is the Playboy Web site. Although Playboy gets an incredible number of hits, we wonder if the stories and ads are actually being read, or if the viewers are jumping directly to the internal pages to see the pictures. (We know, they just read it for the articles.)

3. Caching of Web documents (the browser keeping the file in local memory so it need not download it again, or private crawlers that grab pages for the individual viewer and then store them offline for later viewing) proves to be another problem when using hit counts to determine viewer counts. As more and more offline readers are used, the number of raw hits received by a site becomes less representative of the number of times a viewer might actually see those pages, although this is usually to the advertiser's benefit.

Some companies are now improving their tracking of viewers by using means other than hit counts. One of the ways is to require a registration and log-in sequence to access the site. This is a good option in that it identifies the viewer as an actual human being and can also provide demographic information (based on what is requested during the registration process), which some companies make available to their advertisers. While this does require another step for the viewer (which they may find annoying), it can be indispensable to you in assessing and justifying costs.

Another fairly new trend is to charge the advertiser on a "per forward" basis. This method only charges for viewers who actually follow the paid link in order to arrive at your page. If you can find a company that charges in this way (and you can afford it), this may be the best way to test the waters.

DEVELOPING LINK PARTNERSHIPS

A method many people use to gain publicity for their site is to create link partnerships. It works like this: "Hey Joe, how about I put a link to your site on my page, and you put a link to mine on yours?" You should only create link partnerships with companies that your viewers would be interested in (such as a service related to your product), and you should always be aware of the possibility that they may actually go to that site, never to return to yours again. In other words, be careful.

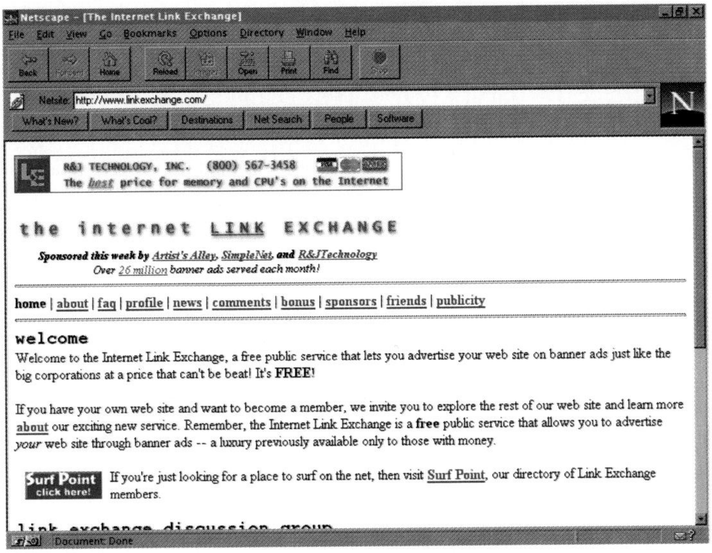

Figure 21.7.
The Internet Link Exchange.

Link partnerships have become so popular, companies have actually jumped in to facilitate the process. One such company is the Internet Link Exchange at `http://www.linkexchange.com/`. (Refer to Figure 21.7.)

The problem with trading links broadly is that you are often giving more than you are getting. Someone who came to your site specifically is more valuable than someone who is just surfing around and skipped over from another site. In most cases, you are looking for customers, not surfers.

If you do decide to trade links, you should proceed with the same caution as you would in networking personally. You wouldn't trade leads with someone who doesn't share a client base in the real world, and you shouldn't do it in cyberspace. If you're selling Bibles, you probably wouldn't get much business from a link on a XXX adult site (but they might get quite a few clients from you!). Remember, your resources are limited. You don't want a bunch of looky-loos slowing things down for real prospects.

USENET GROUPS

It may be beneficial to also post an announcement of your site on *appropriate* Usenet groups. This is a very sticky issue and may cause you to get some harsh responses if not handled responsibly. You should make your

announcement as short as possible, and only post it to groups you feel would truly benefit and appreciate this information.

You can browse through a listing of Usenet newsgroups at `http://miso.wwa.com/~boba/news.html`. (See Figure 21.8.)

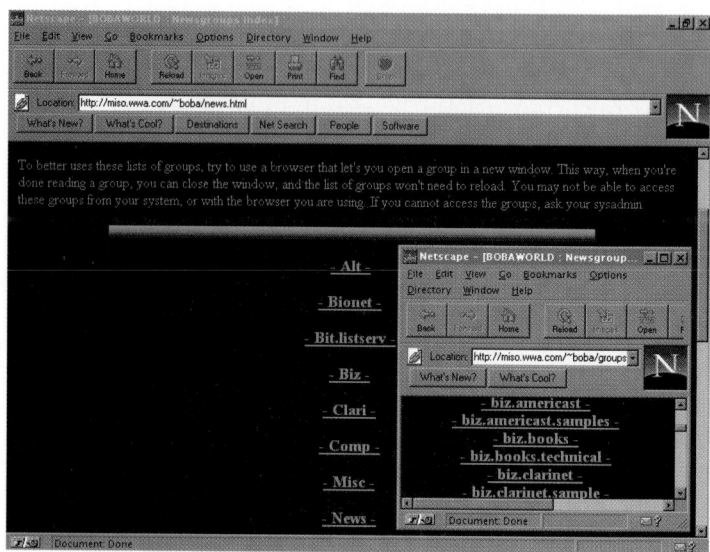

Figure 21.8.
Searching through a listing of Usenet newsgroups.

Note:
A news server is both faster and more accurate than accessing Usenet via the WWW.

Some people try to trick Usenet users by holding mock conversations. They'll start a discussion string about a "cool new site" and create different users to carry on the conversation. Usenet folks are notorious for exposing this type of scheme and rewarding the schemer with all kinds of not-so-fun prizes, like flames, mail bombs, and even viruses.

MAILINGS

E-mailings can be a good way to jump-start the traffic to your site. But how do you get an e-mail mailing list if you haven't had any visitors yet?

Enter PostMaster Direct (`http://www.netcreations.com/postdirect/`), which keeps a mailing list database of more than 400 targeted topical lists containing a total of more than 1.7 million names, all voluntary. They offer a quick, affordable (e-mail addresses can be rented for 10 cents a name, and even less if over a certain volume), and PC (politically correct) way to distribute commercial messages to prospective customers via e-mail. Unlike other services or techniques that "spam" users with junk e-mail that they don't want or need, PostMaster Direct sends messages to only those users who have specifically requested information about certain selected topics. Now Internet marketers can harness the power of e-mail without fear of a recipient backlash (see Figure 21.9).

Figure 21.9.
The PostMaster's subject area list (this list goes on and on).

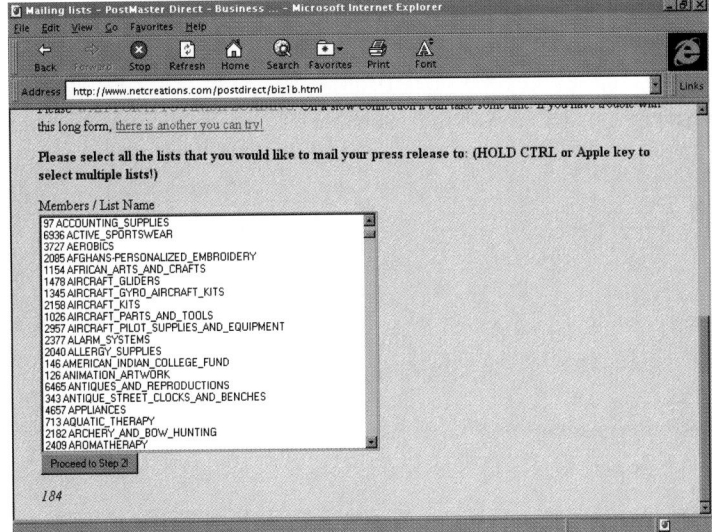

QUICK & DIRTY GUIDE
Register with More than 200 Search Engines in Under 30 Minutes

There are services on the Web that offer a free one-stop promotion page (and sometimes offer expanded services for a fee). You simply fill in a form with all the details of your page, and then a robot goes off and enters this generic information into the more popular search engines. If you are really busy, this can be handy. However, these services do not allow you to tailor your submissions for the individual engines, so your results will most likely not be as effective as they would if you entered the information into each system yourself. We often register with the larger search engines (Yahoo!, Lycos, Excite, and so on) by hand, and then register with the smaller ones via one of these services.

Q&D Register with More than 200 Search Engines in Under 30 Minutes

Let's go through this process step-by-step with Submit It!, so you can get it done quickly.

1. Gather your information. Writing this down and saving it in a text editor will save you time in the future. You will need

   ◆ Your company's e-mail address

   ◆ The title of your site

   ◆ The site's URL

   ◆ Keywords (words or phrases separated by commas)

   ◆ Your business name

   ◆ The company's address (including street, city, state/province, zip/postal code, and country)

   ◆ Your name

   ◆ Your e-mail address

   ◆ Your phone number

   ◆ Your fax number

   ◆ A description of your site (a single paragraph, 25 words or less, that describes your site)

2. Get online with Submit It! (http://www.submit-it.com/).

3. Decide which service you wish to use:

   Submit It! (Free)
   Includes 16 search engines and directories, for companies and individuals submitting URL(s).

   Submit It! Gold ($59.95)
   Includes up to 200 search engines and directories, provides access to the service for a year, organizes search engines and directories by category, saves your submission information, prints reports by URL with time/date stamp for each directory submitted, recalls information by URL to make changes and updates, submits to new search engines added to the service, and provides support via the Web for companies and individuals submitting URL(s).

   Submit It! Pro (10 companies for $199.95; 20 companies for $299.95)
   This service is for Internet service providers submitting URLs on behalf of their clients. It provides access to the service for one year, includes the same features as Submit It! Gold, and enables you to manage multiple customer URLs from one password-protected area.

4. For this example we use plain old Submit It! (see Figure 21.10). The next step is to fill out the Submit It! form and click the "OK, move on to the submitting area" button.

5. In the submitting area, you can view the information you've just entered. Make sure this information is correct.

6. Move down the page to submit to the individual search engines. Use your browser's Back button to return to this page (see Figure 21.11) each time.

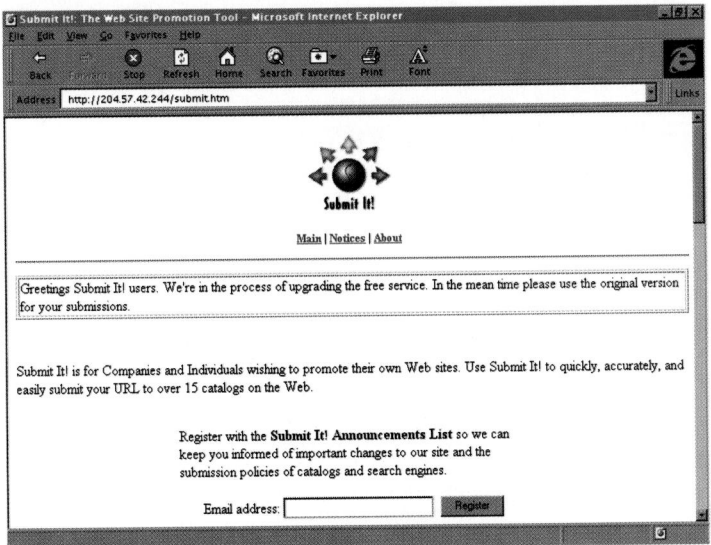

Figure 21.10.
Submit It! home page.

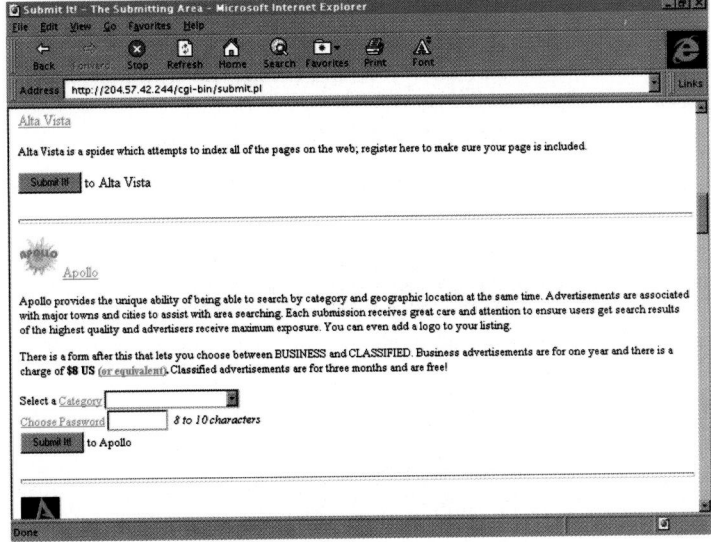

Figure 21.11.
The search engine page.

7. That's it! Now, if you would like to submit your URL to other search engines, you can either visit them individually or try the other services of these types (see Figure 21.12). Three other services like Submit It! are

PostMaster
`http://www.netcreations.com/`
`postmaster`

SubmitAll
`http://www.hometeam.com/`
`addurl/`

Pointers to Pointers
`http://www.homecom.com/`
`global/pointers.html`

Q&D Register with More than 200 Search Engines in Under 30 Minutes

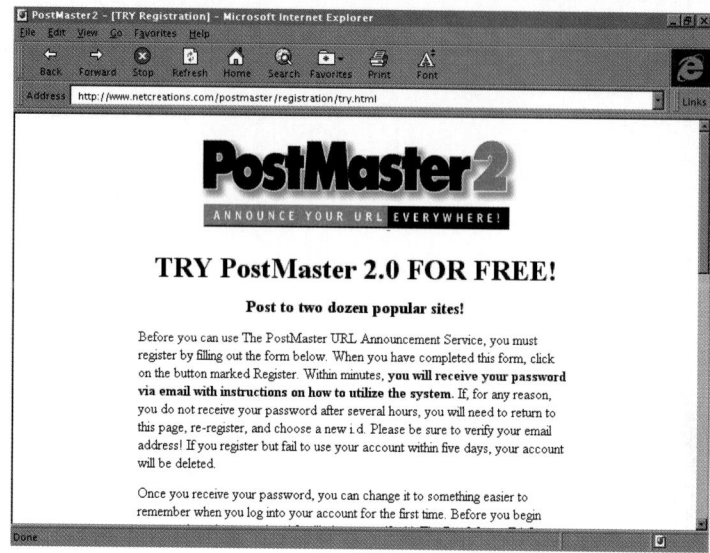

Figure 21.12.
The PostMaster submission service.

SUMMARY

In this chapter, we have discussed how to market your site online using the following:

◆ Search engines

◆ Banner advertisements

◆ Paid links

◆ Directory listings

◆ Link partnerships

◆ Usenet groups

◆ E-mail mailings

Now everyone knows where to find you, everyone in the world! Which leads us to our next subject: international markets.

International Markets

As the names imply, the Internet and World Wide Web are international forms of communication. Anywhere there is a decent phone system, there can be some form of Internet access, and direct satellite communication is available almost everywhere. So, as mentioned earlier, your Web site will be available globally.

## CHAPTER twenty-two

Once you start checking your logs (Chapter 24, "Tracking Page Success"), you'll notice some funny-looking computer names, ending with things like .nz, .uk, and .nl. These are the codes for the country of origin (New Zealand, United Kingdom, and the Netherlands, in this example), and tell you that the world is looking at your site.

> **Note:**
> While a .us name is available for the United States, it is rarely used. The United States is currently considered the default nation of origin. This may change, but for now it can be considered standard.

So, the world is looking at your pages. If you are selling something of interest, the world may even be buying from your Web site, without you having considered this in your design. Therefore, the simplest way to approach international markets may just be to create for the United States, and let whatever happens happen. The United States is likely to be your largest market, and if that spills over, so much the better!

But, what if you are looking at other markets specifically? What if your widget might have a wide open market in the Czech Republic? What special steps can you take to help reach consumers overseas? There are at least three things you need to consider if you are entering overseas markets specifically: language, access, and transactions.

LANGUAGE BARRIERS

Well, first of all, we need to point out that English is the language of the Internet. Only a tiny fraction of the WWW is in any other language, and this is simply the way things have evolved. The vast majority of Internet accesses are from the United States, and a good part of the balance are from Canada, the United Kingdom, Australia, New Zealand, and other English-speaking nations. Furthermore, many other accesses are from satellite offices (sales offices and manufacturing plants) of companies based in English-speaking countries.

There's also something else to consider. Anyone who has become accustomed to using the Net, regardless of where they are, probably reads English. This is for a couple of reasons: First, the Net wouldn't hold a lot of value for someone who couldn't understand English (obviously); and second, most people who access the Net are familiar with computers and programming, which generally requires some English (most programming languages are English-based).

So, do you really need to design HTML pages specifically for any other language? Probably not, but that will depend on your goals. If someone were trying to sell you something, and they were forcing you to deal with them in a language you were uncomfortable with or didn't understand at all, you would need to be pretty motivated to want to deal with them at all. The same holds true for the WWW.

PRESENTING OTHER LANGUAGES (CHARACTER SETS)

If you are trying to market your widgets in say, Germany, you might be best off designing your pages in German. While there are certainly many people in Germany who read English, there are many more who speak German, and you will clearly be reaching a larger market in this language. So what can you do?

Well, as it now stands, you will need to use a special character set to display many other languages. Those languages that share the same alphabet as English can sometimes be presented with the standard character set, but when you start to get into the languages of Asia, Eastern Europe, and other regions and countries that don't use the same alphabet, you will absolutely need to rely on nonstandard character sets.

Currently, you need to write the code in this special character set (which depends on the particular language), and the viewer's browser must also be set to translate this character set. In other words, a browser set for U.S. English won't automatically present a Russian page in Cyrillic (as Figure 22.1 illustrates). Luckily, this should soon be changing.

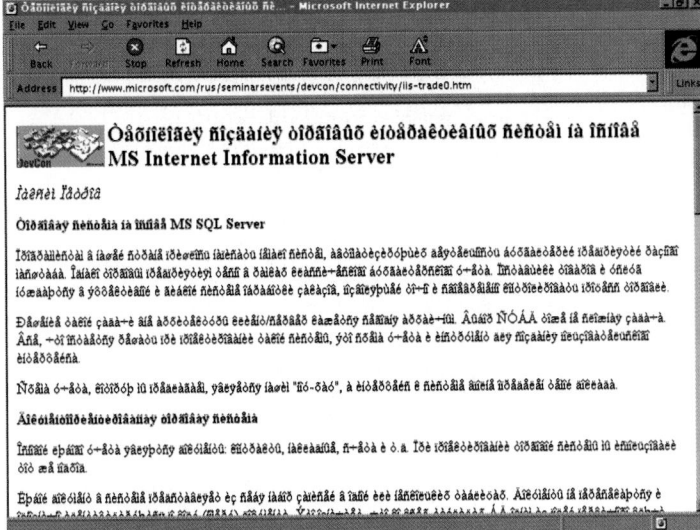

Figure 22.1.
An HTML document using a foreign character set not supported by the browser.

A proposal is to include the character set designation within HTML code, as well as an automated link to the character set itself. This means that if you were to load a Korean page on your browser, the browser could not only recognize that it was in Korean, but would download the appropriate character set and typeface (if it wasn't already on the system) to present the page. Pretty cool, eh?

Note:
As of the date of this writing, both Microsoft and Netscape beta browsers will accept character set designations in the <META> tag, which looks something like this:

```
<META HTTP-EQUIV="Content-Type"
CONTENT="text/html;
charset=Windows-1234">
```

The 1234 would be replaced by the actual character set designation. This can be assumed to be the standard for specifying character sets, until something better comes along. However, this will not automatically download the character set in question.

TRANSLATING

OK, so if you can write in Greek (or whatever language you're working toward), you don't have much of a problem, but what if you don't know the language you're trying to design for? Aren't there programs that will translate for you? Well, sorry, but no such luck.

There are many companies working on translation software, and some are making great headway. You can translate single words and even phrases fairly accurately, but it will be a while before you can rely on a software application to take your thoughts and translate them into another language.

The differences between syntax, grammar, and especially the nuances of different languages are just too broad. A beverage touted as being "cool, wet and effervescent" might be turned into something "clammy and gaseous" by even a human translator—think of what a computer might do to your wonderful sales copy.

Basically, you'll need to find a professional translator for each language. Furthermore, you will want to check this translation with someone familiar with both your company and the language itself. This is definitely a headache, but is unfortunately the only way to provide reliable translation of your communication.

MULTILANGUAGE SITES

If you do choose to present your site in another language, you may opt to branch out to multiple mirror sites from your main page. If possible, you may even wish to use separate hosts for the different language sites, located in the (main) country you expect to have accessing each particular site. While this is probably beyond the means of many small companies, it's the best bet for companies with satellite offices, as it will allow faster access from each individual nation.

Regardless of the mechanics, a multilingual site is simple enough to achieve on the main-page level. Just designate the links in the actual language (not the English version of the language). In most cases, you will need to make a graphic to designate the different languages, as even the latest browsers won't handle multiple character sets (you can't have Japanese and Russian text on the same page).

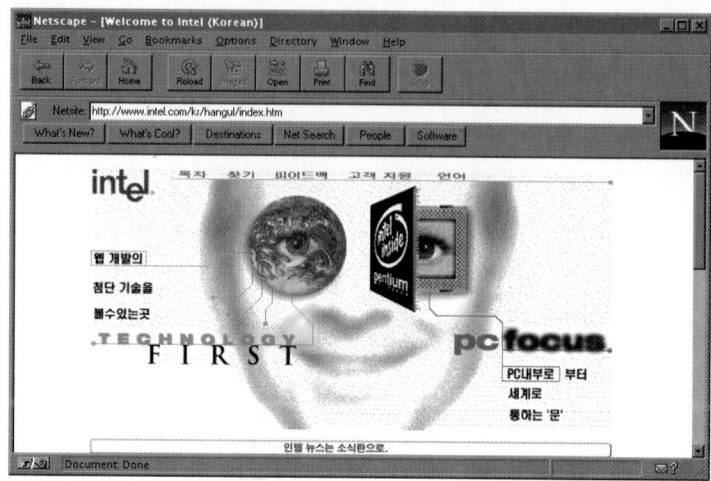

Figure 22.2.
Intel's Web site in Korean.

ACCESS

The speed and quality of Internet access is something that we have had to take into account constantly in our design. The bandwidth bug is a limitation we just can't get away from, and in international markets, things get even more difficult.

As we've mentioned, you can assume with some level of certainty that most people will be accessing your site with a minimum speed of 14.4Kbps. This is in the United States and Canada. Outside of North America, however, this lowest common denominator may be as low as 9.6Kbps, as we've heard from a few sources that some of their European customers access at this speed.

Now, this definitely doesn't mean that all connections outside of North America are at 9600 baud. High-speed connections exist almost globally, and don't think for a second that everyone else is creaking away at this slow speed. But also understand that the compulsion to buy the newest and fastest may not be quite as strong elsewhere as it is in the United States, and that it often takes a while for the latest products to reach other markets.

So you may need to tone down pages directed toward home users and small businesses outside of the United States. A little less sizzle may be appreciated by someone accessing at a third less speed—something to consider if you are marketing retail products abroad.

INTERNATIONAL TRANSACTIONS

There are entire industries based around the legalities and practices of international commerce, and it is way beyond the scope of this book to discuss tariffs, international banking, global shipping and the multitude of other stumbling blocks involved in this type of trade. A good starting point for information of this type would be a search for the keywords *International*, *Business*, *Trade*, and *Commerce* on any of the major search engines.

The way some companies escape many of the technical problems associated with international trade is to simply use credit cards, ship via mail, and to leave the payment of customs and tariffs in the hands of the buyer. The credit card is simply billed in U.S. dollars (if it's a U.S. company), and the merchant banks handle the conversions.

If you (or your client) are considering selling any technology products, or are considering overseas sales of much size, it will be in your best interest to hire an international trade consultant and/or international trade attorney to look things over and instruct you. You do not want to have $10,000 in product sitting in a customs office because you didn't know about some special tax (or how to avoid it).

WHY YOU SHOULD MAKE CONTACTS OVERSEAS

It has been said that 250 U.S. companies handle more than 80 percent of the nation's international trade. The instant communication offered by the Net and WWW can go a long way toward upsetting this monopoly and increasing overseas trade. As the "global village" makes way for the "global marketplace," more and more opportunities will arise for international trade via the Internet.

Even if you don't intend to sell much outside of the United States, it may still be in your best interest to build overseas relationships. A request for information from another country may very well merit a personal response, as building a relationship with even a single person from another nation may help you gain insight that could some day come in handy. Maybe you had no idea that your widget fits perfectly in an Australian mudsucker, or that it is worn as jewelry in Upper Slovobia. If a little e-mail can help open new markets, it's a small price to pay.

SUMMARY

The World Wide Web and Internet are truly international forms of communication, and your Web site, whether or not it's your intent, will be viewed by the world. This chapter has addressed some of the considerations of directing sites for specific international markets, and some of the considerations you should make if you plan on doing business overseas.

The next chapter briefly discusses two applications of HTML design that exist outside of the WWW and Internet.

N ow What?

PART IV

Intranets and Kiosks

The technologies developed for Internet communications, especially the WWW, are beginning to be applied in new ways. While the main focus of HTML design is on the Internet, there are at least two other applications you should be aware of, and this chapter provides a brief overview of each.

INTRANETS

Interstate commerce means the sales of goods and services across state boundaries, and intrastate commerce refers to business within a state. Similarly, the Internet crosses many networks, while an intranet resides on a single network. Clear? OK then, we continue…

You may have noticed that *intranet* has become a buzzword over the last several months, mostly because many software companies have seen an easy transition to this type of system, and because it is one of those solutions that was "there all the time, and nobody noticed."

So, what is an intranet? Well, first of all, it's a misnomer. The name itself simply implies a closed-end network, and LANs and WANs (Local or Wide Area Networks, respectively) have existed for quite some time. An intranet is actually the way this LAN or WAN network is used—just as the WWW is a way the Internet can be used.

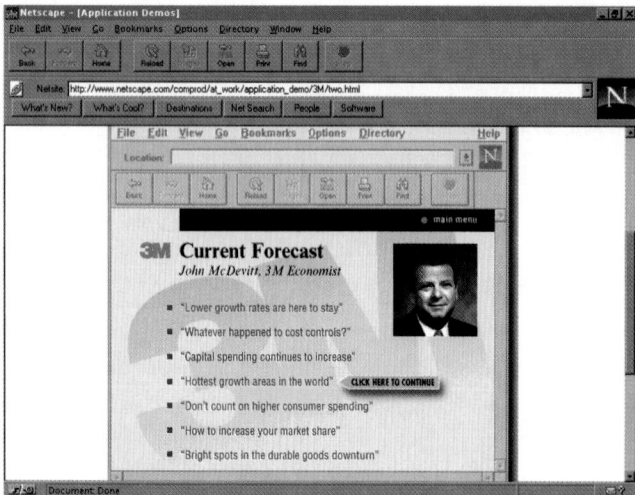

Figure 23.1.
Netscape's intranet development site depicting 3M's intranet.

Now, doublespeak aside, here's the scoop: The WWW has expanded so quickly, with so many companies racing to apply their own advancements, and so much effort has been put into things like cross-platform compatibility and user-friendliness, that existing network protocols and tools pale by comparison. An intranet is basically the application of Internet tools and technologies to a local network—or the creation of a mini-Internet.

The advantages to this are many:

◆ TCP/IP is, obviously, an excellent and proven protocol for connecting multiple platforms.

◆ The open-ended architecture of the Internet enables MIS/IT managers to install a system that can evolve as quickly as the Internet, and make use of many new features immediately.

◆ Internet server software (easily converted to intranet use) is extremely low in cost compared to many LAN or WAN client/server software packages.

◆ Using a WWW browser for information sharing (the main focus of most intranet implementations)— including everything from newsletters, to training manuals, to reports and sales updates—enables an internal network to take advantage of the same instant access, interactivity, updateability, and paper-saving qualities that make the Web so powerful.

◆ The user-friendly design of Web browsers facilitates simple, self-led training—a dream come true for most IT technicians.

◆ There's no need to train users twice. If someone can operate on the intranet, they can function on the Internet, and vice versa. To internal users in most applications, the intranet and Internet can be seamless (so much so that some office workers can't understand why they aren't able to load a specific URL from home—"it works fine at the office").

◆ The intranet can operate at the speed of the network—giving every user high-speed access, and allowing the design of high-bandwidth features that might operate too slowly on the Internet.

Now, what does this have to do with you? Well, basically, if you can design pages for the Internet, you can design them for an intranet. In fact, since you will usually be designing for a single browser on a high-speed connection, designing for an intranet is in many ways easier than designing for the "big one."

KIOSKS

A *kiosk* (for those who don't know) is basically a computer in a box. The idea is to provide a multimedia, interactive, user-friendly interface for the general public. To assist the user-friendly design, most kiosks use touch-screen monitors and very simple navigational controls (see Figures 23.2 and 23.3).

Kiosks generally run a multimedia presentation application (made in something like Authorware) on a closed system. Most applications are for trade shows and corporate lobbies (replacing human-run information desks), as retail applications seem to be pretty hit-and-miss. Kiosks are continuing to prove themselves as communication tools, enabling people to view a presentation at their own pace.

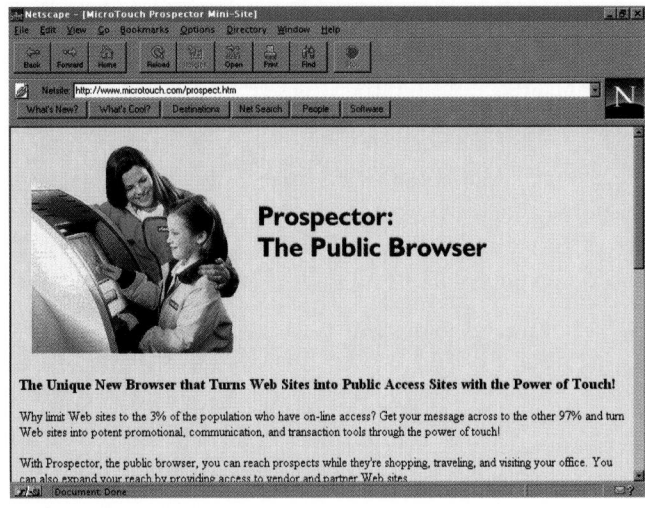

Figure 23.2.
The Microtouch Prospector's Web site (`http://www.microtouch.com/prospect.htm`). Prospector is the maker of Web Kiosk software.

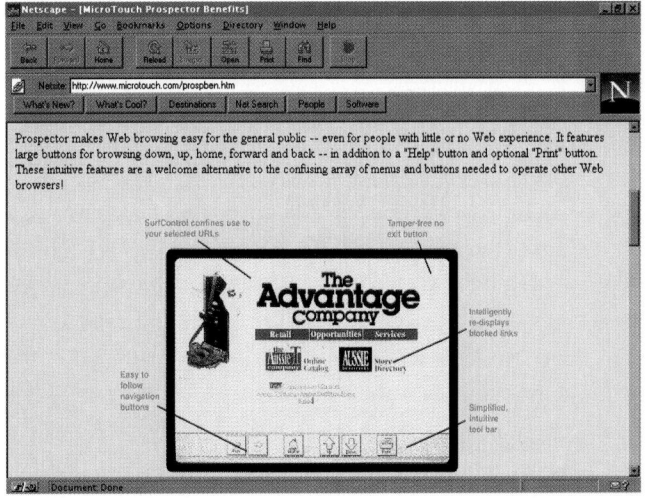

Figure 23.3.
A sample of what Prospector does.

So, what does this have to do with HTML? Well, as HTML begins to incorporate more multimedia, navigational, and interactive features, and as it allows more control over page layout, it will have more applications. Microsoft has already announced that IE4 (a.k.a. Nashville) will provide an entire

HTML desktop GUI navigation for their Windows 95. The HTML designer may have all sorts of new opportunities both on and off the Net.

Because HTML is portable, cross-platform, and easily updated, it is being discussed as the possible future of kiosk-type presentations.

Some advantages to this are

- Continuity. Your presentation can look (exactly) like your Web site.

- Updateability. Your presentation can be updated as often as your site, or can even be a direct link to your site.

- Development cost. Why develop a separate multimedia platform for a kiosk, when you can just use your Web site?

- Equipment cost. You don't need a fast, high-graphic, touch-screen, RAM-intensive machine to power a WWW kiosk (though it would, of course, help).

- Education. Anyone familiar with the Web will feel comfortable with the interface.

- Multiple lines of access. If users don't have time to get all of the information they want, it's not a problem. They can look it up at home.

There are some considerations that need to be taken into account when designing a closed-ended HTML

system. For instance, it would be a good idea to refresh all pages with the home page (or presentation starting page) after a certain length of time—five minutes, for example. This way the system will "restart" after someone has walked away from the kiosk.

It's also a good idea to take into account the fact that many people who are using the system may be unfamiliar with WWW terms. Naming your home link Start Over, for instance, would make things clearer to everyone involved. A help page, describing how to navigate, may also be very useful.

Finally, if you are designing a kiosk system that doesn't necessarily match your WWW system, you can take advantage of the bandwidth available in a closed system. Sounds, animations, and other bandwidth hogs that you wouldn't put online can easily be incorporated into a closed system—giving you the ability to do all the "wish-I-could" things that the Net doesn't yet allow.

ANYTHING ELSE?

Well, there are already several bars and cafés that have replaced the pretzel bowls and ash trays with multimedia computers and charge for people to use them. Similarly, the advent of Internet Appliances ($500 simplified systems made specifically for accessing the WWW) will bring more and more people onto the WWW. This spells growing markets for advertisers and designers alike.

The heavy investment that large corporations have made from their wallets, and that the media has made with its mouth, seems to make it a safe bet that technology is following the path of the WWW. Will the Internet soon support 5,000,000 TV channels? Well, perhaps not, but it's now more likely that the future of TV (and many other technologies) will lie in Internet technology than the interactive TV technology being touted a few years ago.

Even if the Internet is just a big laboratory—even if it's the steam engine of this decade, and will be eventually replaced by an as-yet-unknown technology—it is the future. Just as the internal combustion engine was based on the steam-piston, future communications technologies will undoubtedly grow from what has been developed up to this point.

SUMMARY

In this chapter we have addressed additional uses for the Web design skills you now possess. We have discussed the expanding markets of intranets and kiosks and have attempted to predict what the future may hold. There will undoubtedly be many other avenues to explore as this technology continues to evolve.

In the next chapter, we return to the Internet to investigate who has been visiting your site.

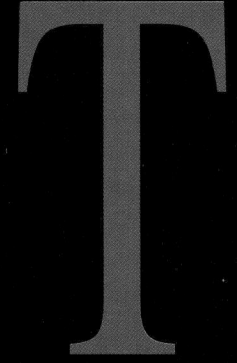

Tracking Page Success

So, your site is up and running—now you're probably wondering if anyone is visiting. There are a few ways to find out: by using a counter, by accessing your virtual host's online statistics system for your site (if you have one), by using a program on your server for this purpose (again, if you have one), or by accessing your raw access logs.

COUNTERS

We have already warned you about the use of counters. In all but very rare instances, we advise against them. However, we know some of you will either wish to disregard this advice, or will have clients who insist you do so, which is why we cover them here.

A SIMPLE COUNTER

A CGI that creates a simple text counter is provided on your CD-ROM. This counter is very simple to set up. Here are the steps:

1. Copy the CGI script (`counter.pl`) into a working directory.

2. Follow the instructions in the `readme` file contained in the same directory.

3. Add the code for the counter into your HTML file. It should look something like this (with your own URL of course):

```
<!--#exec cgi="http://www.hampton.org/scripts/textcounter/counter.pl"-->
```

4. Upload your CGI script and your HTML file (see Figure 24.1) to the server.

5. Test, test, test. If you have any trouble, refer to Matt's Web site at `http://www.worldwidemart.com/scripts/textcounter.shtml`.

Figure 24.1.
A simple text
counter.

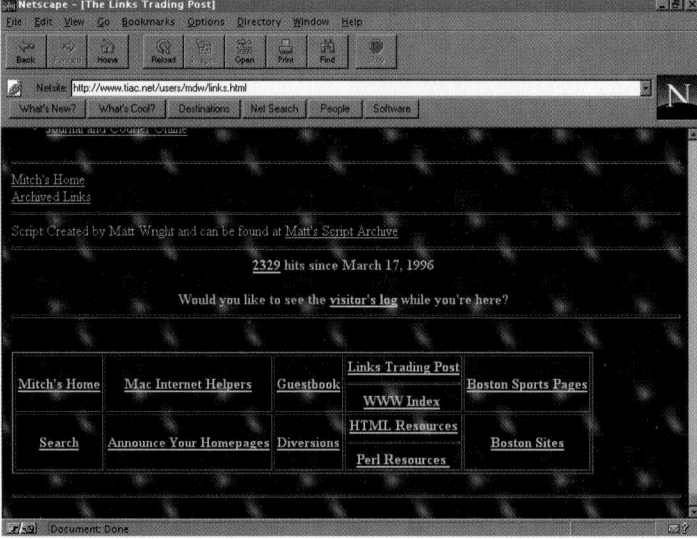

If you are interested in creating a more complex, odometer-style graphical counter (see Figure 24.2), you can refer to Matt's graphical counter at http://www.worldwidemart.com/scripts/counter.shtml.

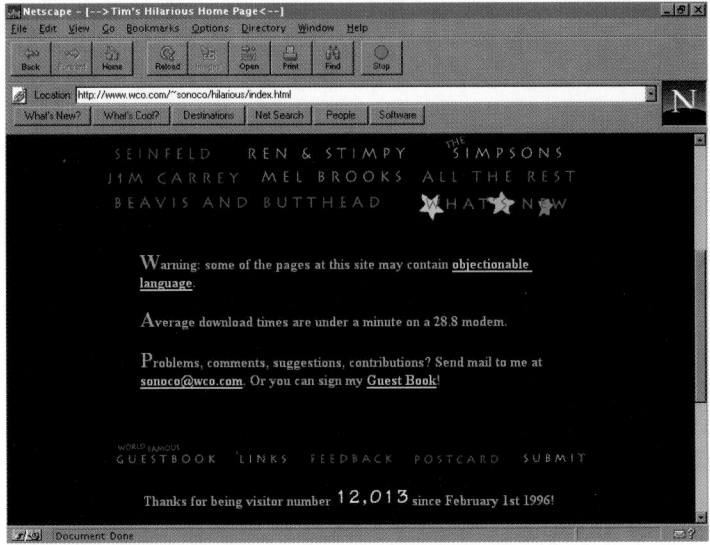

Figure 24.2.
A more complex graphical counter.

There are also many other references online for counter creation. The only times we have used counters are when clients have demanded them, and we're usually successful at talking clients out of this. You wouldn't answer your phones by telling people that they're the twenty-five-thousandth caller.

Note:
A counter might be a good alternative if you have a client who calls you daily to check on their hit count. You may even wish to have one page being counted, and another containing the display. This way you can have an easy reference for your client without having a counter display on the home page.

USING ACCESS LOGS FOR SITE ANALYSIS

Using access logs to track your site is by far the best option. Access logs not only tell you how many times your site has been accessed, they contain other valuable information as well.

WHAT ARE ACCESS LOGS?

When a viewer visits your site and requests a document, a record of that request is written into a log by the Web server. Most servers support the CLF (Common Log Format). This format was derived from an old version of the NCSA Web server in order to keep simple request information; it was not designed for in-depth site analysis. The CLF contains only the viewer's hostname, the HTTP requested from your server (containing the URL), the time and date of the request, a return code for the request, and the number of bytes returned.

An access log consists of lines of text that look like this:

```
lucifer.me.wig.org - - [07/Aug/
1996:15:31:32 -0700] GET /
graphics/banner.gif HTTP/1.0" 200
3021
```

This shows an access from host lucifer.me.wig.org on August 7, 1996 at 3:31 PM PST requesting the document /graphics/banner.gif using the usual `GET` method. The server returned an "OK" status code of 200, then transferred 3021 bytes of data.

Note:
The `-0700` following the date is telling you that the local time zone is seven hours earlier than Greenwich Mean Time, in this case Pacific Standard Time.

For most commercial purposes, you will want some additional information, which is why many servers also support the new Extended Common Log File (also from NCSA), or their own additional extended log formats. Extended log formats record additional useful information. Most often these extended log formats include information like the name of the viewer's browser and a field indicating which Web page referred the viewer to the site (where they came from).

Interpreting Log Files

Access logs are very complex; although you can read through them, they might make little sense unless you use a product developed to translate these logs into another format. (See Figure 24.3.)

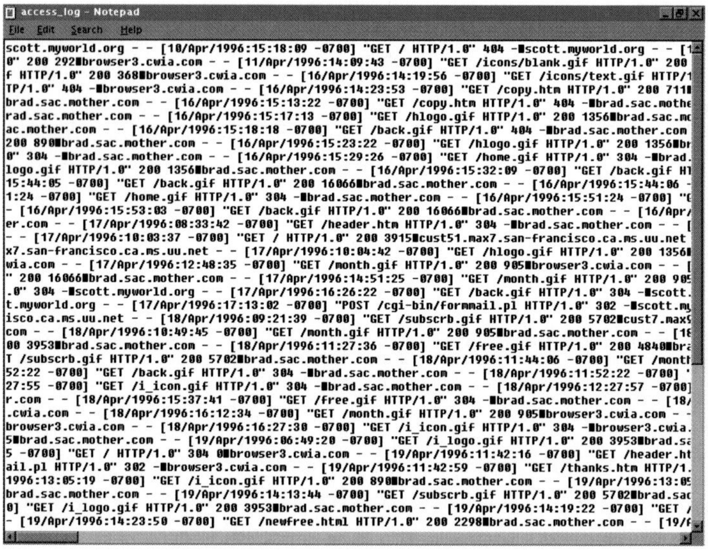

Figure 24.3.
A "raw" access log as viewed through Notepad.

Products for this purpose can directly extract or interpret your log file data into different categories. Commonly available categories include hit counts for each file, breakdowns of requests based on hostname (or IP address), server performance statistics, where the viewer came from (the referring URL), and often an analysis of the correlations between these categories.

ON YOUR OWN SERVER

If you are using your own server, there is most likely a special program already residing on your system for viewing your site statistics. Check your server's manual for information on setting this up. If you have no luck there, try your server manufacturer's Web site.

If your server did not include an application for this purpose, there are add-on software solutions available to you. Commercial software tools like Marketwave Hitlist (see Figure 24.4), net.Analysis, and WebReporter are available on various platforms, allowing on-demand analysis of your Web site by generating detailed reports. Some of these products even enable you to "zoom in" on information in order to generate even more detailed reports. A listing of these types of applications are maintained by Yahoo! at `http://www.yahoo.com/ Business_and_Economy/Companies/Computers/Software/Internet/World_Wide_Web/ Log_Analysis_Tools/`.

Figure 24.4.
The Marketwave
Hitlist report
dialog box.

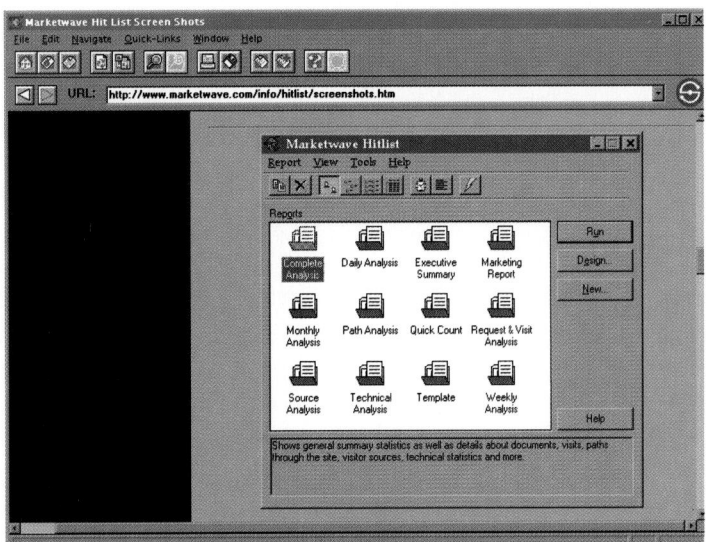

THROUGH YOUR VIRTUAL HOST

If you are using a virtual host that offers online site statistics, this will be your best option for seeing who is accessing your pages. Simply e-mail your host, asking where your statistics are located. Most ISPs that offer hosting services will have anticipated your needs and developed user-friendly access log reports, as shown in Figure 24.5.

Figure 24.5.
A sample of an online site statistic report via a virtual host.

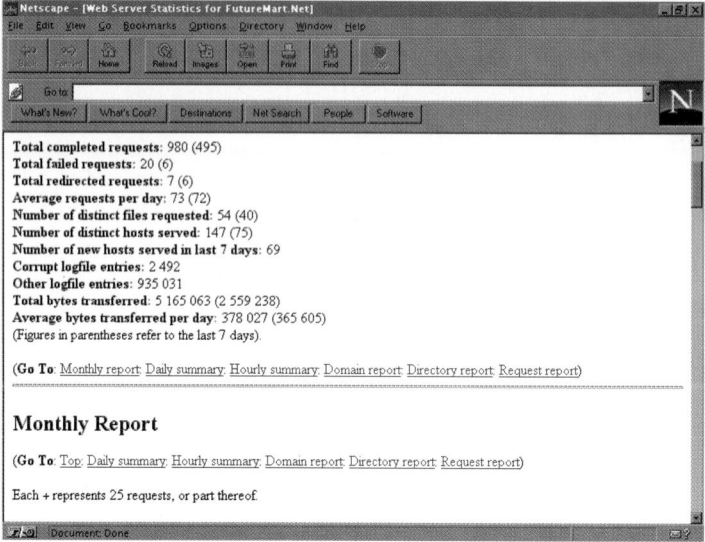

DEALING WITH RAW ACCESS LOGS

If you're not fortunate enough to be using a host that offers online site statistics, it will be necessary to gain access to your "raw" access logs. Your host will know where these are located.

Unless you're excited about dealing with those monstrous raw logs, your next step will be to translate these into a more usable format. There are many public-domain and commercial log-analysis tools that enable you to output these logs into HTML and various other document formats (even comma-delimited text formats are available, enabling easy importation to a database). One such tool, WebTrends, is shown in Figure 24.6. A listing of log-analysis tools is available through Yahoo! at `http://www.yahoo.com/Business_and_Economy/Companies/Computers/Software/Internet/World_Wide_Web/Log_Analysis_Tools/` or at Stroud's shareware archive at `http://cws.wilmington.net/stat.html#access`.

A new option is using an online Java-enabled system, like Bazaar Analyzer. These systems can

- ◆ Work with any Java-compatible browser
- ◆ Support standard server logs
- ◆ Provide interactive graphical data analysis
- ◆ Report total number of accesses
- ◆ Alert you to specific accesses
- ◆ Create reports that can be customized
- ◆ Offer complete automation of reporting

Figure 24.6.
WebTrends, a program that translates "raw" access logs.

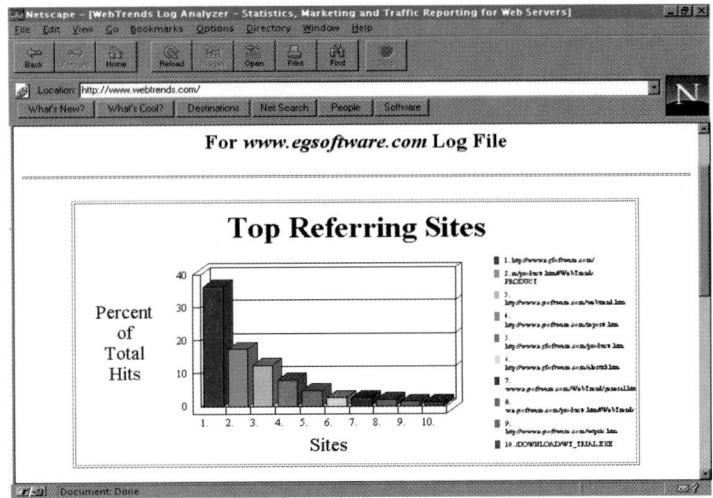

Although Bazaar Analyzer (shown in Figure 24.7) is currently only available for Solaris systems, you can use it online through their server at http://www.bazaarsuite.com/webdemo/index.htm to check a site on any server. Although we have experienced some bugs when using this system, it seems like a good option if you're really under a time crunch.

Figure 24.7.
Part of a report we created online using Bazaar Analyzer.

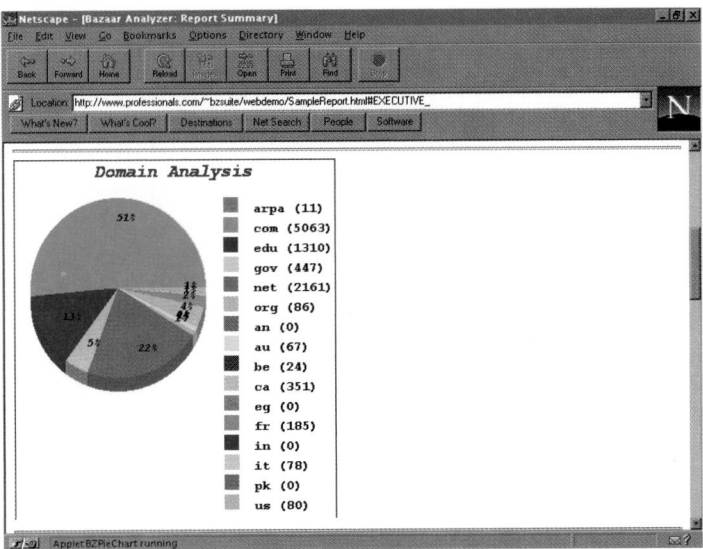

SHOULD I PUT MY SITE STATISTICS ONLINE?

Well, do they contain information you wish to advertise? In most cases there is no reason to put your site statistics online. An exception to this would be if you have a widely used site and plan to sell advertising on it, or if for some other reason you wish to publicize the success of your site (if it were a site for an association, for instance, and you wanted the members to know how active their association is).

SITE STATISTICS SERVICES

Using an off-site analysis service provided by companies like NetCount (`http://www.netcount.com/`, see Figure 24.8) and I/Pro (`http://www.ipro.com/prod.html`) can save you time and system resources. Using such a service eliminates the task of having to maintain a database on site with the associated large disk space consumption, but of course there's no such thing as a free lunch. These services generally charge from $95 to $600 a month. A "free" service such as this is provided by the Internet Audit Bureau (`http://www.internet-audit.com`), but they require that you include their logo on your Web site.

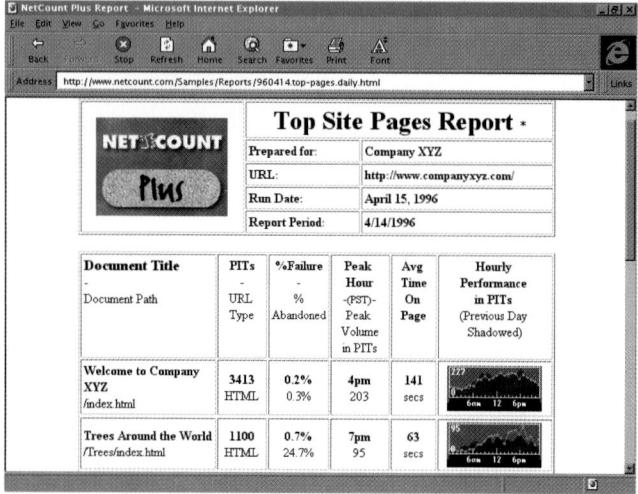

Figure 24.8.
NetCount, a site statistics service.

WHAT DOES THIS REALLY MEAN?

Now that you have your access logs in a nice format, you would probably like to know what it all means. Well, access logs track hits (in addition to other information), not individuals. What is the difference between a hit and an individual? A *hit* is any request on the server (including HTML files, graphics, sound files, and so on). For example, an HTML page with four graphics counts as five hits, even though only one person viewed that one page. An *individual* is the individual user—the person receiving your communication.

So, how can you tell how many actual people are viewing your pages? One way is to approximate the number of unique hosts that are accessing your Web documents. This will give you a pretty inaccurate picture, though. You see, server logs use IP addresses (`210.86.5.21`) or hostnames (`ha.net`) to describe where viewers are coming from. This refers to the computer or dial-up account the viewer is using. When viewing your logs, looking at the IP addresses and hostnames may seem a good indicator of how many people are visiting your site, who your viewers are, and where they are located. Unfortunately, there are many distortions that can occur in an analysis of this information:

1. It assumes that each IP address or hostname is unique to one person. We're not sure what goes on with you and your computer, but we know of many computer labs, coffee shops, and offices that have *many* more than one person using a single computer.

2. If you see a hostname of ucsc.edu (University of California at Santa Cruz), you can probably assume that viewer is from Santa Cruz, California. But what if they come from intel.com? Intel has offices all over the globe, many of which use the intel.com domain. Also consider the millions of viewers who use national service providers like America Online. They can be located all over the United States, but your log states them all as coming from aol.com.

3. Proxy servers pose yet another dilemma. A primary function of the proxy server is to act as a liaison from within the security firewall to the Internet. A request from within the firewall goes first through the proxy server, which in turn makes the request to the Internet server. Server logs will normally list all of these requests under the proxy server's domain name (or IP address), and not that of the original host.

4. Dynamic IP addressing (a means of spreading a large user demand for IP addresses across a few machines) is yet another stumbling block. This usually affects users of dial-up accounts. It means that one day a viewer came from 210.86.5.21 and the next day from 210.96.5.56. You could easily make the mistake of thinking this is a new visitor to your site, when in actuality the viewer was visiting just yesterday.

So, taking all this into account, what is the scientific method you should use to assess your access logs? Educated guessing is really the only option. When analyzing one of our own sites, we "guesstimate" the number of times our site is being accessed rather than the number of people accessing it. We call these visitors *session users* rather than *new visitors*.

We do this by counting the hits on our home page as new session users, but if we see the same address access the home page in a short amount of time, we figure it is the same viewer returning to the home page. If an IP address or domain name shows up out of the blue on another page of our site, it is counted as a new session user as well. When a line of request from a certain address stops for a period of time (say 15 minutes), we assume the viewer has left our site.

If your site has a huge number of hits (lucky you), you will need to analyze more details, such as the browser or referrer information, to get a more accurate picture of when one viewer leaves and another with the same address enters. If you see one address on your site for a very long time (requesting new pages over an extended period), this may indicate more than one viewer from the same address. All this will give you a very rough picture of how many times your site is being accessed (of course, this number may be underestimated due to caching).

Now that you have a rough picture of how many times your site is being accessed, you can move on to the really important stuff: how your viewers are using your site. You can see that there is really no foolproof way to track individual viewers as they visit your site, but you *can* see what individual viewers are doing when they get there.

As a new IP address (or hostname) appears in your log, you count it as a new session user. When the requests appear within a short span of time, this indicates the session user is navigating your site. You can then analyze the choices that user made. This is called session analysis and is one of the very best ways to improve your site.

Using Logs to Improve Your Site

Your logs are full of valuable information. The trick is asking the right questions.

Access Logs

To use access logs to improve your site, ask yourself the following, based on your site statistics and session analysis:

- ◆ How many people are viewing my site?
- ◆ How are those viewers using the site?
- ◆ Which pages are being requested the most?
- ◆ Where did the viewers come from (the referring URL)?
- ◆ How am I listed there?
- ◆ Who are my viewers? (.com = businesses, .edu = schools, and so on)
- ◆ Which countries are the viewers coming from?
- ◆ Which countries visit my site the most?
- ◆ Which areas in my site are of interest to international visitors?
- ◆ What browsers are the viewers using?
- ◆ What page on the site do viewers visit first?
- ◆ Based on the pages requested, what information are they looking for?
- ◆ Are viewers contacting me, or just viewing my site, never to be heard from again?
- ◆ How long does a viewer usually stay on the site?
- ◆ How are viewers navigating?
- ◆ What is keeping them there (where are they spending the most time)?
- ◆ Where do I lose them (what page were they on when they left)?
- ◆ Is there a document that receives an abnormally low number of visitors?
- ◆ Are viewers filling out my HTML forms, or just looking them over?

Error Logs

Your site's error logs also contain valuable information. The error log, as its name implies, logs your Web site's problems: requests for documents that don't actually exist, attempts to access protected documents, and internal errors from CGI scripts and the server itself. There are two types of entries in the error log: the warning and error messages generated by the Web server itself, and the error messages generated by any running CGI scripts. A typical error log consists of text like this (see Figure 24.9):

```
[Tue Aug 6 23:22:08 1996] httpd: connection timed out for hr25.snm.org
[Tue Aug 6 22:02:03 1996] httpd: malformed header from script
[Tue Aug 6 22:10:11 1996] killing CGI process 638
```

Figure 24.9.
A raw error log
viewed through
WordPad.

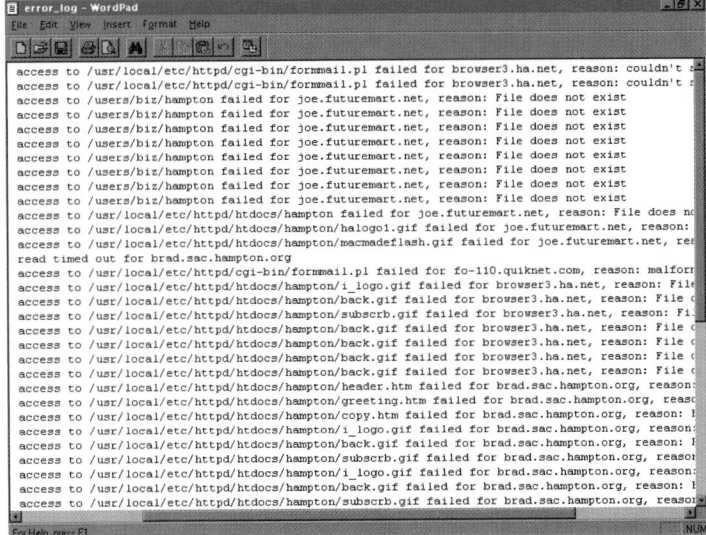

The messages that begin with the label httpd are generated by the HTTP server itself, and follow a standard format. The other is a warning message generated by a CGI script (such as killing CGI process 638).

Make it a point to check out your raw error logs from time to time (especially if you or your viewers are experiencing problems). Most software programs that translate these for you do not give as much detail as the raw logs themselves, so familiarizing yourself with them is a very good idea. Things to watch for include the following:

Connection timed out

This occurs when the browser breaks the connection before receiving the entire requested document. This usually means your viewers are leaving (pressing the Stop button) before your page is loaded. If so, maybe the file takes too long to download, and you should cut down its size. This message could also indicate that your server is prematurely timing out connections to users on slow machines. If so, and if you are running your own server, consider increasing the time-out values in the server's configuration files.

Client denied by server configuration

This usually means one of two things:

1. When access to a directory is restricted to only certain IP addresses, a user other than those allowed tried to gain access.

2. Someone attempted to gain unauthorized access to the system.

File does not exist, or no multi in this directory

This indicates that someone attempted to access a nonexistent URL. Tip: If this warning occurs frequently, you probably have a broken link.

Malformed header from script

This is warning you that a CGI script is producing poor output and the server can't interpret it (usually caused by a bad script). Normally, this is followed or preceded by a CGI error message from the script itself.

Password mismatch

This is telling you that a user typed an incorrect password when attempting to access a protected document. Tip: A long series of these may indicate an attempt to gain unauthorized access to your protected documents; it might be a good idea to see who was on your system at that time if this is a concern.

QUICK & DIRTY GUIDE
Get a Counter Up in 20 Minutes

If you're interested in setting up a counter, but don't have time to deal with a CGI script, there is a very simple solution: Use a Web-counter service. One that we have used from time to time is Web-Counter. The process is really simple—here goes.

1. Go to `http://www.digits.com` and read the policies page.

2. Decide whether you can go with the free service or should upgrade to the commercial service (if you have more than 100 hits per day).

3. Fill out the online form (`http://www.digits.com/create.html` for the free service, see Figure 24.10) and click the Create Counter button, which will send you to the response page.

Figure 24.10.
Completing the Web-Counter's online form.

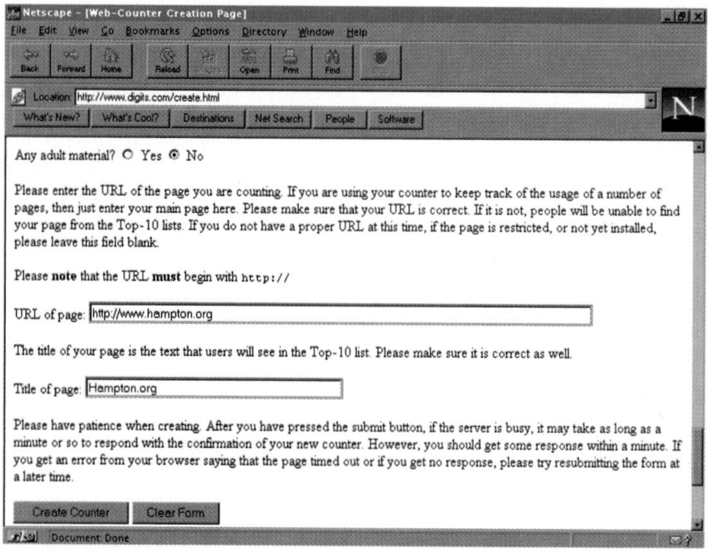

4. Cut and paste the code they suggest into your HTML document (see Figure 24.11).

Figure 24.11.
Copying the suggested code for use in your HTML document.

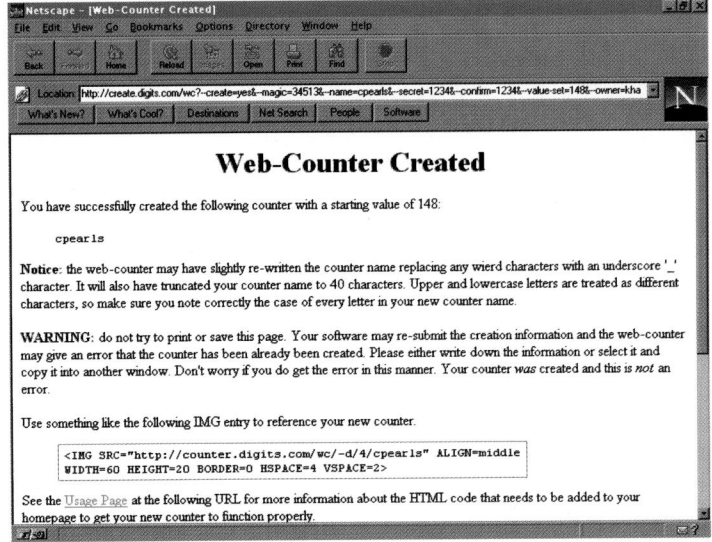

5. Upload your new HTML document.

6. Test it out, and you're done. (See Figure 24.12.) We completed this in under 15 minutes.

Figure 24.12.
Testing the counter.

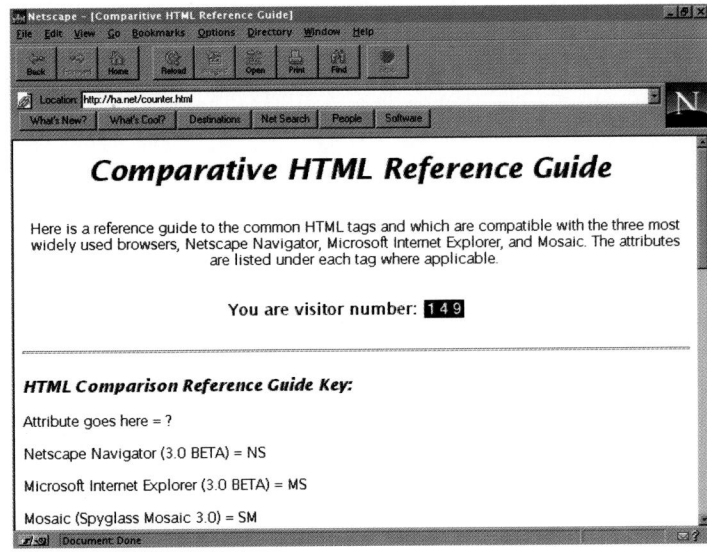

SUMMARY

In this chapter, we've addressed the inexact science of studying access logs. We've also gone against our own opinions and have offered two different ways to include counters on your pages—in case you find it absolutely necessary.

As you should now understand, there is no way to know exactly who is accessing your pages (unless you require everyone to log in). You can, however, gain some valuable insight into the usage of your site by reviewing and compiling server statistics.

In the next chapter, we move on to ways of maintaining your system and working with multiple authors.

Maintaining Your System

System maintenance is a rather broad subject. A simple system may require little maintenance, whereas maintenance on a large, multiple-author system can be a full-time job. Whether it takes you 5 minutes per week or 50 hours, there are steps you can take to help facilitate effective system maintenance and time management.

C H A P T E R
twenty-five

Your primary goal will obviously be to keep the site's links current and make sure that no files have become corrupt. While there are specific software programs that can help with this (InContext WebAnalyzer, for instance), you can also simply go through the system on a weekly basis to make sure everything's running and loading correctly.

The fact that "nothing *should* go wrong" is little help when something *does* go wrong. So, even if you're contracting out *everything*—including the HTML design, site administration, and the whole ball of wax—check your system regularly.

KEEPING ON TRACK

After you've got your site up and running, and have come to understand the concessions you've made, you will be in a better position to reassess the long-range goals of your site, based on your original ideas and the obstacles you've found along the way. This reassessment will continue as you see what works and what doesn't, and should never really be set in stone, but can act as a benchmark of sorts as your system continues to evolve. Some of the key issues you will want to address are

- ◆ The overall communications objectives
- ◆ The system's look and feel
- ◆ Bandwidth considerations
- ◆ Navigation and operability

For example, you might say that the communications objective of a site is to create public awareness; that the look and feel will incorporate a certain page layout, color scheme, and text treatment; that you won't create pages over 50K for bandwidth considerations; and that you will include a site-wide navigation bar on all pages.

Now, this won't mean that you will have to restrict your creativity to meet these standards, but that you will have something to go off of as you assess new additions to your site. If you are the only author for a system, you can keep these standards in your head. If, however, there will be several sources providing pages, guidelines and standards will become necessary.

MANAGING MULTIPLE AUTHORS

Marketing wants to post a product demo, sales wants to be able to update prices weekly, customer service wants an ongoing FAQ page, technical support wants to post updated diagrams, and the CIO wants everything to mesh seamlessly. What a nightmare!

If you are the webmaster for a large corporate site, you may find it beyond your ability to meet everyone's needs yourself. Or, if you are heading a design team, you may need a way to guide all of the different designers. Either way, managing multiple authors requires some special considerations, and there are some things you can do up front to make life a whole lot easier for everyone.

KEEPING THE CONTINUITY

Your first goal in designing or implementing a multiple author site is to achieve continuity. You don't want your site to look piecemeal, even though it is. Viewers should be able to navigate through the site easily, using the same navigation tools throughout. They should be able to know that the information they're looking for will be available in a certain format, and that charts, links, and tools will be laid out in some standard. Most importantly, someone should be able to access your site at any point and know that he or she is on your site.

This requires that you set standards of authoring that specify exactly how a page will be laid out. This may sound like your site is going to lose some of its pizzazz, since you are trying to make each page look like the rest, but don't worry about it. The point is not to make your site generic, but to make each page work within the structure. You can set whatever standards you want, as long as those standards can and will be met by each page on the system.

When you start getting into sites with hundreds or even thousands of pages, the concept of individual creativity starts to lose its appeal. Your focus should be on making the entire site an effective communications tool—not to make each page sizzle. In short, don't lose sight of the forest for the trees. Now, to keep control of that big picture, you will need to set up some kind of authoring pecking order.

ESTABLISHING A CHAIN OF COMMAND

Your first step in managing multiple authors is to set up some sort of managerial system. The reason for this is simple: You don't want just anyone accessing your WWW directories. Early on, many large site webmasters gave authoring privileges to anybody who wanted them. Not many people knew or wanted to deal with HTML, and page ownership wasn't an important issue.

It wasn't long before some of the largest systems on the Net began suffering from too many cooks spoiling the broth. One person wanted to set up pages one way, someone else another. WYSIWYG editors and HTML converters screwed things up even further by making pages with sloppy code, self-serving <META> tags, improper formatting, and the like. Pretty soon, webmasters began pulling the plug on open access.

As it now stands, most if not all large systems have a structure set up for document submission, testing, and page ownership. While security is obviously a factor, the main reason for this type of protocol is to keep people from submitting mistakes and to make those who do responsible. If you are working with multiple authors, you too will want to implement a protocol of this type.

You will probably want to have no more than one approved author for each department. While others can work on the HTML, only the author will have the clearance to post. You can password-protect the upload directories on the server to enable you to track access, and thereby give ownership to each file. It's also a good idea to separate the directories for each author (for example, /sales, /custserv, /product1, /product2) so as to allow for even better control—keeping the root directories for yourself.

Be warned—you are likely to face some opposition. However, no matter how much of a pain it might be to set up some sort of chain of command, it will never compare to the problem of having 20 different people screwing around with your system, updating links, deleting each other's pages and the like.

DEVELOPING SITE GUIDELINES

As mentioned in the section "Keeping on Track," establishing guidelines for a site not only helps to keep things in control, but allows a site to evolve more effectively. A few simple rules may assist you in working on a small or single-author site, but for a large commercial site, detailed guidelines will be a necessity.

If your company has an intranet, your first option is to set up an internal site that gives precise guidelines on content, formatting, colors, acceptable sizes, procedures, and even hints. You can also use an intranet to set up a mirror site. This site can have the exact same structure and content as your public Web site, and can act as a testing area for new pages (better to find a bad link before it goes public).

If you don't have the luxury of an intranet, you may have to produce some kind of printed or electronic manual to act as a reference. Regardless of the medium, your site guidelines should include

- WWW mission statement (the overall goals and objectives of the site)
- HTML formatting standards (what code to use, and what not to use)
- Navigation standards (maps, links, cross-referencing, and so on)
- Information standards (how to place text, tables, and so on)
- Layout standards (headers, footers, graphic placement, and so on)
- Size (no pages larger than ?? bytes)
- Graphic standards (formats, sizes, color palettes, and so on)

Each of these topics should be addressed in detail, with examples and hints where necessary. As you can probably imagine, this manual can get pretty lengthy. You also have probably come to understand that there may be several ways to use HTML code to achieve the same effect in many instances. So, in an effort to keep things as simple as possible, and to assure the best success of a multiuser site, you may want to rely on templates.

WORKING WITH TEMPLATES

With templates, you can give your authors a starting point, but you stay in control of the major issues. Furthermore, by having standardized HTML code across all pages, you can easily make sweeping changes to the entire system without changing each page's code. You can also use robots to search/replace code across standardized files, to implement even more drastic changes on a site.

First things first—you'll need to nail down a format for each page, as well as a root directory structure. Once this has been accomplished, you can begin structuring your templates. For the purpose of example, we'll make a basic master template.

Let's suppose that we want a master graphic, a standard page background, a navigation map, a standard title and headline scheme, a main supporting graphic placement scheme, and a standard copyright and mail footer. Our objective is to make a fill-in-the-blanks type of template. Here's the code:

```
<HTML>
<HEAD><TITLE>

+++++++++ENTER TITLE HERE

</TITLE></HEAD>

<!-- begin Standard Header—do not alter or remove -->
<BODY BGCOLOR="#FFFFFF">
<A HREF="/main/main.map">
<IMG SRC="/main/header.gif" BORDER=0 ISMAP ALT="[XYZ navigation]"></A>
<!-- end Standard Header -->
```

```
<H1><CENTER>

+++++++++ENTER PAGE HEADLINE HERE

</CENTER></H1>
<BR><HR>

<!-- insert main graphic between quotes below -->
<IMG SRC="graphic.gif" ALIGN=RIGHT>

+++++++++ENTER CONTENT TEXT HERE


<!--begin standard footer—do not alter or remove below this line -->
<P>
<HR>
&copy; Copyright 1996, the<A HREF="mailto:cs@xyz.com"> XYZ Corporation</A>, all
rights reserved.
</BODY>
</HTML>
```

You'll notice that the code here is pretty straightforward, and that we've used carriage breaks to help set the editable areas apart from the standard areas. We've also used comment tags to give instructions and warnings. The resulting page would look like Figure 25.1.

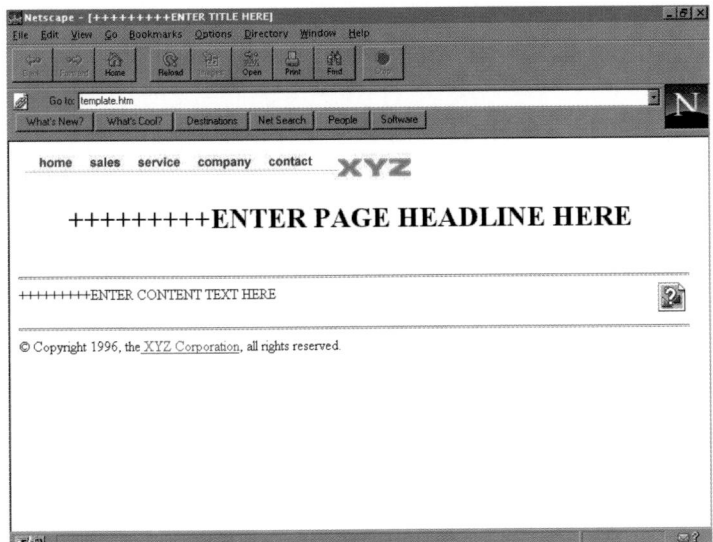

Figure 25.1.
Our template viewed through a browser.

You'll notice that in this case we didn't specify the size of the header graphic, and that we used an externally referenced map. This is so that we can replace this header with whatever we choose, without having to change the code. This is one of the nicest features of using standardized templates (or standardized components); you can make system-wide changes immediately.

Seasoned HTML authors would be able to pick up on the structure of this template and could build very extensive pages based on this simple design, while preserving the basic, system-wide elements. HTML novices, on the other hand, can see this as a paint-by-numbers project—place the graphic here, type the title there, lay in the text, add a few formatting commands, and voilà!

Obviously, people using WYSIWYG HTML editors will never see the comment tags and can very easily do something to compromise the code. While you can possibly go over each individual's software application and make sure that it is customized to work within your code structure, who wants the hassle? Our philosophy on this subject is simple: If you can't write pages in a text editor, you aren't an HTML designer, and you shouldn't be working on a commercial site.

Where to go from here is up to you. You can make a master template, or you can make individual templates for each type of page you foresee on the system (like product info sheets, ordering forms, section pages). What you choose to do will depend on the system, its goals, and with whom you're working.

Even if you're the only author, you might find templates a great tool—especially for crash-and-burn projects, where something needs to be posted within a matter of hours. You might, for instance, make a press release template, as shown in Figure 25.2.

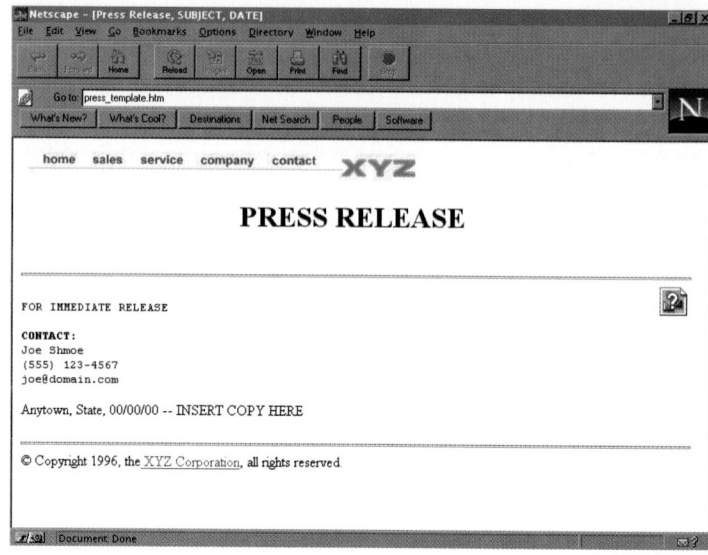

Figure 25.2.
A template for press releases.

Using a template like this, you could convert a press release to HTML in a matter of minutes. The point is that a standard template will help keep you and others on track and will give you a good start on page production. They are great tools that you won't want to do without.

Note:
Most HTML-enhanced text editors allow you to work from a template, and many will even allow you to automatically open a template at start up.

CHECKING UP

No matter how thorough you try to be, using guidelines, templates, threats and the like, someone is going to mess things up. Whether it's accidental, or the result of someone getting a wild, creative hair, your code and standards will become compromised. Because of this, you will need to check your pages.

There are ways you can make programs to automatically check for specific components. You can even simply run a search for text strings that match your template header, for instance. The truth of the matter, however, is that there's no substitute for just opening the file and taking a couple of minutes to check the format.

Don't be a hard-nose. Remember that your site should continue to evolve, and it's easy to get in the habit of the lazy manager who won't accept anything that's the slightest bit out of the norm. Other authors may have some great ideas that won't detract from the overall system, even though they stray from a template.

There may also come a time when the template(s) won't work with some feature of a page (like a standard header in a channel-background page), and you may need to help set up an alternative. You'll need to carefully track these aberrations so you can change them individually as the system changes, and the more there are, the more difficult it can be to make changes.

BEWARE OF DRASTIC CHANGES

Let's suppose that you've developed a 50-page system with multiple authors. Let's also suppose that you've used templates, standard navigation headers, strict guidelines, and the like. You've taken care to assure the broadest compatibility of your system, and

the simplest system-wide editing. Now, you have an entirely new plan for the system's front end, and you want to change all of the supporting pages to match.

If your new scheme will stray only very slightly from the current system, you can probably make some universal changes without many problems. For instance, if you are just replacing the navigation header in the previous example, you may run into no problems at all. If, however, you are making drastic changes, you may run into some tremendous problems.

We'll make an example of a page designed on the earlier template. Let's suppose that one of your authors got a little creative and wanted to use a drop-cap effect (see Figure 25.3) with a little text graphic.

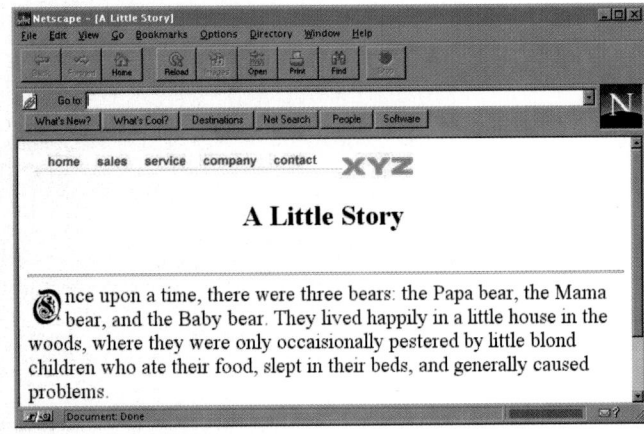

Figure 25.3.
A drop-cap effect before changes.

Now, this page is still very simple, and hardly deviates from the standard template. But we want to make system-wide changes that will affect this and every other page. To make these changes, we'll be using a new main header image (and corresponding map), and we're going to change the background and text colors.

To accomplish this, we are simply going to change the header section of each page from this:

```
<!-- begin Standard Header—do not alter or remove -->
<BODY BGCOLOR="#FFFFFF">
<A HREF="/main/main.map">
<IMG SRC="/main/header.gif" BORDER=0 ISMAP ALT="[XYZ navigation]"></A>
<!-- end Standard Header -->
```

to this:

```
<!-- begin Standard Header—do not alter or remove -->
<BODY BGCOLOR="#000000" TEXT="#FFFFFF" LINK="#00FFFF">
<CENTER><A HREF="/main/main.map">
<IMG SRC="/main/header.gif" BORDER=0 ISMAP ALT="[XYZ navigation]"></A></CENTER>
<!-- end Standard Header -->
```

This can be done manually, by search and replace, or can be accomplished with a spider (robot) automatically. Either way, this should be fairly simple, right? Well, as you can see in Figure 25.4, even the smallest, least noticeable things can cause problems.

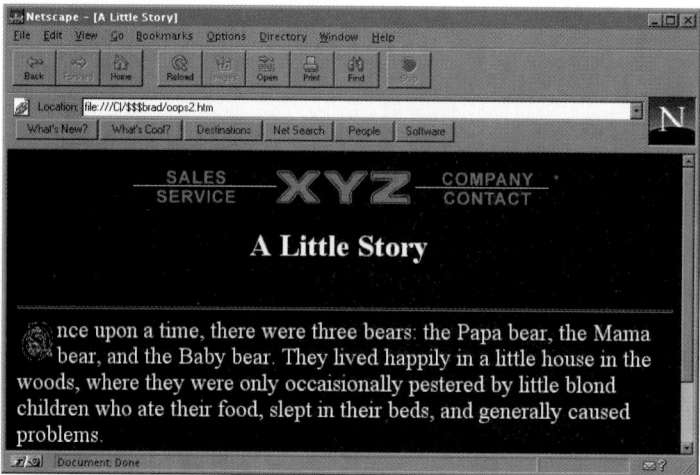

Figure 25.4.
Oops!

You'll notice that the drop cap now just looks like a blob. Had it not been antialiased, it wouldn't show up at all. Oops! Now, had we tried to do a more subtle change, like using a light-colored background, for instance, this problem would not have been as noticeable.

This is a very simple example. Just imagine what it would be like if many authors had relied on a white background/black text design for their graphics, table backgrounds, and so on. Many graphics and even entire pages might need to be redesigned.

Since the nature of HTML requires designers to use creative tricks (like using a transparent GIF to create a drop cap), design elements may depend on the overall page layout. Drastically changing the page layout can and will have adverse effects on these "tricks," and will therefore affect the system as a whole.

So, regardless of how well you set guidelines and stick to templates, making major changes to your system will require that you and your team go over everything at least twice. First, you will need to try and anticipate problems, so that you can make changes in either the pages or your revision plans. Second, you will need to go over the pages after the revision, to find the trouble spots you missed earlier (and you will miss some).

As a rule, the more sweeping and profound the change, the more problems you'll run into.

SUMMARY

In this chapter, we've addressed some of the techniques that can help to control the expansion and evolution of a site—especially a site with multiple authors. We've also discussed problems associated with the implementation of sweeping changes on a large system, and ways to avoid some of these problems. Our main goals have been to

- Establish guidelines
- Create and use templates
- Make use of common elements like headers and footers
- Manage multiple authors and access privileges
- Anticipate and avoid the problems associated with drastic changes

In the next chapter, we discuss some of the ways to market your newly acquired Web skills.

Marketing Your Newly Acquired Web Skills

We hope that you have gained some valuable information throughout this book. It has been our goal to relay our experience in this field to help you understand how to use the WWW as a marketing tool, and to give you some of the tips and tricks we've learned the hard way.

CHAPTER.
twenty-six

So, can you now consider yourself a commercial Web designer, hang out a shingle, and start making huge sums of money? Well, of course not. While we hope that this book will help in your future, you'll need to learn from your own experience. Regardless of what your future plans are, however, the skills you've learned in this book can help you on your way.

THE HIGH DEMAND FOR COMPETENT PROFESSIONALS

Now that you have knowledge of the mechanics of HTML and have designed a Web site, you possess skills that are in high demand. Whether you are a receptionist, executive, computer programmer, graphic designer, entrepreneur, or whatever, you now have a skill that others are seeking.

While there is an increasing number of Web designers on the marketplace, there are very few who actually possess the skills and knowledge necessary to create effective Web marketing campaigns. You are now well on your way to becoming one of these few. Whether you are planning a new career, or just looking to make yourself more valuable to your current employer, you may find a very bright future ahead of you.

MOVING UP THE LADDER

If you currently hold a position at a company, it's important that you let your superiors know what you've been up to. Revise your résumé, ask for meetings, and make it known that you have a new and valuable skill. There are few business people who wouldn't be intrigued if you said, "I've been studying commercial WWW design, and I have a few ideas for the company." In short, get yourself noticed.

You may be surprised by what you find out when you start spreading the word. Many companies are either on the Web or are considering it, but very few have internal people who really understand the medium—and fewer still have people who understand Web marketing at the level you have learned here. A big promotion may be in your future.

Now, how you handle this is all up to you. Some companies may recognize the value of your expertise, and some may not. Maybe you'll get a promotion, maybe you'll be asked to start creating Web pages, and maybe you'll be ignored. The point is that you'll never know unless you try. If you don't like the response you get, don't forget that there are companies all over the world looking for WWW designers.

LOOKING FOR WORK

The best way we have found to let people know you're available is by posting your résumé online. There are hundreds of Web sites out there for this purpose, and they are widely used by headhunters and corporate personnel departments.

Recruiting on the Internet has been going on for many years. It began through Gopher and newsgroup postings, and has now branched onto the Web. Sites like the Online Career Center, The Monster Board (see Figure 26.1), Career Mosaic, and CareerWeb can be invaluable for recruiters as well as those seeking employment. By utilizing search engines and directory listings, these sites have brought the job search to a whole new level.

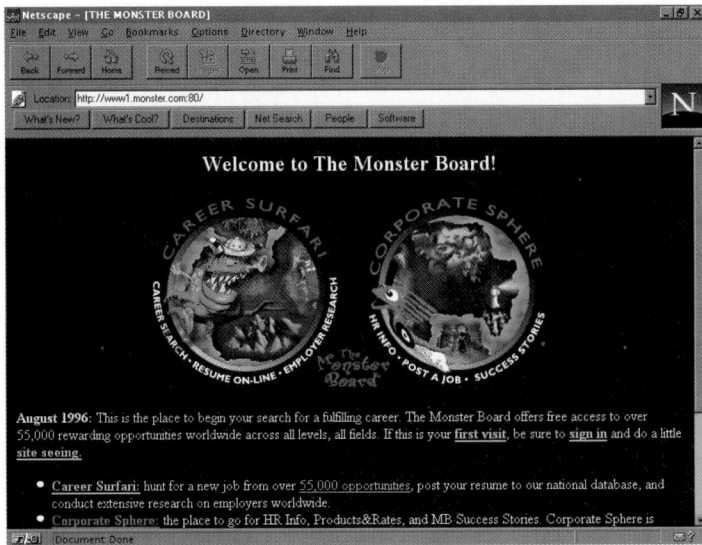

Figure 26.1.
The Monster Board, a Web career center.

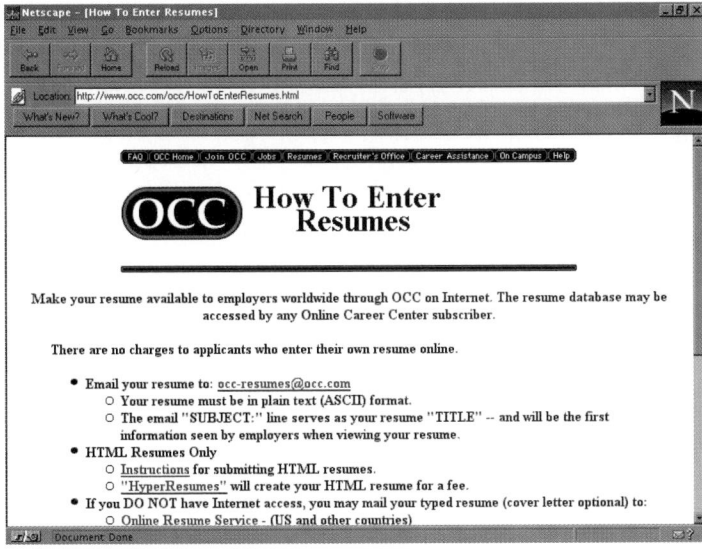

Figure 26.2.
Posting your résumé at OCC.

The first step in using these services is to adapt your current résumé to include your new skills and save it as a text file. You may also wish to make an HTML document from this, as many services allow you to post your résumé in this format.

The next step is to post your résumé on the major services, with some of those being:

♦ Online Career Center (see Figure 26.2)

    `http://www.occ.com/`

♦ The Monster Board

    `http://www.monster.com/`

♦ Career Mosaic

    `http://www.careermosaic.com/`

♦ Internet Job Locator

    `http://www.joblocator.com/jobs/`

♦ Adam's Job Bank

    `http://www.adamsonline.com/`

After this, you will want to search for jobs that interest you, and to contact the companies offering these positions. Most of the above services also have job postings and offer a search engine to help you sift through the information (see Figure 26.3). You will want to prepare a simple e-mail cover letter to include with your résumé when sending to these recruiters.

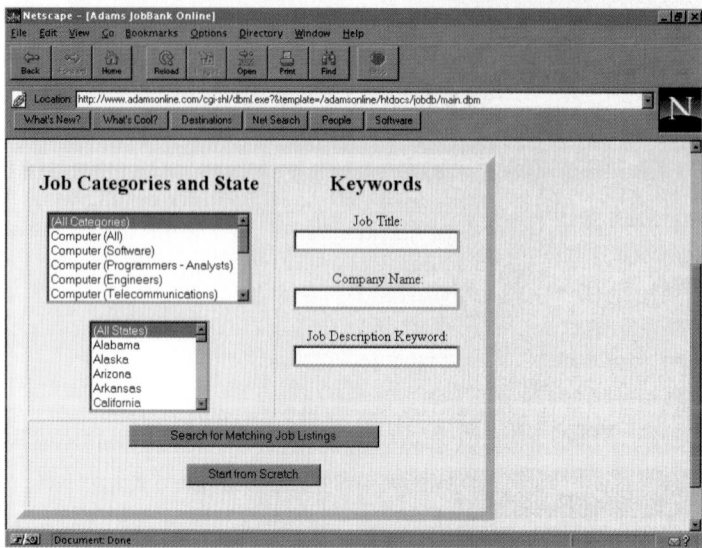

Figure 26.3.
Searching for a job
at Adam's Job Bank.

You can also search the newsgroups for job postings under your specific industry. A good listing of these is provided by Yahoo! (see Figure 26.4) at `http://www.yahoo.com/Business_and_Economy/Employment/Jobs/Usenet/`.

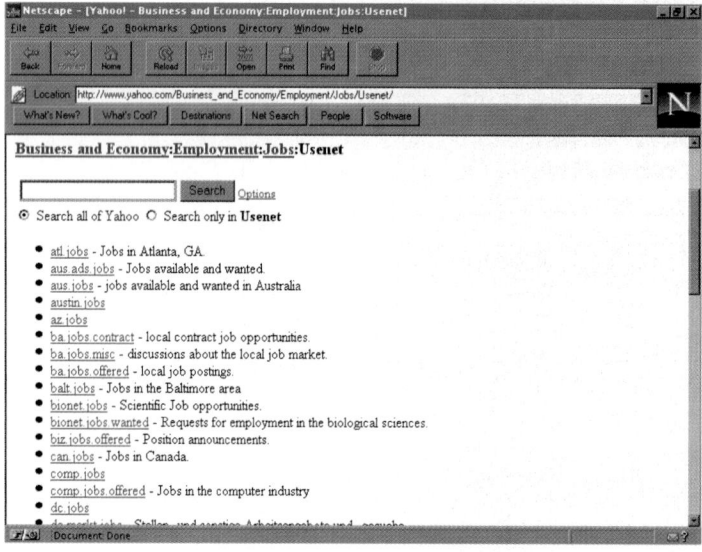

Figure 26.4.
Yahoo!'s list of
newsgroups listing
job openings.

Having a knowledge of HTML may mean more to employers than the fact that you can make Web pages. Many people will see that you have recognized a leading-edge technology and have had the self-determination and courage to learn about it on your own. When job descriptions say "motivated" and "self-starter," this is what they are talking about.

So, even if you are looking for a job that has nothing to do with HTML, don't forget to put it on your résumé. You never know what it might mean to someone else, or where it may lead you.

THE PROCESS OF BECOMING AN INTERNET MARKETING PROFESSIONAL

If you have studied this book as a way to better approach the commercial Web design industry, you may be looking at the possibility of offering Web design services to clients directly, either as a freelancer or through a design firm. If you have experience in business, and have practiced enough to have gained some skill at design, you may very well find a market.

If you are already a business professional, you probably know what it takes to gain and keep clients, to manage people and resources, and to get the job done. You will have seen the opportunities available for truly professional HTML designers, and you are probably preparing to hit the streets. You'll find that the next chapter is geared specifically toward you, as it gives some tips on handling clients. Aside from this, there is probably little we can do for you except to give you encouragement, so go get 'em!

SUMMARY

In this chapter we've covered a few things that may help you apply your new skills, either to excel in your current job, or to get a new one. We've emphasized that you need to let people know that you have some good insight into a leading-edge industry, and we have given you some resources for getting the word out on the job market.

The next chapter deals with handling clients and is directed specifically to those who will be responsible for negotiating Web site projects. However, it may also be useful for those who want to breach the subject of Web site creation at their current company, as it gives some hints on educating and communicating in regard to WWW design. This final chapter also covers some key ideas regarding professionalism, which we have found lacking in this field— a problem we hope you will help change.

Handling Clients

The XYZ Corporation of Anytown has asked you to meet with them. They've decided that they need to create a presence on the Internet and believe that you may be the person for the job. Your meeting is next week.

If you are working in a company where you have been called upon to head Web design, the issues discussed here may very well help you in communicating with your higher-ups. Just replace the word "client" with "boss," and you'll have a good starting point for progress meetings.

PREPARATION

Your first step in preparing to meet a client is to assess the situation. You'll want to get as much information on the company as you can. Check the Web, of course, to see what they are doing there (if anything). Then check with any contacts you might have. The more thorough your search, the better you will be able to assess the situation.

Your next step will be to talk with the client (though this may come first, if the client has called you out of the blue to set up a meeting). Having some good questions for the client will often put you in a good light, as it will make you appear more professional. Some key information that can help you prepare for your first meeting will often be necessary, and you really shouldn't be afraid to ask.

Some companies are pretty open when it comes to answering your questions. They usually understand the position you are in, and that any help they can offer will aid in streamlining the whole sales process. Other companies are downright paranoid, and may say things like, "We'll discuss that when the time comes." This is often the case with small- to medium-sized businesses that are unaccustomed to hiring contractors.

Should you run into this tight-lipped situation, your first step may be to offer to sign a nondisclosure agreement (NDA). This agreement usually states that you may not divulge or in any way make use of information provided by the company, unless and until you are under contract to do so. If the agreement is worded in such a way as to be unclear to you or is obviously going to limit your future, consult an attorney. Usually, however, these are pretty straightforward.

Should this fail to pry open the "box of secrets," you may need to make a tough decision. We live by an old adage that says that people who are always suspicious deserve suspicion. In business, people who are always thinking of ways in which they might get cheated are usually also thinking of ways to cheat others. Sad but true.

We've worked with some very, very large companies, and have never had any problem getting information (once we've signed an NDA). On the other hand, we've been called out to meet with small companies who have refused to even tell us what they do. You will almost never make any money from this second type of company.

If you are just sitting in your office, watching the paint peel, and you have an opportunity to meet with a secretive client, it will probably be worth it just for the experience. If, on the other hand, you would be taking time away from even marginally profitable efforts, it may be best to just tell the client you're booked. We generally explain to them that we are busy professionals and that we'd be happy to sign an NDA, but that they'll have to give us some more information before we can arrange a productive meeting.

More often than not, we're able to pry some information out of a company after doing this. Many times, however, these companies are trying to pull a fast one (either trying to get you to work on spec, or just trying to get free information from you so they can assign the task in-house); this happens all the time with multilevel (pyramid) marketing companies. You're better off spending an hour watching TV than wasting it with these bozos.

So, what kind of information will you want? What questions should you ask? Here are a few we find useful:

1. **Who is in charge of the project?**

The best answer is "me." If your contact is just a lackey, you may wish to talk with the real person in charge. Any answers you get may be incomplete or downright wrong. In some cases, the person in charge will be too busy to talk with all of the prospective contractors, but it shouldn't hurt to ask.

2. **What does your company do?**

Even if you already know what a company does, it's often a good idea to ask them. The way in which they explain it will help you understand how they think of themselves. You might even go so far as to ask for a sales pitch on their products/services. Most marcom professionals will anticipate this and will give you a good overall feeling for their company's position.

If your contact acts like you should know what they do, you might just say, "I'm familiar with your organization, but hearing it in your words would really help me out."

3. **What do you see as your needs and goals?**

Obviously, knowing precisely what a company does is the first step in assessing their needs. What clients see as their needs, however, will help you position yourself. They may be looking to you to assess their needs, in which case, they'll probably say something like, "We just feel like it's time we got on the Web," or "Clients have been asking…"

In other cases, you might get a detailed description of what exactly the company hopes to accomplish. Either way, this gives you a starting point.

4. **Who are your main clients?**

This will be the audience for your work. Knowing what your intended market is will, of course, help you define the project goals. Even the broadest descriptions ("large corporations") are going to narrow down your presentation. If your question is answered with starry-eyed hype like, "Everyone needs our product," you may need to rephrase the question: "Who are your current clients?"

5. **What are your current marketing efforts?**

This will not only give you an idea of how well-structured the company is, but of what the budget might be. If they say, "Right now we've got a classified ad, and we're thinking about a brochure," you can be fairly confident that this is a small-time business. If, however, they start talking about direct mail, print, radio, and so on, you may have a pretty savvy prospect.

Beware of companies who want to pour all of their budgets into the WWW. If they think that a Web site will be the miracle cure for slumping sales, they may come back at you when the cure fails to make them millions overnight. Be honest with them, give them the facts—not a pipe dream.

6. **What is your corporate image and market position?**

This is important in assessing the communications needs of your clients, as well as their growth potential. This will obviously need to be addressed in great detail once you get going on the project, but it's never too early to hear it from the horse's mouth.

This is, in many ways, a rephrasing of earlier questions. Take note of how well the answer matches those of what they do, and who their clients are.

7. What is driving the project?

This is sort of a rephrasing of the needs and goals, but it may give you some insight into the organization. While the answer to the needs/goals question might be, "We want to establish a presence," the answer to this might be, "Our competition is online, and the boss says we should be too."

This is to give you some insight into the company's motivation and may give you some key points for your first meeting.

8. What is the timeframe for the project?

Obviously, this will have an effect on your own scheduling. It will also give you an idea of how well-organized and how desperate the client is. If the answer is ASAP, the project may be yours for the taking, but it might be a nightmare. If the answer is, "We'd like to

have this completed by the end of next quarter," you might be bidding on a very large project.

9. What is the budget?

You'll almost never get a straight answer on this one, but it's worth asking. If they come back with, "How much do you usually charge?" be prepared to respond. There is no way to accurately assess a project's cost without knowing every detail, and giving a ballpark estimate is almost never in your best interest.

This also applies to people who call out of the blue and ask what a Web site costs. A couple of our favorite answers are, "How long is a rope?" and, "How much does it cost to build a house?"—but you can also answer this by saying that a Web site can cost as little as $100, or as much as $1,000,000.

10. Who will be attending the first meeting?

This not only allows you to prepare mentally, but also with your supplies. How many handouts will you need? Should you bring a laptop, or a projector? Along with some of the other questions, it will also let you know whether the main players will be in on the meeting, or whether you'll need several meetings to make the sale.

11. Whom will we (I) be working with?

Whether there will be a team or a single contact will affect how you will need to work with the client. If every decision is going to go through committee, you can bet that the project will be late and over budget.

12. Who makes the final decision?

In many cases, the highest-ranking person you'll be meeting will only be able to make recommendations. Sometimes though, you'll be meeting with the decision-maker. For obvious reasons, you'll want to know.

13. Who else is bidding on the project?

Knowing your competition is very valuable when it comes to pricing, as well as preparation. Whether you're up against a Madison Avenue firm or Joe's Bait Shop and HTML Design will dictate the form and content of your presentation. Unfortunately, many companies will play this pretty close to their chest.

14. **How did you hear about us?**

This not only gives you some idea of what they may expect, but will also give you insight on your own marketing efforts. Furthermore, it gives you an opportunity to close this little inquisition on a good note, by helping to reinforce whatever it was that led them to the decision to call you:

"I got your name from Joe at World Wide Widgets."

"Oh yeah, Joe's a great guy. I really enjoyed working with him—he really knows his stuff."

Once you've bled all of the information you possibly can, you can begin to prepare for the first meeting.

DISCOVERY

The first time you meet with a client on a project is often called the discovery phase. This is where you and your client assess the possibility of working together and find out more about each other. If you are responding to an RFP, you may be submitting your proposal in your first meeting. Otherwise, this is the time when you will be getting all of the details necessary to draw up your proposal.

PREPARATION

You'll want to be as prepared as possible. Decide on what equipment you'll need, prepare handouts, slides, examples, and so on. Plan for the worst-case scenario—that you'll be sitting in front of 20 people who have no idea what to ask you. Imagine that you may be the only person talking for an hour.

Try to anticipate any questions, concerns, or objections the client may have. And prepare to answer even the dumbest questions patiently. The CEO may be able to put together multimillion dollar deals in her sleep, but be dumbfounded by her VCR. Making her feel stupid is not in the plan.

Also be prepared to be challenged by at least one person in the room. Almost as a rule, you can expect that someone will try to stump you in some way. This is often the token geek, but can be anyone. It's usually someone who is in constant fear of losing his or her place in the pecking order, and can only make himself/herself look good by making others look bad.

Be prepared to answer questions like, "Isn't this whole WWW thing a scam?" and, "How can you call yourself an expert when you've only got a year's experience?" as well as questions that contain only strings of acronyms.

> **Note:**
>
> Befriend the head geek. Because of the fact that the Net is a new technology, most companies will have their "head computer person" (who may just be the person who understands how to clean the track ball of a mouse) come to your meetings. Often, this person either wants the job as Web designer or has a friend who does.
>
> Try to find this person as soon as possible and befriend him/her. Talk about what kind of systems the company is running, what he or she has at home, Star Trek, games, whatever. This person's recommendation may be the most important, and his/her help may be invaluable in completing the project.

Don't hope that your portfolio will be the main focus of the meeting. It's usually better to show a few examples, going into detail about the scope of each project, the goals, and how those goals were met, than to show page after page of HTML design.

THE DAY OF RECKONING

If you've never been in a sales meeting, you may have a hard time keeping focused. It's a natural tendency to either clam up or to blather away. Obviously, avoid either case. Be friendly, but not too familiar; reserved, but not snobbish. Respect your prospect's time, but expect them to respect yours as well. If you're kept waiting for a half hour, don't let it pass without mention.

There will probably be a round of introductions; if not, instigate one. You should be introduced to everyone in attendance. Remember, you have something of value.

Next, there will usually be a brief synopsis of why you are there, and it will then be your turn to speak. After a few niceties ("nice day, nice office, blah blah"), go over a brief description of everything you've learned about the company and what you understand to be the project. Then ask if your facts are correct.

This sets the stage for two-way communication and forces the prospect to get involved in your presentation. It will also help to clarify who the key players are (usually the ones whom everyone turns to when you ask a question). You can always fall back on a question or two if people seem to be losing focus or if you're starting to feel like a bug under a microscope.

By the end of the meeting, you should be asked to submit a proposal. Make sure that you have a contact for any questions, that you have a firm understanding of the scope of the proposal, and that you know the exact date for when the proposal is expected.

THE PROPOSAL

In most cases, the written proposal will reflect the size of the project. A quick "crash and burn" project may only deserve a one-page proposal, whereas a large project may require a lengthy write-up. You'll have to guess what your prospect would like to see.

Regardless of its size, a proposal should not include any creative work on your part. You don't work for free, and most clients won't respect you if you do.

Most proposals will include the following:

◆ **Executive Summary**—A synopsis of the proposal
◆ **Background**—Key issues that have led to the need for the project

◆ **Scope of Proposal**—The nuts and bolts of what will be accomplished, and by whom
◆ **Timeline**—Detailing the beginning and ending of each phase of the project
◆ **Projected Costs**—Your fees for the work
◆ **Terms**—The contractual details of the agreement

Other items that might be included in a proposal are a glossary of terms, a historical look at the Internet, and other items that may help in your communication to an audience unfamiliar with the medium.

There is no set way to present a proposal, but if you can, present it in person to the main decision maker, and go over it with him or her. This will help you address any immediate issues and may enable you to get some feedback on the spot.

THE MOCK-UP

It's generally not a good idea to present a mock-up of any kind until the deal is closed. This isn't in any way sneaky—you're not pulling a fast one. You get paid to make mock-ups; you get paid for your creativity— so giving either before you've been hired is counter-productive.

Once you've been contracted, a mock-up may be the best way to communicate your ideas for approval. Now, there are several ways in which you can mock up the "look and feel" as well as the mechanics of your system, and which you choose will depend upon your own skills and resources, as well as what you perceive as the client's needs.

STYLEBOARDS

A styleboard is basically a piece of foamboard or cardboard upon which you've laid photos, rough art, and text that give the overall impression of a page or system's look and feel. You can use photos, tissues (or layout paper), artwork, font treatments, and the like to help define what the message will be, without actually going into the mechanics of how a page or system will look in HTML. The key elements of a styleboard can include

- Photographs (if available)
- Basic color schemes
- Bulleted text for key points
- Text treatments for headers
- Key graphic elements
- Navigational concepts

Using a styleboard can be difficult, in that it often takes more time to describe its contents and each feature than it's worth, especially if you're dealing with a company that has never worked with a design agency. All in all, we generally avoid styleboards for two reasons:

- In HTML design, the final medium is (still) very limited, and styleboards can give clients the impression that they will be able to achieve more than the medium allows.
- A styleboard can be very subjective, and two different designers can create two entirely different pages based on what each sees in a styleboard.

Styleboards can, however, allow clients to see into your creative "engine," and can help them feel like they have some control over the way in which their system is being designed. For this reason, it may be best to think of styleboards (and other proofing tools) as methods for client communication and involvement, rather than actual creative processes.

STRUCTURE DIAGRAMS

A structure diagram is somewhat like a flow chart, and somewhat like a site map. It is a tool with which you can describe the functionality of the site. Now, we've addressed the issue of actually trying to show every link within a page and system—with a mass of lines running every which way—and this is definitely not the purpose of a structure diagram.

A structure diagram is meant to show the relation between the main pages of a system and the main navigational structure as it pertains to the core messages of the site. In most cases, this will be achieved by a simple hierarchical diagram (as a tree or as concentric circles) that will give you something to refer to as you describe a system.

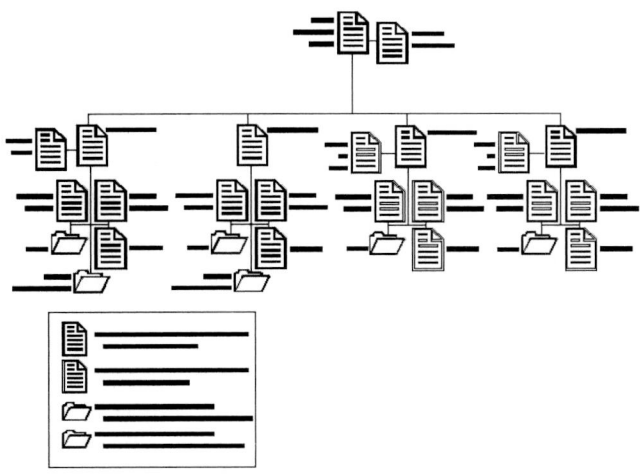

Figure 27.1.
A simple structure diagram.

STORYBOARDING

A storyboard is a tool most often used in video production, but it can be adapted for use in presenting a WWW system's message. A storyboard is simply a series of rough sketches that depict the actions and flow of a presentation, and can be useful when attempting to show a client the flow of a sales argument.

As a structure diagram shows the navigation and structure of a system from a "30,000-foot" view, and a styleboard shows the look and feel of a page or system, a storyboard can help you communicate how both the look and feel and navigation will lead to the presentation of the message(s).

JUST GOING FOR IT

There's a lot to be said for just using your HTML work-in-progress for communicating with the client. First and foremost, it allows the client to see the limitations that you face throughout the process, rather than at the end. Second, it allows you to stick to the project and not waste time designing, explaining, and trying to follow mock-ups and diagrams. Third, it helps to circumvent the possibility of a client getting vague or unreasonable expectations based on mock-ups.

EXPLAINING LIMITATIONS

Have we mentioned that HTML is still very limited? Well, be prepared to do the same yourself. Whether you are going to work as a commercial designer within a company, or on your own, a big part of your job will be explaining the limitations of the medium.

As often happens in a sales meeting, a potential client will ask whether or not you can put such-and-such on a Web site. Now, you can take at least two approaches on this. You can explain the limitations up front, as we do, or you can wait until after you've got a contract.

Suppose someone asks whether or not you can include a video on a Web site. You can answer, "Absolutely," and then later explain why the client's system is always bogged down, or you can say, "Yes, but there are some issues associated with doing that," and then explain the issues, allowing your client the opportunity to make an informed choice.

There is no doubt that we have lost sales for doing this. Some designers will go into a sales meeting and tell a client everything they want to hear. In comparison, we sometimes go into a meeting with some hard news for clients unfamiliar with the WWW. Sometimes, it can appear to the client that we just don't have the expertise necessary to pull it off.

On the other hand, by describing limitations up front, and by explaining issues like browser market share, bandwidth, audience, and the like, we are able to avoid frustrating our clients down the road. In our opinion, this is the more professional way of doing business.

There have been more than a few occasions when we've lost sales to designers who painted a rosy world, and have later been called by a sheepish client to "fix" the Web site for them. The other designer pocketed some fast cash, but we gained the client.

BE A PROFESSIONAL

Just as inexpensive computers and ignorant clients made everyone with a laser printer and a clip-art collection a "desktop publisher," the media hype and onslaught of "point-and-click" HTML editing programs have caused thousands of people to think they can call themselves webmasters.

Half-baked ideas of virtual malls and unlimited income, and the would-be entrepreneurs pushing these ideas, are causing a lot of people and businesses to get burned. Carpetbaggers abound in this industry, and the dashed hopes and bad feelings resulting from their unprofessional work reflect on all of us.

Don't enter this business with the idea that everyone needs a Web site, or that you are going to make a killing overnight. You are in a new industry, and you are a pioneer—be professional about it.

Overall, you should follow these simple business rules:

- Be honest.
- Meet deadlines.
- Communicate clearly.
- Return phone calls and e-mail promptly.
- Stick to your proposed budget.

BE HONEST

Don't give clients unreasonable expectations of what a Web site will accomplish for their business, don't lie about deadlines, and don't misrepresent the medium as a "limitless frontier." You're not a used-car salesman, you're a professional—act like one.

Lying not only makes you a dirtbag, it makes the entire profession look bad. It's also fraud and can have life-long ramifications. The corner donut shop probably has no place on the WWW, and trying to persuade them otherwise is in no one's best interest.

MEET DEADLINES

Hmmmm, let's see: "dead" and "line"—this would seem to mean that if you cross that line, you're dead. This appears to be a fairly straightforward concept, so why is it that so many people misinterpret it as meaning "approximate completion date" or some vague concept of an ideal goal?

Well, in fairness to many programmers-turned-designers, a deadline doesn't mean the same thing in programming as it does in advertising. In programming, a deadline is often as vague as having "something working by spring," whereas an advertising deadline would be more like "have it printed and delivered by December 8."

If you work with businesses, you'd better meet your deadlines. Don't set unreasonable goals that you know you can't meet, and don't ever try to whine your way out of a deadline. If you make a commitment, you keep it.

If you are relying on a client to provide information, input, or approval, and that client is lax in getting back to you, then you have every right to extend the deadline. Make sure you include in any agreements that you are not responsible for the delays caused by the client, and that you reiterate this when necessary.

Now, sometimes clients will make you work with one of their subcontractors (like a designer), and this person may put your needs at the bottom of a very large pile of priorities. If this is the case, document everything—you can't be expected to control this person, and the client should know this up front. If it's your own sub that's dragging you down, however, it's your problem.

COMMUNICATE CLEARLY

Again, it's often the geek-turned-designer who screws this up. Many geeks have poor social skills, which may be the reason why they were originally drawn to an industry where they don't need to interact much. Maybe this type of left-brained mentality lends itself well to working in a digital environment. Who knows?

The facts of the matter are that the moodiness, mutterings, and tirades of the "fragile genius" geek don't hold water in the boardroom. Nor does the pretentious practice of burying people in acronyms. You are an expert, and part of your job is to explain what it is you are doing.

Now, there is certainly some wisdom from the way programmers interact that can be applied to specific situations. There may be a time when you will want to rely on acronyms to shut up an offensive yes-man. This is one of those people who feel that they need to constantly keep a high profile to justify their job and will read a magazine article just before a meeting so that they can throw questions at you to make themselves look better at your expense. This may also be a person who knows just enough about HTML to think that he/she should be getting the project for himself or herself. Feel free to squash this person like a bug, but make it appear as if you are honestly trying to answer his/her question.

Example:

Brown-nose: "Isn't the new SQRL going to completely replace the standard XYZ1?"

You: "Well, the SQRL is still in beta testing, and everyone seems to agree that both the TFP and RQQ will need to be beefed up before there is any commercial viability. For this project, the XYZ1 seems to be the lowest cost and best-tested option. Is there some specific reason why you want to use the SQRL?"

Brown-nose: "…er, um, …yeah. I just wanted to bring it up—I heard something somewhere…"

You: "Oh."

Let the awkward silence rest on their shoulders. This shouldn't be your overall communication style, but it really can come in handy.

> **Note:**
> Don't fake it. If someone presents you with an acronym or concept that you aren't familiar with, ask that person what it means. If you try to fake it, it might blow up in your face.

RESPOND TO PHONE CALLS AND E-MAIL

This should go without saying. Clients expect a service from you, and part of that service is communication. Communication is, after all, the whole point of the WWW. If a client wants to get in touch with you, don't lie, don't hide, and don't try to shift blame. If you do, you won't have a client for very long.

For example, a certain software company was supposed to provide us with specific information in this book. We were given a contact (a project manager) and sent her an e-mail message requesting the information. A few *weeks* after it was due, we called this "manager" to see what the delay was.

Well, first she wouldn't return our calls, then she claimed that she'd only just gotten the e-mail—though we knew the exact date and time that the e-mail was delivered. Next she told us that e-mail isn't really reliable—though one of her company's focuses is on e-mail client software, and again, she had the e-mail. Finally, she said that it really wasn't her job, though we'd been referred to her by the company's top brass.

So, this person tried to lie her way out of just telling us that she hadn't done her job. It took us days to get the information from other, more reliable sources, and caused us to pull a few all-nighters to make our deadline. We made the deadline and have included the information, but we now honestly tell clients that we doubt the longevity of that company because of its poor managerial resources and business skills.

STICK TO THE BUDGET

Don't fall into the bait and switch routines that have become commonplace in so many businesses. You've seen the magazine ads that say "$5 Web site" by companies that will nickel and dime every feature until that "$5" becomes $5,000—for a site that isn't even worth the original $5.

A big part of your job is to anticipate expenses. Don't leave out features that you know will be necessary to an effective site, just so that you can give an apparently low bid: "Oh, you wanted graphics with that? Well that's gonna cost you!"

PAYMENT ISSUES

What, you want to get paid? Isn't staring at code and massaging graphics all day payment enough? Nah, us either.

For the most part, payment issues are legal issues, and you should consult an attorney to help you develop your contract. There are, however, some key issues you will want to keep in mind.

First, you'll want to split up your payments. You'll want to bill the client for at least a third of the projected cost before you start work. Clients who balk at this are generally either very small and unused to doing business, or they are dishonest.

Second, you'll want to leave room for addenda that will affect both the cost and deadlines of a project. This way you can add new facets to the project without the need to rewrite the contract.

Third, you'll want to specify payment terms. If you want money up front, a net-30 payment schedule isn't going to cut it. Some companies assume net-30 on everything, and you'll need to make sure you both agree on the terms before you start work.

SUMMARY

We've really stood upon the soapbox in this chapter and put ourselves in the position of presuming to tell you how to do business. Well, this is the last chapter, and it's about time we mouthed off.

Ethics and honesty are the marks of a true professional, and failure to live up to these standards derides the whole profession. Every profession has its black sheep, but in a technology as new as this, a few bad eggs can make us all stink.

We've parted with some hard-earned knowledge in writing this book, and we hope that it will inspire you to build upon your own skills and creativity. We hope that you will succeed, and that you will help push this industry in new directions. Above all, it is our hope that you will help elevate this profession from the level of the get-rich-quick opportunists who are threatening to drag us all through their muck.

Now, go out there and make us proud—we'll see you on the Web.

Appendixes

PART V

Internet Statistics Resources

Cyberculture Survey
http://www.tanisys.com/~joshk/survey.htm

D.I.T. Web Marketing Survey
http://www.internet-eireann.ie/dit/survey.htm

Geography of Cyberspace
http://info.cf.ac.uk/uwcc/cplan/martin/geography_of_cyberspace/geography_of_
cyberspace.html

Nielsen Interactive Services—Internet Surveys
http://www.nielsenmedia.com/demo.htm/

Survey on Electronic Information Commerce
http://survey.infj.ulst.ac.uk/

Yahoo!'s Internet Statistics and Demographics
http://www.yahoo.com/Computers_and_Internet/Internet/Statistics_and_Demographics/

Virtual Hosts Resources

The List
http://www.thelist.com

Yahoo!'s List of Internet Access Providers
http://www.yahoo.com/Business_and_Economy/Companies/Internet_Access_Providers/

Yahoo!'s Web Presence Providers
http://www.yahoo.com/Business_and_Economy/Companies/Internet_Services/
Web_Presence_Providers/

Server Resources

APPENDIX C

Apache HTTPD Server

`http://www.apache.org`

Apple

`http://www.apple.com`

CERN's HTTPD

`http://www.w3.org/hypertext/WWW/Daemon/Status.html`

Cisco (Routers)

`http://www.cisco.com`

Compaq Online

`http://www.compaq.com`

Computer Data Networks

`http://www.kuwait.net/~cdn/servers.html`

Dell

`http://www.dell.com`

Digital Equipment Corporation

`http://www.digital.com/`

Epson

`http://www.epson.com`

Hewlett-Packard

`http://www.hp.com`

IBM

`http://www.ibm.com/`

Intel

`http://www.intel.com`

Intergraph

`http://129.135.1.3/webserver`

MacHTTP

`http://www.starnine.com/machttp/machttpsoft.html`

MacHTTP Frequently Asked Questions

`http://arpp1.carleton.ca/machttp/doc/`

Microsoft Internet Information Server

`http://www.microsoft.com/infoserv`

NCSA's HTTPD

`http://www.ncsa.uiuc.edu/InformationServers/`

Netcraft's survey of the most popular servers
http://www.netcraft.co.uk/Survey/Reports

Netscape
http://www.netscape.com

O'Reilly and Associates WebSite
http://website.ora.com/

SGI (Silicon Graphics Incorporated)
http://www.sgi.com

Sun
http://www.sun.com/

WebCube
http://www.pacnet.com/pacnet/wcube/home.html

WebSTAR
http://www.starnine.com

WinHTTPD
http://www.city.net/win-httpd

Yahoo!'s Turn-key server packages listing
http://www.yahoo.com/Business_and_Economy/Companies/Computers/ Networking/Consulting/

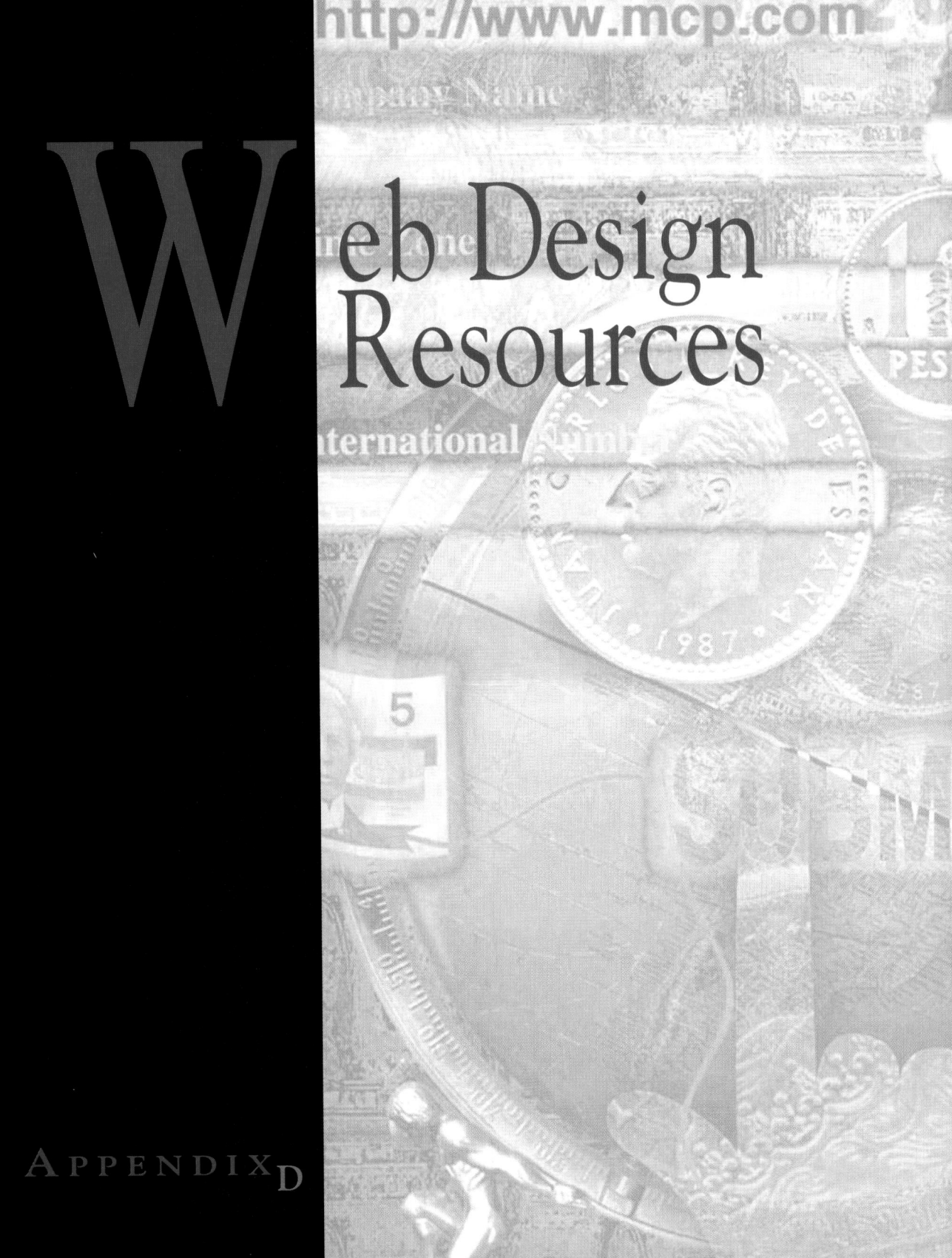

Web Design Resources

The Bare Bones Guide to HTML
`http://werbach.com/barebones/barebone_html.html`

Bibliography of HTML Reference Documents
`http://www.utirc.utoronto.ca/HTMLdocs/NewHTML/bibliography.html`

Extensions to HTML
`http://home.netscape.com/assist/net_sites/html_extensions.html`

HTML Fancy Stuff
`http://www.hal.com/~barry/Links/html.html`

HTML Station
`http://www.december.com/html/`

The HTML Writer's Guild Website
`http://www.hwg.org/resources/`

Macmillan's HTML Workshop
`http://www.mcp.com/general/workshop/index.html`

NetMind Free Services Home Page
`http://www.netmind.com/`

Sun's Web Development Information
`http://www.sun.com/styleguide/`

The Toolbox
`http://member.aol.com/royalef/toolbox.htm/`

Tools for WWW Providers
`http://www.w3.org/hypertext/WWW/Tools/`

The Web Designer
`http://www.kosone.com/people/nelsonl/nl.htm#FRAMES`

The Web Developer's Virtual Library
`http://www.stars.com/`

The Web Masters' Page
`http://miso.wwa.com/-boba/masters1.html`

Webmaster Reference Library
`http://www.webreference.com/index2.html`

The World Wide Web Consortium (W3C)
`http://www.w3.org/`

Graphics Resources

FIGLET Service (ASCII text design)
http://www.inf.utfsm.cl/cgi-bin/figlet

Graphics Viewers, Editors, Utilities, and Info
http://www2.ncsu.edu/bae/people/faculty/walker/hotlist/graphics.html

Icons for Use in WWW HTML Documents
http://www.infi.net/~rdralph/icons/

Interactive Graphics Generation Page
http://www.eece.ksu.edu/IGRNEW/

Photographer's Alley Home
http://204.162.147.30/photodisc/html/photo/phohome.htm

Ventana's Clip Art Archive
http://www.vmedia.com/archives/clipart/index.html

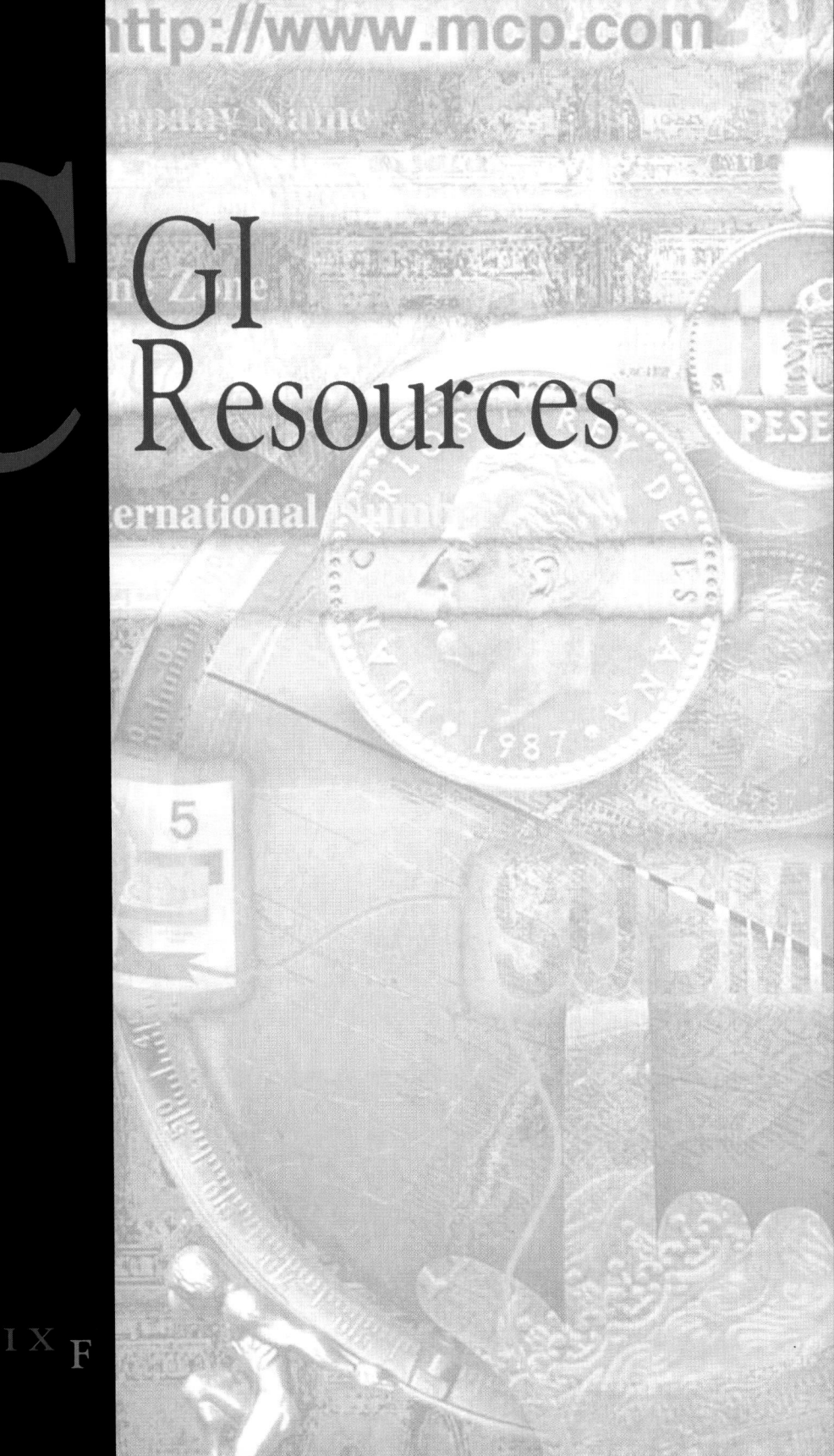

CGI Resources

APPENDIX F

An ANSI C Library for CGI Programming
`http://sunsite.unc.edu/boutell/cgic/cgic.html#images`

CGI for Applescript
`http://www.comvista.com/net/www/cgilesson.html`

Matt's Script Archive
`http://www.worldwidemart.com/scripts/examples/formmail.shtml`

A Perl CGI Library
`http://www59.metronet.com/cgi/`

Public Domain CGI script archive
`http://www.eff.org/~erict/Scripts`

Search for CGI Documentation
`http://hoohoo.ncsa.uiuc.edu/docs/Architext/AT-CGI_Informationquery.html`

Yahoo!—Common Gateway Interface
`http://www.yahoo.com/Computers/World_Wide_Web/CGI___Common_Gateway
_Interface/`

Places to Market Your Site

AltaVista

http://www.altavista.digital.com

EINet Galaxy

http://galaxy.einet.net/cgi-bin/annotate?Other

Excite

http://www.excite.com

Expose (links to hundreds of other places to submit your URL)

http://www.dev-com.com/~cmg/expose1.htm

Infoseek

http://www.infoseek.com:80/doc/FAQ/_How_do_I_get_my_Web_page_inde.html

Inktomi

http://inktomi.berkeley.edu/addurl.html

Lycos

http://www.lycos.com/lycos-register.html

NCSA's What's New page

http://www.ncsa.uiuc.edu/SDG/Software/Mosaic/Docs/whats-new.html

Open Market

http://www.directory.net

Open Text

http://www.opentext.com:8080/omw/f-omw-submit.html

Point

http://www.pointcom.com

SubmitAll

http://www.hometeam.com/addurl/

Submit It!

http://www.submit-it.com/

Pointers to Pointers

http://www.homecom.com/global/pointers.html

PostMaster

http://www.netcreations.com/postmaster

WebCrawler

http://www.webcrawler.com/WebCrawler/SubmitURLS.html

WebPost 96

`http://www.webpost96.com/`

Web Promote (this one charges a fee)

`http://www.webpromote.com`

WWW Worm

`http://wwwmcb.cs.colorado.edu/home/mcbryan/WWWWadd.html`

World Wide Web Yellow Pages

`http://www.mcp.com/newriders/wwwyp/submit.html`

Yahoo!

`http://beta.yahoo.com/bin/top1?424,11`

Comparative HTML Reference Guide

Here is a reference guide to the common HTML tags that are compatible with the three most widely used browsers: Netscape Navigator, Microsoft Internet Explorer, and Mosaic. The attributes are listed under each tag where applicable.

HTML Comparison Reference Guide Key

After the tags and attributes listed in this appendix are letters indicating the browsers the tags and attributes can be used with. The letters stand for the following:

NS = Netscape Navigator (3.0 beta)

Source: `http://www.netscape.com` and from Netscape Communications.

MS = Microsoft Internet Explorer (3.0 beta)

Source: `http://www.microsoft.com/intdev/author/newhtml/ie30html.htm`. (A great reference. We wish all the browser software companies could arrange their HTML information so well.)

SM = Mosaic (Spyglass Mosaic 3.0)

Source: Contact with Spyglass, Inc.

HTML Tags and Attributes

`<!>`   NS, MS, SM

This tag can be used anywhere in your document to place a comment within the HTML code. A comment affects the document in no way other than enabling you to place a comment within it. The most common use for this is within the `<HEAD>` tag for providing information about the document, such as

```
<!--Author: you -->
```

`<!DOCTYPE ?>`   NS, MS, SM

This tag is the first to appear within an HTML document and declares which HTML version your page is using.

For HTML 2.0, use this tag: `<!DOCTYPE HTML PUBLIC "-//IETF//DTD HTML 2.0//EN">`
For HTML 3.0, use this tag: `<!DOCTYPE HTML PUBLIC "-//W3O//DTD W3 HTML 3.0//EN">`
For HTML 3.2, use this tag: `<!DOCTYPE HTML PUBLIC "-//W3C//DTD HTML 3.2//EN">`

<A ?>...</A>   NS, MS, SM

These anchor tags specify a hypertext link.

HREF   NS, MS, SM

HREF is used to define the URL of your linked image or document. A common usage looks like this:

```
<A HREF="http://www.hampton.org/index.html">Jump to hampton.org</A>
```

You can also use this tag to signify an address for e-mail by using the Mailto: tag, like this:

```
<A HREF="mailto:you@yourdomain.com">Email</A>
```

METHODS   NS, MS, SM

This rarely used attribute specifies the method with which the document should be retrieved (Gopher, FTP, and so on). The value of the METHODS attribute is a comma-separated list of HTTP methods supported by the object for public use.

NAME   NS, MS, SM

This attribute is used to associate a name with a part of a document that can be linked to, like this:

```
<A NAME="chapter1">Chapter 1</A>
```

You can create a link from within the page to this part of the document by using this code:

```
<A HREF="#chapter1">Jump to Chapter 1</A>
```

TARGET   NS, MS, SM

Since browser windows can have names associated with them, links in any window can refer to another window by name. Click on the link and the document you requested will appear in that named window. (If the window is not already open, the browser will open and name a new window for you.)

The syntax for the targeted windows is

```
<A HREF="home.htm" TARGET="window_name">Click here to open home.htm into a new
browser window</A>
```

Note:

If the targeted document is part of a frameset, there are various implicit names you can use for that purpose. The implicit name is determined by the frame's relationship to other frames; implicit names are reserved words that all begin with an underscore (_). These reserved words are

◆ "_blank"

This specifies to load the link into a new browser window (your frames site will remain open as well). Example:

```
<A HREF="document.htm" TARGET="_blank">Clicking here will load this link
into a new blank browser window.</A>
```

◆ "_top"

This specifies to load the link into the full body of the window. Use this for links outside your frames system. Example:

```
<A HREF="document.htm" TARGET="_top">Clicking here will load the link into
the whole body of the window.</A>
```

◆ "_parent"

This specifies to load the requested item into the linking document's immediate parent. Example:

```
<A HREF="document.htm" TARGET="_parent">Clicking here will load this link
into this page's parent window.</A>
```

◆ "_self"

Use this to load the link into the same window the link was clicked in. Example:

```
<A HREF="document.htm" TARGET="_self">Clicking here will load the link
into this same window.</A>
```

TITLE   NS, MS, SM

The TITLE attribute is for informational purposes only. If used, it should provide the title of the document whose address is given by the HREF attribute.

REL   NS, MS, SM

This attribute gives the relationship(s) described by the hypertext link from the anchor to the target. The value is a comma-separated list of relationship values. The REL attribute is only used when the HREF attribute is also present.

REV   NS, MS, SM

The REV attribute is the same as the REL attribute, but the semantics of the link type are in the reverse direction. A link from A to B with REL="X" expresses the same relationship as a link from B to A with REV="X". An anchor may have both REL and REV attributes.

URN NS, MS, SM

This attribute specifies a uniform resource name (URN) for a target document.

<ADDRESS>...</ADDRESS> NS, MS, SM

This set of tags is used to specify information such as address, signature, or authorship, and is usually rendered in an italic typeface. This element implies a paragraph break before and after and is generally used at the end of a document.

<APPLET ?>...</APPLET> NS

This set of tags enables you to embed a Java applet into an HTML document. Its attributes are presented in the following sections.

ALIGN

This attribute is required and specifies the alignment of the applet. Possible values are

```
RIGHT
LEFT
BOTTOM
TOP
TEXTTOP
MIDDLE
ABSMIDDLE
BASELINE
ABSBOTTOM
```

ALT

This attribute is optional and specifies the text that should be displayed if the browser understands the APPLET element yet can't run applets written in Java.

CODEBASE

This attribute specifies the base URL of the applet (the directory that contains the applet's code). The default is the document's URL.

CODE

This attribute is required and gives the name of the file containing the applet's compiled applet subclass. The file is relative to the base URL of the applet and cannot be absolute.

NAME

This attribute is optional and specifies a name for the applet instance, making it possible for applets within the same page to find and communicate with each other.

VSPACE/HSPACE

These specify the number of pixels above, below, and on the sides of the applet. These attributes are optional and are used the same way as the IMG element's VSPACE and HSPACE attributes.

WIDTH/HEIGHT

These attributes describe the initial height and width (in pixels) of the applet's display area (not including any windows or dialogs that the applet brings up). These attributes are required.

<AREA ?>   NS, MS, SM

This tag is used to describe the shape of a hot spot (clickable region) in a client-side image map.

COORDS   NS, MS, SM

This attribute defines the hot spot's shape, like this:

```
<AREA SHAPE="RECT" COORDS="40, 20, 140, 120" HREF=http://www.yourdomain.com>
```

HREF   NS, MS, SM

Indicates the destination of the hot spot (its URL) like this:

```
<AREA SHAPE="RECT" COORDS="40, 20, 140, 120" HREF=http://www.yourdomain.com>
```

NOHREF   NS, MS, SM

Indicates that clicks to this area cause no action.

SHAPE   NS, MS, SM

This attribute indicates the type of shape like this:

```
<AREA SHAPE="RECT" COORDS="40, 20, 140, 120" HREF=http://www.yourdomain.com>
```

Options are

```
CIRC
CIRCLE
POLY
POLYGON
RECT
RECTANGLE
```

<B>...</B>   NS, MS, SM

This set of tags specifies bold type.

\<BASE ?>   NS, MS, SM

This tag specifies the name of the file in which the current document is stored. It is useful when link references within the document do not include full pathnames (that is, are only partially qualified). The \<BASE> element should appear within the \<HEAD> element.

HREF   NS, MS, SM

This is a required attribute that is used to identify the URL, like this:

```
<BASE HREF="http://www.yourdomain.com">
```

TARGET   NS, SM

Enables you to pick a default-named target-window for every link in the document that doesn't have an explicit TARGET attribute, like this:

```
<BASE TARGET="default_target">
```

\<BASEFONT ?>   NS, MS, SM

This tag sets the base font's value.

SIZE   NS, MS, SM

This changes the size of the BASEFONT (the default is 3), and is the size all relative \<FONT SIZE ...> changes are based on. It looks like this:

```
<BASEFONT SIZE=4>
```

You can use a number from 1 to 7.

\<BGSOUND ?>   MS, SM

This tag enables background sounds to accompany an HTML document. The "soundtracks" can be in MID (SM uses an external player for MID files), AU, or WAV files.

DELAY   SM

Used to delay the playing of the sound for x number of seconds.

LOOP   MS, SM

This attribute specifies how many times a sound will loop. You can use a number for this value as in

```
<BGSOUND SRC=sound.wav LOOP=4>
```

or make the sound loop on forever as in

```
<BGSOUND SRC=sound.wav LOOP=INFINITE>
```

SRC　MS, SM

Specifies the URL of the sound (see preceding example).

`<BIG>...</BIG>`　NS

These tags specify a large font. Please use *sparingly*.

`<BLINK>...</BLINK>`　NS, SM

These tags specify blinking text. A little goes a long way with this one.

`<BLOCKQUOTE>...</BLOCKQUOTE>`　NS, MS, SM

Used for long quotes or citations, these tags are usually rendered with indented margins.

`<BODY ?>...</BODY>`　NS, MS, SM

These tags contain within them the contents of the document (tags and the text) and can be used to describe optional attributes of the document, such as those presented in the following paragraphs.

ALINK　NS

Describes the color of an active textual link (in hexadecimal code or by name). This is the color that appears while the user is selecting the link (for a split second).

BACKGROUND　NS, MS, SM

Describes the name (if within the same directory) or URL of the graphic that will be tiled to create a background for the page. The viewers will not see this image if they are using a non-compliant browser, if they have chosen the option of overriding background images, or if their image loading is turned off. Never use in conjunction with the BGCOLOR attribute.

BGCOLOR　NS, MS, SM

Defines the background color of the page, which is specified using a hexadecimal color code (for example, white = "#FFFFFF"). The color wizard included in the HTML library on the CD-ROM is a very useful tool for determining these codes. You can also use a few select color names for this attribute: blue, fuchsia, gray, green, lime, maroon, navy, purple, olive, aqua, black, silver, red, teal, white, and so on. Never use this attribute in conjunction with the BACKGROUND attribute.

BGPROPERTIES　MS

Specifies a watermark (a background picture that does not scroll).

CLASS   NS

Identifies and further specifies the characteristics of an element, thereby allowing the extension of HTML tags for different purposes. This is especially useful in the construction of style sheets. You can specify multiple classes for an element by separating class names with a period. It appears like this:

```
CLASS="type"
```

ID   NS

Designates a location in the document as a destination for a link (replaces the `<A NAME>` tag) and appears like this:

```
ID="keyword"
```

LEFTMARGIN   MS, SM

Used to specify the left margin for the body of the page, like this:

```
<BODY LEFTMARGIN="30">
```

LINK   NS, MS, SM

Describes the color of textual links (in hexadecimal code or by name).

TEXT   NS, MS, SM

Describes the document's text color (in hexadecimal code or by name), like this:

```
<BODY TEXT=#FFFFFF>
```

It's better to use only hexadecimal color names with SM.

TOPMARGIN   MS, SM

Specifies the top margin for the body of the page, like this:

```
<BODY TOPMARGIN="5">
```

VLINK   NS, MS, SM

Describes the color of previously visited textual links (in hexadecimal code or by name).

   NS, MS, SM

This tag is one-sided and is used to force a line break. Unlike the `<P>` tag, the `<BR>` tag can be used over and over, resulting in a carriage return with each use.

CLEAR   NS, MS, SM

Used to insert vertical space so that the following displayed text will appear past left or right aligned images. Options are

```
LEFT
RIGHT
ALL
```

<BQ>...</BQ>   NS

These Block Quote tags identify an extended quote.

<CAPTION>...</CAPTION>   NS, MS, SM

This set of tags can be used to put a label on a `<TABLE>`.

ALIGN   NS, MS, SM

Used to align your caption, as in `ALIGN=TOP`. Possibilities for this attribute include

```
BOTTOM (NS,SM)
TOP (NS,SM)
LEFT (MS)
RIGHT (MS)
CENTER (MS)
```

VALIGN   NS, MS (TOP, BOTTOM), SM

Specifies whether to place the caption on top or below the table, as in `VALIGN=TOP` or `VALIGN=BOTTOM`.

<CENTER>...</CENTER>   NS, MS, SM

Text contained within these tags is centered.

<CITE>...</CITE>   NS, MS, SM

This tag is normally used for citations or references to other sources.

<CODE>...</CODE>   NS, MS, SM

This set of tags is used for extracts from program code.

<COL>...</COL>   MS

These tags can be used to specify the text alignment for table columns.

ALIGN

Defines the text alignment within the column group (CENTER is the default).

SPAN

Is occasionally used to set the number of columns upon which the ALIGN attribute is to act.

<COLGROUP>...</COLGROUP> MS

This set of tags can be used to group columns together to set their alignment properties.

ALIGN

Used to specify the column group and text alignment (the default is CENTER), like this:

```
<COLGROUP ALIGN=RIGHT>
```

Options for this attribute are

```
JUSTIFY
CENTER
RIGHT
LEFT
```

VALIGN

Used to specify the vertical alignment of text within the column.

<COMMENT>...</COMMENT> MS, SM

This set of tags indicates a comment.

<DD> NS, MS, SM

This tag specifies a definition within a definition list (see <DL> for an example).

COMPACT NS

This is used to reduce spacing between text elements, thereby displaying the text more compactly.

<DFN>...</DFN> MS

These tags mark a defining instance of the enclosed term.

<DIR>...</DIR> NS, MS, SM

This set of tags indicates a directory list. (MS appears without bullets.)

\<DIV>...\</DIV>   NS

This is used to group related items together and can be used with the ALIGN attribute, as in

```
<DIV ALIGN=LEFT>
```

ALIGN   NS

Used to align the grouped items; options are

```
LEFT
RIGHT
CENTER
```

\<DL>...\</DL>   NS, MS, SM

This set of tags specifies a definition or glossary list; it contains \<DT> elements that give terms and \<DD> elements that give the corresponding definitions. It is commonly used like this:

```
<DL>
<DT> Term to be defined #1
<DD> Definition of term #1
<DT> Term to be defined #2
<DD> Definition of term #2
</DL>
```

\<DT>   NS, MS, SM

This tag specifies a term to be defined within a definition list (see \<DL> for an example).

\<EM>...\</EM>   NS, MS, SM

This set of tags specifies the basic emphasis, normally rendered in an italic font.

\<EMBED ?>   NS, SM

This tag enables you to embed documents of any type (the user needs to have an application that can view the data installed on his or her system) directly into an HTML page; it is used like this:

```
<EMBED SRC="sound/embed.wav">
```

Embedded objects are activated by double-clicking them within the browser, causing the application that supports that embedded object to be launched, with the object present. For instance, if a TIF graphic file was embedded into an HTML document, when the user double-clicks, Netscape would launch the graphics program that supports TIF files (such as PSP, included on your CD-ROM) with the object already loaded and ready for editing.

The attributes for this tag behave differently with different plug-ins, so before using this tag
and associated attributes, we suggest you visit Netscape's plug-in site at

`http://home.netscape.com/comprod/products/navigator/version_3.0/developer/`
`newplug.html`

or the site of the particular plug-in you intend to use for the latest information.

Some of the attributes you can use with this tag are

ALIGN (NS)
AUTOLOAD (NS)
AUTOPLAY (NS)
AUTOSTART (NS)
BORDER (NS)
CONSOLE (NS)
CONTROLS (NS)
CONTROLLER (NS)
CORRECTION (NS)
ENCTYPE (SM)
ENDTIME—NS
FOV (NS)
HIDDEN (NS)
HEIGHT (NS, SM)
HREF (NS)
LOOP (NS)
MASTERSOUND (NS)
NAME (NS)
NODE (NS)
PALETTE (SM)
PAN (NS)
PARAMETER_NAME (NS)
PLAYEVERYFRAME (NS)
PLUGINSPACE (NS)
SRC (NS, SM)
STARTTIME (NS)
TARGET (NS, SM)
TILT (NS)
VOLUME (NS)
WIDTH (NS, SM)

<FONT ?>...</FONT>   NS, MS, SM

This set of tags enables you to change the font color, size, and face of the enclosed text. Colors are defined in hexadecimals or one of the understood color names.

COLOR   NS, MS, SM

Specifies the font color, as in

```
<FONT COLOR="#FF0000">This text is red</FONT>
```

FACE   NS, MS

Specifies the font face, as in

```
<FONT FACE="Lucida Sans,Arial,Times Roman">This text will be in either Lucida
Sans, Arial, or Times Roman, depending on which fonts are installed on the
viewers system, trying each in order.</FONT>
```

SIZE   NS, MS, SM

Specifies the font size, as in

```
<FONT SIZE=+1>This font is bigger than the previous</FONT>
```

<FORM>...</FORM>   NS, MS, SM

These tags are used to define a fill-out form within an HTML document.

ACTION   NS, MS, SM

Describes the URL of the query server to which the form contents will be submitted.

ENCTYPE   NS, SM

Specifies the encoding of the form contents. Only applies if the METHOD attribute is set to POST.

METHOD   NS, MS, SM

This is the method used to submit the form to the query server (which method you use depends mostly on your server). Options for this attribute are

GET   Causes the form contents to be appended to the URL as if it were a normal query

POST   Causes the form contents to be sent to the server in a data body (not as part of the URL)

For most purposes, using POST is preferable.

<FRAME ?>   NS, MS, SM

This tag is used to describe an individual frame within the <FRAMESET> tag. Unlike many tags, the <FRAME> tag does *not* occur with a closing </FRAME> counterpart.

BORDER   NS

Enables you to change the characteristics of the frames border.

BORDERCOLOR   NS

Defines the color of the frames border in hexadecimal or by name.

FRAMEBORDER   NS, MS

This enables the option to display or not display a border for a frame, as in

```
<FRAMEBORDER="NO">
```

FRAMESPACING   MS

Is used to create additional space between frames (specified in pixels).

NAME   NS, MS, SM

This provides a target name for the frame. The name should always start with an alphanumeric character.

NORESIZE   NS, MS, SM

This is used to prevent the user from resizing the frame (as is usually allowable).

MARGINHEIGHT   NS, MS, SM

This controls the margin height of the frame in pixels.

MARGINWIDTH   NS, MS, SM

This controls the margin width of the frame in pixels.

SCROLLING   NS, MS, SM

This enables you to choose the scrolling option for the frame. Choices are YES, NO, or AUTO (which automatically enables scrolling only if necessary).

SRC   NS, MS, SM

This describes the source file of the document contained within that frame. It is advisable to make your source files containing information HTML 2-compliant (containing no HTML 3, Netscape, or Microsoft extensions). This will enable you to make your frames site compatible with non-frames-capable browsers.

<FRAMESET ?>...</FRAMESET> NS, MS, SM

These are the tags that set the layout for your frames page. This is also the container that hosts the FRAME, FRAMESET, NOFRAMES tags. The opening <FRAMESET> tag must include either a column list or a row list, taking the form "COLS=column_list" or "ROWS=row_list". Row or column lists are always separated by commas.

COLS NS, MS, SM

Used to separate the frame document into vertical columns. You can specify the column dimensions by pixels, percentage (%), or a relative size (*), for example

```
<FRAMESET COLS="140,*">
```

This means make the first column 140 pixels wide, and the other column as wide as the remaining browser screen.

ROWS NS, MS, SM

This creates a frame document with horizontal rows. You can specify the row dimensions by pixels, percentage (%), or a relative size (*), for example

```
<FRAMESET ROWS="65,*">
```

<H#>...</H#> NS, MS, SM

This describes a heading, as in <H1>.

ALIGN NS, MS, SM

Enables you to set an alignment for your heading, like this:

```
<H1 ALIGN=CENTER>This heading is centered</H1>
```

Options for this attribute are

CENTER (NS, MS, SM)
LEFT (NS, SM)
RIGHT (NS, SM)
JUSTIFY (NS)

<H1>...</H1> NS, MS, SM

Heading 1.

<H2>...</H2> NS, MS, SM

Heading 2.

`<H3>...</H3>`   NS, MS, SM

Heading 3.

`<H4>...</H4>`   NS, MS, SM

Heading 4.

`<H5>...</H5>`   NS, MS, SM

Heading 5.

`<H6>...</H6>`   NS, MS, SM

Heading 6.

`<H7>...</H7>`   MS

Heading 7.

`<HEAD>...</HEAD>`   NS, MS, SM

These tags contain within them the document head elements. A common head element
looks something like this:

```
<HEAD>
<TITLE>A common head element</TITLE>
<!-- Author: Kim and Brad Hampton -->
<!-- Revision: 2.0 08/08/96 -->
</HEAD>
```

`<HR>`   NS, MS, SM

This places a horizontal rule (line) across your page and does not have an end tag.

ALIGN   NS, MS, SM

Specifies whether the line should be centered, aligned to the left margin, or aligned to the
right margin.

COLOR   MS

Specifies the color of the horizontal rule (by color name or in hexadecimals).

NOSHADE   NS, MS, SM

Draws the horizontal rule without a 3-D shadow.

SIZE   NS, MS, SM

Specifies the thickness of the horizontal rule in pixels.

WIDTH   NS, MS, SM

Specifies the width of the rule in pixels.

<HTML>...</HTML>   NS, MS, SM

All of your text and HTML tags go within the <HTML> tags. These tags indicate that the file is an HTML document—they tell your browser what to expect.

ROLE   NS

This identifies the type of document, such as a table of contents:

```
ROLE="name"
```

URN   NS

Used to designate the universal resource name for the document, like this:

```
URN="name"
```

VERSION   NS

Specifies the DTD version to an application. For instance, for HTML 3.0 the tag would look like this:

```
<HTML VERSION="-//W30//DTD W3 HTML 3.0//EN">
```

<I>...</I>   NS, MS, SM

These tags specify that the text within them should be displayed in italics.

<IMG ?>   NS, MS, SM

This tag inserts images into the document and requires no ending tag. A common usage looks like this:

```
<IMG SRC="flower.gif" ALT="[A Flower]">
```

ALIGN   NS, MS, SM

Specifies the alignment of the surrounding text (in relation to the image). Options include

```
TOP
BOTTOM
MIDDLE
LEFT
RIGHT
```

(SM uses middle, top, and bottom only.)

ALT   NS, MS, SM

This specifies the text that will be displayed in place of the graphics in case:

1. The viewer is using a text-only browser.
2. The viewer's browser cannot read a graphic of that type.
3. The viewer has chosen not to load images.

It is a very good idea to always include this attribute.

BORDER   NS, MS, SM

Specifies the size of the border drawn around the image.

CONTROLS   MS

If a video clip is present, this attribute specifies that a set of controls will be displayed under the clip.

DYNSRC   MS

This specifies the address of a VRML world or video clip to be displayed in the window.

HEIGHT   NS, MS, SM

Specifies the height of the image.

HSPACE   NS, MS, SM

Specifies the horizontal margins for the image.

ISMAP   NS, MS, SM

This identifies the image as a server-side image map.

LOOP   MS

Specifies how many times a video clip will loop (repeat) when activated.

LOWSRC   NS

This attribute makes it is possible to use two images in the same space and is used like this:

```
<IMG SRC="highres.gif" LOWSRC="lowres.jpg">
```

This code line will load the image called `lowres.jpg` on the first pass through the document. Then, after the page (and all of its graphics) are fully loaded, NS will load the image called `highres.gif`. This enables the user to have a very low-resolution (poor quality) version of an image loaded initially (to speed download time), and if the user stays on the page after the initial layout of the page, a higher-resolution version of the same graphic will fade in and replace it.

If the images are of different sizes (which isn't a good idea) and a fixed width and height are unspecified in the IMG element, the second image (in this example highres.gif) will be scaled to the dimensions of the first (LOWSRC) image (in this example lowres.jpg).

Browsers that do not recognize the LOWSRC attribute will just ignore it and load the image called highres.gif.

MOUSEOVER   MS

This attribute is for video clips and specifies that the video clip should start playing when the user moves the mouse cursor over the animation.

SRC   NS, MS, SM

Specifies the URL of the graphic to insert.

START=FILEOPEN   MS

This attribute is for video clips and indicates to start playing the video as soon as the file is done opening.

USEMAP   NS, MS, SM

This is used to identify the picture as a client-side image map and specifies a MAP to use to interpret user clicks.

VRML   MS

This attribute has the capability to include inline embedded VRML (WRL) worlds. (The viewer may need the VRML add-on, available from the Microsoft Windows 95 Web site, to view it, though.) You can also use this tag to embed XAF ActiveVRML files. These allow for animated VRML objects to be freely manipulated in 3-D space, to respond to user events, or to change with time. This attribute supports many of the attributes of the <IMG> element, like HEIGHT and WIDTH, and is used like this:

```
<IMG SRC="graphic.gif" VRML="house.wrl" HEIGHT=200 WIDTH=150>
```

This example will embed the VRML world house.wrl into the HTML document, with the navigation controls below the embedding pane. The pane is displayed as 200 pixels high by 150 pixels wide. For browsers incapable of reading the VRML file, the graphic graphic.gif would be displayed.

VSPACE   NS, MS

Specifies the vertical margins for the image.

WIDTH   NS, MS, SM

Specifies the width of the image.

<INPUT ?>   NS, MS, SM

This tag is used within the FORM tag and specifies a form control.

ALIGN   NS, MS, SM

Specifies the vertical alignment of the next line of text in relation to the image. For use only with TYPE=IMAGE. Possible values are the same as for the ALIGN attribute of the <IMG> element.

CHECKED   NS, MS, SM

This is used for checkboxes and radio buttons and indicates that they are selected. The options are TRUE or FALSE and it is used like this:

```
<INPUT NAME="control2" TYPE=CHECKBOX CHECKED=TRUE>
```

MAXLENGTH   NS, MS, SM

This indicates the maximum number of characters that can be entered into a text control. It appears like this:

```
<INPUT NAME="control2" TYPE=TEXTBOX MAXLENGTH=20>
```

NAME   NS, MS, SM

Specifies the name of the control, like this:

```
<INPUT NAME="control2" TYPE=CHECKBOX CHECKED=TRUE>
```

SIZE   NS, MS, SM

Used to specify the size of a control in characters (for TEXT AREA controls both height and width can be specified), like this:

```
<INPUT NAME="control2" TYPE=TEXTAREA SIZE="25,5">
```

SRC   NS, MS, SM

Used in conjunction with TYPE=IMAGE, this attribute specifies the address of the image to be used.

TYPE   NS, MS, SM

Specifies the type of control to use, like this:

```
<INPUT NAME="control2" TYPE=TEXTBOX SIZE=25>
```

The following are options for this attribute:

> CHECKBOX   This is used for simple Boolean attributes or for attributes that can take multiple values at the same time. It is represented by a number of checkbox fields, each of which has the same name. Each selected checkbox generates a separate name/value pair in the submitted data, even if this results in duplicate names. The default value for checkboxes is on.

HIDDEN   This specifies that no field is seen by the viewer, but the content of the field is sent with the submitted form. This value is often used to transmit information about client/server interaction.

IMAGE   Enables you to use an image rather than a browser-driven button. The coordinates of the selected point are measured in pixel units from the upper-left corner of the image and are returned (along with the other contents of the form) in two name/value pairs. The x-coordinate is submitted under the name of the field with .x appended, and the y-coordinate is submitted under the name of the field with .y appended. Any VALUE attribute is ignored. The image itself is specified by the SRC attribute, exactly as for the IMAGE element.

PASSWORD   The same as the TEXT attribute, except that text is not displayed as it is entered.

RADIO   Used for attributes that accept a single value from a set of alternatives. Each radio-button field in the group should be given the same name. Only the selected radio button in the group generates a name/value pair in the submitted data. Radio buttons require an explicit VALUE attribute.

RESET   When clicked, this button resets the form's fields to their specified initial values. The label to be displayed on the button can be specified the same way as for the SUBMIT button.

SUBMIT   When clicked, this button submits the form. You may use the VALUE attribute to provide a noneditable label to be displayed on the button (such as Clear Form). If a SUBMIT button is clicked to submit the form, and that button has a NAME attribute specified, then that button contributes a name/value pair to the submitted data. If the button has no name, a SUBMIT button makes no contribution to the submitted data.

TEXT   Specifies a single-line text-entry field. Use in conjunction with the SIZE and MAXLENGTH attributes. See TEXTAREA for text fields that can accept multiple lines.

TEXTAREA   For multiple-line text-entry fields. Use in conjunction with the SIZE and MAXLENGTH attributes.

FILE   This option (which is currently supported by Netscape) enables the inclusion of files with form information.

VALUE   NS, MS, SM

Required for radio buttons, this attribute is used for numerical/textual controls and specifies the initial displayed value of the field or the value to be returned when the field is selected, if it displays a Boolean value.

`<INS>...</INS>` NS

This set of tags identifies Inserted Text.

`<ISINDEX ?>` NS, MS, SM

This tag indicates a searchable index; used for simple keyword searches.

ACTION MS

Specifies the gateway program that the string in the textbox should be passed to.

PROMPT NS, MS

Specifies a prompt to be used; example:

```
<ISINDEX PROMPT="Please type in keywords here">
```

`<KBD>...</KBD>` NS, MS, SM

These keyboard tags are used to indicate text to be typed by the viewer.

`<LI>` NS, MS, SM

This tag denotes a list item.

TYPE NS, MS

Specifies the style of an ordered list. Options are capital letters (TYPE=A), small letters (TYPE=a), large Roman numerals (TYPE=I), small Roman numerals (TYPE=i), or numbers (TYPE=1)—the default.

VALUE NS, MS

Changes the count of ordered lists as they progress, like this:

```
<OL>
<LI>This is item #1
<LI VALUE=4>This is item #4
</OL>
```

`<LINK ?>` NS, SM

This tag defines a relationship between a document and another element.

HREF NS, SM

Identifies the link's destination.

METHODS   NS, SM

This specifies a list of HTTP methods for accessing an object in the destination and is used like this:

```
METHODS="method1,method2,method3,... "
```

REL   NS, SM

Defines the link's relationship like this:

```
REL="value"
```

The following are options for this attribute:

BOOKMARK   Associates the link with a direct location in an extended document

COPYRIGHT   Specifies a copyright for the current document

GLOSSARY   Associates the link with a glossary

HELP   Indicates the link is to a help document

HOME   References a home page

INDEX   Associates the link with an index

MADE   Indicates that the destination document includes information on the author of the current page

NEXT   Specifies that the link is to the next page in a sequence

PARENT   Defines the current page as the parent of the destination document

PREVIOUS   Indicates the link is to the previous page

STYLESHEET   Specifies that the link is to a style sheet

TOC   Associates the link with a table of contents

UP   References the immediate parent page in a sequence of documents

REV   NS, SM

This defines a reverse relationship between the current page and the destination and appears like this:

```
REV="value"
```

The values are the same for the REL attribute, though they specify the relationship from the destination. Therefore, the parent value defines the destination page as the parent of the current page.

TITLE   NS, SM

This contains information about the title of the destination page and is used like this:

```
TITLE="Text"
```

URN   NS, SM

This attribute provides a permanent address for the destination and appears like this:

```
URN="name"
```

\<LISTING\>...\</LISTING\>   NS, MS, SM

These tags specify to render the text in fixed-width type.

\<MAP ?\>...\</MAP\>   NS, MS, SM

These tags enable the definition of client-side image maps, and contain one or more AREA elements used to define the hot zones (linked areas) on the associated image and to bind the hot zones to specified URLs.

NAME   NS, MS, SM

The name specifies the name of the map so that it can be referenced by an \<IMG\> element.

\<MARQUEE ?\>...\</MARQUEE\>   MS

These tags enable the creation of a scrolling text marquee. Here is an example of one:

```
<MARQUEE BGCOLOR=#FFFFFF DIRECTION=LEFT BEHAVIOR=SCROLL SCROLLAMOUNT=15
SCROLLDELAY=150><FONT COLOR="RED">Here is a scrolling marquee.</FONT></MARQUEE>
```

ALIGN

Specifies that the text surrounding the marquee should align with the top, bottom, or middle of the marquee.

BEHAVIOR

Describes how the text should behave. Options are

> ALTERNATE   Means bounce back and forth within the marquee
>
> SCROLL (the default)   Means start completely off one side, scroll all the way across and completely off, and then start again
>
> SLIDE   Means start completely off one side, scroll in, and stop as soon as the text touches the other margin

BGCOLOR

Specifies a background color for the marquee, either as a hexadecimal or one of Microsoft's accepted color names.

DIRECTION

Specifies which direction the text should scroll. Options are LEFT or RIGHT (the default is LEFT, meaning the text scrolls from left to right).

HEIGHT

Specifies the height of the marquee (in pixels or as a percentage of the screen height) and is used like this:

```
<MARQUEE HEIGHT=25% WIDTH=75%>This marquee is a quarter the height of the screen
and 75% of the width.</MARQUEE>
```

HSPACE

Specifies left and right margins for the outside of the marquee, in pixels.

LOOP

Specifies how many times a marquee will loop when activated (described as either a number or INFINITE, which means it will loop indefinitely).

SCROLLAMOUNT

This specifies the number of pixels between each successive draw of the marquee text.

SCROLLDELAY

This specifies the number of milliseconds between each successive draw of the marquee text.

VSPACE

This attribute is used to specify the top and bottom margins for the outside of the marquee (in pixels).

WIDTH

This sets the width of the marquee (either in pixels or as a percentage of the screen width).

<MENU>...</MENU>   NS, MS, SM

This set of tags defines a menu list and contains one or more <LI> elements, which represent individual menu items. It is used just like <OL> and <UL>, and can also be used without <LI>, to indent text. MS rendered this without bullets.

<META ?>   NS, MS, SM

This tag is used to supply meta-information; this is often used to associate keywords to documents (readable by search engines). Meta-information is generally in name/value pair form and should be within the <HEAD> tag.

CONTENT   NS, MS, SM

This tells the browser to reload in a certain number of seconds. If a URL is specified, the browser will load the URL (after the time specified has elapsed); if no URL is specified, it will reload the current document.

HTTP-EQUIV   NS, MS, SM

This causes a document to be automatically reloaded on a regular basis (specified in seconds); used like this:

```
<HEAD><META HTTP-EQUIV="REFRESH" CONTENT="4; URL=http://www.yourdomain.com/
page.htm">
<TITLE>This Will Load The Next Document ("http://www.yourdomain.com/page.htm")
After 4 Seconds</TITLE>
</HEAD>
```

NAME   NS, SM

This indicates the meta-information name (if the NAME attribute is not present, then NAME can be assumed equal to the value HTTP-EQUIV).

<MULTICOL>...</MULTICOL>   NS

The MULTICOL tag is a container, and all the HTML between the starting and ending tag will be displayed in a multicolumn format. Multicolumn text layout displays text in multiple columns, similar to print newspaper columns. It is used with the COLS, GUTTER, and WIDTH attributes to control the number of columns, the space between the columns, and the width of individual columns, respectively. This tag can be nested.

The attributes of this tag are presented in the following sections.

COLS

The COLS attribute is mandatory and controls how many columns the display will be split into. Layout will attempt to flow elements evenly across the columns to make each column about the same height. Unless the WIDTH attribute is specified, column width is adjusted to fill the available view.

GUTTER

The GUTTER attribute controls the pixels of space between columns. It defaults to a value of 10.

WIDTH

The WIDTH attribute controls the width of an individual column.

<NEXTID ?>   NS, SM

This tag creates a sequential hierarchy of documents and indicates the next document following the current one. Use this tag only within the <HEAD> tag.

<NOBR>...</NOBR>   NS, MS

This tag is used to turn off line breaking.

<NOFRAMES>...</NOFRAMES>   NS, MS, SM

Within this tag is contained the page that viewers with non-frames-capable browsers will see. For best results, use only HTML 2 tags (for the widest audience) and have textual links to your contents pages.

<OBJECT>...</OBJECT>   MS, SM

This tag is an HTML 3.2 specification and requires both start and end tags. <OBJECT> is used to insert an object (ActiveX, applets, plug-ins, components, media handlers, and so on) into an HTML document. It provides a general solution for dealing with new media while providing for effective backwards compatibility with existing browsers. <OBJECT> enables the HTML author to specify the data and/or properties/parameters for initializing objects to be inserted into HTML documents, as well as the code that can be used to display or manipulate that data.

The data can be specified in one of several ways: a file specified by a URL, inline data, or as a set of named properties. In addition, there are a number of attributes that enable authors to specify standard properties such as width and height. The code for the object is specified in several ways: by an explicit reference or indirectly by the object's class name or media type.

Attributes include the ones presented in the following sections.

ALIGN   MS, SM

This determines where to place the object. The ALIGN attribute enables objects to be placed as part of the current text line or as a distinct unit aligned to the left, center, or right, and is used like this:

```
ALIGN=TEXTTOP
```

The following are options for this attribute:

```
    TEXTTOP
    MIDDLE
    TEXTMIDDLE
    BASELINE
    TEXTBOTTOM
    LEFT
    CENTER
    RIGHT
```

BORDER   MS, SM

This attribute applies to the border shown when the object forms part of a hypertext link, as specified by an enclosing anchor element. The attribute specifies the suggested width of this border around the visible area of the object. The width is specified in standard units and appears like this:

```
BORDER=2
```

CLASSID   MS, SM

This is a URL that identifies an implementation for the object. In some object systems this is a class identifier.

CODEBASE   MS, SM

Some URL schemes used to identify implementations require an additional URL to find the implementation. CODEBASE enables you to specify that URL.

CODETYPE   MS, SM

This specifies the Internet media type of the code referenced by the CLASSID attribute in advance of actually retrieving it. User agents may use the value of the CODETYPE attribute to skip over unsupported media types without needing to make a network access.

DATA   MS, SM

This is a URL pointing to the object's data—for instance, a GIF file for an image. In the absence of the CLASSID attribute, the media type of the data is used to determine a default value for the CLASSID attribute. The implementation is then loaded as if the CLASSID attribute had been given explicitly.

DECLARE   MS

This is used to imply objects that are not created until needed by something that references them (that is, late binding). Each such "binding" typically results in a separate copy of the object (this is class-dependent). In other words, the OBJECT DECLARE is treated as a declaration for making an instance of an object.

If the declared object isn't supported, or fails to load, the user agent should try the content of the OBJECT DECLARE element, which is currently restricted to another OBJECT DECLARE element. The TYPE attribute can be used to specify the Internet media type for the object as a hint for this situation.

HEIGHT   MS

This gives the suggested height of a box enclosing the visible area of the object. The height is specified in standard units. User agents may use this value to scale an object to match the requested height if appropriate.

HSPACE   MS

This specifies the width of the space to the left and right of the box enclosing the visible area of the object. The width is specified in standard units. This attribute is used to alter the separation of preceding and following text from the object.

ID   MS, SM

Is used to identify the specific label with a unique name, allowing interaction with and dynamic updating of the object's properties via active OLE scripting.

ISMAP   SM

Defines the object as an ISMAP.

NAME   MS, SM

This provides a way for user agents that support forms to determine whether an object within a FORM block should participate in the submit process. If NAME is specified and the DECLARE attribute is absent, then the user agent should include the value of the NAME attribute and data obtained from the object along with the information derived from other form fields. The mechanism used to obtain the object's data is specific to each object system.

SHAPES   MS

The presence of this attribute indicates that the contents of the OBJECT element contains anchors with hypertext links associated with shaped regions on the visible area of the object.

STANDBY   MS

Enables you to specify a short text string the browser can show while loading the object's implementation and data. It can include special characters.

TYPE   MS, SM

Specifies the Internet media type for the data referenced by the DATA attribute in advance of actually retrieving it. In the absence of the CLASSID attribute, this enables the user agent to retrieve the code implementing the object concurrently with the data and to skip over unsupported media types without needing to make a network access.

USEMAP   MS, SM

Specifies the URL for a client-side image map.

VSPACE   MS

Specifies the height of the space to the top and bottom of the box enclosing the visible area of the object (in standard units).

WIDTH   MS, SM

Specifies the width of a box enclosing the visible area of the object (specified in standard units).

<OL>...</OL>   NS, MS, SM

An ordered list (1,2,3,...). Contains one or more <LI> elements, which represent individual list items.

START   NS, MS

This specifies a starting number for the list.

TYPE   NS, MS

You can add a TYPE attribute to the <OL> tag to specify whether the list items are marked with: capital letters (TYPE=A), small letters (TYPE=a), large Roman numerals (TYPE=I), small Roman numerals (TYPE=i), or numbers (TYPE=1)—usually the default. Here's an example of code that will make a lettered list:

```
<OL TYPE=A>
<LI> First item in the list
<LI> Last item in the list
</OL>
```

VALUE   NS

Used to change the count, for that list item and all subsequent list items.

<OPTION>   NS, MS, SM

This tag indicates one choice in a listbox.

SELECTED   NS, MS, SM

This item is the default.

VALUE   NS, MS, SM

This indicates the value that will be returned if this item is chosen.

<P>...</P>   NS, MS, SM

This tag denotes a paragraph. The end tag is optional.

ALIGN   NS, MS, SM

Aligns the paragraph. Options are CENTER (NS, MS, SM), LEFT (NS, SM), and RIGHT (NS, SM).

`<PARAM NAME/VALUE>`   NS

Used in conjunction with `<APPLET>`, this tag specifies an applet-specific attribute and is used like this:

```
<PARAM NAME = the_applet_attribute VALUE =the_value>
```

`<PERSON>...</PERSON>`   NS

This set of tags defines text as the name of a person.

`<PLAINTEXT>...</PLAINTEXT>`   NS, MS, SM

These tags enclose the text to be rendered in a fixed-width type (MS and SM allow a closing element).

`<PRE>...</PRE>`   NS, MS, SM

These tags indicate elements to be rendered with a monospace font and preserve the layout defined by spaces and line break characters.

WIDTH   NS, SM

This specifies the maximum number of characters for a line (a width of 80 characters is the default).

`<Q>...</Q>`   NS

This stands for Quote and defines a short quotation within a paragraph.

`<S>...</S>`   NS, MS, SM

This renders the text in strike-through type.

`<SAMP>...</SAMP>`   MS, SM

These are used to display sample output from scripts, HTML code, programs, and so on.

`<SCRIPT ?>...</SCRIPT>`   NS

This set of tags enables a script to be embedded into an HTML document.

LANGUAGE

This attribute specifies the scripting language and is used like this:

```
<SCRIPT LANGUAGE="JavaScript"></SCRIPT>
```

This is mandatory unless the `SRC` attribute is present.

SRC

This attribute specifies a URL that loads the text of a script, like this:

```
<SCRIPT SRC="http://www.yourdomain.com/the.JavaScript"></SCRIPT>
```

<SELECT>...</SELECT>   NS, MS, SM

This set of tags indicates a listbox or drop-down list.

MULTIPLE   NS, MS, SM

Specifies that multiple items can be selected.

NAME   NS, MS, SM

Gives the list a name.

SIZE   NS, MS

Used to specify the size of the list control.

<SMALL>...</SMALL>   NS

This set of tags specifies a small font.

<SOUND ?>   SM

This is used for playing inline sound. It enables the playing of WAV, AU, or AIFF files in pages.

SRC

The URL of the sound file.

DELAY

Used to delay the play of an inline sound for a certain number of seconds; appears like this:

```
<SOUND SRC="sound.wav" DELAY=5>
```

<SPACER>   NS

The SPACER tag provides control over the vertical and horizontal white space appearing on the HTML page and appears like this:

```
<SPACER TYPE=HORIZONTAL SIZE=25>
```

You can control the horizontal white space that appears between words in a line and the vertical white space that appears between lines on a page, and you can also set up arbitrary rectangular spacing elements (often placed in margins to make text flow around them).

ALIGN
Sets the alignment of the spacer.

HEIGHT
Defines the height of the spacer.

SIZE
Specifies the size of a spacer.

TYPE
Specifies the spacer type. Options are

> HORIZONTAL
>
> VERTICAL
>
> BLOCK

WIDTH
Defines the width.

<STRIKE>...</STRIKE>   NS, MS, SM
This specifies strike-through text.

<STRONG>...</STRONG>   NS, MS, SM
This specifies strong emphasis; generally it is rendered in a bold font.

_{...}   NS, SM
This specifies subscript text.

^{...}   NS, SM
This specifies superscript text.

<TABLE ?>...</TABLE>   NS, MS, SM
This set of tags contains all the other table elements (table elements will be ignored if they aren't wrapped inside of <TABLE> ... </TABLE>). Every table begins with an optional CAPTION, which is followed by one or more <TR> elements defining the table's rows. Every row has one or more cells that are defined by <TH> or <TD> tags.

ALIGN   NS, MS, SM

This specifies the alignment of the table, as in ALIGN=RIGHT. Other possibilities for this attribute include ALIGN=LEFT and ALIGN=CENTER.

BACKGROUND   MS

Specifies a background graphic. The graphic is tiled behind the text and graphics in the table.

BGCOLOR   NS, MS, SM

Defines the background color (as a hexadecimal number or a recognized color name).

BORDER   NS, MS, SM

This causes a border to be placed around the table, specified by a numerical value (1,2,3...).

BORDERCOLOR   MS

This defines the color of the border, as in: BORDERCOLOR=#ff0000. You can either use a hexadecimal color or use one of Microsoft's specified color names (for example, BORDERCOLOR=RED). This attribute must be used in conjunction with BORDER=; otherwise, there is no border to color.

BORDERCOLORDARK   MS

Sets independent border color control over one of the two colors used to draw a 3-D border (as a hexadecimal number or as a recognized color name); opposite of BORDERCOLORLIGHT, this must be used with the BORDER attribute. It is used like this:

```
<TABLE ALIGN=RIGHT BORDER=1 BORDERCOLORDARK=RED width=20%>
```

BORDERCOLORLIGHT   MS

Sets independent border color control over one of the two colors used to draw a 3-D border (as a hexadecimal number or as a recognized color name); opposite of BORDERCOLORDARK, this must be used with the BORDER attribute.

BORDERSTYLE   SM

Specifies the type of table border. Options for this attribute are

NONEMPTY   The default, this produces a frame around the table and individual borders around non-empty cells.

ALL   Draws boxes around the frame and all cells without regard to their contents.

FRAME   Draws a frame around the table, but not around the individual cells.

NONE   Draws no borders.

CELLSPACING   NS, MS, SM

Indicates the amount of space inserted between individual cells in a table.

CELLPADDING   NS, MS, SM

Specifies the amount of space between the border of the cell and the contents of the cell. It is used like this:

```
<TABLE BORDER=2 CELLSPACING=1 CELLPADDING=1>
```

FRAME   MS

This attribute affects the display of the table borders. (It requires the BORDER attribute to be set.) It accepts any of the following values:

ABOVE   Displays external borders at the top of the table only

BELOW   Displays external borders at the bottom of the table only

BOX   Displays a box around the table

HSIDES   Displays external borders at the horizontal sides of the table (at the top and bottom)

LHS   Displays external borders at the left hand edges of the table exclusively

RHS   Displays external borders at the right hand edges of the table only

VOID   Removes all the external borders

VSIDES   Displays external borders at both left and right edges of the table

HEIGHT   NS, MS, SM

Describes the height of the table (in pixels, or as a percentage of the display window).

RULES   MS

This attribute affects the display of the internal table borders ("rules"). The body section of the table must be specified using the <TBODY> tag. The following values are accepted:

NONE   Removes all the internal rules

BASIC   Displays horizontal borders between the <THEAD>, <TBODY>, and <TFOOT> sections

ROWS   Displays horizontal borders between all rows

COLS   Displays horizontal borders between all columns

ALL   Displays all the internal rules

VALIGN   MS

Specifies the vertical alignment of text within a column. Options are

```
="BASELINE"
"BOTTOM"
"MIDDLE"
"TOP"
```

WIDTH   NS, MS, SM

This species how wide the table will be, either in pixels or as a percentage, as in

```
WIDTH=30%
```

<TBODY>...</TBODY>   MS

This set of tags is used to specify the body section of the table. It is required if RULES wish to be set in the <TABLE>.

<TD>...</TD>   NS, MS, SM

This set of tags defines a table data cell, as in

```
<TD>info a</TD>
```

ALIGN   NS, MS, SM

Specifies whether the text inside the table cell(s) is aligned CENTER, to the LEFT side of the cell, or to the RIGHT side of the cell.

BACKGROUND   MS

Describes the image that will be tiled behind the table data cell specified.

BGCOLOR   NS, MS, SM

This is the background color of the data cell (in hexadecimal or one of the recognized color names).

BORDERCOLOR   MS

Specifies the border color of the data cell (in hexadecimal or one of the recognized color names). The BORDER attribute must also be present in the main <TABLE> element for border coloring to work.

BORDERCOLORDARK   MS

Sets independent border color control over one of the two colors used to draw a 3-D border (as a hexadecimal number or as a recognized color name); opposite of BORDERCOLORLIGHT, and must be used with the BORDER attribute.

BORDERCOLORLIGHT   MS

Sets independent border color control over one of the two colors used to draw a 3-D border (as a hexadecimal number or as a recognized color name); opposite of BORDERCOLORDARK, and must be used with the BORDER attribute.

COLSPAN   NS, MS, SM

This can appear in any table cell (<TH> or <TD>) and specifies how many columns of the table this cell should span (the default being 1).

HEIGHT   MS

Used to describe the height of the table (as a pixel value, or as a percentage of the display window).

NOWRAP   NS, MS

Specifies that the lines within this cell cannot be broken to fit the width of the cell.

ROWSPAN   NS, MS, SM

Specifies how many rows of the table the cell should span (the default being 1).

VALIGN   NS, MS, SM

Defines how the text inside the table cell(s) is aligned. Options are

```
TOP
MIDDLE
BOTTOM
BASELINE
```

WIDTH   NS, MS, SM

Describes the desired width of the cell (as an absolute width in pixels, or as a percentage of table width).

<TEXTAREA ?>...</TEXTAREA>   NS, MS, SM

This set of tags enables users to enter more than one line of text within a form.

COLS   NS, MS, SM

Determines the width of the field in characters.

NAME   NS, MS, SM

Used to give the TEXTAREA a name; looks like this:

```
<TEXTAREA NAME="address" ROWS=40 COLS=6>
```

ROWS   NS, MS, SM

Determines the height of the field in characters.

WRAP   NS, SM

Specifies how to handle word-wrapping in the text input area and appears like this:

`<TEXTAREA WRAP=OFF>`

Options for this are

> OFF   Wrapping doesn't happen. Lines are sent exactly as typed (this is the default).
>
> VIRTUAL   The display word-wraps, but long lines are sent to the server as one line.
>
> PHYSICAL   The display word-wraps, and the text is transmitted at all wrap points.

<TFOOT>...</TFOOT>   MS

This set of tags specifies the footer section of a table.

<TH>...</TH>   NS, MS, SM

This set of tags identifies a table heading cell. Optional attributes are the same as for `<TD>`.

<THEAD>...</THEAD>   MS

This set of tags describes the table heading section of a table.

<TITLE>...</TITLE>   NS, MS, SM

This set of tags contains the document title. (Note: This is the title of your HTML page and appears within the browser, but not as text on your page.)

<TR>...</TR>   NS, MS, SM

This stands for Table Row; the tags contain a row of table cells. All tables must include at least one `<TR>` element.

ALIGN   NS, MS, SM

Specifies whether the text inside the table row(s) is aligned CENTER, to the LEFT side of the cell, or to the RIGHT side of the cell.

BACKGROUND   MS

Describes the image that will be tiled behind the table row specified.

BGCOLOR   NS, MS, SM

This is the background color of the table row (in hexadecimal or one of the recognized color names).

BORDERCOLOR   MS

Specifies the border color of the table row (in hexadecimal or one of the recognized color names). The BORDER attribute must also be present in the main <TABLE> element for border coloring to work.

BORDERCOLORDARK   MS

Sets independent border color control over one of the two colors used to draw a 3-D border (as a hexadecimal number or as a recognized color name); opposite of BORDERCOLORLIGHT, this must be used with the <TABLE> BORDER attribute.

BORDERCOLORLIGHT   MS

Sets independent border color control over one of the two colors used to draw a 3-D border (as a hexadecimal number or as a recognized color name); opposite of BORDERCOLORDARK, this must be used with the <TABLE> BORDER attribute.

VALIGN   NS, MS, SM

Specifies how the text inside the table row(s) is aligned. Options are

```
TOP
MIDDLE
BOTTOM
BASELINE
```

<TT>...</TT>   NS, MS, SM

This set of tags specifies monospaced or teletype text.

<U>...</U>   NS, MS, SM

This set of tags specifies underlined text.

<UL>...</UL>   NS, MS, SM

Specifies an unordered bulleted list. An unordered bulleted list contains one or more <LI> elements, which represent individual list items. Here's an example:

```
<UL>
<LI> First item in the list
<LI> Last item in the list
</UL>
```

TYPE   NS

Netscape adds a TYPE attribute to the `<UL>` tag, which can describe whether the bullet used is a CIRCLE, DISK, or SQUARE, and is used like this:

```
<UL TYPE=circle>
```

`<VAR>...</VAR>`   NS, MS, SM

This set of tags is used for variables or arguments to commands.

`<WBR>`   NS, MS

This tag stands for Word Break and is used when a `<NOBR>` section requires an exact break (can also be used any time to tell Netscape Navigator where a word is allowed to be broken). Important note: This tag does not force a line break (like `<BR>` does); it simply lets the browser know where a line break is allowed if needed.

`<XMP>...</XMP>`   NS, MS, SM

This set of tags is used to presents blocks of text in fixed-width font, and so is suitable for text that has been formatted onscreen (normally rendered as a fixed-width font with white space separating it from other text).

Note:
Only MS has the capability to translate special characters included within `<XMP>` elements (that is, if a character like `&copy;` is used, it will be translated to ©).

And that's about all you can do with shrimp!

What's on the CD-ROM?

Most of the software included on the CD-ROM is either freeware or shareware. Freeware means just that—it's free (yippee!); shareware, on the other hand, is not free. Shareware used to mean any software offered expressly to be shared between users, but for some time has meant try-before-you-buy software. The idea of shareware is to give the user a free trial period with the software (usually 30 days) before requiring that payment be made by those who want to keep it. In other words: try it; if you like it, buy it.

FTP Client for Windows 3.x and Later Systems

CuteFTP is one of very few programs that enable novice users to utilize the capabilities of FTP without having to know all the details of the protocol itself. CuteFTP's strongest point is that it can gather almost every available bit of information about the files and directory structure of a remote system and present it to the user in an easy-to-use file manager-like browsing screen. CuteFTP also keeps data transfers to a minimum by storing all the data it can to a temporary file. One of the best things about this client is that you don't have to do separate transfers for 7- and 8-bit files—it's automatic.

Requirements

CuteFTP requires MS Windows 3.1 or later, WinSock 1.1 or later network interface library, and ctl3dv2.dll (included). You also need at least 2MB of memory.

Known Problems

CuteFTP doesn't work with SunSoft PC-NFS or some versions of the AOL WinSock. Many problems have been reported when running CuteFTP with SLIP emulators (for example, Twinsock, TIA, Slirp). However, in most cases using PASV Mode fixed them. (In Options | Firewall set FireWall Type to PASV Mode and put a check in the Enable Firewall box.)

GIF Construction Set for Windows 3.x and Later Systems

GIF Construction Set for Windows is a powerful collection of tools to work with multiple-block GIF files. It will enable you to assemble GIF files containing image blocks, plain text blocks, comment blocks, and control blocks. It includes facilities to manage palettes and merge multiple GIF files. It will make the extensions of the GIF specification work for you. Among its other functions, GIF Construction Set for Windows can

- Create Netscape animations
- Create transparent GIF files
- Create interlaced GIF files
- Add, edit, and delete comment blocks
- Add nondestructive text to images as plain text blocks
- Create multiple-image GIF files
- Serve as a fully compliant Windows GIF viewer application
- Be a GIF viewer helper application for a World Wide Web browser or Mosaic client

This is *the* gif89a animation tool.

Requirements

GIF Construction Set for Windows requires a minimum of 4MB of memory to run reliably, with 8MB preferable. Larger images may require more memory still.

HTML NOTEPAD VERSION 2.0 FOR WINDOWS 3.x AND LATER SYSTEMS

HTML Notepad is an editor with the capability to produce HTML coding for World Wide Web pages. Simple and fast, it comes with full explanation of how to create professional pages. HTML Notepad provides a simple interface for nearly every HTML tag used by the professional Web page designer. It includes most of the HTML 3.0, Internet Explorer 3.0, and Netscape 3.0 tags. An editor like this is usually our first choice.

REQUIREMENTS

Windows 3.x systems use `htmln231.zip`.

Windows 95/NT systems use `htmln295.zip`.

HTML REFERENCE LIBRARY v2.2 FOR WINDOWS 3.x AND LATER SYSTEMS

This reference software, using the Internet RFC as an information base, is a nonline reference library of currently supported HTML elements—their syntax and use. It is extremely helpful in searching for HTML tags or to see which tags are compatible with which browsers. HTML Library also includes the HTMLib Colour Wizard, which can be used to get an idea of what different color schemes will look like when used in HTML documents (and helps decipher the 6-digit code).

REQUIREMENTS

Windows 3.x systems use `htmlib22.zip`.

Windows 95/NT systems use `htmlib9522.zip`.

HTML TRANSIT

Using a template-based architecture, HTML Transit automatically generates Web-ready publications from word processing files, including long documents like sales brochures or technical manuals.

INCONTEXT SPIDER AND INCONTEXT WEB ANALYZER

Though it doesn't easily allow for direct code input, Incontext Spider does enable you to open one of more than 30 ready-to-use Web pages, drag and drop your choice of over 300 images and backgrounds, and even point and click to embed a Macromedia Shockwave animation file or Java applet. When you're finished, One-Button Publishing gets your pages up on the Web in seconds.

InContext Web Analyzer diagnoses Web sites, finding broken links and ensuring your Web site functions correctly.

THE INTERNET LEXICON FOR WINDOWS 3.*x* AND WINDOWS 95/NT SYSTEMS

With nearly 1,500 acronyms and terms described, defined, and cross-referenced, Free Internet Lexicon and Networking Dictionary for Windows is the only known resource of its kind. A sample of the PC/Internet Lexicon contains the complete Internet Terms and Internet Acronyms modules, the Top Level Domains List, and way too many smileys. This is a self-extracting, auto-installing EXE file with uninstaller. It's in Windows Help format, with some surprising features.

REQUIREMENTS

    80386-SX or higher
    Windows 3.1 enhanced mode
    2MB system memory

KNOWN PROBLEMS

The graphics and opening screens will not display properly on systems using CGA, EGA, or large-font VGA, SVGA, and XGA systems. This is because of the way Windows Help handles graphics when large fonts are selected, and you will find that 90 percent of Windows help files have the same problem. This bug occurs on Windows 3.1/3.11 and Windows 95. We recommend the following as a fix:

Windows 3.1/3.11

If your main problem is the small size of icon titles, add the following line to your WIN.INI file under the [Desktop] section:

IconTitleSize=12

You can change this line incrementally to suit. This should enable you to use small fonts and have better visibility of icon titles as well as graphical compatibility with Windows help tools.

Windows 95

The same applies. It's probably the size of your Start menu text and dialog box text that prompted you to select large fonts. We recommend obtaining a program called TWEAKUI.EXE, one of the free power tools from Microsoft for Win95, from Microsoft's Web site or one of several locations on the Internet. Using a search engine such as Yahoo! or Webcrawler, try a search for WINDOWS 95 POWERTOYS or WINDOWS 95 POWER TOYS.

This utility may be used for fixing a lot more than just the size of the Start menu and dialog text, and if you're a heavy Windows user, you will find it very useful.

JDESIGNERPRO

JDesignerPro is a database wizard for Java. The screens you build with JDesignerPro are "databound" from the start, so when you have completed a screen, it is ready to deploy.

MAP THIS FOR WIN32S (FOR WINDOWS 3.1), WINDOWS 95, AND WINDOWS NT

Map This is a program designed to create mapping files for clickable image maps (ISMAPs) for the World Wide Web. This can simplify the process of creating ISMAPs, but you should still understand the code in the map file (which can be created and accessed via a text editor).

REQUIREMENTS

Map This is a 32-bit program. This means it runs as a native Windows NT or Windows 95 application—much faster than a 16-bit program. In order to get Map This to run under Windows 3.1 or 3.11, you must have the Win32s extension (available from Microsoft) installed. The normal function of Map This does not require an Internet connection or even WinSock to be installed.

KNOWN PROBLEMS

- Map This is, as mentioned, a 32-bit program. Its creators feel this is not a true limit because of the proliferation of Windows NT, Win95, and Win32s.

- Map This only uses a mouse as input. It's a semi-CAD (x,y coordinate) program, after all.

- Map This does not perform stringent checking of the values for the areas. You can have offscreen areas that will never be hit, and illegal HTML commands.

- Each polygon area is allowed up to 64 points. Some Web servers put a lower limit. We know of one that only allows up to 16 points.

- The scrolling of the image when you are zoomed in is slow.

PAINT SHOP PRO FOR WINDOWS 3.12 AND WINDOWS 95/NT SYSTEMS

Paint Shop Pro is a powerful Windows graphics program that provides painting, photo retouching, image enhancement, editing, and color enhancement functions. An image browser, batch image conversion, image viewing and printing, screen capture, and scanner support (TWAIN-Compliant) are also provided. Enhance your other applications with Paint Shop Pro's OLE support.

Paint Shop Pro is a raster format image-editing program, a type of software more commonly known as a bitmap editor. Raster image formats break a picture into a grid of equally sized pieces, called pixels, and records color information for each pixel. Common examples of raster formats include the Windows BMP format and the CompuServe GIF format.

Unlike most bitmap editors, Paint Shop Pro isn't confined to a short list of raster file formats. It provides full support for all of the most popular raster formats, full or partial support for many less popular raster formats, and can read nine meta and vector image formats. It is also our favorite shareware graphics program. While this isn't nearly as feature-rich as the commercial applications of its type (Photoshop, PhotoPaint, and so on), it's a great start.

REQUIREMENTS

System requirements for Version 3.12:

◆ Minimum: 386 CPU or faster; Windows 95, NT, or Win32s; 8MB RAM or higher; 16-color resolution or higher

◆ Recommended: 486 or Pentium CPU; Windows 95 or NT; 16MB RAM; 24-bit color (True Color)

System Requirements for Version 3.11:

◆ Minimum: 386 CPU or faster; Windows 3.1 or higher; 4MB RAM or higher; 16-color resolution or higher

◆ Recommended: 486 or Pentium CPU; Windows 3.11, Windows 95, or Windows NT; 16MB RAM; 24-bit color (True Color)

SNAGIT

SnagIt enables Windows users to capture an entire screen, an individual window, or a user-defined portion of the screen. SnagIt also accepts input directly from the Windows clipboard or a Windows bitmap (BMP) file. After the image is captured, SnagIt will send it to the printer, the clipboard, a graphics file, or to e-mail.

STIKRZ!

StikrZ! provides the ability to add instant clarification to e-mail and other Windows applications you use daily. This simple pop-up utility is composed of more than a hundred separate emotional icons (emoticons), or graphical icons, suitable for including in your electronic communication. It includes images of faces showing emotion, business-oriented graphics, and fun stickers.

THUMBSPLUS

ThumbsPlus is an effective way to locate, view, edit, print, and organize your image and multimedia files in Windows 95, NT, and 3.1.

WEBFORMS FOR WINDOWS 3.x AND WINDOWS 95/NT SYSTEMS

WebForms is a World Wide Web forms generator that automatically creates HTML forms and reads their responses, enabling you to conduct surveys, collect orders for your products—anything you can think of! Responses are automatically sent to your mailbox, then read by WebForms and collected in a response database. It's all controlled by you, and all you need is an e-mail address. NO CGI REQUIRED!

Be aware, though, that this software will sign your HTML (this form created by…). This has become a problem with many software applications, but it's simple enough to go back to the raw code and delete this information.

REQUIREMENTS

Processor: 25Mhz 386
Minimum Operating System: Windows 3.1
Standard RAM: 4M
Hard Drive Space: 3M

Video Graphics Array (VGA)
Additional Software: `VBURN300.DLL`

WEBMANIA

WebMania is a full-featured HTML editor that includes unparalleled support for frames, forms, and now client-side image maps. It also includes 60 user-programmable toolbar buttons, which enable you to add new HTML tags as you learn them, or as HTML standards evolve. This software signs its name in your code. The minimum operating system necessary to run this editor is MS-DOS 3.3.

REQUIREMENTS

Processor: 16Mhz 386
Minimum Operating System: MS-DOS 3.3
Standard RAM: 4MB
Hard Drive Space: 4MB
Expanded or Extended memory
Video Graphics Array (VGA)
Additional Software: `vburn300.dll`

WINZIP FOR WINDOWS 3.x AND LATER SYSTEMS

WinZip brings the convenience of Windows to the use of ZIP files without requiring PKZIP and PKUNZIP (except for special features, like spanning multiple floppies). It features an intuitive point-and-click, drag-and-drop interface for viewing, running, extracting, adding, deleting, and testing files in archives. ARJ, LZH, and ARC files are supported via external programs. WinZip interfaces to most virus scanners.

REQUIREMENTS

The Windows 3.1 Version (`wz16v61.exe`) requires Windows 3.1 or Windows for Workgroups. The Win32 version (`winzip95.exe`) requires Windows 95 or Windows NT 3.5 or later. While no other programs are required for basic operations involving ZIP files, optional features require one or more external programs, including PKZIP and PKUNZIP products from PKWARE, Inc., LHA.EXE from Haruyasu Yoshizaki, or the Shareware ARJ product from Robert

Jung. WinZip interfaces to several programs to access ARC files and optionally runs most virus-scanning utilities.

WIRL LITE

WIRL Lite is the first true virtual reality Web browser. WIRL takes VRML to a new level. With it, you can experience fully interactive virtual reality worlds on the Web with support for more than 100 features not available in other conventional 3-D browsers.

TEMPLATES ON THE CD

The HTML templates on the CD are located in the directory `d:\templat` (where `d` is your CD drive). They are meant to serve as examples and to be adapted for your personal use. You can either alter the original file to suit your needs, or cut and paste the code into your own file.

◆ The home page template (`d:\templat\home1.htm`): The basic home page template to get you started

◆ The frames template (`d:\templat\frames`): A complete frames/noframes system to be adapted for your use

◆ The tables template (`d:\templat\tables.htm`): An HTML file containing 30 different tables templates

Index

Laura Lemay's Web Workshop: Creating Commercial Web Pages

Laura Lemay and Daniel Bishop

In her classic, clear style, Laura Lemay, author of the best-selling *Teach Yourself Java*, not only details how to use HTML, CGI, and Java to create Web pages, but shows how to apply proven principles of design to make the Web pages effective marketing tools. Filled with samples, this book illustrates the various corporate uses of Web technology—catalogues, customer service, and product ordering. CD-ROM includes all the templates in the book, plus HTML editors, graphics software, CGI forms, and more.

Price: $39.99 USA/$56.95 CDN
ISBN: 1-57521-126-2   400 pages

Building an Intranet

Tim Evans

The first book to focus on using Web technology to provide information for a company internally, *Building an Intranet* explains how to choose hardware and software, set up a secure Web server, and make a company's applications Web-aware. Shows how to design, build, and deploy information and applications within an organization. Covers security issues and the Internet. CD-ROM contains source code from the book and valuable utilities.

Price: $55.00 USA/$74.95 CDN
ISBN: 1-57521-071-1   720 pages

Building an Intranet with Windows NT 4

Scott Zimmerman and Tim Evans

This hands-on guide teaches everything you need to know to set up and maintain an efficient intranet with Windows NT. Includes complete specifications for several of the most popular intranet applications for group scheduling, discussions, database access, and more. CD-ROM provides a complete Windows NT intranet toolkit with a full-featured Web server, Web content development tools, ready-to-use intranet applications.

Price: $49.99 USA/$70.95 CDN
ISBN: 1-57521-137-8   600 pages

Paul McFedries' Windows 95 Unleashed, Premier Edition

Paul McFedries

Best-selling author Paul McFedries has created a Windows 95 user's masterpiece! In the traditional style of the *Unleashed* series, every new feature is discussed in detail, leaving the reader fully informed and completely ready to function within the new operating system. Discusses multimedia topics, internetworking, and communication issues. This updated and revised edition includes coverage of soon-to-be-released Microsoft Internet products, such as Visual Basic Script, Internet Studio, and Microsoft Exchange—topics not covered anywhere else. The CD-ROM contains an easy-to-search online chapter on troubleshooting for Windows 95.

Price: $59.99 USA/$84.95 CDN
ISBN: 0-672-30932-7   1,376 pages

Windows NT 4 Server Unleashed

Jason Garms

The Windows NT server has been gaining tremendous market share over Novell and the new upgrade—which includes a Windows 95 interface—is sure to add momentum to its market drive. Written to meet the needs of that growing market, *Windows NT 4.0 Server Unleashed* focuses on using Windows NT as an Internet server and provides information on disk and file management, integrated networking, BackOffice integration, and TCP/IP protocols. Also covers security issues and Macintosh support. CD-ROM includes source code from the book and valuable utilities.

Price: $59.99 USA/$84.95 CDN
ISBN: 0672-30933-5   1,100 pages

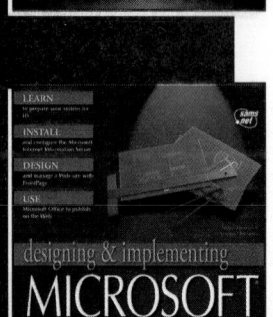

Designing and Implementing Microsoft Internet Information Server 2

Arthur Knowles and Sanjaya Hettihewa

The specific tasks involved in setting up and running a Microsoft Internet Information Server are presented in detail. You'll learn troubleshooting, network design, security, and cross-platform integration procedures.

Price: $39.99 USA/$56.95 CDN
ISBN: 1-57521-168-8   336 pages

Teach Yourself Web Publishing with HTML 3.2 in a Week, Third Edition

Laura Lemay

This updated edition of Lemay's bestseller, *Teach Yourself Web Publishing with HTML in 14 Days, Premier Edition,* explores the use of CGI scripts, tables, HTML 3.0, the Netscape and Internet Explorer extensions, Java applets and JavaScript, and VRML. You'll find all the advanced topics and updates—including adding audio, video, and animation to Web pages.

Price: $29.99 USA/$42.95 CDN
ISBN: 1-57521-192-0   600 pages

Programming Windows NT 4 Unleashed

David Hamilton, Mickey Williams, and Griffith Kadnier

Programming Windows NT 4 Unleashed will give you a clear understanding of the modes of operation and architecture for Windows NT. Execution models, processes, threads, DLLs, memory, controls, security, and more—everything is covered in precise detail. Teaches OLE, DDE, drag and drop, OCX development, and the Component Gallery; explores Microsoft BackOffice programming. CD-ROM contains source code and completed sample programs from the book.

Price: $59.99 USA/$84.95 CDN
ISBN: 0-672-30905-X   1,200 pages

Add to Your Sams.net Library Today
with the Best Books for Internet Technologies

ISBN	Quantity	Description of Item	Unit Cost	Total Cost
1-57521-126-2		Laura Lemay's Web Workshop: Creating Commercial Web Pages (Book/CD-ROM)	$39.99	
1-57521-071-1		Building an Intranet (Book/CD-ROM)	$55.00	
1-57521-137-8		Building an Intranet with Windows NT 4 (Book/CD-ROM)	$49.99	
0-672-30932-7		Paul McFedries' Windows 95 Unleashed, Premier Edition (Book/2 CD-ROMs)	$59.99	
0-672-30933-5		Windows NT 4 Server Unleashed (Book/CD-ROM)	$59.99	
1-57521-168-8		Designing and Implementing Microsoft Internet Information Server 2	$39.99	
1-57521-192-0		Teach Yourself Web Publishing with HTML 3.2 in a Week, Third Edition	$29.99	
0-672-30905-X		Programming Windows NT 4 Unleashed (Book/CD-ROM)	$59.99	
		Shipping and Handling: See information below.		
		TOTAL		

Shipping and Handling: $4.00 for the first book, and $1.75 for each additional book. If you need to have it NOW, we can ship product to you in 24 hours for an additional charge of approximately $18.00, and you will receive your item overnight or in two days. Overseas shipping and handling adds $2.00. Prices subject to change. Call between 9:00 a.m. and 5:00 p.m. EST for availability and pricing information on latest editions.

201 W. 103rd Street, Indianapolis, Indiana 46290

1-800-428-5331 — Orders   1-800-835-3202 — Fax   1-800-858-7674 — Customer Service

Book ISBN 1-57521-169-6